Story Sense

*Writing Story and Script
for Feature Films and Television*

Story Sense

Writing Story and Script for Feature Films and Television

Paul Lucey

The McGraw-Hill Companies, Inc.

New York   St. Louis   San Francisco   Auckland   Bogotá   Caracas   Lisbon
London   Madrid   Mexico City   Milan   Montreal   New Delhi
San Juan   Singapore   Sydney   Tokyo   Toronto

McGraw-Hill

A Division of The **McGraw·Hill** Companies

This book was set in Palatino by The Clarinda Company.
The editors were Cynthia Ward and John M. Morriss;
the production supervisor was Diane Ficarra.
The cover was designed by Top Desk Publisher's Group;.
cover illustration was done by David Flaherty.
Project supervision was done by The Total Book.
R. R. Donnelley & Sons Company was printer and binder.

STORY SENSE
Writing Story and Script for Feature Films and Television

This book is printed on acid-free paper.

4 5 6 7 8 9 0   DOC   DOC   9 0 9 8

ISBN 0-07-038996-9

Library of Congress Cataloging-in-Publication Data

Lucey, Paul.
   Story sense : writing story and script for feature films and
television / Paul Lucey.
       p. cm.
   Includes index.
   ISBN 0-07-038996-9
    1. Motion picture authorship.   2. Television authorship.
   I. Title.
PN1996.L745   1996
808.2'3—dc20   95-41425

About the Author

PAUL LUCEY has written scripts for all the major studios and television networks. His work has been honored by the Writers Guild of America, which nominated him for their Best Anthology Script award. He has served as chairperson of the WGA's Academic Liaison Committee and has done extensive tapings of various Guild activities. He has taught screenwriting since 1968 at colleges in the United States and Canada. In 1984 he was designated Senior Instructor and was voted Outstanding Teacher in the UCLA Extension Writers' Program. For ten years he taught screenwriting in the School of Cinema-Television at the University of Southern California, where he headed graduate and undergraduate screenwriting programs. Dr. Lucey has earned degrees from Duke University, UCLA, and USC. He lives in Santa Monica.

Contents

Part Two
WRITING THE SCRIPT

APPENDIXES

Acknowledgments

We wish to thank and acknowledge the following companies and writers for permission to reproduce the material indicated:

Quote on page 7 by Edgar J. Scherick, used with permission.

Quotes on pages 58 and 158 from *Word Into Image: Writers on Screenwriting: Transcripts of Award-Winning Film Series*, Los Angeles: American Film Foundation, 1981. Available from American Film Foundation, P.O. Box 2000, Santa Monica, CA 90406. Used with permission.

Quotes on pages 61, 145, 146, and 337, copyright (1994, 1983, 1994, 1995) respectively, *Los Angeles Times*, Reprinted with permission.

Quote on page 193 from "The Hunter and the Hunted," by Jeremy Gerard, March 8, 1987, copyright © 1987 by The New York Times Company. Reprinted by permission.

Table on page 319, Revenue estimates of Paul Kagan Associates, Inc., Carmel, CA, reprinted with permission.

Quote on page 327, used with permission of Laurin Shuler Donner.

Quotes page 332 and Appendix F, page 366, reprinted by permission of the *Journal of the Writers Guild of America*, West.

Excerpt from the screenplay of BASIC INSTINCT reprinted with permission of Carolco Pictures Inc. and Le Studio Canal + S.A.

Excerpt from the screenplay of RAMBLING ROSE reprinted with permission of Carolco Pictures Inc.

Excerpts from the screenplay of THE SHAWSHANK REDEMPTION © 1994 Castle Rock Entertainment. Courtesy of Castle Rock Entertainment and Frank Darabont.

Excerpts from the screenplays of IN THE LINE OF FIRE, FIVE EASY PIECES, and SINGLE WHITE FEMALE. Courtesy of Columbia Pictures.

Excerpts from the screenplays of OUT OF AFRICA, ON GOLDEN POND, and JURASSIC PARK. Copyright © by Universal City Studios, Inc. Courtesy of MCA Publishing Rights, a Division of MCA Inc. All rights reserved.

Excerpts from MOONSTRUCK and THELMA & LOUISE screenplays courtesy of MGM.

Excerpts from the screenplay of SILENCE OF THE LAMBS used with permission of Ted Tally, Thomas Harris, and Orion Pictures Corporation. Courtesy of Orion Pictures Corporation, All Rights Reserved.

Excerpts from the screenplays of FATAL ATTRACTION, SERPICO, and WITNESS courtesy of Paramount Pictures.

Excerpts from THE QUIET MAN screenplay courtesy of Republic.

Excerpts from SLEEPLESS IN SEATTLE, screenplay by Nora Ephron, David Ward, and Jeff Arch, based on a story by Jeff Arch. Courtesy of TriStar Pictures, Nora Ephron, David Ward, and Jeff Arch.

Excerpt from CASABLANCA screenplay courtesy of Turner Entertainment Co.

Excerpt from the screenplay of WORKING GIRL, written by Kevin Wade. "Working Girl" © 1986 Twentieth Century Fox Film Corporation, All Rights Reserved.

Excerpt from the screenplay of ALIEN, written by Walter Hill and David Giler. "Alien" © 1979 Twentieth Century Fox Film Corporation, All Rights Reserved.

Excerpt from the screenplay of YOUNG FRANKENSTEIN, written by Mel Brooks and Gene Wilder. "Young Frankenstein" © 1973 Twentieth Century Fox Film Corporation, All Rights Reserved.

Excerpt from the screenplay of THE VERDICT, written by David Mamet. "The Verdict" © 1982 Twentieth Century Fox Film Corporation, All Rights Reserved.

Excerpts from the screenplays of UNFORGIVEN and DAVE courtesy of Warner Bros. Inc.

Excerpt from GREEN CARD screenplay courtesy of Peter Weir.

Preface

This book teaches the two essentials of screenwriting: how to plot a story and how to write the plot into a dramatic script. The book also teaches how to analyze scripts and the movies made from them so that you can apply these lessons to your work. Because there is no commercial payoff for amateurish movie scripts, the book deals with professional standards of work, which means creating scripts that promise an entertaining movie. In all, *Story Sense* lays out a complete guide to screenwriting, from locating a dramatic idea, spinning it into a story, writing the incidents of plot into a script, rewriting, and selling the work. There is overlap and flexibility to the advice, so if a particular strategy doesn't work, others can be used, enabling you to create any story, style, or genre of movie script imaginable, from *Becket* to *Babe* to *Baywatch*.

The lessons of *Story Sense* are based on my three decades of teaching in film schools, on writing screenplays, and on seminar discussions by writers, filmmakers, and movie executives who addressed craft forums sponsored by the Writers Guild of America (WGA). As chairperson of the WGA Academic Liaison Committee, I helped organize many of these sessions, which we began taping in 1969. Insights taken from the WGA meetings were tested in my screenwriting classes at UCLA, the University of Southern California, and other schools. Lessons that proved most useful became part of sit-down-and-do-it writing strategies and practical advice for creating scripts and solving writing problems. Overall, the book teaches a feel for what is dramatic in stories, scripts, and movies. It teaches you how to express your heart and mind and how to play with ideas until a notion, which at first glance might seem ordinary, refracts into something fresh and original. The movie industry term for these skills is *story sense*.

ORGANIZATION OF THE BOOK

Chapter 1 discusses how to locate dramatic story ideas and how to expand a notion or character into the beginnings of a plot.

Chapters 2 and 3 continue the discussion of plotting. Although there is no magic formula that eliminates this work, story construction is my teaching specialty, so you can count on more than enough instruction on conflict, theme, frame, style, emotional slant, dramatic problem, and related topics for solving this crucial aspect of the work. Like the mass of the iceberg that lies below the surface, these values interlock to form the structure and spine of the plot. One of the strategies used in this thinking is a snippet of advice that seems easy enough: *Write simple plots and complex characters.* This advice, one of hundreds of writing strategies that are part of the web of story sense, may seem simple, but it has profound implications, for if this proposition is reversed, there is an excellent chance that the story and its script will fail. The discussions will enable you to fully understand this thought and to incorporate it into your sense of story.

Chapter 4 reveals how the scripting process uses three dramatic units (*bits, scenes,* and *sequences*) to build stories, characters, and drama. Particular attention is given to how scenes and subplots are driven by conflict and how they are structured and dramatized. To demonstrate how professionals critique motion picture material, the chapter analyzes a commercial movie scene.

Chapter 5 explores one of the primary lessons of this book, which deals with writing characters who have interior lives, histories, and motivations. Emotionally dimensional characters are created when they are thought through and imagined so vividly that they come to life and drive the story. To guide you into this level of imagining, you will be given techniques for accessing your unconscious mind where your characters dwell, waiting to be brought to life.

Chapter 6 continues the exploration of character by examining how dialogue advances the narrative and reveals the inner being of the characters. The chapter also discusses subtext and "actable" dialogue, that is, what the characters feel but do not express overtly.

Chapter 7, on dramatization, presents dozens of strategies for charging stories and scripts with energy, tension, and drama.

Chapter 8 examines how screenwriters tell stories with images rather than with dialogue and talking heads. This chapter on visual storytelling and those on plotting, scene construction, and dramatization look closely at topics that are often neglected.

Chapter 9 is about writing stage directions that communicate the movie imagined by the screenwriter. Examples from noteworthy screenplays illustrate.

Chapter 10 explains script format and how to write scripts according to the standards that the movie industry expects.

Chapter 11 is based on another piece of enduring movie advice: *Screenplays are not written; they are rewritten.* Accordingly, this chapter serves as a point-by-point checklist that reviews everything discussed previously, so you can use it to troubleshoot all aspects of your story and script.

Chapter 12 presents career counseling for new writers, plus advice on securing a literary agent, pitching and selling scripts, story conferencing, and other matters connected to launching and sustaining a writing career.

Although the chapters present more than enough content to create stories, characters, and scripts, a writer's skill package contains elements that must come from the writer. These include emotion, sensitivity, and story sense that chooses ideas and stories with artistic and commercial appeal. The writer also must be willing to knock on doors, to face rejection, and to endure the stress that is part of life in the arts. Such resiliency is part of *willfullness*, which is perhaps the most important arrow in the screenwriter's quiver. To these writerly contributions, add the wild card of dumb luck that can arrive through a chance meeting, a script that catches a reader in the right mood, or whatever happenstance launches a career. In the end, the surest way to become lucky is to write good scripts—and to continue writing them until they sell. This is more likely to happen when one focuses on creating good scripts rather than worrying about whether they will sell. Because hope and energy are so important to new writers, it is important to believe that good screenwriting is recognized and tends to get discovered; therefore, anyone who can create a page-turner script should expect that the work will come to the attention of movie professionals who are eternally vigilant for good material. (Traits of such scripts are described in the first chapter.)

STORY SENSE: *A SCREENWRITING COURSE IN A BOOK*

The chapters explain how to find movie ideas and how to develop them into plots, scenes, and scripts. Each chapter concludes with a summary and exercises for reinforcing the discussions. The book also contains an extensive glossary and appendixes that present recommended films, movie clips, media to illustrate the discussions, plus studio reviewing forms, commercial and professional information, and other screenwriting documents.

Individually, the lessons are easily understood, but they are numerous, so plan to spend about ten hours per week to complete each of the twelve chapters (including the exercises). A chapter per week is enough time for the lessons to sink in. Apply the lessons to the movies you watch, the scripts you read, and especially to your screenwriting, which I hope will be inspired by *Story Sense*. If you work through the book in the manner described, you will approximate the experience of a full-blown, semester-long screenwriting course. One good course is all you need; additional courses only provide another perspective plus repetition and practice aimed at teaching what was not learned earlier.

Throughout, the discussions are illustrated by examples from scores of well-known films.[1] To ensure that major concepts are fully explained, the discussions are also tied to four mainstream films that represent a range of story styles: *The Verdict* (character study), *The Terminator* (action story), *Witness* (action and character), and *Sleepless in Seattle* (romantic comedy).

[1]The terms *films, movies, motion pictures,* and *TV* refer to feature films, narrative television, and short films, even when (for brevity) references in the text are mainly to feature films.

Various schemes for connecting the four main study films to the discussions were tried, and the most useful approach was to briefly describe the moment that illustrates the point being made in the text. Additionally, all references to the four study films are keyed to shot numbers in the scripts, which allows readers who secure one or more of the four titles to quickly locate the moment referenced. Shooting scripts of the four main study films can be secured from Movie Media, P.O. Box 1544, 11420 Santa Monica Blvd., Los Angeles, CA 90025, or from other commercial sources.

ACKNOWLEDGMENTS

Of the many kind people who have given direction to my life in screenwriting, my wife Sally must be mentioned first. Perhaps I could have selected a more arduous profession—bomb disposal, or teaching eighth grade as she did for many years—but she has been my rod and my comfort for almost four decades. Bless this dear woman.

From the professional side, I would like to acknowledge the cooperation of Metro Goldwyn Mayer, Warner Brothers, Republic Pictures, Walt Disney Studios, Paramount Pictures, Turner Broadcasting, Columbia Pictures, Universal Pictures, United Artists, Hemdale Productions, and Zanuck-Brown Productions for permitting me to print excerpts from their motion picture scripts. Appreciation and respect also extend to the men and women who wrote the scripts cited; their work is the inspiration and standard for new writers everywhere. Quoted screenwriters are individually acknowledged in the text.

To colleagues in the Writers Guild of America, who have shared their hard-won writing skills over the years, I am also most grateful. There are too many names to cite, although Richard Brooks, Philip Dunne, Louis Pelletier, E. Jack Neuman, David Dortort, Jaron Summer, and Nelson Gidding must be singled out for their support.

Additional cooperation came from my colleagues at the School of Cinema-Television at the University of Southern California. Mort Zarcoff, Woody Omens, Frank McAdams, John Morrill, and Bob Enders are among many who reviewed, counseled, and encouraged me; I am grateful to them as well.

Valuable help also came from students from my writing classes. Their arguments, questions, and comments inspired much of what went into this book. I am grateful to these fine men and women.

Thanks too to colleagues from other schools who reviewed this book—Lew Hunter at UCLA, Andy Horton at Loyola New Orleans, and Bonnie Engdahl at Cal Arts. The publisher's reviewers were also a source of helpful advice for making the book work in the classroom: Linda Anthon, Valencia Community College; Jeffrey Chown, Northern Illinois University; Walter F. McCallum, Santa Rosa Jr. College; Peter Moller, Syracuse University; Eran Preis, Temple University; James B. Steerman, Vassar College; Fred P. Watkins, University of North Texas; and Paul Younghouse, Indiana State University.

Additionally, I am indebted to McGraw-Hill editors Cynthia Ward, Annette Bodzin, and Linda Biemiller for shepherding the book through its many revisions.

Finally, my appreciation goes to friends and students who reviewed the manuscript. They include Polly Cohen, Eric David, Paul Duke, Raul Fernandez, Susan Komisaruk, Beatrice Palicka, Gregg Rossen, Dan Sullivan, John Tarver, and especially Professor Malvin Wald of USC and Malcolm Palmatier of The RAND Corporation.

Paul Lucey

PART ONE

Writing the Story

Most screenwriters find that creating a three- or four-page story for motion pictures is an unnaturally difficult task, so brace for it. This is true despite earnest teachers, broadsides from famous screenwriters, promises of fame and fortune to those who master story, and a considerable tonnage of books that explain how wonderfully simple screenwriting is. Because developing a viable plot is the essential first step of screenwriting—writing the script is step two; rewriting and selling are step three—almost half of this book concentrates on writing stories for feature films and television,

I wish I could announce that all this attention has tamed the dragon of story, but this is not the case, because there are too many styles and genres of stories, too many styles and genres of writers, and not enough ways to be fresh and original. But this

is an ancient lament, and what writers need are strategies to make plotting more productive. To help with this, I have gathered a number of insights that have demonstrated their story value. The first you've already been told—plotting is hard work. Another perspective views screenwriting as a left-brain/right-brain activity in which the story is worked out mainly in the rational side, while writing the script is done in the imaginative side. Although this division means that plotting is, for the most part, a thinking process, you should leaven your work with a degree of creative anarchy. This will allow your instincts and intuition to fire off the occasional lightning bolts that can punch through the membrane of what is ordinary and get you into what is fresh and imaginative. The egg tooth for breaking into the imaginative realm resides within your unconscious, and so a primary goal of this book is to lead you to this interior domain. The unconscious is where screenwriters use imagination to pull forth the emotionally complex characters needed to bring simple stories to life.

There is no magic formula to tapping into the unconscious or to writing a story. As you will see, the first four chapters will press you with dozens of story insights, commercial considerations, creative challenges, and assorted do's and don'ts. This is dense material, so do not rush through the discussion or become intimidated by the time and effort needed to work out, motivate, and justify what happens in your plot. A key story lesson is that good work takes as long as it takes, for if writing stories were easy, everybody would be doing it and movies would be much better than they are.

CHAPTER 1

Selecting an Idea for a Motion Picture Story

*This chapter examines how writers organize an idea
into a feature film or a television story and also
examines the traits of a good motion picture story idea.*

Because a viable story is the surest way to sell scripts and movies, this chapter deals with the characteristics of good story ideas and how to locate them. *Story* and *plot* are used interchangeably throughout this book, since both terms refer to the sequence of dramatic incidents. The definitions can be sharpened somewhat when *story* is viewed as containing implications of character and motivation. *Plot,* by comparison, refers mainly to incidents that reveal what happens in the drama. To illustrate: Stated as a plot summary, *The Verdict* is about an alcoholic lawyer who uses a surprise witness to defeat the most powerful lawyer in Boston. Stated as a story summary, *The Verdict* is about an alcoholic lawyer who is motivated by old grievances against enemies who, years earlier, ruined his life. The hero defeats his opponents after locating a witness whose life was also wrecked by their common adversary.

In most cases a movie plot/story presents a history of what happens when characters are confronted by a challenge of some sort—winning a prize, defeating a villain, finding love, and the like. Screenwriters complicate the narrative by inventing incidents of plot that have an impact on the characters and on the values that have been invested in the story idea. As will be discussed, these values form the structure that supports the three acts of the story.

To help you sort through the story possibilities that swirl about early in the writing, you will be introduced to the six story archetypes that are the ancient models of most narratives. Understanding the archetypes and the special nature of motion picture plots can enrich your story notion until it begins to shape into a plot. To this end, you will be encouraged to create temporary characters who add a human dimension to the developing story.

Locating a story idea begins when a writer takes a shine to a character, an image, a situation, a notion, or whatever attracts his or her interest. Story ideas can come from the daily press, from people we know, from personal experience, or from any of the sources to be cited shortly. An idea also can bubble up from the unconscious, which happened to Callie Khouri: as she parked her car one night after work, the idea for *Thelma and Louise* came to her. Khouri thought about the notion for a year or so before she sat down to write it. Although she had never written before, she completed her script in six months, sold it within weeks for a million dollars, and went on to win the Best Original Screenplay Academy Award in 1991. Note the two lessons here: First, Khouri recognized the value of her idea and wrote it into a professional script. Second, good stories sell, whether written by professionals or by beginners.

Movie ideas take shape when a screenwriter devises a way to combine ordinary characters and situations into something extraordinary. There is, for example, nothing remarkable about a weary gunfighter struggling to escape his violent past. *Shane, The Gunfighter,* and many other westerns are based on such a situation. David Webb Peoples combined this notion with an appreciation of the terrible nature of gunfighting and the strange ability of some men to endure this hellish life. The result was the Oscar-nominated script *Unforgiven.*

Another example: Screenwriters William Kelley and Earl W. and Pamela Wallace took a familiar situation—police corruption tied to a fortune in drug money—and gave it a fresh spin by staging the story among the Amish, where the hero finds romance with a young widow. *Witness,* the script based on this notion, won the Best Original Screenplay Academy Award in 1985.

These examples raise questions about which story ideas lead to good scripts and good movies. Certainly, the idea should be fresh, which means we have not heard it before—not exactly. Also, stories usually benefit when the action takes place in interesting locations. The characters should be people we want to know better because they are quirky, interesting, and unpredictable. The story should have a few surprising twists and turns that keep it from becoming predictable. Also, the story should be believable and worth the audience's time because it has something to say.

I have tried to sharpen these generalities by asking studio and network executives what they look for in a story, but in each case the person questioned has put on a serious face and said straight out, "I'll know it when I see it." Screenwriters are in a similar position. Endless prospects present themselves, but the idea undertaken is usually based on a personal sense that the notion is worth writing into a story; that is, writers also rely on knowing a good idea when they see it.

In most cases our story judgments are based on a complicated mix of personal values and our understanding of how the motion picture industry operates. Because the reader's sense of story is a personal value that this book intends to strengthen, let us take a closer look at what goes into a good story idea.

CHARACTERISTICS OF GOOD STORY IDEAS

Simplicity

Most movie executives respond to ideas that offer unique characters and dramatic situations that are thoughtful, different, and, most precious of all, *inter-*

esting from beginning to end. I have wrestled with the concept of what characterizes an interesting story idea and have come up with a few observations. It seems that some story notions are interesting because the writers have conceptualized them in an original style, as in *Raising Arizona, Pulp Fiction,* or *Ghostbusters.* Others are powered by a strange creature *(Alien),* an exotic setting and/or circumstance *(The Shawshank Redemption),* an offbeat character *(The Last Seduction),* an unusual situation *(It Could Happen to You),* or a factor that has not been tried recently (the magic realism in *Like Water for Chocolate* or the slapstick of *Dumb and Dumber).* In most cases, the originating idea is presented as a simple plot that puts interesting characters through a major ordeal of some sort.

In the Line of Fire illustrates some of these points. The story idea involves a Secret Service agent who survived the Kennedy assassination in Dallas and who must now prevent an assassin from killing the current president. That situation is complicated by the intensity of both the hero and the villain as they conflict over who will prevail. This brief statement summarizes the movie. Many films are equally simple when reduced to a sentence or two in this way. Let this be our first lesson: *Movie stories are usually simple.* This book advocates using the story idea to form a sentence summary of the plot, which is then developed in more detail.

New writers often do not recognize the simplicity of movie stories because of the intense nature of the motion picture experience, which moves audiences out of real time and into *reel* time, where their attention is controlled by the tension and the pace of the on-screen story. In this way, intensity and dramatic focus allow movies to gradually reveal incidents of plot that draw attention to the characters. This observation ties into one of the main points of this book: *Write simple stories and complex characters.*

Dramatic Contrast

Interesting story ideas usually involve characters who oppose each other in ways that create *dramatic contrast.* In most cases the contrast results from two strong personalities who conflict over a problem, as in *A Man for All Seasons* or *Midnight Cowboy.* Dramatic contrast allows writers to dramatize the story by exacerbating the situation until it creates a worst-case scenario. This means that whatever can go wrong for the hero goes wrong, until there seems to be no way for this person to survive the problem and/or to defeat the stronger villain. This is called dramatizing—raising the stakes and getting the hero into trouble—and it is discussed at length in Chapter 7.

Screenwriters impale characters on the horns of the problem and use the ensuing struggle to create a dramatic plot, as in *Sleepless in Seattle,* one of our four main study films. The problem of the story seems simple enough—getting Sam and Annie together from opposite coasts. The problem became difficult when the writer put the matchmaking in the hands of an eight-year-old boy and a radio call-in show. As the characters become caught up in resolving this problem, the drama intensifies in a way that puts the principals through a life-shaping dramatic ordeal. Most American movies are built around problems that are life-shaping and/or life-threatening.

Dramatic contrast arises from disparities in social standing, economic or career opportunity, intelligence, or a power or an ability. *Natural Born Killers* presents characters from gruesome backgrounds who contrast with the world around them. Whether the character is special *(Edward Scissorhands, Tootsie)* or the situation is special *(Speed, Mississippi Burning)*, dramatic contrast can produce an interesting story. The range of this contrast is immense: *Forrest Gump* relates how a mentally disadvantaged young man wins fame and fortune; Mickey and Mallory in *Natural Born Killers* are the dark side of Gump, naïfs who become mass murderers as they too blunder on to fame and a life of sorts; and the two bozos in *Dumb and Dumber* are comic versions of Mickey and Mallory. Thus all three stories present characters who contrast dramatically with the circumstances of their lives.

Dramatic contrast creates tension by presenting a hero who takes on a task or a situation that turns out to be impossibly difficult, if not dangerous. The situation is presented in ways that make the audience expect that something disastrous will occur, which causes viewers to tense up and connect to the ordeal of the characters. *The Terminator* evokes this tension because the cyborg contrasts violently with the world it has entered. The tension in *Forrest Gump* arises from the audience's worry about how a mentally challenged man will be able to survive in a dangerous world. Although Forrest's prospects seem impossible, the inventions of the story enable him to emerge victorious.

Another perspective on dramatic contrast is how it creates tensions that unbalance the status quo. The screenwriter creates incidents to cause the unbalance and then invents additional incidents that lead to an improved status quo at the end of the story. In *The Verdict* the status quo is unbalanced after the hero decides to take on the establishment that destroyed his life years earlier. The idea of the story is to give Galvin a final chance to even the score—if he can defeat a mighty foe. Worry over the hero's ability to win the case causes dramatic tension, but in the end, a more equitable status quo is reached after the hero defeats the establishment's top lawyer.

At the heart of using dramatic contrast is an ancient narrative ploy: *Confront a relatively weak hero with a more powerful adversary and/or problem.* This is the single most dramatic strategy available to screenwriters. Note how it shows up in our four main study films. The contrast in *The Verdict* involves an uneven battle, a drunkard lawyer pitted against the most outstanding lawyer in Boston. *The Terminator* sets a young waitress and a soldier from the future against an indestructible creature that has been programmed to kill them. The problem in *Sleepless in Seattle* is finding a way for a young boy in Seattle to unite his father with a woman who lives in Baltimore. *Witness* presents dramatic contrast by partnering a tough cop from Philadelphia and an unworldly Amish widow; the pair must hide from the police conspiracy that intends to murder them. Their plight is made more dramatic because the hero is wounded and seemingly without allies, because the Amish who are hiding the hero are unarmed pacifists. In each example, the dramatic contrast is based on some form of inequality between the main characters and the circumstances of their situation.

The situation of the story can create drama that forces normal people to take radical action when confronted by danger and confrontation. We see this happen in *Jurassic Park, Schindler's List,* and *The Bridge on the River Kwai.* One of the traits of good story ideas is how they support dramatic situations that drive the characters and create tension. In most cases, as will be explained, the tension is caused by the audience's fear that the hero will be defeated by the villain and/or will be unable to resolve the dramatic problem of the story.

News stories with dramatic contrast occur daily. Not long ago I came across such a notion in the sports pages (an excellent source of story ideas). The item concerned an all-star college athlete whose father, a drug-addled derelict, mopes about town. This sad situation presents strong dramatic contrast because the athlete is moving toward stardom, while the father's destination is death and disgrace—unless something happens. A story could be built around making that "something" happen dramatically. The difficulty of doing this in a positive way and the life-or-death stakes involved with the idea bear the promise of a story with drama and heart.

Humanism

The father-athlete item touches on how dramatic stories usually challenge the main characters with an overwhelming test. In the end, the hero endures the ordeal and is a better person for it. This dynamic—the struggle to realize our human potential—is found in many American movies, as noted by veteran producer Edgar Scherick (*They Shoot Horses Don't They*):

> Audiences respond to, are touched by yarns spun around men and women who act in response to their humanity. And when touched, the audience will leave the theater anxious to share their experience with others. The yearning, thrilling, healing—whatever it is—that we bring to a boil within their hungry soul makes people proud of their humanity. Give them pictures that remind them that they are made of better stuff than what they see on our streets, in our newscasts, and populating our government. Picking pictures is plucking heartstrings. My heart leaps up when I am told a story of the triumph of the human spirit. I assure you that I am not alone.[1]

Good scripts reveal the world because they are invested with thematic content that has relevance and importance. Call this point *humanism.* Humanism suggests that the story connects to our struggle to be fully human; dramatic contrast suggests that there is an inequality in the way the hero and villain deal with that human struggle. Later, we will discuss how the hero manages to win against greater odds, but first note how these values show up in *The Verdict.* Dramatic contrast results when a lowly hero

---

[1]Writers Guild of America seminar, February 4, 1994.

takes on the Boston establishment. In terms of humanism, the story idea concerns the hero's struggle to reclaim his life and his belief in the law. Considerable thinking goes into animating a notion such as this, which brings up another characteristic of a good idea, the writer's perspective on the material.

Writerly Perspective

Good stories result when writers come up with ethical and/or social values that connect to the organizing idea. Initially vague or remote, this value usually must be teased out of the work through careful thinking. Call this fourth aspect of a good story the *writerly perspective*. Experience teaches that story ideas seldom jump out and hug us; rather, they must be searched out and buffed to a shine as we ponder what the notion means and what we are trying to say with it. When we think long enough and hard enough, profound meaning can be extracted from the core idea and how the dramatic situation affects the characters. It is through such thinking that writers turn ordinary notions into extraordinary movie ideas.

A few examples of how this works may help nail down this point. *Glory's* writerly perspective was how it saw the black soldiers who marched to their death during the Civil War as brave men rather than former slaves. Screenwriter Kevin Jarre realized the significance of their sacrifice to future generations, and his writerly perspective on a remote historical incident created a simple story with dramatic contrast that touched our common humanity.

Writerly perspective can be grand, as in *Lawrence of Arabia,* or modest, as in Horton Foote's redemption story, *Tender Mercies.* The latter concerns a wrecked country-western singer (Robert Duvall's Mack Sledge) who is reformed by a good woman, so that her son accepts him as a father. The movie ends as man and boy toss a football back and forth. That precious moment was Foote's writerly perspective on the story, for it represented one of God's tender mercies for living a good life. His take on the material was part of why Foote won a best screenplay Oscar in 1983 for this script.

Stories enriched by the writer's perspective usually have something to say. Such stories touch the hearts of moviegoers by refracting ordinary life experiences and turning them into drama. Working at this level requires writers to invest thought and energy in the story idea and its characters. Unless the writer's heart is open during this work, it is unlikely that the story will open the heart of the audience. The point here is that *the screenwriter is the source of the best story ideas and scripts.* When a simple idea has been thought through regarding the story goal and includes a hero-villain conflict that contains dramatic contrast and humanism, then the notion has acquired four perspectives of a good story. This is by no means the end of the thinking that goes into an idea; for example, writers must also decide which audience will find the story appealing.

Consideration of Intended Audience

Will the story appeal mainly to youngsters, to young adults, or to adults? Once this has been determined, the screenwriter should develop the story idea in ways that appeal to its targeted audience. Each age group favors a different type of story, with only the occasional *Jurassic Park, Ghostbusters,* or *Mrs. Doubtfire* drawing large cross-over audiences from all three age categories. Selecting a particular age group for which to write is a judgment call that depends on the writer's sense of which segment of the audience will find the story most entertaining. In most cases, the main characters and the audience are similar in age and in their interests.

The Youth Audience

Children up to about age twelve are drawn to stories that are not too intense emotionally, not too sexy, and not too violent. The main characters in movies made for this age group are often children or animals (as in *The Lion King* and *Free Willy*). The writer creating a story for children should not allow the narrative to drift into a different audience-age category; if it does, the tale may lose its appeal. This happened with *Last Action Hero,* which spoofed itself and the action genre before a youth audience that was not amused. Similarly, Ridley Scott's 1985 film *Legend* lost its youth audience when, halfway through, it drifted from unicorns and a damsel in distress to a story with devilishly sexual overtones. Do not confuse stories *for* children with films *about* children; the latter are aimed at older audiences, as in *King of the Hill, Pelle the Conqueror, The 400 Blows,* and the like.

The Young Adult Audience

Young people ages twelve to twenty-four like a range of stories that runs from coming-of-age yarns (*Pretty in Pink*), to horror and gross-out stories (*Halloween, Police Academy*), to stories about superheroes. They also like "date" stories (*Some Kind of Wonderful*), adventure stories (*The Fugitive*), action pictures (*Speed*), and broad comedies (*Dumb and Dumber*). Occasionally, a quality film may break away from the pack to address youthful problems, as in *Dead Poets Society, Zebrahead,* or *Boyz N the Hood.* Unfortunately, many excellent films made for this age group do not draw audiences.

The Adult Audience

Moviegoers eighteen years of age or older are drawn to a wide range of stories, from blockbusters and epics (*Dances with Wolves*) to low-budget thrillers (*The Last Seduction*) to character stories (*Born on the Fourth of July, Apollo 13*). The situations, language, and sexuality of these works, which include foreign films, tend to be adult.

Style of the Story (Unreal, Real, or Surreal?)

Screenwriters must decide whether an idea will be written in an unrealistic, realistic, or surrealistic style. The story style chosen will influence how the idea is imagined and how the beats[2] of the plot are written. The three styles are defined below.

Unreal Stories

Unreal stories impose a prescriptive point of view on the work, which means that the screenwriter romanticizes, alters, and skims over negatives that might jeopardize the story's commercial intentions. For example, *Pretty Woman* was originally a realistic story about a junky prostitute who is hired by a wealthy businessman for a week. Although Jonathan Lawton's original script was effective, Disney decided they could make more money on the project by prettying it up, so they had the script rewritten. Their instincts paid off, and this commercial confection grossed several hundred million dollars. Numbers such as these are on the minds of the executives who buy scripts; writers—especially successful writers—think about such matters as well.

Real Stories

Real stories deal realistically with love, families, health, drugs, and other aspects of the human condition. Real stories tend to rely on characterizations and the power of drama for effect, rather than on puffed-up make-believe and the flash of complicated plots. Writing these stories means dealing with substantive issues in ways that do not depress the audience—that is, there should be some sort of a positive or hopeful ending. *Born on the Fourth of July* and *McCabe and Mrs. Miller* are examples of realistic, entertaining stories told honestly. This topic raises the hot-button issue of upbeat endings. Although this subject is discussed in Chapter 3, for now I would advise new writers to avoid stories that end with the defeat of the main characters. Audiences do not find

---

[2]A story *beat* is an incident in the story. For example, *The Verdict* opens with a one-minute incident in which the hero hustles business in a funeral home. The barn raising in *Witness* is also a story beat (or incident), but it plays for about eight minutes. To distinguish between their differing lengths and content, beats of a story are sorted by length into bits, scenes, and sequences. These terms will be explained in Chapter 4, but some abbreviated definitions will do for now: *Bits* play for about a minute; they deal mainly with the plot. *Scenes* usually play for about three to four minutes; they deal mainly with character. *Sequences* make major story points such as introducing the main characters and the problem; sequences are composed of bits and scenes and usually play for five to fifteen minutes.

such works to be entertaining. Producers[3] are aware of this, which is why they seldom buy downer scripts. The few that are tried *(Last Exit to Brooklyn, Iron-weed, Mr. Jones)* usually do not attract an audience. As with everything in this book, there are exceptions to this advice. *Raging Bull* is one of them. This realistic story about a prizefighter plays in the mean streets of New York during the 1950s. It presents characters and a story universe that are raw and powerful, yet the film attracted a sizable audience because it had a slightly upbeat ending. Movies that conclude on a hopeful note, however slight, have a better chance of selling.

Surreal Stories

Surreal stories present a distorted, often spooky view of reality, as in *Blue Velvet* or *The Man Who Fell to Earth*. The style does well with offbeat humor, as in *Dr. Strangelove* and *Groundhog Day*. Surreal films are an interesting eddy in the movie mainstream that are favored by directors such as David Cronenberg *(Videodrome)*, Roman Polanski *(Repulsion)*, and the Coen brothers *(Barton Fink)*.

The Emotional Slant

A successful plot makes audiences feel sad, makes them feel worried, or makes them laugh. Unless the story provokes a strong emotional response on at least one of these points, it may end up as earnest, preachy, or angry.

Certain ideas seem made for humor: the two loonies in *Dumb and Dumber* scream out to be written comically, as do the notions that led to *Dave, Mrs. Doubtfire,* and *Young Frankenstein*. Writing such stories requires situations, incidents of plot, characters, and dialogue that are comical. As with almost everything connected to film, there are variations: humor can be screwball, black, dry, offbeat, slapstick, satiric, domestic, sardonic, and so on. Appreciating when an idea proposes humor will incline your thinking in that direction, thus sparing you from swatting at endless possibilities. This is another small decision that writers use to develop a story idea.

Scripts that make the audience fearful also have a considerable range. At one end are shock-horror stories *(Night of the Living Dead)* and ghost stories *(The Uninvited)*. At the other end are straight dramas *(In the Name of the Father)*

---

[3]A *producer,* as used in this text, refers to someone who works for a movie studio or a production company. There are several hundred of the latter firms in the United States that buy movie scripts that they develop and often sell to one of the seven major studios. The studios, who also buy scripts, have the resources to fund, produce, and distribute movies (in exchange for a share of the profits). Studios and independent production companies who have earned a reputation for good work often form affiliations that endure for years. Some of these production companies are owned by actors and directors—Universal Studios funds and distributes movies developed by Steven Spielberg's production company, Amblin Entertainment, as well as those of Robert Redford's company, Wildwood Enterprises. Movie ads often list the production companies and their studio affiliations. Sometimes called the seven sisters, the major studios are Warner Brothers, Disney, Universal, Paramount, MGM/United Artists, Columbia/TriStar, and 20th Century-Fox.

that cause audiences to worry about a hero who seems headed for defeat. In between is a range of stories that causes audiences to be fearful about whether the hero will emerge victorious *(Kramer vs. Kramer, In the Line of Fire, Braveheart)*. The audience worries because it has been persuaded to root for the hero and to oppose the villain. Evoking this response involves writing tasks that will be discussed in later chapters.

Sad stories *(My Life, Dying Young)* work best when the pathetic emotion is earned by the ordeal of the drama and when there is emotional uplift at the end. These stories sometimes give audiences that rarest of treats—a tragedy with a happy ending, as in *Butch Cassidy and the Sundance Kid, Viva Zapata,* and *Thelma and Louise.* These stories pleased audiences because the main characters were willing to die to honor their beliefs. In the end their courage won them a form of immortality—why else would we remember someone like Bonnie Parker or Clyde Barrow?

Many stories combine several or all three of these emotional slants. Humor and fear can create a dramatic ambiance, as in *Dr. Strangelove. My Favorite Year* and *Forrest Gump* combine laughter and tears. *The Elephant Man* combines fear and compassion for Merrick's tragic deformity and his sweet soul. *Sleepless in Seattle* uses clever dialogue, charming characters, and a needful situation to make the audience laugh. At the same time the movie causes worry (fear) about whether the hero and heroine will get together. Sadness comes in because of the plight of the lonely father and his motherless son.

Investing a story with a strong emotional slant is essential to dramatizing the material. Unless the story idea is developed so that its emotional slant is strongly stated, there is a good chance that the work will fail.

Having introduced simplicity, dramatic contrast, humanism, writerly perspective, audience, and emotional slant as aspects to consider when working up a story idea, we shall now explore the sources that screenwriters use to locate story ideas.

ADAPTATION

Out of the gate, my advice on adaptation is to avoid it. The need is for new vision, new energy, and new passion; there is already too much recycling of old work. Adaptation, especially of novels, tends to be demanding work that can defeat the most experienced screenwriters. Even so, many of us are driven to adapt, so here is a short tour of the subject in terms of adapting fiction, stage plays, and items from the press.

Adapting Works of Fiction

William Kennedy, who refers to himself as "a practicing novelist who once in a while writes a screenplay [*Ironweed*]," has worked both sides of the street regarding adaptation, and his comments are relevant to our topic:

Film . . . yearns for coherence. The novel does also, but the novel can tolerate sideshows and excrescences that wouldn't be allowed by most modern film-makers. Because the novel requires an exercise of the intellect, an intimacy with the reader's mind and reasoning powers, it can luxuriate in language alone, and gain in depth from these excursions. But because film is an exercise in immediacy, in raw life perceived in the instant that it happens, these meanderings are judged to be irrelevancies that dilute or divert the principal focus of the story. Stay in the center ring and never mind the sideshows, is the revered wisdom.[4]

Kennedy's remarks touch upon a primary difference between prose and cinematic writing: movies usually require a strong, externalized action line (plot). Keep this in mind when a book or a short story charms you with its cinematic possibilities. Also ask whether the story is worth the trouble. Ask whether the characters are interesting. Is the story cinematic, or does it bog down in the internalized thoughts and feelings of the characters? Does the yarn present an entertaining plot? Does it have interesting locations and a strong action line?[5]

Figure out why the source material is appealing, then ask whether those elements can be used to create a "new and improved" version of the story. If truth be known, many genre standards are reworked from earlier stories that are themselves adaptations of earlier stories. This is not plagiarism; it is a strategy that was old when Shakespeare "adapted" *Romeo and Juliet* from the works of earlier writers. Turnabout being fair play, *The Tempest* was rewritten into *Forbidden Planet*, with Walter Pigeon's Dr. Morbius serving as the science fiction version of Prospero. Robby the robot is a stand-in for Ariel, and Morbius's daughter (played by Anne Francis) is a stand-in for Miranda. The beast Caliban is Morbius's incestuous Oedipal impulse, and the crew of the stranded spaceship are stand-ins for the mariners in the original work.

Writers adapt familiar stories by inventing new characters, new locations, new actions, different time settings, and a fresh emotional thrust or interpretation. Steve Martin was on this tack when he rewrote *Cyrano de Bergerac* by turning Rostand's soldier of ancient France into the contemporary American fire chief that we meet in *Roxanne*. (Martin also rewrote *Silas Marner* into *A Simple Twist of Fate*.) Also note similarities between *Body Heat* and *Double Indemnity*, and how closely *Pale Rider* follows the plot of *Shane*. *The Front Page* has been redone as *His Girl Friday*, *Switching Channels*, and other variations.

Certain literary works read beautifully but turn out to be mainly style and a past-tense, internalized plot based on what the characters are thinking. Such

---

[4] *American Film*, January 1988, p. 25.
[5] Action movies appeal to production companies because these stories translate well to foreign audiences, whereas comedies do not. Richard Munchkin, a producer of low-budget action movies, makes the point: "When we go overseas, we sit down with the buyers and say what do you want to see? and No. 1 is action. Comedies don't translate. What we think is funny they won't think is funny in Turkey or Malaysia, but a car chase is a car chase in any language." Overseas markets now account for about one-half of the gross income of American movies and TV, which is why many producers are drawn to action stories.

content may not offer the focused storyline that motion pictures require. Screenwriters compensate for this by pressing the characters with a dramatic problem that intensifies until it is resolved in the climactic scene. Even when movies ease up on their dramatic focus, it is usually done to set the audience up before hitting it with an even more powerful surge of drama.

Screenwriters respect literary quality, but they know that movies must pull people into the theater and entertain them. The difficulty of doing this was apparent in the adaptation of John Updike's *The Witches of Eastwick*. Although *Witches* is a sparkling little novel, it lacks a clear storyline that could sustain a two-hour movie. To fix this problem, screenwriter Michael Cristofer made so many changes that the movie on screen is more his work than Updike's. In this case, Cristofer used the source novel as the takeoff point for what is almost an original work of fiction.

The example makes a simple point: screenwriters are hired to write a movie script, and though they do their best to honor the source material, their obligation is to create an entertaining motion picture story. I have discussed this point with a number of screenwriters, including Nelson Gidding, an accomplished screenwriter who has adapted *The Andromeda Strain* and other works. He feels that his obligation as adapter is to use the source material to write a script that can be made into an entertaining motion picture. Gidding's thoughts are similar to those of the late Philip Dunne, who adapted several dozen novels and historical works for Darryl Zanuck. Dunne told me that he tried to be true to the source material but that this is not always possible. Like Gidding, Dunne felt that his job was to use the source material to create a strong unitary storyline that would accommodate a traditional three-act structure.

Dunne's experience with *How Green Was My Valley* is instructive here: he spent months trying to structure a story from Richard Llewellyn's sprawling novel about life in a turn-of-the-century Welsh mining town, but the story would not come together. Dunne was ready to give up on the project when the young actor (Roddy McDowell) who was to play the lead character (Huw Morgan) arrived in Los Angeles from England. Upon meeting McDowell, Dunne immediately solved the book's story problem: he tossed out the second half of the novel, in which Tyrone Power was to play Huw as an adult. Instead, Dunne based his script on Huw's life as a boy living with his family. Dunne had a similar adaptation experience when he extracted a storyline from the mass of John O'Hara's *Ten North Frederick*. Dunne, whose story was based on a portion of the book, noted that "some books cannot be adapted as written, and you use what you can to tell the best story possible."

Although filmmakers try to remain true to the original material, radical solutions may be needed to adapt it to the screen. Barry Reed's novel upon which the movie *The Verdict* was based spends a great deal of its time on lawyerish disputation and exposition. Such dialogue, however well-written, seldom does well in movies. To adapt the book, David Mamet added personal drama to a routine court case by weakening the hero with a betrayal that ruined his life and turned him into a legal lowlife. Once this point was established, the story allowed the character (Paul Newman's Frank Galvin) to be jerked around by the psychological string connected to the betrayal.

Adaptation Rights to Another Writer's Work

Rights to literary material are secured by contacting the publisher for the name and address of the writer's literary agent, who is the person to contact regarding the adaptation request. The agent and the author of the source material then negotiate an agreement aimed at giving the screenwriter exclusive rights to the source material for six months, or for whatever time is agreed upon. Most options involve fees that can range from $100 to many thousands of dollars—the price depends on the market and what the writer will pay. Several years ago a student (disregarding my advice) paid $3,000 for an 18-month option on a minor detective novel. Unfortunately, nothing came of this investment, and when the option expired, the agent asked for another option fee. Other writers are more ingenious, securing rights that require payment only after the adaptation sells.[6]

Adapting Works in the Public Domain

The U.S. Copyright Act of 1978 protects the rights of authors during their lifetime, plus fifty years from the date of publication. These rights involve legal protection to reproduce the work, to create derivative copies of the work, and to distribute copies of the work, as well as the right to perform and to display the copyright-protected work. For works published anonymously or as a "work for hire" (as movie and TV scripts are categorized), protection extends to the copyright holder for seventy-five years from the date of publication. (In most cases, the production company, *not* the writer, holds the copyright to TV and movie scripts.) Works published before 1978 have copyright protection for twenty-eight years with a right to renew for twenty-eight or forty-seven additional years, depending on the original date of publication. Older works that are beyond these windows of coverage no longer have copyright protection, and they can be adapted or excerpted without compensation or legal encumbrances.

Adapting Stage Plays

Certain stage plays appeal to filmmakers because of plot, dialogue, characters, and/or spectacle. Today's filmmakers have become skillful in "opening" stage plays so they have more visual content and so they do not bury the script in dialogue. Such an adaptation should have a strong storyline, it should contain visual potential, and (in most cases) it should not take place in a limited number of visually restricted interior locations.

---

[6]Screenwriters sometimes write directly to the author for permission. In some instances adaptation rights are given for a fee or a promise of future payment—or for nothing!

As will be discussed in Chapter 8, although it is possible to re-stage works so the story is more visual, a larger problem is adapting dialogue scenes so their dramatic points are made with images and action. Peter Shaffer confronted this problem when he adapted his stageplay *Amadeus* for the screen. Shaffer not only reshaped the relationship of the two main characters but also created scenes of rich visual content that were hardly suggested in the stage version. Alfred Uhry's adaptation of his play *Driving Miss Daisy* was also skillfully done for the screen. It is worth comparing the theatrical text of these two plays with their movie versions to see how the authors managed the shift from stage to screen. Both adaptations won Oscars for the writers.

Adapting Stories from the Press and the Public Record

Sometimes so many ideas are buzzing in our heads that we cannot decide which one to develop. At other times we may feel we have gone dry—forever! You can avoid the latter twinge—mere writer's panic—by always having one or two projects simmering in the back of your mind. This way, when a current project is finished, you can take up one of the back-burner items. Some writers stoke this process by accumulating a file system of news items that have been snipped from newspapers and magazines. File your gatherings in folders labeled as you wish. The topic categories in my clip file are biology, book reviews, characters, crime, drugs, environment, ethics, ethnic, history, homeless, immigration, love, medicine, money, nature, occult, occupations, oceans, psychology, race, religion, science, sex, space, sports, war, weird, and westerns.

You should be able to find at least one story idea every day in *The Los Angeles Times, The New York Times,* or similar papers. Human interest and sports stories, character sketches, articles on history, and book reviews are recommended. Writers find ideas by searching for them, and even when the news items are ignored (as most will be), the search process encourages story awareness. You will also be pleased to discover how dissimilar items often combine synergistically into an original story idea.

As you read the press, appreciate the human drama that spills into the public record every day. Often, the most useful news items are those containing specific details about characters, their backstory, and how they came to public attention. When you feel that your heartstrings have been plucked, when you feel anger or sadness, the news item may have value.

That stories taken from court cases, governmental hearings, and newspaper stories can be written into movies, is evidenced by such films as *Silkwood, All the President's Men,* and *The Positively True Adventures of the Alleged Texas Cheerleader-Murdering Mom.* However, there are legal concerns attached to many of these stories. One is that the principals in the actual event retain their right of publicity, even though their right of privacy has been set aside. Because of this, the parties cannot be named in the script unless they grant permission to do so.

Release forms and story rights open a vast legal swamp that is beyond the scope of this brief discussion, but you should know that the courts try to balance a citizen's right to publicity and privacy against the public's right to know about public business. Laws concerning privacy and publicity vary from state to state, so there are fifty different sets of laws. To avoid legal entanglements when adapting a story from a press item, screenwriters often secure signed releases from the principals. The goal here is an agreement that takes effect when the script sells and/or when it is made into a movie. It is advisable to pay a nominal fee (for example, $10) in exchange for a signed release; this applies even when claimants offer to waive payment and sign over their rights of privacy and publicity. The legal protection is worth the expense, in case the parties change their minds when they discover that their lives will be portrayed by Demi Moore or Jack Nicholson. It is advisable to have a lawyer handle these negotiations because production companies wish to avoid lawsuits. This also protects screenwriters, who should not commit months of work to a script that may be subject to lawsuits and injunctions that tie it up in court.

Legal entanglements can be sidestepped by rewriting the characters and the circumstance of the story until the scripted version bears scant resemblance to the source material. Screenwriters use this second approach to create fictional characters who have different names and backstories. Writers may also change the locations, the circumstances, the settings, and the context of the story. Such actions may lead to a script that is merely suggestive of the original news item story. Often this happens naturally as the inspiring event is reworked into an entertaining story and script.

A few examples of how this form of adaptation works will help illustrate the point. Wes Craven created his *Nightmare on Elm Street* movies after reading a news item in *The Los Angeles Times* concerning young Asians who died mysteriously in their sleep. The strangeness of their deaths so fascinated Craven that he began thinking about what might cause healthy youngsters to die this way. Craven's solution was to invent a killer who comes to life in the dreams of teenagers and kills them. This story concept—nightmares energized by the recurring demon figure of Freddy Kruger—was so expansive that many sequels have been made. The series struck a nerve with young adult audiences who identified with the hapless youngsters being tormented by Kruger. Nowhere does the series mention the original news item, since only the death-while-dreaming element was taken from it.

A somewhat more realistic use of a news story arose from a piece written by magazine writer Richard Preston for *The New Yorker* (October 2, 1992), which concerned a biohazard incident in a research lab. Hollywood picked up on the piece, and before long two production companies were bidding for the rights. The news item had movie appeal: A deadly virus contaminates a laboratory in Maryland and threatens the surrounding region with a monster plague; when the government is informed, a biological strike team is dispatched to contain the threat. In essence, the article reported a real-life version of *The Andromeda Strain*. The story, even in simple telling, suggests a three-act structure: the outbreak, the battle to contain the virus, the final victory. Such a techno-thriller has appeal because it is fresh, brainy, exotic, and visual, and it deals with an invisible, deadly menace.

When its bid for the rights to the source material fell short, one of the companies was advised by its legal department that it could fictionalize the original article; according to one executive, the advice was that "as long as we stayed away from the characters portrayed in the Preston article we could develop our own fictional story."[7] The company hired screenwriters and made its movie. The adaptation of the Preston article invented the details of the incident, changed the locations, and created a cast of fictional characters. The resulting movie *(Outbreak)* imagined a worst-case scenario that was based on the escape of a deadly virus that threatens the planet. To enliven the melodrama, the story roped in a ruthless military commander, germ warfare skullduggery, a broken marriage, and even the family dog. Manipulative or not, the mix of ingredients helped the movie to do well at the box office. The production company did all this without paying a penny to the parties mentioned in *The New Yorker* piece or to the author of the source article. This was possible because the incident reported by Preston was a true story that was duly reported in the public record, that occurred in a public facility, and that did not violate national security.

The second production company was less fortunate, for it paid $400,000[8] for the rights to Preston's article, the same story the other company picked up for the price of the magazine. Perhaps the second company felt that the payment would give it exclusivity, or perhaps it believed such a payment would impress the actors. Or the fee might have been a signal that indicated their desire to own bragging rights that would allow that company's version to be advertised as the *"true* story." In the end, both versions of the virus story experienced script problems because the screenwriters had to rush their work. To patch things up, "script doctors" were brought in for rewrites (top hands are paid $100,000 per week for such fix-ups). Ultimately, one of the scripts could not be whipped into shape, which caused the stars (Robert Redford and Jody Foster) to bail out. The collapse of the project cost the production company a reported $8 million, which is a measure of the high-stakes games that Hollywood plays.

The virus story contains several lessons: First, bad scripts seldom turn into good movies, even when they have the best actors. Second, to write a good movie, even when the story idea is outstanding, the writer must be given enough time to research and to write the script. Third, the virus story validates that the press is a source of good ideas but the story selected should be free of legal encumbrances.

The virus-story experience also points out that the rights to certain stories can be costly, but payment can be sidestepped when the characters, details, and locations are altered, which was the case with *Outbreak.* Again, this is not

---

[7]*The New York Times,* June 23, 1994.

[8]Apparently Preston's agreement with the production company was to pay off in full only after the movie went into production. When the project collapsed, he ended up with a front-end payment of $100,000. Preston earned considerably more when his original article was expanded into a best-seller.

plagiarism, for the common-law basis of the copyright statutes aims to encourage an open society where artists are free to use the public record to create works that serve the public interest. The value of this protection goes beyond entertainment, as evidenced in the virus story, which deals with a menace festering in an anonymous laboratory that was in the midst of millions of unsuspecting citizens. This is information that the public should know. Other stories have taken audiences into corporate boardrooms (*The Firm*), into government bureaucracies (*All the President's Men*), and other surroundings (*China Syndrome, Mississippi Burning, Apollo 13*) to tell tales of public concern. In most stories, the original news item is but the starting point for the screenwriter. Also in most cases, the resulting scripts were more dramatic and imaginative than the source material. This rarely happens automatically, and most press stories require considerable rewriting before they are worth making into a movie.

ADDITIONAL SOURCES FOR STORIES

Writing About Personal Experience

Miss Berry, my sixth grade teacher, advised us to use personal experience as a story source. She also told us to pay close attention to the people we observe, the stories we hear, and the incidents that happen to friends and acquaintances, for they too may have story value. This good advice still applies, as when two Runyonesque characters showed up at my health club. Both men were in their sixties and looked as if they might have been professional football players. Observing this pair, I began to wonder who these men were, where they came from, how they became friends, and what they did for a living. From such musings, a story idea dawned—what if the two men were retired gangsters? This notion set my story wheels to spinning: What might happen if the two were unhappy about forced retirement and were planning revenge on the mob? What if one of the men met a woman at the club and fell in love for the first time, threatening his lifelong friendship with the other fellow? What if these two dinosaurs bought the club with their retirement bonus and then had to run a business catering to mineral-water yuppies? In this way, casual observation of two strangers suggested story possibilities.

The example brings to mind advice that screenwriter Louis Pelletier (*Big Red*) offered during a visit to my class: "There are very few new plots; most of us use new and interesting characters in old plots." Crafty writer that he is, Pelletier appreciated the way active characters bring seemingly ordinary story ideas to life. Pelletier also urged the class to pay attention to people and to tune in on their story potential. He suggested speculating about people encountered in everyday life, inventing experiences for them that seem believable. Some writers record their character musings in a journal, while others record TV news shows to build a gallery of character types. I advise students to add one unique character to their rogues' gallery every month. Describe each character briefly, as in Frank Nugent's sketch of Victor McLaglen's Will Danaher, the nominal villain of *The Quiet Man*:

```
DANAHER is a giant of a man with a close-cropped bullet
head, tremendous shoulders, arms like a gorilla and
fists the size of catcher's mitts.  We already know of
him that he is a skinflint, a large farmer and—by some
freak biology—the brother of lovely Mary Kate.
```

Writing about Family Members

Observing people is an activity that also applies to one's family, so seek out those in your clan who might have stories worth dramatizing. Recently, a student who had been unable to come up with a story was asked to write a history of her family that began with both sets of grandparents and extended to the present. The following week, when her eight-page history was discussed in class, it was found to contain three excellent story ideas. Because the family-history approach usually means talking to relatives who can contribute to the narrative, promote your family history as a work in progress that encourages additional revelations. You may need to dig for the good stuff that the family would rather leave buried—they might prefer a story that glorified Grampie Dan and how he founded the feed store rather than one about what happened to awful Aunt Minn, who ran off with a knife-thrower and ended up working in a sardine factory in Alaska. Often families must be persuaded that tales of the black sheep are merely the takeoff point for a fictionalized story and that the finished yarn will have little resemblance to actual events or characters.

The only problem with this approach is that family stories have a way of reaching out of the grave and demanding that they be told *as they happened.* When that bony hand cannot be shaken off, the family approach to a story idea may lose its appeal. The same may be true for personal stories that are too painful to be contained in a script, although in some cases writers spend their careers trying to excise difficult life experiences, returning to certain themes through the years.

Pay attention to stories told by neighbors, hearsay stories, local legends, and interesting ideas and incidents that you come across; all are grist for the mill. Writers collect stories, anecdotes, jokes, odd names, and tidbits that might have future use. Writers are scroungers, snoops, eavesdroppers, and junk collectors who hoard whatever experience can be stuffed into a folder, written into a journal, and used to create stories. A spiral notebook is useful for jotting down observations, characters, incidents, and whatever tickles your fancy. It has been said that *creativity is the ability to perceive relationships*—and a sizable data base will give you more to relate.

Story Genres

Some writers back into a project by first deciding to write a story in a particular genre, or story type. Next they locate an idea that fits the story type. There are many lists of movie genres; the one I use includes vengeance, science fiction, western, comedy, fantasy, thriller, romance, whodunnits, fish-out-of-water, crime and police, coming of age, family, horror, monster, ghost, journey, sports, war, school, animals, modern angst, action-adventure, high adventure, and quest and search stories.[9]

Genre writing involves understanding the form. If the writer is drawn to vengeance stories, a week or so should be spent analyzing the genre. This study would reveal that the first acts of these yarns typically introduce someone who is minding his or her business when the bad guys show up on horses, on motorcycles, in spaceships, or whatever, and unmercifully abuse the protagonist. Somehow, the hero escapes and uses Act II to recover and to learn how to shoot a gun, wield a sword with the good hand, or whatever is appropriate to the story. After the knives are sharpened, the Act III showdown occurs when the hero confronts the villain and, Odysseus-like, defeats his or her opponent. (The final showdown usually occurs during a one-on-one battle between hero and villain.) Thus, the three-act structure of the vengeance genre follows an abuse-recovery-vengeance progression, as in *Witness*.

Often the hero of a vengeance story has a secret strength or experience that makes this person more formidable than appearances indicate, as in *Straw Dogs, Unforgiven,* and *On the Waterfront*. Action stars thrive on vengeance stories. Clint Eastwood has built his career on them, as in *Unforgiven, A Fistful of Dollars, The Outlaw Josey Wales, Hang 'em High,* and other films in which he is knocked around before turning on his tormentors.

Vengeance stories slide into the action-adventure genre *(Die Hard, Under Siege),* which gives the audience an exciting ride without revealing much about the characters or the story's social context. For their part, action-adventure stories lack the thoughtfulness and moral thrust found in the high-adventure genre *(The African Queen, The Treasure of the Sierra Madre)*. High-adventure stories are often set in isolated places where memorable characters deal with complex social or political issues. Although these story types come in many varieties, close study will reveal how they are organized and how they are driven by a task, quest, or conflict. (The breakdown of *The Verdict* provided in Appendix C and various discussions throughout this text explain how to analyze scripts and movies.)

Another interesting genre is one that places the main character in a strange surrounding or situation. These "fish out of water" stories can have considerable

[9]For more on movie genres, see Thomas Schatz, *Hollywood Genres*, Random House, New York, 1981. Schatz lists six main genres—gangster, hard-boiled detective, screwball comedy, musical, family melodrama, and western—but there are many other categories. For example, westerns splinter into spaghetti westerns, revisionist westerns, epic westerns, buddy westerns, comedy westerns, gothic westerns—and the list extends.

appeal, as in *Crocodile Dundee* and *E.T.: The Extraterrestrial*. One reason for the success of this story type is that the main character, by his or her nature or the situation, creates dramatic contrast. Aspects of this genre show up in many films: *Witness*'s John Book (Harrison Ford) is a fish out of water in Amish country. *The Terminator*'s Kyle Reese (Michael Biehn) and the cyborg (Arnold Schwarzenegger) are fish-out-of-water aliens in Sarah's world. The hero of *The Verdict* is an outsider to the inner circle of lawyers that he must battle. And the ultimate fish-out-of-water story is *Splash*, which concerns a mermaid who steps onto dry land!

Favorite Actors

Some writers develop a story by imagining famous actors playing their characters. Should you need a lanky young cowhand, cast Gary Cooper or John Cusack in the role. The actor chosen will become invisible by the time the script is finished, but in the meantime the energy of his or her persona may help you to write the script. This strategy is handy because movie stars are well-known types who are easily cast into whatever roles the writer imagines. Also, almost any conceivable personality type can be cast from the catalogue of actors. If you decide to pair Susan Sarandon and Jack Lemmon as thirty-something bons vivants, do it. While you are imagining, think about sitting in a rehearsal room when these actors read your work, and ask yourself if your script measures up to their talent. The point here is to appreciate that actors do not merely recite lines of dialogue; their goal is to create a unique character who displays emotional complexity and experience. Meryl Streep expressed her feelings on this point by saying she was "interested in the interior lives of the characters, what they were grappling with beyond their physical challenges."[10] Here Streep refers to backstory motivation that unleashes emotions that connect to the actor's experience. Such feelings are intimated by dialogue, by an action or response, by the stage directions, or by the actor's intuitive response to the script.

Characters from Literature and History

If ordinary people hold no interest, write about characters from literature or history, and cast them in your story. In Nicholas Meyer's *The Seven Percent Solution*, Sigmund Freud helps Sherlock Holmes solve the latter's drug habit. Famous figures from sports *(Cobb)*, business *(Tucker)*, medicine *(The Story of Louis Pasteur)*, science *(Fat Man and Little Boy)*, and the arts *(Amadeus)* can also be the source of biographical stories.

Locations

Growing up, many of us heard stories about a local haunted house or some other mysterious location that inspired excitement and now could perhaps inspire an idea for a script. Powerful memories often attach to such sites, and

---

[10]*The Los Angeles Times*, September 25, 1994.

walking the grounds might suggest a story. Photographic essays can also inspire a story or a sequence in a story.

Fairy Tales and Myths

These ancient yarns have an enduring hold on audiences. *Jack and the Bean Stalk, Cinderella, Little Red Riding Hood, Beauty and the Beast,* and *Sleeping Beauty* are reflected in such stories as *Star Wars, Working Girl, Sleeping with the Enemy, On the Waterfront,* and *Pretty Woman.* Fairy tales and myths are often archetypal metaphors for major life stages.[11]

Sequels and Prequels

Stories can be based on an admired film that the writer feels deserves a sequel or a prequel. For example, a writer might imagine a prequel based on Eastwood's Dirty Harry Callahan when he was twelve; the story might explore what caused this boy to fall into a life of solitude and violent action. Yarns can be spun from such speculations. The *Young Indiana Jones* TV series is based on this character's youth. *The Long Kiss Good-bye* concerns an ex-assassin who finds herself beset with mental problems, which sounds suspiciously like a sequel to *La Femme Nikita* or its American remake, *Point of No Return.*

Any movie or fictional character is fair game for this approach. Could not *Dances with Wolves* sustain a sequel? What happens to Stands With Fists and John Dunbar after they escape the army? That seems like a yeasty question. For a time, a friend of mine toyed with writing about what happened to *The Wizard of Oz's* Dorothy when she became middle-aged. However, Geoff Ryman's novel *Was* (Alfred Knopf, New York, 1992) addressed this topic before my friend could write his version of Dorothy's later years.

Historical Events

Although history is humanity's megastory, it is often necessary to personalize war, social upheaval, and grand events by focusing on how they affect the individuals of a family, a neighborhood, or a village. The Great Depression, for example, is shown through its impact on the Joad family in *The Grapes of Wrath; Memphis Belle* uses the experiences of a single bomber crew to tell the tale of the air war over Europe during World War II.

Images

Story ideas can spring from images from art, dreams, experience, or the subconscious. The idea for *Miller's Crossing* originated when the screenwriter (Ethan Coen) was struck with the image of a hat blowing across a forest floor.

---

[11]For more about fairy tales and myths, see Bruno Bettelheim, *The Uses of Enchantment: The Meaning and Importance of Fairy Tales,* Vintage Press, New York, 1977. Also see Joseph Campbell, *The Hero with a Thousand Faces,* Princeton University Press, Princeton, New Jersey, 1949.

The drill on this approach is to think about the image until its significance emerges. Check out *The Family of Man* for story ideas (Edward Steichen, Simon & Schuster, New York, 1983). It presents great photographs on fundamental life themes.

Radio and Television Reality Shows

Radio and TV reality programs present all manner of characters and situations. Some writers videotape and index TV segments that they feel have story potential. Again, to stay clear of privacy and publicity laws, such items may require extensive reworking. At the least, these shows can help you to build a collection of character types.

Stories Based on Music and Song

Classical, pop, period, or folk music can trigger an idea or induce a writing mood. A script I wrote for *The Virginian* was inspired by an Irish folk song. *The Gambler* and *Ode to Billy Joe* were scripted from country-western songs.

Speculation

Intriguing stories can be imagined when one asks *what if?* What if a spaceship landed on the lawn of the White House? What if we found a way to communicate with the dead? What if we learned how to travel in time? What if we could do brain transplants, double our intelligence, recreate dinosaurs, see angels? Story ideas can emerge from such fancies.

USING THE SIX STORY ARCHETYPES TO DEVELOP THE IDEA

Somerset Maugham noted that there were only three rules for writing a novel but that unfortunately no one knows what they are. Similarly, people in the movie business wave off the task of writing stories by asserting that there are only five or nine or thirty-seven basic stories—and they have all been done. Unfortunately, there is no agreement on what the master story models are, even though movies are endlessly studied by genre, style, social content, and other analytical approaches. Such listings are valuable to a point, but I have found that new writers resist complex narrative theories. What they need, especially early on when beset with endless story possibilities, is an overall sense of where the story idea seems to be heading. Knowing a story's general direction would make it easier for them to figure out what needs to be said in the story. Several years ago I came upon such a tool, thanks to David Dortort, a screenwriter and teacher in the UCLA Extension Writers Program. As executive producer of various television series, including *Bonanza*, Dortort had worked with hundreds of writers and their stories. Over time, he noticed that the yarns pitched his way tended to sort into one of six archetypal stories: the Hero archetype, the Buddy/Friendship archetype, the Impossible Quest archetype, the Breaking-Away archetype, the Medea archetype, and the Faust archetype. Interestingly, these six archetypes, explained below, will fit almost any idea imaginable. Dortort's strategy is easy to learn, so writers can quickly acquire a sense of which way their stories seem to be heading and how to organize their work.

The Hero Archetype

In European culture, hero stories are modeled after the myth of Theseus, who sought out and killed the Minotaur in the Labyrinth of Crete. Fittingly, heroes cast in the Theseus mold are brave souls who take on a dangerous task. The audience must be encouraged to root for the hero, whose perseverance and appeal make him or her the audience's surrogate. The hero gains favor because this person (or team) maintains the moral high ground, which connects humankind to what is decent and good. The hero is bound by this moral imperative; if it is abandoned, the cause (and the story) may fail. (Ironically, the motion picture entitled *Hero* was not successful because the main character was ambiguous about holding the moral high ground.)

In a successful rendition of the Hero archetype, the main character is interesting and moral, but not perfect. Superheroes, on the other hand, do everything right and are so invulnerable that there is no need for audiences to worry about them. Writers can avoid this audience response by creating heroes who are vulnerable, imperfect, and human.

Somewhere between the hero and the nonhero is the antihero, a person who follows a personal code of honor, rather than society's standard. Bogart, Garfield, and Eastwood have portrayed loners who operate according to a hard personal code of honor. Sigourney Weaver's strong-willed character in the *Alien* movies is also an antihero who lives according to a stern personal code. Woody Allen often plays a tentative antihero who is pressured into reluctant combat. Of the six archetypes, the hero story is used most often in movies.

The Buddy/Friendship Archetype

This archetype is based on the Damon and Pythias myth and often features two friends who take on the world (*Midnight Cowboy, Of Mice and Men*). The archetype may deal with comedy teams whose variations include "I can do it better than you" (*The Odd Couple*) or working together against a common enemy (*Romancing the Stone*). The buddies may display a love-hate relationship as they battle enemies (*Outrageous Fortune*), or they may become dependent on each other (*White Men Can't Jump*).

Variations to these stories may involve two equals (*Lethal Weapon*), two characters who are not equal (*Twins*), a male and a female (*The Pelican Brief*), or an adult and a child (*The Champ*). Buddy stories can also involve a gang of heroes working together for a worthwhile but risky cause (*Sneakers*).

The archetype can become a triangle when one of the buddies becomes romantically involved with a third party *(The Cutting Edge)*. Some stories defuse the sexual rivalry inherent in such a triangle by fizzing the material with music or style, as in *Butch Cassidy and the Sundance Kid.* The primary goal of many of these yarns is to conquer a foe or to win a prize, as in the hero story. This archetype can also thrust toward individuation, even when the buddies are of the opposite sex. In this case one or both become strong enough to go their separate ways *(The Gauntlet)* or progress to a more promising relationship *(Klute)*.

The Impossible Quest Archetype

The quest archetype relates to characters who undertake a noble adventure, search, or journey, rather than setting forth to defeat a villain. Such stories, based on the Icarus and Daedalus myth, can be humorous, innocent, tragic, and uplifting at the same time *(The Right Stuff, Boys on the Side, Searching for Bobby Fischer)*. Stories using the Impossible Quest archetype often set up an objective (help E.T. escape, cure the disease, find the treasure) and then show how the characters either achieve the goal or fail in their quest. However done, quest stories use the main characters to demonstrate the nobility and resiliency of the human spirit.

Because there are elements of the hero story in all of these archetypes, the protagonist should maintain the moral high ground; otherwise, the noble quest may be debased. When this archetype is applied to the hero in, say, a treasure hunt story, the character should be inspired by more than greed, since that is not heroic motivation. *Romancing the Stone* escapes this trap by having the hero care more for the heroine than for the jewel that everyone seeks. In *The Treasure of the Sierra Madre*, Bogart's character succumbs to the lure of gold, abandons the moral high ground, and comes to a bad end. Similarly, the hero in *Days of Thunder* becomes so obsessed with being the champion driver that he fails to respect the heroic mythos of the sport and so appears greedy, thereby forfeiting the moral high ground. Because they needed a hero to root for, audiences turned to Robert Duvall's noble mechanic, who held fast to the moral high ground. This shift defocused the narrative and undercut the movie's effectiveness because the audiences should have been tracking the hero, not the hero's pal.

The Breaking-Away Archetype

Also called "the king must die," this archetype deals with the conflict between parent and child, or with situations in which the old order must yield to the new. Breaking-away stories take many forms, as when parents wish to hold on to their children *(The Heiress)* or a husband-wife rivalry requires the child's presence *(Irreconcilable Differences)*. The archetype shows clearly in *Breaking Away,* in which a boy turns from his family's blue-collar traditions by enrolling in college. Another example is sexual rivalries between parents and the child's loved one *(Class)*. The Breaking-Away archetype can be laden with blood memories *(The Trip to Bountiful)*, Oedipal conflicts *(Psycho)*, sibling rivalries *(The Fabulous Baker Boys)*, and abandonment fears *(Paper Moon)*.

This archetype ties into two major life moments—separation of son or daughter from parents, and individuation, which is our need to achieve a sense of self. Separation and individuation are among humankind's most powerful drives; when a person is denied this growth, mental illness, loneliness, anger, impotence, drugs, gangs, and other problems may result. In life it often takes years for a person to earn his or her identity, which is why the struggle to individuate is the basis for many fine scripts *(Five Easy Pieces, What's Love Got to Do with It, Postcards from the Edge)*. To determine whether this archetype fits your notion, ask whether the main character has a need to become his or her own person by breaking away from a controlling force of some kind. When the answer is yes, you may have a useful fix on where your story is heading. Knowing this direction can aim your thinking and help to develop the story.

The Medea Archetype

The first four archetypes grew out of Hellenistic traditions that envisioned humans in an uneasy relationship with watchful gods who were alert for signs of human pride or arrogance (called *hubris*). The Medea archetype came from a later tradition that is based on the idea of womanly power. Legend has it that Medea helped Jason secure the golden fleece, became his wife, and bore him two sons. When Jason spurned her for another woman, Medea invoked her sorcery, murdered her rival, and punished Jason by destroying what he loved most: his sons. The Medea archetype thus veers away from earlier patriarchal archetypes by presenting an independent woman who is unfettered by male dominance. Regina in *The Little Foxes* connects to the Medea archetype, as do the powerful women in *The Last Seduction, Disclosure, Fatal Attraction, The African Queen, The Joy Luck Club*, and other films.

The Faust Archetype

This archetype is based on a sixteenth-century German legend concerning a man (Johann Faust) who reputedly gave his soul to the devil for gifts of magic, beauty, and youth. This archetype usually deals with the extremes to which people will go to get what they want.[12] There is a devilish quality to many Faustian stories because the wealth, knowledge, and power that flow to the main character often spring from corrupt sources. On this basis, Faust stories often struggle with moral values.

---

[12]Some writers follow a more redemptive view of Faust, seeing him as a symbol of humanity's heroic striving for knowledge and power. This approach was pursued by Goethe in his epic poem, *Faust*, which inspired operas, plays, and other literary works.

The corrupting power source can be a corporation, a military group, a bureaucracy, a church, a school, or any organization or individual that demands obedience, regardless of morality. *The Firm, Clear and Present Danger,* and *A Few Good Men* illustrate. *Jurassic Park* and *The Fly* (in which ambitious science plays the role of the devil) are also Faustian stories. *Unforgiven* is Faustian because the hero betrays his dead wife for money needed to save his farm. Faust stories sometimes involve master-student or master-slave relationships *(The Servant, Wall Street),* in which the underling must escape the dominant partner.

As should be clear from the preceding discussion, story ideas are developed because they appeal to writers, not because they fit an archetype or any other system. The archetypes are but a scheme for deciding which way an idea seems to be heading. When this direction is determined, it becomes easier to focus attention and to develop the idea. For example, the archetypes suggest directions for developing the notion of the two old gangsters in the health club (mentioned earlier in the chapter). When the idea is conceived as an impossible quest story, the archetype points the material and the two men toward achieving some sort of goal *(Tough Guys)* that is strong enough to test the characters and to drive the plot. When we aim the notion toward a buddy story, the archetype suggests a development similar to *The Odd Couple* or *Scarecrow*—that is, a relationship story. The two gangsters notion could be developed as a breaking-away story—if they wished to escape the Mafia. When developed as a Faust story, the material could steer the pair toward a conflict with the mob, suggesting a story about escaping a criminal past, earning an honest living, protecting old-age assets, maintaining dignity, and the like. When done as a Medea story, a female character would be added to create a triangle. Such a work could be developed as a comedy *(Grumpy Old Men),* as a drama *(Prizzi's Honor),* as a tragedy *(The Hustler),* or using whatever slant the writer found to be appealing.

Another example: Imagine that the story idea involves a youngster who loves horses, but uncertainty exists over how the notion should be developed. When we whip out the archetypes—Hero, Breaking-Away, Buddy, Impossible Quest, Faust, Medea—we immediately have six directions for developing the idea. It could be done as an impossible quest story *(National Velvet),* a buddy story *(The Black Stallion),* a hero story *(The Man from Snowy River),* a Faust story *(The Champ),* or a breaking-away story *(My Friend Flicka).* This "pointing" does not, of course, mean copying an existing movie; the archetype merely indicates a possible direction and energy for the story. When the direction becomes clear, the confusion of endless story possibilities drops away, allowing the writer to concentrate on a specific line of development. Knowing this direction early in the story process is not a breakthrough strategy that will magically solve the task of plotting; however, it is another modest assist that appears at a time when screenwriters need whatever help is available.

Finally, note that some stories straddle several archetypes. For example, Peter Shaffer wrote his version of the boy-and-a-horse story as a Faust/impossible-quest tale, which he called *Equus*. *The Firm* is both a hero story and a Faust story. *Sleepless in Seattle* contains elements of the buddy story and the impossible quest story. *Prizzi's Honor* is another cross-genre story that combines Medea and Faust archetypes. Whatever the combination, the archetypes offer a handy overview for figuring out how to develop a story idea. Such a perspective can lead to a sentence or two statement that cartoons the overall plot and suggests various ways to develop it.

POPULATING THE STORY IDEA WITH "TEMP" CHARACTERS

Creating "Temp" Characters

Before leaving this discussion of story ideas and the use of archetypes to guide them, I want to recommend that you create a few temporary characters to populate your embryonic story notion. Temp characters populate the emerging idea so it can be imagined more clearly. The retired gangster notion, for example, immediately suggests three characters—the two men and their boss. It is not necessary to develop these characters in detail until the story firms up. Until then they can be treated as sketch characters who are assigned traditional dramatic roles, beginning with hero and villain.

Some easy decisions concerning these characters can be made at this point. Is the hero male or female? How old is this person? Is the hero attractive, plain, likable, cranky, or what? The same general questions can sketch the villain. It should take but an hour or so to sketch a few characters for temp duty.

Some writers cast actors in the temp roles. The goal is to come up with a face or a physique that feels right. In most cases the temporary characters develop as story and script are written.

Using Stock Characters

Temp characters also can be drawn from the stock characters found in most movies. For example, heroes and villains often have sidekicks (trusted companions) who allow the main characters to speak their minds. Jack Warden's Mickey plays the hero's sidekick in *The Verdict*. Often the sidekick is a source of comic relief as well (Rosie O'Donnell's Becky plays such a role in *Sleepless in Seattle*). Some sidekicks advise the main character or provide a shoulder to cry on. The best friend can be a clown figure who becomes poignant when offering counsel on the hero's love interest. This happens when the clown has a crush on the hero. Brokenhearted "best pal" clowns include Jon Cryer in *Pretty in Pink* and Shelley Duvall in *Roxanne*.

The clown stereotype is important when the material is inherently gloomy. Woody Allen often fizzes his stories by creating clown characters (*Hannah and Her Sisters, Crimes and Misdemeanors*). When the clown character dominates the story, the result is a comedy (*The Pink Panther*). Steve Martin writes melancholy clown roles for himself, creating comedy-dramas such as *A Simple Twist of Fate*, *Roxanne*, and *L.A. Story*.

Most of the supporting players in TV sitcoms act as sidekicks who deliver comic relief. Writers on shows such as *Frasier, Murphy Brown*, and *Roseanne* must create stories that provide the supporting players with opportunities to perform as comic sidekicks.

Audiences buy tickets to movies because they pay off in adventure, suspense, and *romance*, which suggests another stock character—the love interest. Eva Marie Saint is the love interest in *On the Waterfront;* Brad Pitt and Michael Madsen play similar roles in *Thelma and Louise*. The love interest can form the third side of a romantic triangle *(Casablanca)*, or the character may be involved directly with the hero-villain struggle *(Fatal Attraction)*. The love interest allows the hero to express inner feelings and to comment on the theme of the story. The villain may have a love interest, too, although this person often comes to an unhappy end when the villain is defeated *(Witness, Dog Day Afternoon)*.

Another stock character for jump-starting a plot is the voice of wisdom, decency, or reason. Ben Kingsley often plays such characters *(Schindler's List, Bugsy, Dave)*. Joe Seneca (as Dr. Thompson) plays the sage in *The Verdict*.

Some stories employ a parental figure or a character who offers good or bad advice to the main characters. The flip side of the parental figure is the street-smart or preternaturally wise youngster who counsels a parent or someone older. Ross Malinger's Jonah in *Sleepless in Seattle* and Tatum O'Neal's Addie in *Paper Moon* play such roles.

Tricksters, another character type, are given to double- or triple-crossing those who trust them. Jack Kehoe is a trickster in *Midnight Run,* as is the newspaper flack portrayed by Saul Rubinek in *Unforgiven*.

A character representing the "average person" often shows up in movies. In *The Verdict*, that voice belongs to the Doneghys. Another character type is the devil's disciple, someone who is a source of lies or bad advice (Rod Steiger in *On the Waterfront*). The voice of authority shows up in many stories; in some instances this person is also the villain, as in *The Firm* and *Klute*.

In addition, stock characters can be summarized as braggart, bully, faultfinder, tease, martyr, sneak, worrywart, lazy slob, wimp, and other types that are a form of dramatic shorthand that immediately tells the audience what to expect. Thus, when a huge man with tattoos and a shaved head saunters into a saloon where the hero is nursing a beer, the physicality of the brutish stereotype signals that he will cause trouble. Even though temp characters are unformed, they can help to firm up the idea and to suggest a plot. The challenge is to expand temps and stereotypes with backstory and psychological understanding until they become dimensional characters.

ENRICHING A STORY IDEA: AN EXAMPLE

The preceding values are not an academic game; they are a plan for finding an idea and working it into the beginning of a plot. To demonstrate how they work, we can use the values to shape up the news item given below. This will be done quickly, for we will be attempting to summarize a complex thinking process that differs with each writer. For this reason, the discussion presents a simplified version of how the values presented in this chapter can enrich a modest story idea until it takes on the first glimmerings of a plot. The following human interest item was clipped from a small newspaper in California:

Wife Feels She Is a "Sports Widow"
By Jenny True

Dear Jenny

I need some advice because I seem to have lost my husband to one sport after another. If he's not off hunting or fishing, he's watching football, basketball, baseball, tennis, or whatever sport is playing, plus he plays first base for his company's softball team. Sad to say, I am grateful for this even, for one of the few times my two children ever get to see him is when he is on the playing field. When I told him that I felt abandoned, he told me to hire a baby-sitter and go back to work. "Make a life for yourself" were his exact words. Jenny, I'm twenty-five and like being home with my kids—is it wrong for me to want my husband here beside me? Isn't that what marriage is supposed to be? Being ignored this way is killing me and our marriage. I'm not bad-looking and I like to have a good time, too, but I feel such anger building up inside me that I don't know what to do. My feeling is to break the TV and tell him to stay home with his family or get out—although I don't know what we'd do if he walked out on us! What advice do you have?

The Sportsman's Lonely Wife

I was initially drawn to the news item because it is a sadly humorous insight into a family in crisis. It also has a human dimension that illustrates how story ideas can spring from modest and homely sources if we think about them. One of the first things I thought about upon reading this item was what the spouse does when he goes out with the boys. Is he jocking it up, or is he doing something else? If he has a secret life, what is it? The item could suggest a story in which a meek young wife must assert herself against a bullying husband, as in *What's Love Got to Do with It*. Or it might deal with a husband who must break away from his buddies and settle down with his wife and children, as in *Diner*. If the husband is an ex-convict or a war veteran, then a darker story could emerge, as in *Straight Time* or *Jacknife*. If the kids are older, the yarn could be about a revolt of the underlings or about how the kids become a cheering section as the husband grabs at glory. The story could deal with the fitness craze, fear of aging, and/or the need for recognition, to name additional story possibilities.

Dramatic contrast can be developed when we invest interesting quirks and traits in the characters, as was the case in *Muriel's Wedding* and *Circle of Friends*. For example, what if we imagined the woman in the sports widow item—call her Mom—to be large and exceptionally strong. What if Mom was born this way, and what if she has struggled from childhood to hide her strength because it was "unladylike"? The notion of Wonder Woman disguised as a frazzled, frilly, helpless female seems to have dramatic contrast. Of course it may not, but this is a decision the writer must resolve. Some of our choices pay off, while others may lead nowhere—in which case we begin again or find another story idea. There are no guarantees with this process, and writers work without a net. What matters most is listening to what your heart says about the idea and then going with that flow.

We can use humanism as an enriching value when we imagine the story as the struggle of removing some sort of pain or burden from this woman, in which case we might show how Mom learns to accept herself and to *individuate*. Acquiring peace of mind and the inner strength that she has sought all her life is a substantial human value that could appeal to audiences.

The story notion could be developed to fit a number of writerly concerns. One perspective might be that women should have opportunities to realize their human potential. Although this is hardly a radical thought, it is as serviceable today as it was when Rosalind Russell, Katharine Hepburn, and other movie actresses helped to define the modern woman. Another perspective might be to examine the seductive lure of media and sports. This could be done by dramatizing how Mom finds herself drawn into celebrity status as the housefrau who becomes an exercise or muscle queen. This development could lead to a dilemma when Mom finds that she must choose between the recognition she has craved all her life and the family that she loves. Whatever is decided will lead to some sort of upbeat ending that connects to how Mom realizes her inner value and saves her family. This points to a *throughline* that tracks Mom's evolution from household drudge to woman of character. Her new attitude could stabilize her family by moving it away from its original patriarchy to an improved status quo that is more of a partnership. This would be a wrenching adjustment that tests the family to its core and creates drama and conflict.

The style and audience for such a story would be easy to work out; it seems suited to adult women and their families, especially if done with humor and pathos. Such a story could be made as a movie-of-the-week or as a family film such as *A Home of Their Own* or *What's Eating Gilbert Grape?* The idea probably would work best if developed in an unrealistic style, that is, gentled, without sharp edges, emotionally on the soft side. At this stage, these values are not carved in stone; they are quick decisions for sorting through the confusions that make this early phase of the work so challenging. Note how the preliminary development of the idea suggests a three-act structure:

I. Mom decides to improve her status.
II. Mom struggles to achieve this goal, only to find herself in a predicament that is even more threatening.
III. Mom saves herself and her family from the lures of the celebrity trap and takes up her new partnership role in the family.

If this notion were to be developed further, one of the questions to ask is whether it felt substantial enough to sustain for two hours; in other words, does the idea have "legs"? To answer this we must decide whether the core idea—saving a family with two young children and changing the lives of four unhappy people—has substance. The setting and milieu of the story deal with middle America, the sports craze, mid-life crisis, kids who crave attention, and the need of a wife and husband to make sense out of their lives. Toss in the visual potential of various sports activities, and the idea would seem to have the potential to entertain an audience for two hours. The idea also proposes a few temp characters—Mom, Dad, the kids, and a few pals.

As discussed thus far, this development favors a character story; to turn the notion into an action story would mean focusing on Mom's athletic career. Although this could be done, for now you should notice how small steps have teased story values and information out of this simple idea. Weeks of such thinking are often necessary before the idea and its characters take on weight and dimension. We pick at the material and pull on whatever story thread we can find, looking for questions, details, business, locations, and especially character insights that can be organized into a plot.

SUMMARY

The most important decision in the entire writing process is selecting a story idea, because this choice will shape the content of the script and determine its salability. The story idea should be simple, yet it should contain dramatic contrast, humanism that touches the heart of the audience, and a writerly perspective that extracts meaning and value, from the material. Character and action stories have equal value, even though this chapter mainly examined the character story. Whatever the style or genre, it is usually the writer's thoughtfulness, rather than the uniqueness of the notion, that creates a good story and script.

Early in the work, most writers determine that some ideas are funny, others are sad, and some create worry and fear. These values suggest an emotional slant that aims the story toward comedy, drama, or melodrama, i.e., the story will make audiences laugh, make them fearful, or make them sad. In some stories (*My Favorite Year, Amadeus, Pulp Fiction*) the story presents combinations of these emotions. Pegging the story to at least one of the three emotional slants is a crucial value that can be completed in a day or so. This key decision will influence how the writer conceptualizes the story and its characters and how the script will be dramatized and written.

As general advice, I recommend that you avoid adapting another writer's novel or short story; there is a need for fresh stories and new characters. News items and other documentary sources can be used for movie and TV stories, but the notion should be freshened and developed so that little remains of the source material.

The story idea should suggest complex emotional characters and believable situations. The idea, observation, character, or situation that initiates the story can come from a photograph or an illustration. It can be based on injustice or revenge, on relative or friend, on legend or history. Story ideas can originate with music, songs, poetry, favorite actors or characters, radio and television news shows, or fairy tales and myths. A good story can arise from a sequel or prequel, or a flight of fancy that takes off when the writer asks *what if?*

To nudge a dramatic notion along, use the story archetypes to point the idea in a single direction. The archetypes—Hero, Buddy, Impossible Quest, Breaking Away, Medea, and Faust—are among the few tools available to writers early in the work; they take but a few minutes to learn and to use.

Another strategy for developing an idea is to employ temporary characters who add dimension to the story idea. Stock and stereotypical characters can also be useful early in the writing.

Exercises

1. Clip news items from the daily press and arrange them into a file. Use subject headings that fit your interests. Major newspapers, *The New Yorker,* and *National Geographic* can be useful sources for story ideas.
2. List your five favorite films and summarize the idea that you feel organizes each of them. (Questions 3 through 7 also relate to the five films you have selected.)
3. How do the film ideas display dramatic contrast, humanism, and a writerly perspective?
4. Select two of the films and note how the locations add to the effectiveness of the stories.
5. To which audiences do the films appeal?
6. Are the stories done in a real, unreal, or surreal style? Explain.
7. Briefly describe two characters from the five films selected. Why are the characters interesting?

(For media that illustrate the points made in this chapter, see Appendix A.)

CHAPTER 2

Building the Story Structure

*With a story idea and a few sketch characters in mind,
we can enrich the notion by thinking about the frame,
the conflict, the dramatic problem, the theme, and other
values that build the story structure.*

Chapter 1 discussed the characteristics of good story ideas, how such notions are located, and how they are developed into the beginning of a plot. This chapter and the next examine how to build a structure that expands the story idea into a plot that segments into three acts. Although writers have many ways of reaching this goal, much of the work centers around important dramatic values that are extensively mulled and pondered. The values are, in no particular order, *frame, event, story concept, problem, conflict, dramatic crisis,* and *theme*. Writers often spend weeks shuffling between the seven values; however, out of necessity, this book examines them sequentially, in an imposed order. When you have absorbed these values, use them in whatever order and fashion that you find most useful. The first value to be discussed is the frame of the story.

THE FRAME OF THE STORY

The *frame* of the story supplies the settings and the locations used in the plot, indicating in which country, region, city, neighborhood, and rooms the action takes place. The frame also includes the mood, the style, and the overall visual look of the movie being imagined. This definition of the frame is expansive because screenwriters visualize an entire movie and capture it on paper. As locations are created for each scene, other values—theme, conflict, crisis—will also appear and add to the story.

When the frame of the story is imagined as dark and sinister (*Chinatown*), then that vision will affect the locations and the overall feel of the script. When a frame is imagined realistically (*Raging Bull*) or modestly (*Ruby in Paradise*), the writer is encouraged to develop the material with a corresponding energy. These elements—the settings, the mood, and the overall look of the film as scripted—combine into the frame, which is also referred to as the *story universe.*

When we apply this value to an idea about a desperate young mother who feels abandoned by her sports-crazed husband, then the frame would need to be set during a given year and season, in a geographic location that serves the story. Thus, the frame/story universe is the writer's blank canvas. Anything imaginable can be part of it—a dust storm, a hellish steel mill, whatever seems dramatic and appropriate. When a setting seems unpromising, the writer must relocate the action to a place that adds to the story and makes writing the scene easier and more dramatic. For this to happen, imagine interesting and dramatic settings; ignore the costs or how the images will be captured. Whatever the writer commits to paper can be filmed; only imagination is beyond price.[1]

The amount of time spent developing the frame depends on how complicated the settings are. An ordinary location—for example, a middle-class neighborhood, as in *Moonstruck*—will be easier to imagine than settings for a story such as *Jurassic Park*. The latter required a unique island location, the layout of the park, and the park's defenses, laboratories, vehicles, personnel, and even the weather. Its elaborate frame is part of why *Jurassic Park* is more than another mad-scientist story like *The Island of Dr. Moreau, Island of Doomed Men, Island of Lost Souls*, and similar potboilers. *Jurassic Park* is also a potboiler, but the pot cost $57 million, much of it spent on making the movie's incredible frame credible. This is why the filmmakers spent most of the first act setting up the story's frame. Then, when the audience is hooked into the island setting and its marvelous defenses and creatures, something goes wrong, the frame cracks, and the entire enterprise falls apart. Escaping the chaos of that story universe occupied the remainder of the tale.

The frame extends beyond generalized physical settings of a story. A town in a thoughtful story universe is not an anonymous Anytown, U.S.A.; the location should have a name, a history, and a downtown with buildings and rich and poor neighborhoods. These combine into a social context that shows up as occupations, clothing, and houses with front yards and cars. Some writers give the towns an economic base (industrial or farming) and a geographic location. Locations come alive in imagination when writers create weather, temperature, and the time span of the story. In sum, the frame is whatever we imagine it to be—even the smells. Hershey, Pennsylvania, has an air of chocolate; Durham, North Carolina, is scented with tobacco. When it seems useful, add an operation that creates a smell in your story—a tannery, an oil refinery, a factory that makes perfume, pickles, or whatever can be used to tell the story. Seemingly minor details of the setting can add interest and drama to a story: note how the police overheard the background sound of the elevated train when the hero of *The Fugitive* telephoned from a public call box. The police then used this train sound to track their man.

---

[1]The only caution here is to use a grand location adequately, so that it justifies its expense. A ballroom full of uniformed naval officers would be an expensive setting, so it should contribute to the movie. It is not enough to have a character pop in on such a gathering for a few seconds of transitional chitchat and then move on without using the setting more fully. Such a grand setting should probably deliver three to five minutes of story.

A dramatic frame can also suggest local history and traditions that affect the characters. The story universe of *Witness,* for example, ranges from the mean streets of Philadelphia, where an other-worldly Amish heroine (Kelly McGillis's Rachel Lapp) meets John Book, to bucolic country settings where Book must take on the ways of the Amish. These frame values lead to scenes in which Book not only dresses like an Amishman but takes on an Amish lifestyle as well. Similarly, much of the action of *Places in the Heart* is influenced by its frame, a 1930s Texas cotton town. *Blade Runner, Alien, The Piano, On the Waterfront,* and *Out of Africa* are but a few of the films that have used carefully drawn frames to pull audiences into their stories.

Settings vary as much as characters. This shows clearly when one compares the story universe of *Rambling Rose* with those of *In the Heat of the Night* and *Mississippi Burning.* The settings of these three films vary because the stories take place during different times, are located in different parts of the South, and involve different issues and problems. The story universe of *Rambling Rose* is benign and nurturing; the other two stories have frames that are racist and menacing. In each case, the settings encourage the characters of these stories to interact and to reveal their lives.

Writers have the first shot at creating the frame. The fake orgasm scene in *When Sally Met Harry* could have been played in the front seat of a car, using two characters. However, the scene is more dramatic when played out in a crowded restaurant because it allows the other patrons to react to Sally's outrageous performance.

As you develop the frame, feel free to map out the town, the neighborhood, the street, the houses, the rooms, or whatever helps you to imagine. The layouts may position furniture, a view from a window, or raise questions about the people next door (who are they? what do they do for a living?). Almost none of this doodling and noodling of the frame will show up in the script, but it can help us imagine the settings.

Researching the Frame

Researching the frame leads to information and ideas for scenes, locations, and action. Research feeds imagination, which responds eagerly to any help that develops story incidents. Research helps us to figure out why hero and villain are in conflict and what the overall goal of the story is. During this part of the process we may worry whether the idea is worth doing—or whether *any* story is worth doing! This condition, which has distressed authors for centuries, is another instance of writer's panic. My concern over such inner nagging is minimal, because years ago during a museum visit I noticed ancient hieroglyphs from the tomb of a mummified Egyptian scribe, which in translation proclaimed that "all stories are told. There is nothing more to be written!" That outburst—a sorry epitaph for a writer—was untrue then and it is untrue now, because stories are based on people, and there is no end to human drives, needs, complexities, and problems. From this inexhaustible and evolving stream of humanity, writers can find ten lifetimes worth of stories.

You will discover this when research sends you into the field to visit locations. As you amble along, check out the town, its energy, and its neighborhoods and hangouts. Observe the people; listen to what they say and how they say it. When necessary, set up meetings or formal visits with appropriate people. You need not promise the locals money or credit, although a free lunch is a graceful way to say thank you. Follow up with a note that acknowledges their help and lets the person or group know the status of the project. Give them your phone number in case additional information turns up. When appropriate, take along a camera, camcorder, or tape recorder, but clear their use with the interviewees beforehand. Do not let such equipment intimidate, inhibit, or annoy the locals. I sometimes use a camcorder to tape exterior settings, but I prefer not to use recording equipment during personal interviews. A small notebook is adequate in most cases. Never record an interview secretly. Also, when the location or the meeting is in a possibly dangerous area, take precautions.

When there is no time for a personal visit, conduct interviews by telephone. Jot down names so you can use them as stepping-stones to additional contacts: "So-and-so at the XYZ Company suggested I call you about a movie script I'm writing—do you have a minute?" Use library research to help you prepare your questions in advance of the interview; interviewees should feel they are dealing with a professional who will not waste their time.

Research questions should be focused. Ask about the history and background of a situation or incident. Ask about the cost of products, how people get into the union, and how items are grown or manufactured. Collect any paper they offer, including journal articles; find out whether the location has ever been used in a movie. Be alert to what kind of work is done and whether it has an effect on workers and residents. Jot down interesting jargon and details that can be woven into the story. Knowledge of your subject allows you to invest precise information into your writing, which adds credibility to the story. Tune in on the subtle, often hidden moods and messages of the location and what the people are thinking but not saying. You may be the only voice of the town and its story, so get the details right and tell the truth. There is usually enough drama in actual events to create a good story; finding that truth and interpreting it is the hard part. Truthful scriptwriting requires thorough research; weak research shows easily in scripts and causes negative reactions.

The amount of time spent on research depends on the topic, how quickly you work, and how much background you need to feel comfortable. Some writers spend months researching and mulling the story, which is also an aspect of writing. The research and story pondering continues until the writer feels charged with energy and begins working out the plot. In some cases the research can go on for so long that it becomes an excuse for avoiding writing. To venture another generalization: most feature stories can be researched in a month or so, and most TV shows can be researched in a week or so. When you are unable to manage a trip to Rome or Paris to do research (as few of us can), work from the library and other sources mentioned in this text.

Marbling Frame Research into the Story

A certain amount of your research may be cited in the script, but it should not be dumped on audiences to impress them. Instead, research should be worked into the story in the same way that the history of the characters and the locations is worked in through a process called **marbling.** This term refers to information that reveals the characters and the plot indirectly, through dialogue and images.

When marbling is done skillfully, audiences are hardly aware that they are receiving exposition, as in this example of dialogue that has been freighted with information: "You said you'd use my money to do something about this dump, but it's falling apart worse than when I went to Nam!" Although brief, the line reveals snippets of information about the speaker and the plot without slowing the story. Writers use such strategies to leak information into their stories so that the audience is informed about the characters and the circumstances of the plot. Marbling through dialogue occurs in most movies, as in Shot 80 of *Witness,* when a delirious John Book mutters profanities that suggest his tortured mental state. (Marbling through dialogue is also discussed in Chapter 4, which analyzes a scene from *The Verdict,* as well as in Chapter 6, "Dialogue and Character.")

For how images can communicate plot and character information, note the opening shot of *The Verdict,* which shows the hero playing pinball. The image arouses curiosity about why a well-dressed older man is wasting his time this way. (The image suggests the character's soul-sickness.) The next beat shows Galvin take a shot of breath freshener, a tip-off that he has a drinking problem. Good movies contain scores of brief expositional moments that enrich the plot and the characters.

DEFINING STORY AND EVENT

Our plan for enriching a story idea so that it expands into a plot now adds a definition of *story* that is simplicity itself:

A story is a dramatic summary of an event.

The key word in this definition is *event,* which refers to the ultimate occurrence of the story, i.e., *what happens after everything happens.* The word *event* here is like the term *action,* as used by Aristotle to mean a summing up of what happens in the course of a drama. The event or action usually can be reduced to a brief statement that indicates what happens in the story. The *Odyssey's* event summarizes as, Ulysses restores his family and their home. In *The Verdict,* the event/action occurs when the hero wins the case. In *The Terminator,* the event is the destruction of the cyborg. Knowing the story's overall direction early on, when we are organizing the quicksilver of the idea, provides a huge directional arrow that points to where the plot is heading. So that you do not miss this key perspective: *Deciding the event means asking, "When the story is over, what will have happened?"* Knowing that the hero will save someone, apprehend the villain, win the love interest, discover a liberating truth, or the like usually focuses the hero's goal and the intention of the story. Because the event supplies the basic genetic material of the story and profoundly affects every aspect of the script that follows, *think through this value carefully.*

Awareness of which way the story is heading can spare you from several creative traps. One trap is writing from discovery, which means letting the material develop as the writing progresses, rather than developing an outline of what happens in the plot. Although writing from discovery may work for a short story, most screenwriters avoid this approach because it causes scripts to wander and thus lose dramatic focus. Writing from discovery seems to avoid the work of plotting, because it eases the writer into the *What if?* mode of writing: "What if she finds a treasure map?" "What if the wimp becomes a sports hero?" "What if . . . ?" Also known as the "spaghetti style" of writing, it allows writers to toss out ideas until, like wet noodles, a few of them stick. This is not plotting; it is rummaging for ideas using a pin-the-tail-on-the-donkey approach to plotting that reduces screenwriting to a guessing game or a gamble that something useful will appear out of the blue. This book proposes that you harness brainpower and passion to write stories and scripts, and it gives you a work plan for making this happen. The story definition, for example, asks you to determine *what happens after everything happens in the story.* This question requires a specific answer, i.e., it makes you write from *perspiration* rather than from *inspiration.* While this most assuredly does not mean that writers should avoid flashes of creative lightning, you should remember that we are called *playwrights* because our work is wrought on the anvil of imagination and we must hammer out our stories. It is this way for all writers, so stay with the work and it will get done.

Certain ideas quickly point toward an event. For example, the crime in *Witness* is so grievous that justice demands the retribution that John Book delivers. Because the cyborg in *The Terminator* has a kill-or-be-killed ethos that must be repaid in kind, such a story logically ends with the death of the antagonist; the cyborg is destroyed and humankind is saved.

The event of *Unforgiven* is less obvious because the story involves an aging ex-badman (Clint Eastwood's Bill Munny) who takes on a bounty hunt to save his farm. Ultimately, the event—what happens after everything happens—is that Munny earns the bounty, though not before he punishes the lawman who killed his friend. For this to happen, Munny must put aside peaceful promises made to his wife, transform into his terrible former self, and shoot it out with a posse of lawmen. Imagine knowing early on that the basic story notion would follow this pathway—how valuable such an insight would be! Then imagine when screenwriter David Webb Peoples began his story and suppose that all he had was the idea of a sodbuster who hears about a bounty that can save his farm. Screenwriter Peoples could have pulled many possible events from this idea, each developing the story differently. One event might have been to save the Scofield Kid from his predatory instincts. Another could have been about racial prejudice because one of the gang is an African-American. The event could have involved rescuing a prostitute held prisoner at an isolated ranch. It could be to defend the sheriff from assassins such as Richard Harris's English Bob. It could be to find someone to take care of Munny's children. This list could be extended, and in each case, a different event would lead to a different story. As it turned out, the screenwriter selected an event that realized the dramatic potential of a unique main character whose internal struggle organizes the story. Mr. Munny, as imagined by the screenwriter, was no ordinary farmer; he was viewed as a sleeping dragon who awakens for one final, terrible roar.

Knowing the event presents a flag that you can see in the distance, signaling the direction that the plot should follow. This bearing will allow you to create incidents of plot that move the story along the chosen path. For example, the idea of *Jurassic Park* concerns dinosaurs who are cloned and brought back to life. These are not cuddly little beasties as in *Baby . . . Secret of the Lost Legend*. *Jurassic Park* is about ravenous creatures that gobble up people! The energy of this idea therefore suggests the event of the story, which is surviving the dinosaurs. Most of the characters survive, and that result is what happens after everything in the story happens. The event in *The Fugitive* occurs when the hero proves his innocence. In *Sleepless in Seattle* the event is bringing the couple together.

The event in some films is less accessible. *Pulp Fiction*, for one, entwines three plotlines, jumbles story continuity, and kills off the main character, all of which makes it problematical to point to the event in this film. Is it Samuel L. Jackson's decision to change his life and wander like the monk in *Kung Fu*? Possibly, but my take on the movie is that this character did not organize the story as fully as did John Travolta's character.

Pulp Fiction is an interesting work that bucks the standard three-act/hero-villain/happy-ending of mainstream movie narrative. Although many new writers find inspiration in such films, it is not easy to invent new story forms that will attract audiences. This is why most movies continue to organize around the traditional three-act structure and why professional screenwriters work intensely to create such scripts. This does not mean that everyone pursues a monolithic paradigm, for there are variations within story traditions that writers use to stretch the narrative envelope. Despite this "wiggle room," some writers feel bridled by market pressures and story traditions that are presented in this book. Even though some of the traditions are fussy and not easily grasped, they work, and production companies expect to find them in scripts considered for purchase. Works that are judged to be out of the mainstream make buyers uneasy. (This is true even though everyone realizes that art *should* cause uneasiness.) Before 2,500 years of dramatic tradition are discarded, simple self-protection advises writers to learn to use what has worked, if only to have a fall-back position in case new forms they invent do not pan out.

It is also worth noting that what passes as innovation is often only a stylistic fancy involving editing or camera technique, sequence shuffling, playing with time, objective-subjective points of view, and digital-computer wizardry. While all this is diverting, writers continue to use paper and pen to organize their visions into stories that reveal the human condition. Perhaps the occasional blips that cross the horizon of story narrative will someday deliver a totally new way to tell stories, but until that time, the movie circus depends on stories that will attract an audience. To create such works, writers use narrative traditions that deliver dramatically and commercially.

Selecting the Event

Imagine a twelve-year-old boy fishing beside a stream when a ship from another world appears and draws him inside. That is not a story. It is a notion, a situation, an incident that could be developed in many ways. It could be about alien experiments, secret missions, military skullduggery, missing children, government agents, or it could take any number of other tacks. These possibilities, each based on a different event, would lead to different stories. The notion could be developed as a docudrama, as in *Fire in the Sky*, in which the event is the safe return of a logger after he is abducted by aliens. The event might be training the boy to become an intergalactic warrior, as in *The Last Star Fighter*. The event might be returning the boy to his family after an adventure, as in *The Flight of the Navigator*, or it might be to send the boy *Back to the Future* or to use him to send a warning message, as in *The Day the Earth Stood Still*. The event could be about establishing contact with aliens, as in *Close Encounters of the Third Kind*, or sending the boy to battle an alien, as in *Enemy Mine*. The list of possible events can be extended, each proposing a different way to develop the idea.

Often the event is shaped by the inescapable logic that backs the idea; in the case mentioned above, this would mean returning the abducted boy to his family. If our thinking angled in that direction, we could tie that event to whatever emotional slant seemed appropriate for the audience and the style of the story we are writing. If we decided to do the piece for younger audiences, we might settle on a not-too-scary emotional slant and an unrealistic style. With these values tacked up, we might think about why the boy was abducted and how long he was with the aliens. Knowing the event would also cause speculations about why the boy was returned, how his parents and the authorities react to his disappearance and reappearance, and so forth. These inklings are not a plot, but they are story moments that are another small step toward a plot.

Incidentally, generating a list of possible events can be done by speedwriting as many possible events as you can manage in thirty minutes. During this period, jot down whatever thoughts pop into your mind. Repeat the half-hour session on two or three of the following days, edit out the junk, and think about what remains. The speed drill should pull in most of the events that attach to your idea; the number of possibilities is usually finite. Writing out possible events objectifies them, so you can think about them and select the one that feels right. I have found that new writers get more from this approach than by waiting for ideas to flash randomly from the unconscious. It should take a day or so to sort through the possible events generated. As you become comfortable with this strategy, you should discover that speedwriting possible events allows you to combine the story idea with temp characters, the frame, and other enriching values that begin to develop the plot.

The Event and the Ending of the Story

Not only does the event point the idea in a single direction, but it also indicates several other interesting developments, including how the story will end. To illustrate: If the event in the UFO story is returning the abducted boy to his family, then chances are that the return will occur in the climactic scene. Because the event in *The Verdict* is Galvin's winning the case, it tells us what happens in the climactic scene—he wins his case. The insight also applies to *The Terminator,* in which the event is destroying the cyborg. What happens in the climactic scene? Sarah (Linda Hamilton) squashes the creature in a hydraulic press.

When students are told about this notion, they become nervous because it sounds too easy. Nothing about screenwriting is easy, but helpmates are available; this one can be used to figure out what generally happens in the final act. In the case of the boy and the UFO, for example, it is enough to know that something happens that allows him to return home. We can figure out what that "something" is later.[2] Selecting an event thus provides two key compass bearings, one pointing to where the story seems to be heading and the other indicating what generally happens in the climactic scene. (I am emphasizing the concept of *event* because new writers have difficulty understanding and applying this value. Despite this, I feel that familiarity with the event is the most useful plotting perspective that I know; I recommend learning how it works and how to apply it to your writing.)

The uses of the event do not end here, however, for it also connects to the *problem* of the story, which is discussed next.

DEVELOPING A STORY STRUCTURE BASED ON THE DRAMATIC PROBLEM

Assume that we have a story idea and that it is attached to an event and the values discussed so far. Now we take a giant plotting step by assigning a dramatic problem to the story idea. In doing so, we are positioned to create a structure that organizes the plot.

---

[2]Here I must ask for a bit of good faith until a central lesson of plotting becomes clear. This lesson states that any story problem that can be stated as a question can be thought through and answered. Coming up with the questions is the hard part; answering them is easier—and much more fun.

Story Structure

Before getting into the advertised topic, some background on story structure: *Structure* is a buzzword with so many meanings that in 1985 the Writers Guild of America (WGA) called a seminar to discuss the term. The writers at the meeting quickly worked through the usual suspects: Some felt that structure meant putting the hero up a tree in Act I, throwing stones at him in Act II, and bringing him down in Act III. Others felt that structure was setup, confrontation, and resolution. Some claimed structure to be a matter of "who wants what and why can't he get it?" While everyone agreed with these old chestnuts, the meeting sought something sturdier, and so after an hour or so of wrangling, the following definition of *structure* was worked out:

Structure is the presentation and tracking of a dramatic problem through resolution.

Because this definition of *structure* seemed skimpy for classroom use, I asked a few senior writers for their thoughts on the topic. One respondent was writer-director Richard Brooks *(In Cold Blood, The Professionals)*. Brooks agreed with the definition, but felt that "it should be supported by the characters and the movie's thematic statement. Writers invest so much in the structure's logic, credibility, and motivation that this work should be part of the definition too."

Brooks appreciated that characters are not disembodied frog legs in a laboratory, twitching to whatever spark the writer supplies. The characters should have lives, experiences, and needs. This content is the life force of the structure, what makes or breaks a screenplay. Repeatedly, Brooks made the point that "screenwriting is structure, structure, structure." Most screenwriters would agree, for obscure and subtle as it is, the thoughtfulness invested in the structure is what holds the story together. When the structure is damaged, it may collapse, destroying the story.

The thoughtfulness that Brooks suggests was taken up by E. Jack Neuman *(Rise and Fall of the Third Reich)*, who also had a useful take on the definition of structure, especially as it connects to the dramatic problem. During a guest lecture before my screenwriting class, Neuman observed that creating problems and solving them are what screenwriters do for a living. Drawing on his experience as a TV long-form writer and a creator of numerous series, Neuman observed that "the problem with writing movies is finding the problem and then solving it." In most cases, the problem is the task that the main character must accomplish. In *The Terminator* the problem is how to destroy the cyborg; in *Sleepless in Seattle* it is how to get the couple together. In these and most movie stories, there seems to be no way for the protagonists to solve the problem—yet they triumph.

When we tease out what Brooks and Neuman have said, it turns out that the dramatic problem usually provides a spine or *throughline* on which the incidents of the plot can be hung. This is illustrated by *The Verdict*, in which the problem is Frank Galvin's struggle to defeat the opposing lawyer in a medical malpractice suit. This problem asserts itself eight minutes into the first act (Shot

8), when Galvin is informed that his case is coming due. He goes through the motions of preparing for a fight, all the while planning to take the insurance settlement and avoid going to trial. However, something happens at the end of the first act, and Galvin decides to contest the case. This decision thus launches the second act, in which Galvin conflicts with the most formidable lawyer in Boston (James Mason's Ed Concannon). Galvin's prospects of winning the case, weak to begin with, seem insurmountable after he is humbled at the end of the second act. In the third act, Galvin locates a rebuttal witness and wins the case. In this way, the problem of how Galvin takes on and wins his case against a powerful opponent organizes the three-act structure and the plot of the story.

This story pattern applies to most movies:

1. The hero takes on the problem in the first act.
2. The hero seems defeated at the end of the second act.
3. The hero solves the problem in the third act.

Simply put, three-act structure asks the screenwriter to create a problem that worsens until the hero's cause seems hopeless. Then, in the climactic scene, the hero finds a way to solve the problem and to emerge a better person. We will talk more about this pattern in the next chapter, but for now, think about it. Admittedly, the strategy seems old and worn, but only because writers have used it for centuries. It continues to work and to challenge writers to devise ways to conceal the mechanics of plot so that the strategy seems fresh. This happens when the writer creates interesting characters and fresh dramatic incidents.

Solving the Story Problem

The plotting strategy can be teased out further to reveal that *the problem is usually a restatement of the event.* In other words, you can determine the dramatic problem that organizes the plot merely by adding the word *how* to the event. To illustrate: The event in *The Verdict* is Galvin's winning the case; the problem is *how* will Galvin win the case? The event in *The Terminator* is destroying the cyborg; the problem is *how* will Sarah and Reese destroy the cyborg? In *Witness* the event is apprehending the corrupt police; the problem is *how* the wounded hero will manage this.

So that you understand how this plotting plan lays out the chalk lines that can help you to organize your story, note the progression:

- The event aims the idea in a single direction and suggests, in a general way, what happens in the story.

- The problem indicates what happens in the climactic scene, during which the problem is solved.

- By adding the word *how* to the event, the problem is defined.

The three steps can be used to determine the problem, the event, and the climactic scene of most stories. They combine into a strategy that you can use to test a number of story possibilities. Although everything surrounding the notion is vague and generalized in this early stage, the strategy presents a watchtower view that can reveal which way the material seems to be developing. This overview approach to plotting is appreciated by writers such as John Huston, who in a television interview said, "You are lost in this business unless you can see the whole movie topographically. You've got to be able to do that or you're going to fall apart, or depend on prayer. This isn't the arena for prayer." The story and structure definitions provide Huston's "topographic" view because they indicate the general direction of the story, what the problem is, and what happens in the Act III climax. Next we will show how this perspective can expand the story idea into a *story concept* that contains the genetic code of both the story and the script.

THE STORY CONCEPT

A **story concept** is a summary sentence that indicates what generally happens in a story. *It is the story idea plus the dramatic problem*. The concept statement usually reads like the log line in a TV guide: it is brief and general, yet suggestive of the overall plot. The story concept is what buyers listen for in a pitch, because it signals whether the notion is fresh and it helps them quickly decide whether they are interested in the notion. If a buyer decides that a story concept has interest and "heat," the project may have a future; when a concept fails to attract a buyer's interest, the buyer will pass on the idea. Whatever the strategy used to develop the notion—inspiration, perspiration, hypnosis, group writing, or you-name-it—almost any project can be stated as a story concept that will suggest the script's commercial appeal. Writers should therefore think very, very carefully about their story concepts. A story concept should be polished and tested repeatedly on confidants and collaborators until it seems as perfect as it can be.

We can see how a story concept is put together by examining our main study film, *The Verdict*. The story idea of this yarn is to give Frank Galvin a court case that will even scores with the establishment that ruined his life. This goal presents a problem, for to vindicate himself, Galvin must defeat the toughest lawyer in town. When the story idea is combined with the problem, the resulting story concept reads:

```
A boozy Boston lawyer receives an easy malpractice
case, but because it is his last chance to vindicate
himself against the establishment that betrayed him,
he decides to battle their premier attorney.
```

When the story concept is squeezed for meaning, like our other values, it suggests story goals and plot incidents. For example, *The Verdict*'s concept statement requires a lawsuit that brings hero and villain together. The concept statement also asks the writer to establish the drunken life of the protagonist and to create the Boston setting and the style of the film. It asks the writer to create a powerful antagonist to oppose the hero and to justify his decision to take on such an opponent. Finally, it asks the writer to devise a legal dispute that brings the contending sides together. In this way, the concept proposes story beats that expand the plot.

In the Line of Fire, a 1993 Oscar-nominated script, presents a Secret Service agent who blames himself for failing to save President Kennedy. The agent, Clint Eastwood's Frank Horrigan, is described as being in his early fifties, ruggedly handsome, but "frayed around the edges." The story gives Horrigan a chance to redeem himself when he learns that an assassin plans to kill the current president. The event of the story occurs when the hero defeats the assassin in the climactic scene. The hero's problem is how to defeat the assassin. When the idea and the problem combine, the result is a story concept:

> An aging Secret Service agent, who feels guilty for failing to save President Kennedy from being murdered, duels a deadly assassin. The outcome of their battle will decide whether the current president lives or dies and whether the agent's troubled past will give way to peace.

The concept statement suggests the tension that runs through the story: will Horrigan stop the assassin? This throughline is what the audience tracks as the hero confronts the problem. To make this happen we turn to the information in the concept statement: it tells us that Horrigan is a veteran of the presidential detail, so he is older, haunted, and capable. We know these things because Horrigan was an agent when President Kennedy was assassinated in 1963, and it is logical that he is haunted by his involvement. We know Horrigan is capable because that tends to be the nature of these agents. Of course we could make Horrigan an insecure tremble-chin type, but that would not suit the mood, the style, or the audience for this story. How do we decide that Horrigan will be in a one-on-one duel with the assassin? Our sense of story tells us that such an arrangement is dramatic. The frame of the story suggests Washington, D.C., government office buildings, or anywhere we wish, since the story is not bound to a particular location. In this way, our plotting strategy teases character and story points from the concept statement.

The problem presents a spine on which incidents of plot can be hung, because the genre of this story suggests that the hero and the villain oppose each other in a deadly duel. Frank Horrigan's introduction demonstrates his credentials—we see him defeat a gang of counterfeiters. After this derring-do, the audience senses that only an extraordinary rival could challenge Horrigan by exceeding all of the hero's abilities. Who might such a villain be? Again, simple logic requires someone with a special background—a secret agent, an FBI type, or a supercop. Screenwriter Jeff Maguire invented such a character—John Malkovich's Chuck Leary, a disgruntled former CIA assassin who was retired by The Company when his work weirded him out. Such a professional could indeed pose a threat to Horrigan and to the president. How does the audience know this? Because additional scenes that show Leary in action demonstrate the murderous skills he perfected as a CIA "wet boy." Additional incidents set up Leary's assassination plan. Add the love interest and the usual problems that a crusty character such as Horrigan might have with bureaucratic superiors, and plot incidents pop into view. They are then sequenced to form the spine of this story, which is based on the event, that is, stopping the assassin.

Note how careful thinking rather than guessing or playing "what if" is used to develop the idea. I realize that this is a huge simplification of the process screenwriters go through when working out a story. Described in words and orderly paragraphs, as here, this thinking process—which often includes "what if" brainstorming—appears much tidier than it is in practice; even so, it suggests the thinking that screenwriters employ when they work out their plots. If the plan in this book seems cumbersome, adapt it to suit your working methods. However, it is a plan, it is not particularly difficult to learn, and it works.

USING THE PROBLEM TO CREATE A DRAMATIC CRISIS

Another useful tool for enriching a story idea is the *dramatic crisis* that grows out of the problem being tracked. I learned this plotting strategy from the late Philip Dunne *(How Green Was My Valley)* during an interview at his Malibu home. When he began his career at Fox in the early 1930s, Dunne was given a handy definition by a senior writer; it is now passed on to you, as useful as ever:

Drama is the reaction of character to crisis.

Dunne liked the drama definition because it provoked questions: Who or what causes the crisis? How do the characters react to the crisis? How did antagonist and protagonist become entangled in it? Who else is involved? Why? What is at stake? What will happen if the crisis is not resolved? Such questions develop the plot because the crisis usually connects to a task that the hero must accomplish. When we create a feature problem, as noted earlier, it should cause a life-shaping and/or life-threatening personal crisis for the main characters. Only major problems are capable of causing a life crisis of such magnitude, so this cue can be used to create the worst possible problem that could befall the hero. For Frank Horrigan in *In the Line of Fire*, nothing could be worse than reliving the nightmare of Dallas by being part of another presidential assassination. To prevent this, he must stop a super-assassin bent on murdering the president.

The crisis in *The Verdict* arises when the hero takes on the most powerful lawyer in town. Galvin is soon outmaneuvered, which threatens him with professional humiliation, loss of his few remaining friends, forfeiture of his legal fee, and disaster for his hapless clients. In both films, the difficulties attached to the problem cause major crises for the heroes. *In the Line of Fire* uses a crisis that is life-threatening, while *The Verdict*'s crisis is life-shaping. A good problem worsens until there seems to be no way for the hero to triumph—or even to survive. Unless the crisis and the problem that causes it are revved to this intensity, the story may lack drama.

Screenwriters, novelists, playwrights, and those involved with dramatic material know that the beating heart of a good story is a problem that causes a supreme crisis for the main characters. Then, when the characters are spread-eagled by the problem, the dramatist uses the opportunity to expose their secrets and fears and to stir them emotionally. That is precisely what the plot and the problem are for: to reveal the emotional secrets and passions of the characters. Novelist John Gardner believed that "the crisis of the plot lets the character discover what he, the character, is really like. [It] forces the character to choice and action, transforms him from a static construct to a lifelike human being who makes choices and pays for them or reaps rewards."[3]

Gardner's thought suggests that the character is transformed when he or she undergoes a life-shaping and/or life-threatening experience because the ordeal forces the protagonist to tap into reserves of courage that solve the problem. The advice here should not be overlooked: *Successful stories are dramatic because of the protagonist's ordeal. The writer must create this supreme life test.*

William Kelley and Earl and Pamela Wallace used such a strategy in *Witness.* The crisis of the story begins when an Amish boy (Lukas Haas's Samuel) witnesses a murder and later identifies a police officer as the killer. The boy's revelation leads to an assassination attempt on the hero, flight to Amish country, and a romance with the boy's mother. Although Rachel and Book go their separate ways, the ordeal of the crisis is life-shaping (the romance) and life-threatening (the police conspiracy). The double nature of the crisis, involving an external threat and internal conflicts as well, is found in most good stories, as will be discussed shortly.

The crisis thus presents another tool for developing a plot because it demands that the writer invent an incident or situation that challenges the protagonist with a life-shaping or life-threatening challenge. When confronted by this problem, the writer is obliged to invent that challenge, which should add content to the developing plot.

USING THE CRISIS TO INTERRUPT THE STATUS QUO OF THE STORY

The status quo refers to whatever conditions and relationships are in place when the story begins. This perspective on story can provide another tool for developing the plot. To use it, the writer need only see the inciting incident as something that interrupts the status quo in a way that initiates a crisis. Often, the interruption is caused by the arrival or departure of a character. In *The Verdict* (Shot 8), the interruption occurs when Mickey shows up in Galvin's office

[3]John Gardner, *On Becoming a Novelist*, Harper & Row, New York, 1983, p. 46.

and announces that their case is coming to trial. The crisis occurs later in the act when Galvin decides to fight the case.

Frank Nugent, one of John Ford's favorite screenwriters (as well as his son-in-law), often began his stories with an interruption of the status quo:

> The writer's first job is to look long and hard at his story and to see whether it can be reduced to terms of the upsetting of the status quo. What is the established situation? What is the new element that affects it? What is the end result? The problem of the opening reduces itself to two alternatives: the writer may begin either by establishing the existing situation or by introducing the new element. *The Caine Mutiny, Marty,* and *On the Waterfront* are examples of the former; *Picnic, The Blackboard Jungle,* and *Going My Way* illustrate the latter. [In *The Quiet Man*] the opening shots are of a train rolling into a station, a lanky American alighting and asking the way to Inishfree—a simple enough request, but one that obviously piques the curiosity of porters, station-master, conductor, local fishwife, and of course the audience. Soon it is shown that this is an Irish-born American who has come home to his mother country in search of quiet and peace. And what happens? He disturbs the status quo, to put it mildly. That was the story and that was the technique.[4]

Some films begin with the status quo already unbalanced, as in *Witness,* which opens when Rachel, newly widowed, sets out for Baltimore to visit her sister. The story continues to "unbalance" when Samuel witnesses the murder, when Book is wounded and nursed to health, and when he and Rachel become romantically involved. A similar pattern occurs in *Sleepless in Seattle,* which opens with the hero brooding by the grave of his dead wife. A short time later (Shot 8) Sam moves to Seattle, but again the status quo unbalances when his son, Jonah, calls a radio psychologist on Christmas Eve. When Annie (Meg Ryan) becomes involved with finding Sam, the disequilibrium intensifies. In most cases, stories can be seen as the struggle to establish an improved status quo for the main characters.

Applying this strategy to the sports widow idea, we could interrupt the status quo by subjecting Mom to a humiliation of some sort. This could be a public scandal played out in front of the team, or it could happen when Mom discovers that her husband is having an affair, abusing drugs or alcohol, squandering money, gambling, losing his mind or his job, or whatever. The writing task here would be to create an incident that interrupts the status quo and inspires a crisis that forces Mom to fight for her family.

In many cases, the interruption of the status quo is some sort of incitement that creates a sense of story "takeoff" and a feeling that the tale has been launched. Experienced writers understand that movies are too intense to tolerate dawdling, so their goal is the earliest possible takeoff. *The Terminator* illustrates this point thirty-one seconds into the movie when the cyborg interrupts the status quo by dropping from the sky. A speedy takeoff is especially

---

[4]Frank Nugent, "The Opening Scenes," in Lola Yoakem (ed.), *TV and Screenwriting,* University of California Press, Berkeley, 1958, p. 21.

important in TV and short films, which should be under way *by the end of the first page.*

The Crisis, the Problem, and the Event

Note how the event and the crisis connect to the problem of the story. *In the Line of Fire* involves the life-threatening problem of how to prevent an assassin from murdering the president. The event of the film—what happens after everything happens—is that the hero saves the president and eliminates the assassin. The crisis unleashed by the problem causes the hero to relive a painful memory and to suffer a brush with death.

In *Sleepless in Seattle* the event is uniting Sam and Annie; the problem is how to get them together from opposite sides of the country. The task of making this happen unleashes the life-shaping crisis that causes Annie to break up with her fiancée (Bill Pullman's Walter) and causes a little boy (Jonah) to fly across the country to find his new mom. In this way, the event, the problem, and the crisis propose meaning and plot elements early in the writing.

THE INTERNAL PROBLEM AND THE EXTERNAL PROBLEM OF A STORY

So far this chapter has dealt with such story values as frame, event, problem, structure, story concept, and dramatic crisis that interrupts the status quo. At this point the discussion becomes more complicated because most movies employ *two* story lines that run parallel to each other. They are called the **A-storyline** and the **B-storyline.** So far we have discussed A-storylines, which deal with some manner of external problem—winning the lawsuit, destroying the monster, or whatever attaches to the external action of the plot. The B-storyline deals with the internal problems of the main characters, which are usually emotional and/or psychological.

The A-storyline has been likened to the meat that the burglar tosses to the Doberman to keep it busy while the house is being robbed. In other words, the action of the A-storyline diverts the audience while it absorbs the inner struggles of the characters and their emotional responses. In *The Verdict,* the court case is the external problem that organizes the A-storyline. While this holds the attention of the audience, the plot thickens when the lawsuit causes Galvin's internal problem to surface. We learn that it is based on a legal scandal that happened five or so years earlier, when Galvin was accused (by his father-in-law) of jury tampering during the Lillibridge case. Even though the accusation is false, the incident destroyed Galvin's marriage and turned him into the disgraced drunkard and legal lowlife that we meet when the story begins. The memory of Lillibridge thus forms a psychological wound that motivates Galvin to even scores with the establishment in court. The A- and B-storylines become interwoven as Galvin achieves his goal when he defeats his enemies in the courtroom. Thus the A-storyline in *The Verdict* is the hero's struggle to win the case and the B-storyline is his struggle to reclaim his life. Without the internal struggle, the trial would be little more than a TV court case where one clever lawyer outfoxes another. Similarly, what matters most in *Witness* is the relationship between Rachel and Book, not the shabby doings of Schaeffer and his outlaw gang.

The psychological conditions that feed the B-storyline are based upon life experiences, memories, and incidents that are usually in place when the story begins. In character-driven stories such as *Moonstruck* and *Kramer vs. Kramer*, the B-storyline usually deals with the protagonist's struggle with a psychological or emotional need, such as learning to love, gaining self-esteem, acquiring independence, or overcoming any of the emotional wounds and inadequacies that people suffer. In most stories, the B-storyline's emotional problem escalates along with the problem of the A-storyline to cause a crisis that almost destroys the hero.

Action movies follow a different construction. As in *Speed, Die Hard,* and similar works, *The Terminator* is organized around action, and less attention is given to the internal struggle of the characters. However, there is a range to these films. *Cliffhanger,* for one, opens with a climbing accident that causes the death of a young woman. Although the hero feels sadness about her death, the matter does not affect the action line or the character. This approach suited the aims of the movie, which were to dazzle the audience with action and special effects; however, its emphasis on spectacle[5] over character gave *Cliffhanger* a cartoonish quality because the characters were too busy leaping through the flaming hoops of the plot to reveal their humanity.

Not all action stories are so devoid of character content. *In the Line of Fire* reveals the psychological torment of the protagonist and the twisted inner life of the assassin. The curious partnership of the two adversaries and their B-storyline pathologies present a psychological dimension that enhances this story. Many action films give the characters a few minutes to talk about life plans, family, experiences, and the like. Such a moment occurs in *The Terminator* (Shot 182) after Sarah and Reese escape the carnage of the police station attack and quietly talk about their lives and the future. In many stories, a few minutes here and there are enough to dimensionalize the characters and to turn a no-brainer script into a more satisfying work.

THE NATURE OF DRAMATIC CONFLICT

The preceding discussion indicates that the dramatic problem of the story pits a hero against an opposing force. As both sides battle, the conflict moves the story toward the climactic moment when hero or villain will triumph. From this perspective, *dramatic conflict* is *the hero's struggle against another person, against a system, against nature, or against an internal psychological force.*

---

[5]*Spectacle* refers to the grandeur of the movie—the quality of the cast, the elegance of the sets and costumes, the number of cavalry in the charge, and the overall scale and visual content of the movie.

Conflict energizes movies, which have little use for characters who sit around agreeing with each other. Such harmony is tolerable only when it is the brief lull before the storm or when it occurs (briefly) at the end of the story. In most instances, movie characters disagree, wheedle, connive, complain, plead, fight, or in some way engage in conflict. Awareness of the varieties of dramatic conflict can help you to figure how it is created and dramatized. This awareness is also a major tool for figuring out what will happen in the story being developed. The following listing of the varieties of conflict can be useful.

Hero-versus-Villain Conflict

This conflict involves a hero and a villain who struggle over a problem or goal. *The Terminator* presents an elemental hero-villain conflict in which the parties fight over who lives and who dies. The hero-villain conflict is more civilized in *An Officer and a Gentleman,* where two good men, Richard Gere (protagonist) and Lou Gossett (antagonist) dispute over the best way to train naval aviators. Both men believe themselves to be in the right, but they have conflicting motives, styles, and personalities. *The Verdict, The Fugitive, Witness,* and *In the Line of Fire* are also based on hero-villain conflicts. Writers can quickly check whether a story idea connects to this conflict, or to one of those discussed below, and use this insight to figure out which way the idea seems to be developing.

Hero-versus-Nature Conflict

Wolfen, Jurassic Park, and many science fiction films illustrate the hero-versus-nature conflict. These stories often involve something that must be defeated, endured, or sent on its way—a disease, a beast, an alien life-form, a storm, a natural power, and so on. Inventing such a natural or technological menace, fact, or projection is essential to stories built around this type of conflict.

When the natural force does not have a dramatic presence, it may be possible to divert the conflict to human characters, as in *Jaws*. Because the filmmakers knew that the audience would have trouble disliking the shark—after all, eating things is what sharks do—the filmmakers encouraged the audience to dislike the greedy business types who ignore the hero's warnings. This manipulation gives the audience something to dislike until the shark shows up and noshes on the boat and its crew.

Another strategy used in these stories is to demonstrate the awesome power of the natural enemy, as in *Outbreak* or *The Andromeda Strain* when the virus kills off an entire town. The category also involves disaster stories, such as *The Poseidon Adventure*.

Hero-versus-the-System Conflict

Stories that pit a hero against a faceless bureaucracy illustrate the hero-versus-the-system conflict. The conflict can involve any system that opposes the hero, whether the organization is military, political, criminal, business, religious, or whatever.

In a typical situation, the hero (by accident or by choice) might become involved with an appendage of the system, as when the hero of *Three Days of the Condor* survives a raid by renegade secret agents. The conflict can pit the hero against a bureaucracy *(All the President's Men)*, an institutional establishment *(Lorenzo's Oil)*, a corporation *(Silkwood)*, a class system *(The Verdict)*, a criminal conspiracy *(The Firm)*, and so on.

Hero-versus-the-Self Conflict

This category features inner conflicts that test the hero's values, beliefs, or morals. Although there is an element of self-conflict in most stories, in some it dominates *(The Man from Snowy River, The Lost Weekend)*.

Screenwriters create the main character's value system and test it by a dramatic problem, as in *Nobody's Fool*, in which the hero struggles against childhood memories that have haunted his life. The main characters in *Amadeus* and *Immortal Beloved* also struggle with memories of abusive fathers. Personal-conflict stories can be difficult to write, and new writers should think carefully before attempting one.

Additional Approaches to Conflict

Lives of characters may also be blighted by social or hereditary evils that cause torment *(The Pawnbroker, Chinatown)*.

Conflict can center on reformers whose values cause them to attack social or personal evils. In these stories, the hero runs into a status quo so unjust that it must be defied *(The Fixer, The Bridge on the River Kwai)*.

Prejudice directed at characters who have been shaped or victimized by geography, race, or class differences can lead to conflict *(El Norte, Boyz N the Hood, Wuthering Heights)*.

Conflicts can develop when characters become lost in foreign lands or when they are driven from their homelands. The characters in these stories are then motivated to find a new home or to return to an old home *(Pelle the Conqueror; America, America; The Quiet Man)*.

Another approach to conflict concerns people living in a geographic region or a mental landscape that is haunted by ghosts, cruel memories, or an unhappy past. Such stories respond well to rich, internalized conflicts *(Five Easy Pieces, Sophie's Choice)*.

A final approach to conflict concerns stories steeped in modern angst, where the hero's need is for meaning and stability *(Fearless, The Rapture, Dead Poets Society)*.

The forms of conflict do not separate neatly like cans of soup on a shelf. Often, the conflict draws from several of the sources listed above. In *The Terminator*, the heroes battle a creature that is a force of nature and part of a system. The hero and heroine of *Sleepless in Seattle* conflict with their ideals of what a relationship should be (the self) and with geography (nature). *Witness* presents a hero-villain conflict, a hero-system conflict, and a values conflict.

This list of conflicts can give you another perspective on your work by helping you figure out the nature of your story's particular conflict, who or what the hero is opposing, and which way the conflict is heading.

Correcting Weak Conflict

The main cause of weak conflict is a weak villain. Cure this by making the antagonist potent. Bette Davis in *All about Eve*, Anthony Hopkins in *The Silence of the Lambs*, Lee Cobb in *On the Waterfront*, or Linda Fiorentino in *The Last Seduction* illustrate. Give your characters drives and needs that make them dangerous. Above all, make the villain formidable enough to threaten the hero.

Successful scripts reveal that every scene is cranked with conflict, even when the beat seems "happy." In *Sleepless in Seattle*, Annie introduces Walter to her family (Shot 18); although this is a friendly occasion, the scene has a subtext of hysterical tension and conflict. This is followed by another supposedly happy scene between Annie and her mother in the attic (Shot 21). The two women are trying on a wedding dress when Annie indicates that life with Walter is not much fun. The moment suggests Annie's internal conflict—should she settle for a conventional life with Walter or seek an ideal marriage? To resolve this conflict, Annie strings Walter along while she checks out the lonely man from Seattle that she heard on the radio.

Another source of weak conflict is skipping over a moment of conflict after it has been set up. Such leapfrogging leaves a blank spot instead of a scene of conflict. Leapfrogging may occur when writers become uncomfortable with the emotions they have stirred up and turn away from dramatic opportunity. Emotional moments heated by conflict are what movies are all about, for this is when the characters speak their hearts and unload their passion. When your story promises dramatic conflict, deliver it. When your story does not promise dramatic conflict, rewrite until it does.

HOW THE VILLAIN CREATES CONFLICT

Good stories often use a strong, active villain to challenge the hero. As mentioned, scripts fail when the villain is too weak to menace the hero. Therefore, one of the surest ways to beef up a weak story is to beef up the villain by making the character or force obsessive, charming, clever, powerful, diabolical, or whatever turns the antagonist into a threat. Villains can be energized when they are given a dose of aggression that overinflates them with motivation. This does not mean turning the antagonist into a lunatic, but the character should menace the hero. Angelica Huston as Maerose, the vengeful daughter in *Prizzi's Honor*, illustrates: she is intelligent, willful, unpredictable, vengeful, and locked into her poisonous family.

Motivating the Villain

Strong villains usually have an agenda, something that they want to happen or want to keep from happening. *The Verdict*'s Ed Concannon is a legal eagle who is aided by a phalanx of lawyers, wealth, and connections to every power center in town. He operates with silky precision, so there is no need for him to raise his voice as he conflicts with the hero. Schaeffer, the main antagonist in *Witness*, is a similar type, except that he is boiling within as he tries to silence John Book and his witness.

Tightly wound villains challenge the heroes, but in the end the antagonists are defeated, partly by their inability to adapt and to change. They behave selfishly and in ways that remove them from the moral high ground that is the domain of the hero. Often the hero's winning advantage stems from an intuitive decision to trust his or her heart and to follow the moral path. Mythologists such as Joseph Campbell hold that this internal compass is what connects the hero to the universal power that has guided humankind from the beginning. Whether the power is called God, conscience, the eternal, morality, the wisdom of the heart, or something else, the protagonist connects to this power and the villain does not.

Stated baldly this way, moral power sounds simplistic, yet it shows up repeatedly in films. *The Verdict*'s Ed Concannon, for example, seems a model of rectitude, yet he fits the villainous pattern because he abandons morality by hiring a spy (Charlotte Rampling's Laura). Things go badly for Galvin until he steps onto the moral high ground and begins to draw on its power. This happens when he yields to conscience and turns down the bishop's settlement offer (Shot 26). Galvin steps closer to the power when (Shot 71) he refuses to quit the case, and from there, armed with what is moral and right, he locates his witness and defeats Concannon. We see the quiet hand of moral power at work when Galvin realizes the importance of the hospital admitting form (Shot 75) and when a propitious mail delivery connects Galvin to his missing witness (Shot 80). In this way, movies argue (perhaps naively) that right defeats might and that those who are honorable will defeat those who lack honor. American mainstream films use this hopeful aesthetic to resolve the external problems and the internal problems of stories. Whether true or not, it is risky for anyone hoping to sell a script to go against this aesthetic, which centers the vast majority of feature films and TV shows.

Conflict and Motivation

Dramatic characters do things for a reason. The lonely geek may try to meet a woman but does so in the wrong way. Why? Somehow the fellow was influenced to behave in a way that causes rejection. That unfelt drive motivates him to fail and to suffer loneliness. Conflict is more interesting when the audience has a sense of such motivation. In *The Verdict*, hero and villain fight for victory in the courtroom. During the trial, Concannon is not a fiend who hurries home at night to torture his dog; rather, he is a skillful lawyer doing his best to defend his client.

Villains have various motives: The cyborg in *The Terminator* is motivated to kill Sarah Connor because it has been programmed for this task. *Sleepless in Seattle*'s Walter is a smug fellow who seems content with his life and his allergies. It is the bulldog nature of Tommy Lee Jones's character in *The Fugitive* to hunt down the hero. Characters can also acquire motivation during the story, as in *It Could Happen to You* when Rosie Perez's character becomes dizzy with fancy airs, divorces her husband, and sues for his lottery winnings.

Motivated characters have backstories, psychological needs, personality quirks, problems, and the like. Without such psychological dimension, characters become hollow mannequins executing incidents of plot. Stories with empty characters usually rely on spectacle and physical action (fights, chases, and derring-do) to entertain. This can be a losing battle because unless the characters' backstories and/or motives are developed and communicated, the audience may not care about what happens to them in the story. To avoid this, writers create multifaceted characters that the audience cares about.

THE THEMATIC DIMENSION OF DRAMA

The next strategy for enriching the plot concerns the **theme,** which is the writerly perspective on the significance of the story (discussed in Chapter 1). In many cases, the theme is the "message" of the movie, what it is really about. Billy Wilder's views on thematic content are instructive here:

> You try to make it about something. I don't think I am writing anything that is going to change the world . . . but if you make the audience talk about it for fifteen minutes after the picture, then you have done something. If you can get people to repeat that talk in the office or with people that you have dinner with, then this is the root of the success of a film.[6]

Screenwriters have issues they believe in, often passionately, and these topics—fairness, freedom, justice, opportunity, war, violence, family values—often provide the thematic content that enriches our stories. Unfortunately, when a script sizzles with one of these issues, the movie studios may back away, fearing such material will alienate audiences. The studios argue that audiences do not buy tickets to be lectured on ethics, politics, reforming the world, vegetarianism, or anything else. Thematically, this puts writers in a bind because controversial issues can be very dramatic.

Despite such timidity on the part of the studios, good movies are made and they say important things about the world. Screenwriters manage this by weaving thematic implications into the script. The skill here is to weave invisibly, so the thematic content is felt rather than noticed outright. When written this way, it is difficult for the movie message to be excised. This is the recommended approach to theme: marble your observation into the material so that it seems invisible. Try not to be dogmatic, preachy, scolding, or obvious when

[6]Billy Wilder, conversation with Charles Champlin, Century Cable TV Interview, Santa Monica, California, February 1991.

you are addressing the theme. The intensity of movies and our natural instinct to assign meaning to art is usually enough to cause thematic content to be noticed, regardless of how deeply it is buried in a script. In many cases the script is written with such passion that the writer does not realize that the work is streaked with thematic content. Writers should also appreciate that they have allies, and that the work of directors, actors, editors, and cinematographers can preserve and enhance thematic content—if it adds to the story.

Writers can be so intent on polishing story, characters, and continuity that theme is neglected. In such cases it may seem that the story has nothing to say. However, most stories contain at least the germ of a thematic statement. To discover what your story's theme might be, talk to teachers, spiritual advisors, family, and friends about your story and solicit their take on what the story is saying thematically. Check out reference books that present thoughtful observations; a few should fit what you are trying to say. (Appendix B presents a list of reference books that you may find useful.) The goal is to give viewers something to think about when the movie is over. Ideally, the movie should change them in some way.

Wherever it originates, the theme can give the story substance and meaning. Writer Carl Foreman (*High Noon, The Guns of Navarone*) became a skillful weaver of complex social themes, although this was not always the case:

> It never occurred to me that the story had to be *about* something. I just thought a good story had a good plot and good interesting characters and lots of action. And when I came out to Hollywood, for example, I was still under that belief. And it took me some time to realize that the plot and the characters and all that were fine and very important, but it really had to be about something . . . and sometimes about something that wasn't even apparent to begin with. . . . A lot of college kids get it confused with themes they write . . . those papers for English. That's what I thought it was . . . a paper. But obviously . . . the story has to be about something, and that thing is not necessarily action. It's what you believe in, or what you have to say.[7]

BACKGROUND, FOREGROUND, AND THEME

Most commercial American movies concentrate on the star actors who appear in the foreground of the story. The stars are used to attract financing, audiences, and publicity. The glitter of these stars often draws attention away from the background settings and locations against which they perform. This relationship is important because the background settings are a primary source of the story's thematic content. *Cliffhanger* plays against stunning mountain scenery that is used merely to show off the muscular heroics of the star. The result is a scenic film that has little to say and is forgettable. *The Verdict,* by

[7]Terry Sanders and Freida Lee Mock, *Word into Image,* American Film Foundation, Santa Monica, California, 1981, p. 33.

comparison, features foreground characters who are less "actorish"[8] as they move through the musty halls of some of the old buildings in Boston. The attention given to this background—public buildings, law libraries, legal offices, hospitals, and courthouse settings—suggests the class-ridden social order of New England and how it compromises the legal system. The film uses background and foreground to intimate the clubiness between Bishop Brophy (Edward Binns), Concannon, Judge Sweeney (Milo O'Shea), the doctors, the insurance company, and the hospital. This cabal was able to send Galvin's star witness scurrying off to the Caribbean for the duration of the trial. The film signals a sense of insider privilege when it shows the posh offices of Concannon and Bishop Brophy and when the court calendar is rigged against Galvin. These values, which bleed into the story from the background settings, contribute to *The Verdict*'s theme, which is that institutional corruption can be overcome when we act with faith and the justice that is in our hearts.

Not all films are as dedicated to pulling theme from background and dialogue as *The Verdict* is. Most mainstream U.S. films load the foreground with stars, spectacle, and emotional content that draw the audience into the story so it shares the on-screen ordeal of the main characters. This aesthetic differs from the practice of many independent and overseas filmmakers, whose work tends toward stronger political and social content. One reason for this is that independents lack money to hire international stars or to mount expensive spectacle. Low budgets mean that alternative films must use small crews and available background settings to tell the story. It often happens that these backgrounds present images of ordinary life that are manipulated so they serve the thematic aims of the story. This point is illustrated by *The Story of Qui Ju*, a Chinese film that chronicles a wife's journey from vast rural landscapes to teeming cities as she seeks legal redress for an insult to her family. The backgrounds suggest that a citizen can fight a modern bureaucracy, which is the thematic message of the movie.

Although it is venturesome to compare how mainstream and alternative films deal with theme, a comparison of three works may suggest the difference. *The Molly Maguires* is a mainstream studio movie about an informer who infiltrates a secret society of miners in Pennsylvania in the 1870s. The French film *Germinal* also deals with coal miners during a similar period. Both stories end violently, and each makes a similar thematic point—that desperate conditions drove early miners to pay dearly for the right to organize and to earn fair wages. Despite these similarities, the two stories differ in how they present the foreground characters and the background social context.

Early in *The Molly Maguires*, a mysterious stranger (Richard Harris) arrives in a coal town looking for work. To win acceptance, he must be approved by

---

[8]The best acting is "invisible," which means the actors are so submerged in their roles that they become the characters and we forget they are acting. Modern actors, especially method actors, have become wonderfully "unactorish." When an actor is singled out for "acting," it usually means that he or she is not "into" the character and we notice the acting technique, which reduces the effectiveness of the performance.

Sean Connery, the leader of the local Molly Maguires (a secret Irish group that bombs operations that they feel deal unfairly with coal miners). Throughout, the story focuses on the foreground relationship of Connery and Harris. The struggle of the miners to organize, as well as how they live, ethnic conflicts, and other historic concerns, is given scant attention. As a result, *The Molly Maguires* comes off as an empty Hollywood spectacle of the time (1970) that does little more than show off the two movie stars who dominate the foreground.

By contrast, *Germinal* uses its background settings to examine a social milieu and to point out the injustices of a system in which mine owners live sumptuously while their workers barely have enough to eat. The movie presents its story through painterly wide-angle shots of marching miners, grand estates, and village life, as well as through vignettes of the rich and poor at home. *Germinal* remains cool and somewhat distant, which prevents the audience from becoming emotionally close to the main characters. This approach allows the audience to pull details out of the rich background settings used in the film and to grasp the story's thematic comment.

A third coal mining film, John Sayles's low-budget alternative film *Matewan*, offers another view of how background and foreground work together to influence thematic content. *Matewan* takes place in West Virginia in 1920, where, once again, miners battle the owners for better wages and safer working conditions. *Matewan* also begins when a mysterious stranger (Chris Cooper) arrives in a coal town looking for work. The film builds predictably toward a showdown between the coal company's hired enforcers and the miners, but then it goes against genre by making Cooper's character a pacifist who opposes violence. His peaceful behavior is the opposite of that of the violent characters in *The Molly MaGuires*. Cooper does not dominate *Matewan*, as Harris and Connery do in *The Molly Maguires*. Instead, *Matewan* allows the audience to register the background of the strike so it can understand the conditions that caused the turmoil.

The production styles of the films differ also. *The Molly Maguires* is shot heroically, like a western. *Matewan*, shot on location in the West Virginia coal country, uses a documentary style that is suited to the bleak lives of the miners. *Matewan* pulls back from melodramatic emotion to permit the audience to think about the ordeal of the miners and about questions of social justice raised in the film. By doing this, Sayles's story acquires social relevance and thematic content.

The point of this discussion is to sketch some of the choices that screenwriters confront when they address thematic issues. The thought police are not in charge, but you should appreciate that movie studios are sensitive about stories that might stir up social discord. Those who finance films spend their money on scripts that they hope will entertain an audience and earn money. They behave this way even though they may be in total agreement with the politics of the script. The front office executives make business decisions that are based on art. Canny screenwriters make artistic decisions that recognize the concerns of business. This is an unending battle which, it is hoped, leads to better and more successful movies.

Today, despite a liberal political slant that tends to grow stronger as it moves up the corporate ladder, Hollywood's mainstream movies are politically timid. This has been the case for decades. The "red scare" of the 1940s and the resulting blacklist that ruined many careers is partly responsible for this caution. Thermonuclear threat and the Cold War so chilled Hollywood that during America's fifteen-year involvement with Vietnam, only one film (John Wayne's *The Green Berets*) was made (in 1968) about a war that cost 58,000 American and millions of Vietnamese lives.

Avoidance of hot-button social issues also shows in the 1990s. One example is the way movies represent the homeless and damaged people who live on America's streets, for somehow films based on this tragedy come to us as comedies! Watching *Down and Out in Beverly Hills, The Fisher King, Life Stinks, The Saint of Fort Washington, With Honors,* and similar fare, one might think that living as a derelict has become a pathway to wisdom and enlightenment. Instead of addressing homelessness honestly, these films twist reality to entertain us. These are not portrayals of a tragic social problem; they are star turns that serve up millionaire movie stars dressed in designer rags and carefully applied Max Factorish dirty faces. The oversize presence of the stars blocks out the background settings so our homeless poor can be portrayed as "martyred visionaries, sages, or chattel," according to film critic Peter Rainer of *The Los Angeles Times:*

> You won't learn much from these films about the real causes and conditions of homelessness, but you will learn a lot about how these conditions are camouflaged and candied and served up for a mass audience. . . . The idealization of the homeless in these movies resembles the ways in which Hollywood tends to idealize minorities in general. There's an element of condescension and special pleading in the attempt, as if we wouldn't be interested in these people if they weren't wiser or purer in heart than we are. The treatment denies their rage—it pastoralizes them. It also represents a kind of charity extended to the homeless. It's as if a more realistic portrayal would seem unnecessarily cruel—yet one more injury inflicted upon them.[9]

Here Rainer points to the essence of theme, which is concern for the human condition in terms of ethics, quality of life, family, and a shared humanity. Movies can tell a solid story and convey a theme that helps us to understand our world and ourselves. That understanding is what we need to grow and to realize the potential of our souls, our nation, and our planet. Many feel that movies could do more on this without warping a good story, as evidenced by *Quiz Show,* a movie about rigged quiz shows in the 1950s. The movie provides a basis for comparing what constitutes scandal in America—for cheating on quiz shows seems petty compared to the escalations of Watergate, Iran-Contra, assassinations, the S&L scandal, and similar public disasters. In any event, thirty-five years after the fact, *Quiz Show* examines a moment of

---

[9]Peter Rainer, "In the Movies Everyone Has a Home," *The Los Angeles Times,* May 22, 1994.

broadcast scandal in ways that prod audiences thematically. Although *Quiz Show* is hardly a revolutionary film, it takes a slap at one of the issues that bedevil our nation and the world—ethical behavior by large institutions that affect the public. There is a moment in the movie when a producer of one of the rigged quiz shows is asked whether he acted illegally. He answers, "Look at it this way: the producers made out, the sponsor made out, the public was entertained. Who got hurt?"

The director of *Quiz Show*, Robert Redford, commented on this line (and paraphrased the film's theme) by observing that the producer presented "a real valid argument from the merchant point of view. But there used to be a thing called ethics. And there was a thing called shame. It doesn't exist anymore, because corruption has become a way of life."

Films with thematic muscle remind us of the gap between what we are and what we could be. They do so without stopping the story, for in most cases, thematic content can be slipped into a story by shading a few lines of dialogue or a few visual moments with thematic content. *The Grapes of Wrath* contains dozens of powerful thematic images that communicate what happened to farmers driven off their land during the Depression. The image of the feather that opens and closes *Forrest Gump* makes a thematic point—that each person is special and touched by God, and we must try to do the best we can with what we have, to act with dignity, and to be kind to each other.

Thematic content is the social observation that the screenwriter (or the director) works into the material. Sometimes the thematic statement is so general and bland that it requires little effort. Crime does not pay, everyone needs to be somebody, hard work pays off, and similar thematic marshmallows will not arouse controversy. Such themes are modest pleas for social justice, fairness, and compassion. When the story attacks racism, religious hypocrisy, social injustice, disparities between rich and poor, corporate control of politics, hopelessness, the loss of opportunity, erosion of the family, and similar topics, the censors may argue that such material is "not entertaining."

To protect against such criticism, screenwriters bury their thematic statements so deeply into the text that the message does not emerge until the movie is over and the people who have seen it talk about it away from the theater, if they are so inclined. Each viewer must ponder the movie and extract its message; writers should not use their scripts as soapboxes or propaganda megaphones.

USING THE STORY TEMPLATE TO ROUGH OUT THE THREE-ACT STRUCTURE

The values we have discussed—frame, event, story concept, problem, conflict, dramatic crisis, and theme—are used by writers to enrich the story idea and to create characters and incidents of plot. Possible story beats are sorted into a rough plot that follows a three-act structure. This is less difficult when one realizes that certain things happen in each act of a story. As mentioned earlier, most stories have the hero take on the problem in the first act and seem defeated by the problem by the end of the second act. In the third act of most stories, the hero solves the problem. Knowing this general pattern—call it the *story template*—provides useful advice early in the work, when the plot is vague and unformed.

We can see how the template works by applying it to *In the Line of Fire*. The hero learns of the villain's plan to kill the president in the first act, and he moves to prevent this from happening. To make the hero's problem more difficult, he must contend with bosses who threaten to remove him from the case. This familiar dramatic ploy allows the hero to step away from the other agents and to act as the solitary warrior-hero. There are many ways the writer could have motivated this: Horrigan could alienate his boss; he could have a death wish to retire in a blaze of glory; he could be cranky and ornery; he could have enemies who conspire against him. Any or all of these attributes could fit Horrigan's history and temperament.

Writers use the three-act structure, genre conventions, and their sense of story to make their plots seem fresh and new. At the same time, more practical matters receive attention, such as who is the target audience and what should the emotional tone and style of the film be. I suspect that screenwriter McGuire knew that *In the Line of Fire* would be written as a realistic story, since assassination stories play well as political thrillers that keep viewers on the edge of their seats, deliberately scaring them. The story's complexity and intensity make it suitable for the young adult and the adult audience. Targeting the movie this way, which takes an hour or so, can shoo away some of the doubt and the confusion that nip at us during the early stages of the work.

Most stories contain a darkest moment that occurs at the end of the second act, when the hero seems defeated by the problem. It is not necessary to work out the specifics of this low point until later. In *In the Line of Fire*, the darkest moment occurs when the hero is outmaneuvered by the assassin, who now has a clear shot at the president; this is exactly where the story should be in such a thriller. To arrive at this point, the screenwriter needed to work out how he could make the assassin most threatening, how he plans to kill the president, and how he will outsmart the hero. Once again we come upon our earlier observation: *Ingenious answers can be determined when the writer works out specific questions that apply to the problem being tracked.*

Finally, the template advises that the hero will solve the problem in the third act. The climactic scene in most assassination films occurs when the villain is foiled at the last possible moment by the hero. Although it is not essential that the story follow this plan, the final showdown between the hero and villain will be what the audience has been expecting, so if it does not appear, something better should be presented.

Dissected this way, the plot of *In the Line of Fire* is not particularly complex. However, it is sturdy enough to accommodate interesting characters, a tense situation, a big-city frame, and secret agent activity that supplies incidents of plot. These include a love interest, behind-the-scenes mumbo-jumbo with the Secret Service, the intersection of the somber worlds of Frank Horrigan and

Chuck Leary, and action to demonstrate the skills of both characters. All of this combines into an entertaining package.

It is easy enough to use these strategies on a finished film, but let us test them on the sports widow idea. The news item describes a woman whose family is threatened by her husband's sports obsession (see page 31). One possible event is that Mom saves her family. That choice seems logical because it deals with preserving the family. The problem in the story is *how* Mom saves her family. This will not be easy because she seems to be without skills or much of anything except the secret she has hidden all her life: her remarkable strength. In the course of the story, this ability could be changed from a liability to an asset that gives Mom status and a new outlook on life. We need not turn Mom into an Olympic star, but she could end up expressing who she really is, rather than pretending to be a weakling. To achieve this, Mom could work out in a gym and develop into a physical wonder.

Or we might choose to have Mom fall under the spell of her job or of sports activities and neglect her family (as in *Mr. Mom*). Or the event could involve Mom leaving Dad and making a new life for herself and her kids (*Alice Doesn't Live Here Any More*). In such a case the problem would be how Mom accomplishes her goal. She could become an exerciser on a TV show or a competitor in an Iron Woman contest. We could choose to scrap the "muscular Mom" idea altogether, making her an average woman who must confront this major life problem unarmed. In such a case, Mom's strength would come from within her character as someone who refuses to give up on her family.

Any one of these events could be the basis of a story, depending on whether our intention was to entertain the audience with humor, pathos, or fear. The approach chosen would be influenced by the audience we hope to attract. The material proposed seems too threatening to appeal to children and too "soft" to appeal to men. Unless we bend the idea to make it quite wacky, perhaps the most appropriate venue for it is TV movie-of-the-week. Such shows target the women who generally control what is seen on home TV during the evening. The demographics for this idea therefore indicate it should be aimed at adult women.

If Dad were the central character, the story could examine how the pressures of job and family crunch down on the average man. This approach would examine how Dad and his buddies use sports to feel young and macho or to achieve personal goals.

Another approach would be to look at the sports-orphaned children who must bring the family back together. Jonah and his friend Jessica perform a similar duty in *Sleepless in Seattle*.

The approach to plot outlined in this chapter allows the writer to entertain a number of possible lines of development, so when one tack fails to work, others can be tried. This work must be done carefully. The decisions connected to our seven values are analogous to the tune that a composer picks out with one finger: as that melody organizes the symphony, so do *frame, event, story concept, problem, conflict, dramatic crisis,* and *theme* organize the story. Most stories can be contained on two or three pages, but unless the pages are done right, the script that follows will not be right.

THE TIME IT TAKES TO WRITE A STORY

As you may have noticed, this text offers occasional advice on how long the main screenwriting tasks usually take. Because writers and their stories vary so much, only an approximate range of times can be offered. They are given so you can pace yourself and not rush the work—or spend too much time on it. The schedules proposed are for someone who is beginning his or her screenwriting training. Ideally, a day of writing should extend for three or four hours, which is best done in the morning when the writer is rested. When this time is not available, do what you can, even when it is only an hour per day. Whatever the regimen, stick to it. It should be pointed out, however, that screenwriting is demanding work. As with dancing, playing the oboe, and, in fact, all of the arts, screenwriting demands a rigorous dedication of time, energy, and commitment. This cannot be faked or shucked off, because the pages tell the tale.

Screenwriting requires us to sustain images that are seen in the mind's eye. To sustain this fictive dream, we learn to focus our imagination. This work is so exhausting that most professionals can only manage to do it for three or four hours each day. The energy put forth during this time is the writer's essence, the life force that creates characters and stories. Pumping out those ergs of energy each day is not like writing a term paper or taking a final exam; it is like sustaining a dream that easily dissolves and is gone. You should expect to spend a year or so learning this imagining ability. Until it is mastered, chances are your pages will be filled with typing rather than writing. Therefore, I advise students not to judge their screenwriting abilities until they have learned to imagine. You will sense that you are working at this level when you see your characters and settings vividly in your imagination and become obsessed with your visions. When you feel that your writing is not happening, it may be because your thinking is not sufficiently focused to imagine. Keep at it, for imagining takes time to learn.

You should also appreciate the challenge of plotting a story and not expect to rush through it. When you feel that your brain is dissolving with fatigue, take it as a sign that you are writing the story. So there is no confusion on this point: Working out a feature-length story can easily take several months of gulag labor. That is the nature of this task, so brace for it.

SUMMARY

As an approach to expanding an idea into the beginning of a plot, seven values were defined: frame, event, story concept, problem, conflict, dramatic crisis, and theme. Writers think through these topics in no particular order until ideas about the characters and the incidents of plot emerge. Organizing this material into a plot and writing the plot into a script are the two main tasks of screenwriting.

The *frame* conveys the style and the settings of a story. The frame is the background against which the foreground characters experience the story. We create a dramatic *event* that presents the history of a problem, challenge, or life moment. The event tells us what happens after everything happens in the story. It suggests that the main character (the protagonist) will be the person who is most involved with solving the problem being tracked in the story. The event leads to incidents of plot that play in whatever style suits the targeted audience and the intentions of the story.

Adding the word *how* to the statement of the event usually reveals the problem that will be tracked in the story. The structure of most stories is based on the presentation and tracking of a *problem* that pits the protagonist against a stronger antagonist in ways that create dramatic conflict. Knowing the event also reveals, in a general way, what happens in the climactic scene, when the problem of the story is resolved.

The *story concept*—the idea plus the dramatic problem—suggests what happens in the story. Because they can be put together quickly, story concepts allow writers to try out many different notions. In the end, however, the story concept selected should be worked out carefully because it will influence all aspects of the story and the script. In many cases, story executives judge the value of a story (during a pitch) by the story concept, i.e., they evaluate whether the story concept seems fresh and interesting. If this is not the case, the executives usually pass on the story.

The problem often interrupts the status quo of the story. The story ends when the problem is resolved and a new, improved status quo is established.

A story needs an interesting hero and a stronger villain, plus an *internal conflict* and an *external conflict*. Stories that combine these four elements in a fresh story concept have the best chance of selling.

The external conflict confronts the characters with a problem—winning the case, the love interest, a political position, etc. The internal conflict burdens the hero with a psychic wound that he or she must repair to be emotionally restored. Dramatic conflict can be categorized: hero versus villian, hero versus himself, hero versus the system, hero versus nature, and conflicts based on values. Familiarity with the types of conflict can indicate where the story seems to be heading. Such direction, even though it is slight, comes at a time when the story is unformed and confused.

Drama is the reaction of character to crisis, which in most cases means creating a life-threatening and/or life-shaping problem. Unless the crisis is escalated to this level, the story may lack drama.

The *theme* of the story is the observation that the writer and/or filmmaker works into or extracts from the material. U.S. filmmakers usually do this obliquely, burying the thematic statement deep within the script so that it emerges when the movie is over, as a thoughtful afterglow. Movie scripts should avoid preachiness and propagandizing. In most cases, the writer's passion toward a topic will work its way into a script. It is then up to the director to decide whether the message should be beefed up or muted. In most cases, the story should be *about* something, and not end up as mere chewing gum for the eyes.

The *story template* followed by most movies is as follows: in the first act the hero takes on the problem; in the second act the hero seems defeated by the problem; in the third act the hero resolves the problem in the climactic scene. These three statements summarize what generally happens in the three segments of a story. However, weeks or months of disciplined work are required to write screenplays and stories.

Exercises

1. Select a short film, a television episode, or a feature film to use to answer the questions in this exercise set. Define the film's frame. How does the frame help to tell the story?
2. Summarize the story concept and the event.
3. Define the problem being tracked. How long did it take for the problem to assert itself? What is the basis of the problem?
4. Who is the hero and what is this person trying to achieve? What motivates the hero and the villain? Why does the hero conflict with the villain?
5. What is the crisis in the story? How does the crisis relate to the dramatic problem of the story?
6. What interrupts the status quo in the film? How soon does this interruption occur? Is a new status quo established when the problem is solved? How? Describe the new status quo and how it differs from what went before.
7. Describe the hero's internal and external problem. Describe how the two problems interact and how they influence the conflict.
8. Describe the conflict in the film. How and why does the climax solve the problem tracked in the film?
9. Define the thematic statement of the film.

(*For media that illustrate the points made in this chapter, see Appendix A.*)

CHAPTER 3

Writing the Plot

*There are strategies available for "blocking" a story
concept into scenes and sequences. This chapter lays out
these strategies and discusses how to expand dramatic
beats into a plot.*

Earlier chapters discussed using frame, event, crisis, story concept, problem, conflict, and theme to expand an idea into the beginnings of a plot with a three-act structure. In this chapter we shall continue to enrich the idea with subplots, a first-act setup, continuity, logic, and other values that writers use to create their plots.

If at times you feel swamped by this drizzle of strategies, relax, for they are merely the craft tools that writers use to develop a plot, and soon enough you will become familiar with them.

The incidents of the plot (called *beats*) tell the writer what must be accomplished to advance the story, reveal the characters, create relationships, and/or explore the theme. As will be discussed in this chapter, many of these tasks are expressed as traditional story beats that can be used to fill in some of the blank spaces in the plot, if only temporarily. Later, you will be instructed on how to flesh out plot beats with characters, dialogue, and stage directions to create a story. The first step in this development is to lay out the incidents of the plot, which is called *blocking.*

Although the dictionary lists thirty meanings for the word *block,* screenwriters use the one that means "to indicate broadly without great detail; to sketch; to block out a plan of action." More specifically, let us define blocking as *laying out a generalized summary of bits and scenes that tell what happens in the plot.* Blocking supplies the plot with narrative direction as it lays out the order and continuity of the dramatic incidents. Blocking also forms a generalized outline of beats that gives the characters room to grow and to contribute to the story in their own way, rather than to twitch mechanically at the end of the writer's string.

These blocking strategies apply to the three-act structure used by most feature films and television shows. Interestingly, they also apply to most alternative films, even those that test the parameters of traditional narrative. Some of these nonmainstream films (*Weekend, Crumb, Hiroshima Mon Amour,* and *Pulp Fiction*) tend to make Hollywood mainstream commercial movie stories seem stale and formulaic—and in some ways they are. Nevertheless, well-told traditional stories are what buyers seek, and delivering an entertaining script remains an immense challenge. To those writers who are intent on reinventing traditional narrative, I can only offer traditional advice: *Learn the rules before you break them,* i.e., after you learn to write commercial quality dramatic stories, you should find it easier to expand or adapt your work into whatever new form strikes your fancy. Meanwhile, you will discover vast opportunities for innovation within the existing dramatic forms used in commercial stories.

You will be given a plan for writing an outline of plot incidents that tell a story from beginning, to middle, to end. The outline of incidents, called a beat sheet or step outline, presents a brief (one- or two-page) summary of what happens in the story, as in: *John learns that Mary is ill, John robs the store for medicine, John is arrested . . .* and so on to the end of the narrative. Screenwriters usually work either from an outline that allows them to move their incidents of plot around as needed or from a prose version of the plot called a **treatment.** Stylistically like a short story, a treatment conveys the style and energy of the story, its characters, and the action. Treatments range in length from a few pages to fifty or more pages, depending on what the writer prefers and what the producer requires. A reasonable length for a feature treatment is five to ten pages of double-spaced typing. If you feel that a longer treatment will present a firmer sense of the story, go for it. Recently, I consulted with a television writer whose twenty-five-page treatment was so precisely written that it could have been used to shoot the one-hour show. Frank Pierson's sixty-page treatment for *Dog Day Afternoon* includes sides of dialogue, partially scripted scenes, and descriptions of characters, action incidents, and settings. Less weighty is the treatment for *Flight of the Navigator,* in which writers Michael Burton and Matt McManus tell their tale on just three pages.

WORKING OUT THE PLOT OUTLINE

There is no end to the ways writers work out their plots. Some spin their yarns around a remarkable character, as in *Forrest Gump.* Others confront the main character with an overwhelming situation, need, or problem that suggests plot incidents as the situation is set up, justified, and resolved. For example, the characters in *The Terminator* and *Jurassic Park* face monstrous dramatic problems that dictate the directions of those stories. Another approach is to work from a true story or a social observation, as in *Silkwood* and *All the President's Men.*

Other plotting strategies include writing from metaphor, where a character or a situation represents a social issue. *Edward Scissorhands* was about being different and about the importance of closeness; *The Crucible* and *High Noon* were metaphors for the "red scare" that savaged Hollywood and the nation during the cold war. Stories can be written to illustrate a philosophical idea or premise, as in Joe Eszterhas's *Jagged Edge,* which dealt with the question of whether we ever really know the person we love.

Plots can also be adapted from an existing movie. The task here is to freshen the basic story idea with new characters, new locations, and new plot incidents until the adaptation seems like an original work. As noted in Chapter 1, it is not uncommon for writers to cannibalize old movies. This does not mean writing a sequel; rather, it means changing the story so completely that the original plot is all but unrecognizable. There are many examples of this strategy, some as obvious as the adaptation of *Shane* (1953) into *Pale Rider* (1985). Time and changes make it more difficult to recognize (or remember) the similarities between *Out of the Past* (1947) and *Against All Odds* (1984), or how *The Underneath* (1995) was adapted from *Criss Cross* (1949).

Even when a source plot is recognized, the adaptation can lead to successful new versions, as demonstrated by *The Manchurian Candidate, The Day of the Jackal, The Package,* and *In the Line of Fire.* Although there are striking similarities between these assassination stories, each was made spiffy with new settings, fresh characters, and up-to-the-minute situations. As a result, they were different enough to attract audiences, despite their plot similarities. The four films also illustrate how accepting moviegoers can be of plots that present interesting characters who go through a major life experience. The origins of this acceptance go back to Greek tragedy and historical drama, where the audience knew what would happen. Even though they know who killed Oedipus's father, for example, audiences were curious as to how Oedipus would react to the fate he sought to avoid.

These strategies will be touched upon occasionally throughout the book, but our attention now turns to our primary plan for expanding an idea into a plot. To do this we shall use the values discussed in the opening chapters as well as new material that begins with a list of the traditional story incidents that show up in most stories.

THREE-ACT STORY STRUCTURE

As noted in Chapter 2, the story template shows how movies and TV shows usually follow a three-act structure. This format is not a straitjacket invented to torment writers; it is the pattern that audiences expect and that most movies follow because it offers enough plot to avoid boring the audience. At the same time, stories with three acts are not so complex that they confuse the audience. The next few paragraphs explain what usually occurs during the three acts.

The first act of most feature films and television stories entangles hero and villain in a problem. In a feature, this process uses up most of the first act, which usually plays for about a half hour. The act ends when something deflects the story in an unexpected direction. This incident is referred to as a plot point, a turning point, a twist, or a complication. Example: The first act of *The Verdict* ends twenty-eight minutes into the movie (Shot 26), when the hero turns down Bishop Brophy's settlement offer.[1] Galvin's decision twists the plot

[1]A cast list and sequence breakdown of *The Verdict* are provided in Appendix C.

because it puts him onto a collision course with one of the most powerful lawyers in Boston.

Second acts usually play for about an hour, during which the hero falls deeper into trouble. Most second acts end when something damaging happens to make the hero's desperate situation seem hopeless. Example: The second-act complication of *The Verdict* occurs when the hero commits a grievous court-room error that seems to doom his case (Shot 68).

Most third acts play for about thirty minutes; they are built around the climactic scene in which the hero-villain showdown resolves the problem.

The length of the acts varies, and the playing times cited above are averages. For example, the first acts of *Rocky* and *Sleepless in Seattle* play for more than fifty minutes, and neither story suffers. Even so, new writers should try to gather their first, second, and third acts into something close to the 30-60-30 (minute) pattern.

To summarize, when traditional three-act structure is used in a movie, what usually occurs in each act is as follows:

In Act I the hero takes on the problem.

In Act II the hero seems defeated by the problem.

In Act III the hero solves the problem.

THE OUTLINE OF TRADITIONAL PLOT INCIDENTS

Figure 3-1 presents the story template along with a list of the traditional story moments and incidents contained in most feature stories. Many new writers have found this list of traditional scenes to be useful because it indicates what generally happens in each act. The template and list of traditional **beats**[2] provide a useful overall pattern of dramatic development that shows up in most feature stories.

Analysis has shown that most first acts contain four main beats, although these beats may not occur in the order listed in Figure 3-1. Additionally, the second and third acts also contain traditional moments. This pattern is a blocking tool because it suggests major plot incidents that appear in most stories. You may not use all of the beats in Figure 3-1, but even a few clues about what happens in your story are worth the few minutes it takes to think about these possibilities. You should also note that some of the beats listed in Figure 3-1 play as *sequences* that are made up of bits and scenes. Because sequence beats can play from five to fifteen minutes or so, the traditional plot incidents cited should take up an hour or so of the total playing time of a feature story.

---

[2]The term *beat* has several meanings. In this discussion it refers to a story point that is made by a bit, a scene, or a sequence; an outline of such points is called a **beat sheet.** The term also refers to a pause that occurs in a scene, when something registers on a character. Used in this way, *beat* is interchangeable with *pause* and is often capitalized and placed in parenthesis in a speech to indicate that a character is thinking or reacting. (See p. 123 for an example.)

ACT I: THE HERO TAKES ON THE PROBLEM

Establishing scene or narrative hook

Introduction of the hero

Introduction of the villain

Introduction of the problem

Complication when the hero takes on the problem

ACT II: THE HERO SEEMS DEFEATED BY THE PROBLEM

Aftermath to the complication scene

Backstory and/or setting scene

Attack on hero or by hero

Moments dealing with B-storyline

Moments dealing with the theme

Romantic interludes

Moments with the antagonist

Complication when hero seems defeated by the problem/villain

ACT III: THE HERO RESOLVES THE PROBLEM

Preparation for climax

Resolution of subplots

Climax

Epilogue (optional)

FIGURE 3-1. Outline of traditional plot incidents.

Helpful as it is, the outline of traditional plot incidents does not indicate *what* to write or *how* to write. Also, the order of the beats will vary from story to story. Even so, the outline of beats shown in Figure 3-1 offers general guidance to writers at a time when even a snippet of help may be welcome. You can use the outline to imagine plot incidents that fit the various acts of a story and to acquire a feel for which beats work and what should be done next. As the story is blocked in this way, writers zigzag back and forth through various strategies as the yarn is woven. If one tack does not work, another is tried, until gradually the dramatic incidents form into a plot that has a beginning-middle-end structure.

Another point to be taken from the story template is how it encourages stories that contain ten or so sequences, that being the approximate number of sequence beats found in most feature scripts. Organizing a story with ten or so sequence beats spares the writer from wrestling with sixty or so scenes and bits, which can be an unwieldy number. A sequence outline, based on the values we have discussed, and the outline of traditional beats, casts its light down the long tunnel that screenwriters confront during plotting.

New writers often fail to appreciate how much story is offered by the template and outline of scenes. This is because they have yet to learn how gradually these plot beats play out. The pace of movies is hidden because of cutting, dialogue and emotional moments, and visual revelation and action. When beats are timed, you will learn another interesting truth: *Movies use a limited number of plot incidents to advance the story and to reveal the characters.* This strategy enables movies to tell simple stories about complex characters. In most cases the incidents of plot explore what the main characters are thinking and feeling rather than dazzle the audience with spectacle and action. Experienced writers also know that audiences are easily confused by complicated plots and they have a huge capacity for characters. It is for such reasons that this book and many others[3] encourage scripts based on character rather than action and spectacle. These two points—the gradual unfolding of story and the focus on character over plot—are key elements of the story sense that this book preaches. Simple as it sounds, writing simple stories and complex characters is one of the most difficult of all screenwriting lessons to learn. Moreover, until the lesson is learned, blocking will remain a mightier chore than it need be. To give you a better appreciation of how these "simple" beats operate, we shall briefly describe them.

TRADITIONAL MOMENTS FOUND IN ACT I

Most first acts employ three or four of the story beats noted in Figure 3-1. They introduce the hero, the villain, and the problem. As mentioned, the order of the beats presented in Figure 3-1 varies. The problem may be introduced first, as in *All the President's Men*; the villain may be introduced first, as in *The Terminator*; or the hero may be introduced first, as in *The Verdict*. Whichever comes first, it should contribute to a primary task of the first act, which is to pull the audience into the story. This task begins with the first incident of the story, which can be written as an action scene or one that establishes the mood, time, and location of the story.

Action Openers

An action opener hooks the audience by means of a visually striking action scene. James Bond films begin this way, immediately hitting the audience with spectacular action that transports viewers to the never-never land of 007. An action opener can be written as a sequence that introduces the hero and/or villain. It can also present a problem or mystery or establish the mood and location of the story—the range is broad.

The opening of *Three Days of the Condor* incorporates all these elements. The movie fades in on a damp day in New York City. We sense something odd happening near a town house as a man checks off the people who are entering and leaving the building. The film cuts inside and introduces the brainy staff (they analyze books for one of the intelligence agencies). Moments after the

---

[3]One of the most interesting of these titles is Andrew Horton's *Writing the Character-Centered Screenplay,* University of California Press, Los Angeles, 1994.

hero, who is part of this staff, dashes through an obscure back door for a quick lunch, assassins enter the building and murder everyone. This shocking sequence, which hooks the audience with action, introduces the hero, and establishes the film's style and location, is made up of numerous bits and scenes that play for nineteen minutes.

Another example of an action opener is the one that introduces the hero and indicates the setting and style of *Roxanne*. Under the opening credits, the scene begins outside the home of a small-town fire captain (played by Steve Martin). He is on the telephone, promising to return a friend's tennis racket. When Martin hangs up, he exits his house and strolls toward town. The ditty he sings turns into stream-of-consciousness concern when he notices trouble-makers heading his way. Martin, who scripted this film, describes them as being "two coked-up hop-heads." Immediately, the two men behave like stereotypical dog heavies by ridiculing the hero's remarkable nose. Their abuse gives Martin an opportunity to use his tennis racket as a sword, and he humorously defeats the two men. This action opener launches the film. As is typical of action openers, this beat plays for about five minutes. (I confess fondness for this charming little movie, and not just because Martin was a student in one of my UCLA screenwriting classes.)

Establishing Openers

Establishing openers begin the story by using images and music to indicate the settings, time, mood, style, and genre of a film. *Places in the Heart* presents life in a small Texas cotton town in a way that draws the audience into a quiet Sunday morning as it might have been in 1934. As is often true of establishing openers, this one does not use dialogue. Instead, it relies on images, sound effects, and music to settle the audience into the story. Most establishing openers play for two to four minutes.

The opening beat usually signals whether the movie will be an action picture, crime story, low-key country, or whatever the genre and style. Once this promise has been struck, viewers commit to it, and it is risky to shift to another style. In other words, deliver the movie promised in the opener. If the promise is to scare viewers, do it. If the promise is to make them laugh, do it. This does not mean tipping off what happens in the story, but the tone should be indicated. We get a sense of what *Forrest Gump* will be like when a feather wafts down and lands on the hero's shoe. The mystical nature of that digitized visual pulls the audience into the movie.

Lucky Lady followed a different path by starting off as a lighthearted story about flappers and rum-running in the 1920s. Halfway through, however, gangsters murder the young deckhand who crews on the *Lucky Lady*. When this happens, the emotional tone of the picture changes from light to heavy. *Beverly Hills Cop III* and *The Shadow* suffered similarly. In each case, the shift away from comedy caused audiences to lose interest, because it is not easy to make viewers laugh when people are being murdered on-screen. That seems like a simple lesson that should have been obvious to the filmmakers who created these problematic films, but Goldman's law applied here: *In Hollywood, nobody knows anything.*

Introducing the Hero

Character entrances can be large or small, depending on which seems appropriate. Also, the character is only *introduced* in the first scene; the person should not be totally explained. Goldie Hawn's modest introduction in *Swing Shift* plays for ninety seconds, which is enough time to introduce us to the dutiful young homemaker (circa 1942) that she portrays. Other scenes are used to track how she copes with the world beyond her home and how those experiences enable her to mature. A longer introduction is given to the hero of *Unforgiven,* which spends most of the first act introducing Clint Eastwood as a teetotaling farmer who seems unable to shoot or ride a horse and who shows no indication of why he carries such a fearsome reputation. Later, we learn the truth about this character.

Some films prepare a grand entrance for the main character. These entrances dramatize the character in a way that makes the audience anticipate meeting this person. The strategy applies when someone talks about or searches for a character in a way that arouses curiosity or interest. *Hud* begins with a full-throated fanfare for its title character by opening with a teenager who is seen driving into town to find his Uncle Hud (Paul Newman). For five minutes, over the opening credits, the boy follows a trail of broken glass and the debris of rowdiness until he finds Hud's convertible. It is early in the morning and the car is parked in front of the home of a married woman. Hud staggers out of the house just as the woman's husband unexpectedly arrives home. A confrontation is avoided when Hud blames his nephew for carousing with the woman. In this way, the opening beat introduces the Texas town and the memorable scamp who will center the film for two hours.

Most movies introduce the hero within the first five minutes or so. Newman's Frank Galvin makes his first appearance in the opening shot of *The Verdict,* as does Tom Hanks's Sam in *Sleepless in Seattle.* But, as with almost everything in the movies, there are exceptions to this advice; *Witness* does not introduce John Book until Shot 30, which is fourteen minutes into Act I. Whether the character introduction is large or small depends on how the writer chooses to spin the yarn, but fanfaring can be an effective opening strategy.

Introducing the Villain

There are as many ways to introduce the villain as there are to introduce the hero. *The Terminator* does it in the first seconds when the cyborg drops out of the sky. Similarly, the villain of *Ruthless People* (Danny DeVito) appears in the opening shot, telling his paramour (Anita Morris) how he plans to murder his wife. Although the scene plays for less than three minutes, it lets us know about DeVito's goofy plan and warns us that we should brace for a movie that is awash with loopy characters. By contrast, we do not meet James Mason's Ed Concannon, the antagonist of *The Verdict*, until Shot 38, early in Act II. Until then, a half hour into the story, we only know of him by reputation.

In a few films, the villain is given a huge introduction. *The Witches of Eastwick* spends twenty minutes fanfaring the first appearance of Jack Nicholson's devilish character. Considerable time is also spent introducing the menace in *Jaws*, *The Andromeda Strain*, and *Predator*. The introduction to the villains in *Three Days of the Condor* is also strung out and suspenseful, and it is not until well into the second half of the film that we meet the shadowy figures who staged the mass killing that opens the story.

Introducing the Problem

The problem can be revealed immediately with an action opener, as in *All the President's Men* when a security guard discovers a break-in at the Watergate headquarters of the Democratic National Committee. The problem can also emerge gradually, as in *Alien*, *The Terminator*, and *Rocky*. Introducing the problem can be a lengthy process that requires several sequences. It can also extend into the second act, as in *The Verdict*, which spends most of its first hour explaining the strategies, the characters, and the legalities connected to the problem being tracked. The measured pace of this story suits the complex case that the hero has undertaken; it also gives the audience time to understand what the hero is struggling to accomplish.

Weaving the Beats Together

These introductory beats are not freestanding. They grow out of each other and interweave as plot and character information is revealed. We see this in *The Verdict* (Shot 8) when Mickey tells Galvin that their case is coming to trial. This leads the hero to visit his brain-dead client, meet with her relatives, and contact an expert witness who agrees to testify. These beats connect with each other like links of a chain. The same unfolding of linked incidents of plot show in *Witness*, when the Amish gather for a funeral. The death of her husband motivates the young widow (Kelly McGillis's Rachel Lapp) to visit her sister in Baltimore for solace. While waiting for a train in Philadelphia, Rachel's son witnesses a murder, which connects her to John Book. In this way, one incident links to another until a plot and story form as characters develop and become involved with each other. Driving this development is the dramatic problem that organizes the structure of the story.

As noted in Chapter 2, disruption of the status quo can begin a story. This happens, for example, when someone arrives or leaves, when a bill comes due, when a disaster strikes or threatens, or when a character is provoked into an action. This is not an automatic process, however, and the incidents must be connected skillfully, which brings up the first main dramatizing task: writing the Act I setup.

THE ACT I SETUP

The second acts of most feature scripts play for about an hour, and this long span is where many stories run out of energy. The cause of this expiration is often a weak first-act setup. A strong first act should connect the hero and the more powerful villain in a way that promises conflict and drama. The setup can address either an action problem to be solved or a personal problem that must be solved. *Speed, The Terminator,* and *Jurassic Park* illustrate action stories that confront their main characters with a physical task. *Moonstruck, The Verdict,* and *The Remains of the Day* are character-driven stories that present personal problems. A few films *(The Bridge on the River Kwai, Witness, Forrest Gump)* challenge their heroes with problems that are both physical and non-physical. *Rocky* is another such film, and it is a handy model for how strong setups work.

To begin with, Sylvester Stallone's screenplay draws the audience into the story universe as it reveals the hero's decent ambitions, his hard life, and his love for Adrienne. After the audience is persuaded to care about this likable lug, he is chosen as a replacement fighter because the champion (Carl Weathers's Apollo Creed) is amused by Rocky's nickname, the Italian Stallion. This is where Act I ends, with the audience fearful that Rocky's moment in the spotlight will destroy his dignity, which is not only his most prized possession but also his only possession. The opening act of *Rocky* points out the essence of an effective setup: it pits a likable protagonist against a more powerful antagonist.

Each of the four main study films contains a strong dramatic setup that follows this pattern. In *Witness,* a brave but wounded hero is an Amish child's only defense against a gang of killer cops. In *The Terminator,* a young woman and a soldier from the future battle an indestructible cyborg. In *The Verdict,* a boozy lawyer gambles with the future of his needful clients to get even with the establishment that betrayed him years earlier. In *Sleepless in Seattle,* a boy parlays a tenuous connection with a call-in radio program so his father can meet an unknown woman who lives on the other side of the country.

The examples illustrate how a good setup places a likable hero in a threatening position against a more powerful antagonist. This happens when the beats of the first act come together as the hero takes on the problem. At this stage you should ignore how to solve the problem (a way can always be found); instead, spend your energy on setting up the problem in the first act. Follow this setup by getting the hero in trouble in the second act until there seems no way for the hero to solve the problem. Contrast and injustice are often lathered over whatever will cause the audience to worry about the hero, who manages to solve the problem in the final scene. Although not all stories work this way, most do, and I recommend that you develop your story with this dynamic in mind.

If your hero is confronted with an impossible problem, be grateful, because its hopelessness will make the audience less likely to anticipate a solution. Screenwriters also know that the real task is not solving the problem; it is setting it up so that a powerful drama is unleashed in the second and third acts as hero and villain conflict over the outcome. *Along with writing a strong story concept, creating a strong first-act setup should be a primary plotting task.*

The First-Act Complication

The first-act setup usually concludes with a twist, plot point, turning point, or complication (the terms are interchangeable) that connects the hero to the problem and to the villain. The complication/twist that ends Act I should put the hero on a collision course with the villain over who will win the case, who will earn the prize, or whatever goal is connected to the story's dramatic problem.

In most cases the first-act complication occurs during one of the traditional plot beats listed in Figure 3-1. In *Witness* (Shot 73B) the complication occurs when Book faints from his gunshot wound and crashes his car into the Lapp family's birdhouse. This twist caps a sequence that sees Book almost killed after he unwittingly tells the main conspirator about a witness who saw a police officer commit murder. After he is wounded, Book spirits Rachel and her son to the safety of their farm, advising that there will be no arrest and trial of the renegade policemen. Moments later, Book faints, forcing him to remain with the Amish. This complication bounces the plot away from the shoe leather of the police story and toward the Book-Rachel romance that will occupy most of the second act.

There is no end to the ways that plot twists can occur. The hero (or the villain) can decide to take on the problem (*In the Line of Fire, Unforgiven*); the hero can stumble or be lured into the problem (*Rocky*); the hero can be pressured into the problem by circumstances (*The Terminator,* Shot 128) or by other characters (*Moonstruck*). Additionally, the hero may take on the problem because of psychological reasons connected to the B-storyline. *The Verdict* (Shot 26) illustrates such a convergence when the hero turns down Bishop Brophy's settlement at the end of Act I because of resentment toward the establishment. Galvin's rejection creates the complication that ends the first act and spins the story toward confrontation with the mighty Ed Concannon. The incongruity of boozy Frank Galvin's taking on such a lofty opponent is a key component in *The Verdict*'s setup, which is dramatic because of the David-and-Goliath nature of the hero-villain conflict. There seems to be *no way* for Galvin to defeat Concannon—yet he does it.

Although you may feel that the David-and-Goliath strategy being proposed is simplistic, it has been used since biblical times because the unfairness of the conflict makes audiences worry about the hero's chances of winning. The popularity of this strategy does not mean that writers have stopped searching for fresh approaches, but the bald fact that first acts have been done this way for centuries indicates the usefulness of the plan. This is the track on which most stories run and though some might characterize this organizing pattern as being formulaic, do not think that it works automatically to create a three-act structure and to set up the story. Most writers expend enormous energy to create first-act setups that are fresh and dramatic. As modest and formulaic as this task seems, it defeats most writers, old or new! The challenge of writing a dramatic setup is to invent its contrivances and to make them believable, invisible, and effective. *The setup is so important that I recommend you not continue with Act II until your first-act setup contains enough dramatic potential to drive the remainder of the story.*

TRADITIONAL MOMENTS FOUND IN ACT II

The story template shows that the second act also contains its share of traditional beats; knowing them can inspire ideas and build confidence. You may not use everything cited below; in many cases you will create incidents not listed. Even so, the traditional beats can help you work out what happens in the second act. The beats listed, however, are not blanks to be filled in. Instead, the list is provided to trigger ideas that may suggest beats that fill in portions of the empty Act II landscape that often confronts writers. As with the first-act beats, the incidents below can occur in any order. Some of them may be bits, others may be scenes, and a few may be sequence beats.

Aftermath Moments

Movies often pause early in Act II to allow the characters to discuss the implications of what happened in the first act, as in *Witness* (Shot 77), when Rachel pleads with the Amish to give Book refuge. An aftermath beat occurs in *The Verdict* (Shot 28) when Mickey upbraids Galvin for turning down Bishop Brophy's settlement offer.

During aftermath scenes, motives may be examined, implications discussed, and plans may be hatched. Because such moments tend to be emotional and personal, they are often written as scenes that explore character and/or theme. As a scene, such a beat may play for two to four minutes in a feature. In a TV show, the length of the beat might be a minute or two.

Hero-Villain Conflict

In the second act of most films, hero and villain engage in one or two major incidents of conflict. In *The Verdict* the conflict is verbal and takes place in the courthouse (Shots 38, 65, 92). In *The Terminator* (Shot 160), physical conflict occurs during an attack on the police station. Because hero-villain incidents are often done as major beats that play for five or more minutes, they are set up by moments that lead to the conflict; beats that follow then comment on the incident of conflict.

When blocking the story, it is not necessary to figure out the details of the confrontation. Often it is enough to jot down a generalized beat that might say "Jill decides to end her affair with Jack" or "Bob has a confrontation with Jack." The specifics of the incident can be figured out after a rough plot has been written. Many writers prefer to keep the incidents of plot light and general at first, knowing that the beats will become more specific as the work progresses. Too many details early on may cause confusion and disguise flaws, so it is advisable not to lose the overview of the outline. Also, a light, airy beat sheet is easier to change.

Think of the process of working out story and script as being like working with a microscope fitted with multiple lenses. The outlining lens provides an overview of the plot so it can be examined on a page or so. As work on story and script progresses, more powerful lenses are used to explore the three-act structure and individual sequences. At last we see into the innermost being of the characters as we work with the highest-resolution lenses.

Sometimes we get so close to our work that we lose the story overview. At such times the summary outline is the guide that keeps the plot on track. This is mentioned because *loss of story focus is a primary cause of story failure, and story failure is the primary cause of script rejection.*

Backstory Moments

Backstory moments allow characters to speak of personal matters, to explain behavior and motivation, and to express how the drama is affecting them. These moments allow for a change of pace that reveals character and/or addresses the theme. An example of a backstory scene in *The Verdict* is when Mickey tells Laura how Galvin was betrayed during the Lillibridge case (Shot 47). The scene is interspersed with three cutaways showing Galvin as he loses his star witness, as he is refused a continuance by Judge Sweeney, and as he is turned down by the insurance company after offering to settle the case. A backstory moment in *The Terminator* is when Reese tells Sarah about John Connor and the future (Shot 182).

The second act may also have a moment or two when characters discuss their values, childhood, life experiences, or why and how they became involved with each other and with the story. In *The Verdict* (Shot 33), Galvin tells Laura of his belief in the law and how he plans to "try to do something right."

Moments That Involve the Setting

Moments that involve the setting can reveal the life-style, history, terrain, dangers, weather, wildlife, and other aspects of the frame. Examples: the barn-raising sequence in *Witness* (Shot 106); the chess tournaments in *Searching for Bobby Fischer*; the Cajun festival and tour of the bayou in *Passion Fish*. Such moments can play for a minute or more. To sustain the momentum of the story, these incidents should connect to the characters and/or to the problem being tracked; they should not be unrelated interludes tossed in to pad the story. Unless each incident advances the plot and reveals the characters, the story may lose its intensity and dramatic rush.

Romantic Interludes

The stress of the drama often drives the romantic leads out of each other's arms or back into them. These scenes may involve a heart-to-heart talk, love-making, a courtship montage of some type, or an adventure. Examples: in *The Terminator* (Shot 211) Sarah and Reese make love before taking on the cyborg in the third-act showdown; in Shot 128 of *Witness*, Book and Rachel embrace. There are several such moments between Annie and Walter in *Sleepless in Seattle* (Shots 60, 102, 115), but they turn out to be unromantic interludes that point out the hopelessness of their relationship. Romantic interludes should serve the plot and the character relationships; otherwise, the incident will be mere titillation that defocuses the story and drains it of intensity.

Private Moments with the Hero or Villain

Private moments show how the main characters live. They deal with motivation, home life, problems, and ambitions. In Shot 134 of *Sleepless in Seattle*, Annie observes Sam and Jonah as they play ball on the beach, and she is touched by their easy affection. *The Verdict* (Shot 24) presents a private moment of Galvin drinking at home, while talking on the phone with his client. The beat reveals the first stirrings of his conscience.

The Second-Act Complication

The second-act complication occurs at the end of Act II when an incident makes it seem that the hero has been defeated. Anything that can go wrong for the hero does go wrong to create the story's "darkest moment." Like its counterpart at the end of the first act, the second act complication is a major plot twist that has been building throughout the story. It is often part of a sequence that ends by making the audience fearful that the hero has been defeated.

In many cases this twist is *the complication to the complication* that occurred at the end of Act I. Example: In *Witness*, the first-act complication occurs when Book faints and crashes his car, which causes the Amish to take him in. Later, Schaeffer learns where Book is hiding and arrives with guns and two men to slaughter Book and the entire Lapp family; thus, the first complication causes the second and more deadly complication.

The Verdict also provides a good illustration of the second-act complication: In Shot 68, Galvin questions the defendant (Wesley Addy's Dr. Towler), who mentions the time required to cause brain damage in the hero's client. Galvin, thinking that Towler has made an error, carelessly asks for an explanation. Towler seizes the opening by observing that Galvin's client could have suffered brain damage in just a few minutes because she was anemic to begin with: "It's right there on her chart!" The movie then cuts to the shocked reactions of people in the courtroom to indicate that Galvin has committed an error that may have cost him the case. This complication ends a thirteen-minute sequence and creates the darkest moment of the story—when Galvin seems defeated. The moment grows out of Galvin's refusal of the bishop's settlement, which occurs at the end of Act I. This complication leads to the trial and the darkest-moment complication that ends Act II. Such causality, linking the Act I and Act II complications, is a mark of excellent plotting.

In many stories the darkest moment at the end of the second act worsens when a love interest or a best friend is injured, killed, or becomes estranged from the hero. Such incidents add drama to the twist and make the hero's task so desperate that radical measures must be taken. The hero's last-gasp actions, which seem beyond the person's normal abilities, are what earn the final victory. *The Verdict* works this way when Laura and Galvin have a spat. Moments such as this often become major story incidents that may require two or three beats to set up.

TRADITIONAL MOMENTS FOUND IN ACT III

Most third acts play for twenty-five or thirty minutes and contain one main beat: the climactic scene or sequence. However, before the final showdown occurs, the story may use one or more of the following beats to tidy things.

Setup for the Climactic Scene

The final act sees hero and villain gird for battle as friends plead, plot, cooperate, and/or disengage from the combatants as the showdown approaches. The beat may involve a quiet personal encounter as the hero contemplates matters of conscience, memory, or values in a way that strengthens or reveals character. Such a moment occurs in *The Verdict* when Galvin broods over Laura's betrayal, refuses her phone call, and resolves to fight on (Shots 90 and 91).

The Climactic Scene

This scene is traditionally the most dramatic beat in the movie, the "topper." It is when the problem is resolved and the hero triumphs (usually). In most cases, the protagonist behaves heroically and marches into battle alone because such behavior is expected of a hero. In action films, hero and villain often confront each other in one-on-one physical combat. Showdowns in character stories tend to be verbal, not physical.

In most cases, the problem resolves in the hero's favor, although writers sometimes have the hero win without winning, in which case the victory is symbolic. For example, *Rocky*'s hero does not win the title fight, but he finishes on his feet for a personal victory. The heroes of *The Professionals, The Wild Bunch,* and *Midnight Cowboy* do not triumph, yet they are ennobled by the courage they show in the climactic scene. When the hero sacrifices himself or herself for a loved one or for some form of "the greater good," the character earns honor that gives the story an upbeat ending.

Movies often follow an eye-for-an-eye symmetry regarding crime and punishment. The hero's humiliation usually leads to an even greater humiliation for the villain. If physical or emotional violence is inflicted upon the hero and his or her allies, a more terrible dose of violence befalls the villain. The hero's retribution, however, should not be so vengeful that he or she outdoes the villain. In David Mamet's *House of Games,* the punishment meted out by the protagonist is more severe than the crimes of the antagonist. The film features Lindsay Crouse as a psychiatrist who is swindled by a con artist (Joe Mantegna). Crouse does not take kindly to this, and in the climactic scene she kills Mantegna. In this instance the villain's punishment seems excessive. Although a modest succès d'estime and appreciated for its chilly realism, the film gave audiences no one to root for, and it was not too popular.

Some stories end when the hero shows mercy to a villain who then uses the opportunity to attack the hero. Movies use such strategies to create a climax that sends the audience home believing that the wrongdoers have been punished and that goodness wins.

A lifetime of movie-going has conditioned audiences to expect certain traditional moments, and the climax is one of them. It is when the hero wins or loses the battle that has been raging throughout the movie. During this, the audience has experienced ups and downs in the hero's cause, but the hero is expected to recover and triumph in the climactic scene. When a story fails to deliver on this promise, audiences feel cheated out of the happy ending that they expected. This happened in *The French Connection,* because the final shoot-out ends inconclusively, the villain escapes, and the climactic scene fails to top the film's earlier car chase. Another film, *Mr. Jones,* presents a love affair between a psychiatrist and a manic-depressive that ends inconclusively because there is no cure for the title character's mental condition. As a result, the problem of the story is not solved and the movie ends when hero and heroine walk off to face a lifetime of uncertainty. This downer ending did not go over favorably with audiences.

Sustaining the Climactic Scene

The climax is what the audience has been waiting for, so *extend* the final peak experience. *The Terminator* presents a masterful climax that demonstrates how this is done. The sequence begins at Shot 214, when the cyborg arrives at the motel where Reese and Sarah are staying. They take off and are chased until their truck crashes and the terminator is run over by an eighteen-wheeler hauling gasoline. This ghastly accident should kill the creature, but it is still ticking! When it commandeers the tanker and pursues Sarah, Reese slips a bomb into the truck, which explodes and incinerates the creature. This seems like the climax, for we have seen the cyborg burn up. Wrong again, for this is a false climax. When the action resumes, in Shot 250/FX, James Cameron describes exactly how the cyborg appears in the movie when it emerges from the flames, with "[its] gleaming structure . . . revealed in all its intricacy. No longer a 'He,' but an 'It.' It looks like death rendered in steel."

The climax continues to build as the skeletal cyborg pursues the heroes into a factory. After more chasing and fighting, Reese stuffs a bomb into the terminator's rib cage, exploding it into a scattering of metal parts. Now surely the creature has been destroyed! Not yet! Reese is dead, but the legless cyborg crawls after Sarah until it corners her in a maze of machinery. Then, just as its metallic fingers reach for her throat, Sarah activates a giant press that crushes the cyborg. This is the climactic moment that the audience has been waiting for. In all, this sequence plays for about fifteen minutes, which takes up most of the third act. The climactic scene in this film—and in most films—depicts the solution to the problem (the *event*) that has organized the story: the indestructible cyborg is destroyed. Filmmaker Cameron comments on how he managed this climactic scene:

> I feel that both in *Terminator* and *Aliens,* there were false climaxes before the true one, but I always gave the audience enough respect to say to myself, they're gonna know that this isn't really the ending; they know it's not over. The threads haven't all been tied up yet. Anybody who's been paying attention will know that the questions have not been answered yet. And when it's finally over, they know it's over, they know that the questions have been answered.[4]

Extending the climax means devising incidents, theatrical business, and actions that will sustain the suspense. *The Terminator* uses vehicles, weapons, locations, stunts (and James Cameron's vivid imagination) to exploit the potential of the cyborg and the locations. You can add visual content to your stories by creating incidents, props, machines, locations, weather, or whatever dramatizes the story. Write the grandest, most dramatic, most exciting climax imaginable. Trust experts in camera and special effects to figure out how to film what you envision.

If your story does not lend itself to action and spectacle, you can still wring juice out of the climax. Check out how *The Verdict* extends its peak moment by making it seem that Concannon has countered Galvin's surprise witness (Shot 93–96). Also note how Bishop Brophy and Alito meet to discuss the case and how the jury announces the verdict. Small as they are, these bits extend the climactic scene that will decide whether the hero or the villain will triumph.

Concluding Loose Ends of Plot

Except for rare ambiguous endings, most films give the audience a sense of closure on points of plot, subplots, and character. Loose ends of plot are snipped off, and characters say good-bye, mention future plans, make peace, or somehow settle matters. Examples from *The Verdict:* Shot 93, when the Bishop Brophy/Joseph Alito subplot concludes; when the jury announces its verdict (Shot 96); and in the final shot of the movie (not scripted) when Galvin ignores Laura's phone call. Each incident concludes one of the subplots.

[4]Karl Schanzer and Thomas Lee Wright, *American Screenwriters*, Avon Books, New York, 1993, p. 65.

Whodunnits often end with a major closure scene in which the great detective summarizes the case, sorts through the clues, and identifies the criminal. This allows the audience to leave the theater feeling sure about what happened in the story and how the problem they had been tracking concludes. Lack of closure is such an easy problem that it seldom shows up in films. Because movie endings are a sensitive topic, we shall discuss this topic next.

THEME AND THE HAPPY ENDING

Movie stories end in one of three ways: inconclusively, pessimistically, or optimistically. Each writer must decide on which ending to use, but mainstream movies favor optimistic endings, which means that these stories have the best chance of selling. Selecting a satisfactory ending for a story is a major consideration, especially since writing a feature script can easily soak up months of a writer's life.

Inconclusive endings fail to close the story, as in *Basic Instinct*, which spends two hours teasing the audience about whether the femme fatale is a murderer. The story ends, however, without answering the question. Although there are films in which inconclusive endings work, most American films do not follow this pattern.

They also do not favor pessimistic stories with downer endings that see the hero ruined, the cause defeated, the love affair destroyed, and/or the world going to hell. Mainstream films avoid such endings because audiences tend not to patronize such stories. Except for an occasional film like *The Remains of the Day*, downer stories do poorly at the box office. *Ironweed, Last Exit to Brooklyn,* and *Sommersby* illustrate.

Audiences prefer stories about characters who struggle through to some sort of victory or self-realization. This aesthetic—the cinema of optimism and a strong narrative line—is a defining trait of American movies. This does not mean that these are all "feel-good" movies, for there is a range of endings. At one end of the happy-ending scale is the rapture of Cinderella winning the glass slipper (*Working Girl*); at the other end are stories that offer minimal hope of a positive outcome (*Raging Bull*). Even when mainstream stories end tragically, it is possible to offer the audience hope or satisfaction. *My Life, Awakenings, Promises in the Dark,* and *Dying Young* are about young people with catastrophic illnesses that will kill them, yet these stories ennoble the human spirit and leave a positive aftertaste.

Two films that illustrate a more negative turn are *Map of the Human Heart* and *Leolo*. In the former, the Eskimo hero ends up an alcoholic who is defeated by internal conflicts. In the latter, the boy we have been pulling for succumbs to the insanity that plagues his family. Both films were critically acclaimed, but they failed to draw audiences. Although it is arguable why these two films proved unpopular, experience indicates that audiences are not entertained by stories that end tragically, and so they do not patronize them.

The reason this text belabors the point about upbeat endings is because writers can convince themselves that the dopiest ideas have commercial possibilities. Some new writers are inclined toward an angry worldview that leads to Götterdämmerung endings in which everyone loses. Before taking on such a story, ask yourself when you last saw a movie with a downer ending and whether you enjoyed it. Such films are rare outside of small art houses because audiences are not drawn to downbeat stories. If you hope to make a thematic or artistic point with such an ending, remember that the people who finance movies are in business to sell movie tickets. Not surprisingly, given the millions that it costs to make a movie, these people seek stories that entertain the audience by presenting characters who struggle through to some sort of a victory or realization, however slight.

I do not wish to overstate the case for happy endings, for an upbeat story does not mean that the hero must tap-dance into paradise. It does mean that audiences should be in a better mood when they leave the theater than when they entered. The endings of the four study films are upbeat but hardly triumphant. In *Witness*, John Book returns to Philadelphia without Rachel and will probably revert to being an action junkie. In *The Verdict*, Frank Galvin is last seen sipping coffee, apparently giving up his long love affair with alcohol. Even so, he is fast approaching sixty with nothing going in his life emotionally. Such a man might resume drinking and perhaps never win another case. In *The Terminator*, Sarah Connor must face the end of the world. In *Sleepless in Seattle*, Sam and Annie, who meet for the first time at the end, may be bored with each other by the time they descend from the top of the Empire State Building. Even so, the protagonists in each film emerge from their ordeals emotionally bruised but stronger, giving each story an upbeat ending.

The four study films are successful[5] because they honor advice that has aided storytellers through the ages: *Make the audience want something, make it seem unattainable, then give it to them.* This thought guides most of the people—screenwriters included—who make and fund movies. The script cannot cheat on this goal, which asks the writer to create a dramatic ordeal that the protagonist wins through courage and suffering. Only then does the hero's victory give the audience the positive ending that it was encouraged to desire.

Working out an upbeat ending can be frustrating because many writers do not enjoy stifling passion for commerciality. To ease you over this hump, please recall stories that succeeded even though their endings offered only a slight degree of hope. *The Waterdance* and *Born on the Fourth of July*, to take two examples, do not invent miracle cures to repair the shattered spines of their heroes, but in both films they recover their will to live. *Thelma and Louise* freeze-frames the two heroes as their car sails into the Grand Canyon. The ending suggests that they were brave enough to die on their terms, thus earning a degree of nobility. Similar "tragedies with happy endings" include

---

[5]The domestic box office gross for *The Verdict* amounted to $54 million. Similar gross figures for the other study films: *Witness*, $66 million; *The Terminator*, $37 million; *Sleepless in Seattle*, $126 million. Overseas, cable, and video sales and rentals doubled or tripled these figures.

Sophie's Choice, Bonnie and Clyde, and *Butch Cassidy and the Sundance Kid.* Such stories, with bittersweet or ironic endings, are different from negative stories that end hopelessly, without escape or a sense of legend or immortality.

LIFELINES AND HOW THEY CAN SOLVE THE PROBLEM OF THE STORY

The **lifeline** is a skill, a tool, a weapon, an ally, or whatever the hero uses to solve the dramatic problem of the story. The lifeline is the hero's (and the screenwriter's) ace in the hole. It is what the hero latches onto at the last moment of the climactic scene to defeat the villain and/or to solve the problem. In *Witness* the lifeline is the bell that Samuel rings to summon the neighbors (Shot 152); in *My Cousin Vinny* the lifeline is the heroine's knowledge of automobiles; and in *Sleepless in Seattle* the lifelines are the son's backpack and references to an old movie. Other lifelines: the spacesuit and loading machine in *Alien* and *Aliens;* the cylinder of gas that blows up the shark in *Jaws;* the mud that renders the hero invisible to the alien in *Predator;* the hero's intercom in *In the Line of Fire.* Although our four main study films use lifelines, not all films do. Brando's Terry Malloy slugs it out with Lee Cobb's Johnny Friendly in *On the Waterfront.* Gary Cooper's Sheriff Will Kane is unable to secure a lifeline—or any manner of help—to fight the outlaws who plan to kill him in *High Noon.* In the end, he does the job the old fashioned way: he single-handedly kills the gang.

The Verdict contains an elaborate example of the lifeline strategy, which Galvin first touches in Shot 75 when he realizes the importance of the admitting nurse (Lindsay Crouse's Kaitlin Costello). Next, Galvin tricks Julie Bovasso's Nurse Rooney into revealing that Kaitlin lives in New York City (Shot 76). This does not solve the problem, because Galvin is unable to locate her. In Shot 80, Galvin's telephone bill arrives, inspiring an idea for finding Kaitlin, which is to steal Nurse Rooney's phone bill and use it (Shot 83) to locate the missing nurse in New York. In Shot 86, Galvin visits Kaitlin and asks her to testify. She shows up in the climactic scene (Shot 92) and helps Galvin to win his case. In all, seven beats were used to create this lifeline.

Obviously, careful plotting is required to weave a lifeline into the story, but it is worth the effort. As you work on solving the problem, you may be convinced that there is no way for the hero to win. At such times, ask yourself what is available. What device, weapon, piece of information, strategy, strength, weakness, ally, or gizmo could unexpectedly, yet logically, appear in the nick of time to help the hero win? There is *always* something, because writers can plant anything they wish in their stories. *Anything!* When James Cameron needed a way to destroy the cyborg in *The Terminator,* his heroes did not run into a lingerie shop; they ran into a factory (Shot 251) that could be turned on by throwing a few switches. Just as the heroine is about to be killed by the critter, Cameron has the cyborg crawl into a hydraulic press that is started by the button that happens to be at Sarah's fingertips (Shot 256). The circumstances of that lifeline, fortuitous to say the least, worked nevertheless. The advice to be taken from this: when you are stuck concerning how to solve the problem in your script, remember that *you* create the world of your story. You can put anything you wish into the story universe, as long as it has credibility and serves the yarn.

The lifeline should be believable and logical. It should be planted earlier in the story so the audience is aware of its presence. Do not make the device so obvious that the audience anticipates its purpose. Similarly, avoid lifelines that suddenly appear when needed, for this smacks of the *deus ex machina* solution. That strategy (literally "God from a machine") was used in ancient Greek and Roman theater to solve the dramatic problem. It sometimes featured a golden chariot or some such contraption that lowered from above, allowing a god to step onto the stage and resolve the story. Although this made life easier for playwrights, audiences felt cheated by the contrived ending because the hero did not solve the problem. With rare exceptions (*Lord of the Flies, The Bad Seed*) movies avoid endings that smack of *deus ex machina*. The vestigial counterpart of this convention is Columbo, Perry Mason, Hercule Poirot, and other brilliant detectives who step onto center stage in the climactic scene, sort through the clues, and identify the villain.

THE EPILOGUE

The epilogue is a beat that tidies up the ending of the story. Epilogues play for two to five minutes. Although not found in all films, epilogues are useful for snipping off loose ends and for commenting on the dramatic action. The epilogue in *Witness* shows Schaeffer leaving with the police (Shot 158); moments later Book says good-bye to Samuel, to Rachel, and to Eli (Shots 161 and 162). Rachel's future is suggested in Shot 163, for as Book drives away from the farm, he passes a buggy carrying an Amishman who is on his way to visit Rachel. The moment closes speculation on what will happen to Rachel. The epilogue of *The Terminator* (Shot 259) shows a pregnant Sarah stopping for gasoline and acquiring the Polaroid snapshot that will become Reese's prize possession. The epilogue concludes with a portentous shot of Sarah driving into a gathering storm. *Sleepless in Seattle*, by comparison, has no epilogue; it ends immediately after Annie and Sam meet.

CONTINUITY OF THE PLOT

The preceding presents possible story beats that may help you write a plot outline. Not counting the odd tale that proves the rule, in most stories one beat sets up the next as the story flows toward the climax. This progression of incidents is called *continuity*. A wise comment on continuity was given to me by Philip Dunne, who compared screenwriting to cabinetmaking because both require careful design and quality materials that are expertly joined. Joinery in screenwriting is continuity—the careful fitting of finely crafted scenes that combine into a plot. There should be logical reasons for why the incidents of plot occur, even when the action seems accidental, as when John Travolta's gun goes off and kills a young man in *Pulp Fiction.*

Witness demonstrates the value of continuity in Shot 119, for this is when Book learns that his partner (Carter) has been murdered; the logic of the story tells Book (and the audience) that Schaeffer is responsible. Enraged, Book telephones Schaeffer and warns him that he will pay for killing Carter. Still anguished, Book hangs up, and moments later he is confronted by three hoodlums who have been hassling the Amish (Shot 122C). When Book is mistaken for an Amishman and teased, he unleashes his rage on the troublemakers and punches them out. A busybody reacts to the fight by telling the local sheriff what happened. The sheriff reacts by calling Schaeffer to inform him that he may have found the suspect that the Philadelphia police have been seeking. Schaeffer's reaction to this news is to drive out to the Lapp farm. The logical flow of incidents continues until the corrupt cops are defeated.

The continuity demands of *Witness* are modest, but this is not always the case. *Sleepless in Seattle,* for example, ping-pongs between Annie in Baltimore and Sam in Seattle. The fragile link between them is managed through Annie's computer (Shot 86), the letter from Becky to Sam (Shot 89), the radio show (Shots 24, 39, 67, 102), and Jonah's connection with a travel agency and transcontinental air travel (Shot 162). All of these moments supply continuity that ties the story together.

Providing continuity in *The Terminator* is also problematic, for in several places (Shots 81, 117, 204) the cyborg loses track of the heroes, which threatens to break the thread of the story. James Cameron sustained the momentum of the chase by using telephones, police radios, answering machines, and an address book to link up the main characters again.

The Terminator also demonstrates how continuity can be stretched so the audience must fill in missing information. We see this (in Shot 204) when Sarah speaks by phone, apparently to her mother. In reality she is speaking to the cyborg, who imitates the mother's voice. At this point the plot trusts the audience to remember the cyborg's ability to mimic, which was planted in Act I when it took over a police car (Shot 117) and duplicated the officer's voice. They must also remember that the creature has Sarah's address book (Shot 83), which (logically) contains the mother's address. The continuity skip ends when Sarah calls her mother. At this point, the scene cuts from Sarah to her mother's house (Shot 205), whereupon the camera reveals the cyborg as it mimics the mother's voice.

By requiring the audience to remember earlier business in the story, the plot turns them into collaborators who fill in missing parts. Knowing what to leave out of a story regarding scenes, actions, and dialogue is an elegant storytelling ability that can be learned by studying films, by asking what can be left out or suggested, and by trusting the audience to remember what has already happened in the story. When a script explains everything, it may

exclude the audience and turn them into passive observers rather than participants in the dramatic ordeal.

Exposition that supports continuity can be slipped in with occasional lines
of dialogue or with quick visuals. The continuity information should not call
attention to itself, although the script should make clear what is happening. For
an example of how this is done, see *Sleepless in Seattle* when Jonah tells his father
that he gave the radio station their phone number (Shot 57). This continuity
information explains how Annie is able to locate Sam's address (Shot 86).

Continuity problems ease when the plot is simple. What is less clear is
knowing when the plot should skip. This is a judgment call that each writer
must make after considering whether the script explains the skip, whether the
skip is necessary, and whether the flow of the story will be improved by leaving something out. The advantage of a skip is that it changes the rhythm and
pace of the story and prevents the narrative from becoming plodding and predictable; the risk of using skips is that they may muddle the storyline. I recommend stories with a steady forward continuity that moves the narrative
toward a climax in which the problem is resolved. Although this sounds simple enough, most scripts are unable to accomplish this task. Good stories avoid
doglegs and *switchbacks* that cause the plot to wander into meanders, diver-
sions, dead ends, and repetitions.

Telephones (especially cellular telephones) have become a continuity aid
that can connect characters in scattered locations. Telephone continuity joins
the characters in all four of our main study films. Phone conversations are
most dramatic when there is conflict and emotion involved, as in Shots 24, 50,
51, and 85 of *The Verdict,* which show only Galvin's side of each conversation
as he talks to his client, to the insurance company, and to Dr. Thompson, and
as Laura talks to Galvin about meeting him in New York. *Witness* (Shot 82)
presents a phone conversation that is intercut between Schaeffer and a sheriff
in the Amish country. Telephone conversations can also be shown on a split
screen that shows both parties simultaneously, as in *When Harry Met Sally.*
There will be more said on this topic in Chapter 6, which deals with voice-over
narration, graphics, and other dialogue and continuity strategies.

STORY LOGIC

It can be awkward to think about narrative matters of logic when a story deals
with invisible men, 50-foot women, emerald cities at the end of the rainbow,
and similar flights of imagination. Although some dramatic plots are incredible, there should be logic and consistency within the story's context, regardless
of how bizarre the premise or frame. The screenwriter sets forth the rules of
the story universe, and if it allows bringing dinosaurs back from extinction,
then the audience will accept that presumption and judge the story accordingly. If the story posits that its characters can turn into wolves or can be
stitched together from body parts, then the audience will accept that premise
and judge what follows accordingly. No matter how extreme the request, audi-

ences usually go along with the storyteller's initial presumption as the price of an interesting ride. They buy into the notion through mumbo-jumbo explanations, magical music, mysterious machines, ancient elixirs, wizards, and similar nonsense. Once the deal is struck, however, the audience has done its part and the film should resist asking it to accept additional improbabilities. Furthermore, the story should develop logically within the established context. In *Big*, the audience accepts that a magical carnival machine can transfer the persona of a child into Tom Hanks's adult body. However, the action that follows the transfer is logical because the story provides motivations for why the characters behave as they do.

In some films, the rules of the story universe are so complicated that they evolve throughout the narrative, which is okay too. *Forbidden Planet*, for example, reveals the mysteries of a vanished civilization as the story plays out. This is not unusual in science fiction, a genre that favors surprises, revelations, and twists. We see this in *Alien* and *Predator* and in similar stories dealing with strange life-forms that gradually reveal their complexity.

In films that are more realistic, logic can falter when unlikely incidents cause the audience to disbelieve what is on screen. For example, in *Far and Away* the hero is about to fight a challenger when a grasping politician begins to paw the hero's love interest. Distracted, the hero loses the fight. This could happen, but it seems manipulative and thus undercuts the credibility of the story. In *The Snows of Kilimanjaro*, Ava Gardner is trapped inside an ambulance on the battlefield and prays for her lover to find her. As hundreds of desperate men run blindly past her, the fellow who shows up in the nick of time is Gregory Peck, the man in Ava's prayers. Although such a thing could happen, this coincidence struck me as weak plotting that undercut the logic and credibility of the movie. Similarly, one of the moments in *Nell* that strains believability occurs when the title character is driven into a large city by her benefactors who allow her to wander into a nearby pool hall, where she encounters the young motorcycle scamps who spied on her when she was in her wilderness home. Also stretching credibility is the fact that Nell's cabin is located next to a large lake, making it likely (in real life) that boaters would have intruded on her privacy, yet the filmmakers ask us to believe in her isolation. Such concerns are often unavoidable, but writers should be picky regarding logic and credibility; otherwise, the story will be riddled with gaps, improbabilities, illogic, and similar dents in believability.

One way to fix a logic problem is to ask if the dramatic moment is truthful. Is it honest? What might really happen in this situation? In most cases, if you test your plot with these questions, they will lead to incidents that work without causing the audience to wince in disbelief. At the same time, ask if the characters are reacting too weakly or too strongly to a provocation. Ask if an important issue is raised or dropped without follow-up. Ask if the characters are motivated. For example, we accept that William Munny in *Unforgiven* would go after a bounty, even though he seems too old for such a venture. Munny's decision is believable because we sense the needfulness of his children, his dying farm, and the legacy of his dead wife. Writers nag themselves about logic and credibility as a hedge against committing to an idea or incident that is sappy and illogical. Most of us also have a huge ability to talk ourselves into believing that the dumbest idea is wonderful, so when a logic question arises, examine the fundamentals of the structure: What is the event? What is the problem? What do the characters want and why can't they get it? Ask what you want to say in the story and whether your story is truthful, logical, and motivated. Once questions such as these are straightened out, it is time to think about the story's characters and how they will arrange themselves in the subplots.

SUBPLOTS

Movie subplots form when the hero and the villain have relationships with the secondary characters. Mickey and Galvin in *The Verdict* are friends, and they form a subplot. In *Sleepless in Seattle*, Meg Ryan's Annie and Rosie O'Donnell's Becky also form a subplot. Most feature stories contain two to four supporting characters who are tied to the hero and to the villain through subplots that heighten conflict, delve into the hero's internal conflict, and/or address the theme. Matters become a bit vague when it comes to determining which characters are part of a subplot, for it could be argued that every character has a subplot. You can figure this out by asking whether the character has a relationship that evolves and intensifies as the drama moves toward the climax. If so, that character probably will have a subplot that sees him or her whipped up emotionally along with the hero or villain.

We find such a subplot in *The Verdict*. It begins when Mickey Morrissey (Jack Warden) lectures Galvin about taking care of business after finding him passed out on the floor of his office. Because the two men are old friends, their personal relationship reflects the tension that arises during the trial. At the same time, the Laura-Galvin subplot tracks a relationship that builds lovingly but crashes in the end. During the building of this romantic relationship, Laura rekindles Galvin's belief in the law. Laura also adds emotional content to the story, while allowing thematic concerns to be expressed.

Emotional and Nonemotional Subplots

Movies do their best to simulate real life, but they are dramatic contrivances. Most films revolve around the main characters in an egocentric way that denies potentially interesting characters a chance to develop in a subplot. For example, the man behind the cigar counter in *The Verdict* (Shot 40) or Schaeffer's wife in *Witness* (Shot 119A) could have been developed and written into subplots, but there was no need. Writers must decide which characters will be given subplots while at the same time making sure that the narrative does not become confused by too many subplots. Experience will enable you to recognize which characters connect in subplots that have emotional content.

You will also learn that certain characters will try to push their way into a story, even when they have nothing to do. These interlopers often charm writers by offering a wonderful subplot that has no purpose in the story. Such disconnected characters can cause the story to meander and to lose intensity. Subplots usually are given to secondary characters who connect emotionally to the protagonist and the antagonist.

A second point concerns nonemotional characters who mainly pass on plot information. Although these types can be useful, too many of them can damage a story because they are expositional conduits who do not relate emotionally to the other characters. Kent Broadhurst's insurance agent (Joseph Alito) in *The Verdict* is an expositional character who shows up periodically to tell Bishop Brophy and Concannon about what Galvin is doing. This is the function of this chilly character, who remains buttoned up emotionally during the story, as one would expect from a corporate apparatchik. Weak scripts are often overpopulated by characters who do not show warmth, frailty, and other emotional traits. Writers must judge which secondary characters deserve emotional roles in the story and which are messengers who pass on exposition. In most cases the problem is not how to develop subplots, it is how to limit their number. Knowing whether the characters deal with emotion or exposition can spare confusion on this point.

Subplots and the Second Act

You will be pleased to learn that subplots can ease the strain of what goes into the second act. In *The Verdict,* the Galvin-Laura subplot takes up thirteen minutes of the second act. A total of fifteen minutes of the second act is given to the Doneghys, Nurse Rooney, and doctors Towler and Thompson. The remaining twenty-two minutes of the second act deal with the pretrial and the trial. This breakdown illustrates how much of a fifty-minute second act can be given over to subplots that examine the dramatic problem from different viewpoints.

Add this perspective on subplots to your sense of story, although this brief discussion is not enough to teach this story insight. To learn it, study scripts and films to see how they introduce their subplots in the first act, how they use them to fill out the second act, and how they build and are concluded in the third act. When you appreciate this dynamic and how subplots reveal character and theme, the task of writing the second act should be reduced. Until this lesson is understood, the characters may lack the subplots they need to develop emotionally. Without emotionally evolved characters, stories become plot-heavy and dependent on action and empty spectacle. (Note that a strong first-act setup that charges the characters emotionally so they can interact is one of the best cures for this condition.)

The Varieties of Subplots

Subplots have agendas. For example, the love-interest subplot allows the hero not only to express his (or her) tender feelings toward a loved one but also to discuss thematic concerns, childhood, family, dreams, values, or whatever.

Laura, in *The Verdict*, seems like a traditional love interest, yet she is freshened by secrets that she cannot share. Laura is also an outlet for Galvin's thoughts about the law and what he is doing with his life (which addresses the theme). The Laura subplot concludes sadly, as does the love affair in *Witness*, which also has a bittersweet ending when Book and Rachel go their separate ways into worlds that will probably never touch again. As in *Witness, The Graduate, Prizzi's Honor,* and other films, the charm of the romantic subplot can be more memorable than the main action line. Most stories are improved by the romantic subplot, even when the romance is platonic, as in the Gene Hackman-Frances McDormand subplot in *Mississippi Burning.*

The variety of subplots allows stories and characters to show different emotional colors and energy. *In the Line of Fire*'s Rene Russo supplies romantic interest that allows the story to shift from white-knuckle tension to a more playful energy. As is often the case, such a change reveals another dimension of the hero and allows the audience a respite until the next surge of conflict.

Another example: the Paul Newman-Jessica Tandy subplot in *Nobody's Fool* presents an overview of the hero's life and what he has been doing since he was a student in Tandy's classroom. The teacher's perspective, based on her lifetime of observing the hero and the town, presents an interesting angle on what happens in this gentle story. Similarly, the Annie-Becky subplot in *Sleepless in Seattle* makes the audience aware that time may be running out for the heroine if she intends to marry.

This final bit of advice: Many subplots deal with the B-storyline, which swings attention away from the A-storyline. This focus can cause the viewer to lose the thread of what is happening in the story. For this reason, I recommend caution when leaving the A-storyline to deal with B-storyline material. Be sure that the narrative throughline of the story is not broken because of too many subplots that involve the B-storyline. Your sense of story must advise you whether this condition is undermining your work.

BLOCKING THE STORY

Up to this point I have dealt with expanding a story idea into a plot, offering advice on frame, characters, internal and external conflict, theme, and related topics. These values can help screenwriters ponder the event, the problem, the story concept, and the dramatic crisis. During this part of the process we sketch temp characters and think about story archetypes and genres. We also think about whether the story will be real, unreal, or surreal; whether it will be plot-driven or character-driven; and which segment of the available audience will be targeted. We also determine the emotional slant of the story—will it evoke humor, sadness, or fear? This thinking, a part of screenwriting, is work that can extend for weeks or months while the writer enriches the story and generates incidents that are organized into a plot. Blocking the plot means arranging the dramatic incidents into a sequence that has a beginning-to-end progression. Blocking is a process that often involves many drafts, each moving the writer closer to the plot that feels most dramatic.

Plot Incidents

Plot incidents occur because of the logic of the narrative and its overall direction, i.e., certain things happen in the story because they *should* happen. For example, the sports widow notion might contain a plot beat that says "Mom decides to take charge of her life." Because the event of the story is based on Mom saving her family, such a beat (or something close to it) is essential. Furthermore, this beat is so important that it would probably be written as a dramatic sequence that plays for five or more minutes. Thus, creating such a beat seems unavoidable, given the nature of the story being developed.

This particular beat—Mom taking charge of her life—might involve a training sequence. If we are unsure of how this might be done, the topic could be researched with calls to a sports club or to the women's athletic department of a local school. Films containing training sequences—*The Cutting Edge, Personal Best,* and the like—might be checked out. Mom's training sequence would require incidents that are emotionally revealing, visual, and entertaining. These generalities suggest that Mom might visit a health club or a TV exercise show, or she might be counseled by an exercise professional. During this incident, Mom's exceptional strength would be revealed. Even though the incidents being proposed sound flimsy, they are typical of those found in early plot outlines. Fleshing them out with interesting character interaction will add to the drama. The goal in the early drafts of the plot outline is a sequence of incidents containing two twists that tests Mom and concludes in a sequence that enables her to solve the problem of the story. The preliminary outlines need not have elegant twists or sequences, merely the feel of a continuous narrative with a three-act structure.

As this work progresses, remember one of the main mantras of this volume: *Write simple stories and complex characters.* Simple stories work because writers invest energy in characters who generate interesting details, twists, and insights that transform seemingly simple story beats into major dramatic moments. The hotdog lunch enjoyed by Book, Rachel, and Samuel in *Witness* (Shot 52B) is such a beat; it is where Rachel tells Book what his sister Elaine said about his life. As played at a fast-food location (the script staged the scene as a picnic on a park bench), the humanity of the characters—Book's scowling toleration of Rachel's charming innocence and Samuel's belch—turns a simple encounter into a memorable movie scene.

Plots, like scripts, are not written. They are rewritten. They evolve. They grow and become complicated as simple incidents are roughed out, often without much detail. The first versions of the plot are usually ragged and spotty, with gaps that must be filled in. The rough outlines of the plot (most can be contained on a single page) are like a painter's charcoal sketch that lays out the cartoon: initial versions are rubbed out and changed until the sketch feels right. Plots evolve similarly—groping, unsure, and searching for a throughline until the span of the plot feels complete. Throughout the early phases of the writing, the malleable plot gives the characters freedom to develop and the writer freedom to try different approaches. If the plot is screwed down too tightly and too soon, the characters may be smothered by lack of freedom. Lillian Hellman once remarked that plot is what the author wants to happen; story is what the characters want to happen. When the incidents of plot refuse to arrange, it might be that the characters are not being allowed into the blocking process.

Creating plot incidents is usually simple enough; more challenging is how the incidents are arranged and dramatized to track characters in conflict. Many writers find this phase of the work so difficult that they try to avoid it by convincing themselves that their story is ready for scripting when it is not. Guard against this tendency. *Do not write the script until you are totally happy with your plot outline.* Weak plots invariably end badly because they contain flaws that swarm up during scripting. When this happens, the writer begins to adjust the plot in an attempt to fix fundamental weaknesses in the story. Although fixes are possible during scripting, more often the narrative acquires a contrived, plotty quality that withers the original story concept. A viable plot outline rewards the writer's hard work by providing an overview that clearly tells if the story works and what must be done in each incident. Many writers contend that the one or two pages of the story outline constitute 70 to 80 percent of the work of screenwriting. Because plotting is so challenging, many writers approach this task by first creating a *story armature.*

Creating a Story Armature

This task usually takes a day or so as the writer decides what happens in the twists that end the first and the second acts. Devising these two complications will reveal the overall layout of the acts and where the story is heading. With this overview in mind, you should find it easier to track the story, to create incidents of plot, and to arrange the beats of the plot. This happens because the armature (aided by the story template and the other values discussed so far) points out what generally happens in the story.

To determine the two twists, you must try out possible incidents that determine what might seem to move the story in a new direction. In most cases the twist that ends the first act occurs a half hour or so into the story when an incident or decision causes the hero to take on or become involved with the problem. As noted elsewhere, the first complication incident in *The Verdict* occurs when Galvin turns down the bishop's settlement offer (Shot 26). This decision requires the hero to take on the problem of the story, which is to defeat Ed Concannon in court.

In the sports widow situation, the first twist incident could occur after Mom experiences an incident that is so humiliating or frightening that she realizes that her family is in jeopardy and thus she is inspired to take action. Coming up with an incident that provokes Mom to take action would require a moment that almost breaks her back emotionally. Such an incident might play most dramatically if it happens before a shocked and watchful audience that includes her children. If the incident is too garish, it can be toned down.

The incident should trigger a major life crisis, when Mom must choose between fight and flight. This tack has Mom deciding to fight to save her marriage. There are many ways to arrive at this point: she could discover that Dad has lost interest in his family, or that he wants to become a bushrat in Alaska, or that her kids are ashamed of her, or all the above. Whatever the incident, it should cause Mom to take on the problem of saving her family, starting a new life, or whatever suits the event of the story.

If we use the advice from Chapter 2 about interrupting the status quo, the incident could begin when one of Dad's college teammates and his lady friend appear at the game. The fellow now earns $3 million a year as a wide receiver for the New York Jets, and he seems to have everything. Envy over Joe Jet's glittery life-style could put Dad in an ugly mood, which motivates the action. If that notion did not start a fire, new ideas would be tried until something felt right.

Working out the twist that ends Act II is done in a similar fashion. The story template advises that Act II ends with the hero seemingly defeated by the problem; therefore, in the Mom story, we should ask what might cause this darkest moment, when it seems that Mom has lost her family. Imagine the worst thing that could befall your hero. In the Mom story the second twist could be that Dad decides to run off with another woman and to abandon his family; or it could be that Mom abandons her family in favor of entering a competition to prove that she is somebody. The darkest moment could occur when Dad and the kids abandon Mom for neglecting them. These and other possibilities would be tacked up while we work out the second twist of the armature that outlines what generally happens in each act. In most cases, the two twists are a test of ingenuity and common sense as we ask, "What could reasonably (or unreasonably) happen?" Write a list of what comes to mind. The possibilities are usually finite, and your list should produce a usable twist or two.

Working out the story armature completes the first main blocking task. What remains is also suggested in Figure 3-1 (see page 72), which notes that the third act is mainly taken up with the climactic scene that resolves the problem. I suggest putting the climax aside until later, since the details of the dramatic showdown will be clearer after the first two acts have been blocked and outlined. The page-or-so length of the outline will enable you to rewrite it until your sense of story indicates that it feels right.

Throughout, this book encourages you to pack your story into a nutshell so that you have an overview that tracks the story as it sets up a problem that causes trouble until the hero solves matters in the final scene. The story armature provides such an overview, which you can use for the next phase of blocking: expanding the armature and preliminary plot outline with dramatic incidents.

Plotting Incidents Based on Action and Reaction

One of the surest blocking strategies is to provoke characters so they respond emotionally, that is, to create an *action* that causes some sort of *reaction*. We see this in Shot 60 of *Witness* when the hero is shot by a fellow officer. The attack causes Book to react because he realizes that he has stumbled onto a police conspiracy. Therefore his reaction is to drive Rachel and her son back to the safety of Amish country. When the corrupt cops realize that Book and the witnesses have escaped, they react by hunting them down.

In Shot 88 of *The Verdict*, Galvin learns that Laura is a spy for the opposition. This motivates him (in Shot 89) to confront her in a cocktail lounge. Here, too, an action causes the character to react. Although the action-reaction is not always as sudden as in these examples (there may be intervening scenes or a delayed reaction), the domino-effect dynamic is a sure way to unfold the story. If the actions and reactions are not strong enough to create drama, turn up the heat, raise the stakes, and create conflict. Do not be timid on this point. If your initial ideas are overblown, they can be toned down. Your goal is to create conflict, drama, and emotion. Tear into the story idea, the locations, the time and weather, the style, and especially the characters, asking, "What could happen in this situation?" If nothing interesting turns up, ask again—*louder!*

In most cases the action-reaction approach will generate more incidents than you can use. The beats can be combined, discarded, sorted, and refined until they reduce to ten or so sequences, at which time the plot outline should be complete and you are ready to begin writing the script. Creating story beats should be done patiently and carefully, so do not rush matters or rationalize that the work is done when it is not.

Speed-writing Story Incidents

This strategy is another go at writing every incident that comes to mind during a set time (a half hour is the recommended daily dosage). The time pressure of speedwriting pushes writers in the direction of intuition and the unconscious, where many of the best ideas are found. Delving into the dark of the mind this way can produce all kinds of fresh ideas, some of which may have story potential. Once or twice a semester I use this drill by giving students a photocopy containing four or five short news clippings (similar to the sports widow item). The class pairs off and is given ten minutes to devise a story based on one of the items. A class of twelve students will usually produce two or three excellent ideas that are often quite different from the original news story.

Psych up for speedwriting sessions. Before beginning, review the event, the story template, and the outline of traditional scenes so you have a solid sense of three-act structure and where your story seems to be heading. When brainstorming, do not hold back. Repeat the drill for two or three days. Do not become tense if this drill turns up only a sketchy story, for mainly you will discover beats that address the A-storyline. The character scenes that attach to the B-storyline as subplots usually come later when you work on the motivation of the characters and the logic of the piece. All you need from this phase of the work is a simple plot that offers a beginning, middle, and ending.

These blocking strategies respond to the story questions we have been discussing:

- Who are the main characters and what do they want?
- Why are they unable to get what they want?
- What is the problem?
- Who opposes the hero's attempts to resolve the problem, and why?
- Did something happen earlier in the plot or in the backstory that could cause the story to take off?
- Is the status quo upset by someone leaving or entering, or could a natural or social disaster set the story in motion?

As you play with these questions, let your mind fly. Crank out ideas and jot them down, regardless of how weird, feeble, or bizarre they are. Later, you may find that you can use one of these odd incidents or details.

Other Blocking Strategies

Screenwriters have no end of strategies for blocking a story. One well-known writer likes to pretend that he is sitting in a movie theater waiting for the premiere showing of his movie to begin. When he has conjured the theater, he envisions the houselights dimming and his movie appearing on the screen. During this he imagines the opening music—scary, lush, modern, pop, lulling, or whatever. He knows who composed it and how it is arranged and orchestrated. When the picture fades in, he imagines the settings in fine detail. He imagines his characters. Most important, he asks himself if the movie in his mind will entertain the hundreds of people in the audience. His advice to new writers is to concentrate on the first five minutes of the movie and how it pulls the audience into the story. If the movie that you have in mind seems dull, reimagine it until it seems entertaining. What is seen in imagination is usually what ends up in the script. When this thought is tied to an old Hollywood insight claiming that 80 percent of what shows up on the screen is in the script, then the importance of these imaginings is clearly essential to the success of the project.

Another game that can ease you into fruitful levels of consciousness is the casting session. This one asks you to cast the story with your favorite actors. Have fun with this by inscribing name cards for each actor; position the cards around a table. Place one copy of your plot outline next to each name card and imagine that the actors are sitting behind their respective name cards reading your plot. Now pretend to be each actor in turn. Ask why things happen in the story. Ask how the story will entertain an audience. Ask what the story is about. Ask who the characters are and how they relate to one another. The object of this drill is to assume the personas of the actors as they test your plot. As the writer you must answer their questions, justify the plot, and persuade the actors to accept their roles. This game can also be done with a writing partner or friends playing the various roles.

I recommend that you carry a small notepad or sheet of paper for jotting down plot ideas or random thoughts that come to mind. The notepad lets your unconscious mind know that there is an outlet for whatever ideas it might care to serve up.

Another aid to imagining plot incidents is listening to music, which may open up your unconscious. Some writers ask their unconscious for story assistance before going to sleep, encouraging the dreaming process to supply ideas and to solve writing problems. Some writers place paper and pencil next to their beds to record whatever bubbles up overnight. Often the unconscious answers questions unexpectedly, at a later time, when the problem is not being considered by the writer's conscious mind.

GROUPING STORY BEATS INTO SEQUENCES

The preceding strategies should generate a few dozen story moments and incidents that look promising. The next step is to group them into ten or so sequences that form a plot with a beginning, middle, and ending. During this process, keep a statement of the story concept and event nearby, to remind yourself of what happens in the piece. As noted earlier, do not panic if the plot seems skimpy, for it will take on weight during the scripting process when the characters evolve and fill out their subplots. This is as it should be, for many stories improve as the writing digs vertically into character rather than sliding horizontally into additional incidents of plot.

The sports widow story might begin with a sequence beat that establishes the frame, which might be in Athens, Ohio; Newton, Massachusetts; or whatever town we set the story in. See the openings of *The Deerhunter, Places in the Heart,* and *Nobody's Fool* for examples of how small-town story frames are introduced.

The second sequence might take the audience to a softball game that reveals the world of middle-aged sports fanatics such as Dad. The scene could also show how Mom and the family are subordinate to the sport. The third sequence could introduce the problem by showing the family's home life. The final beat of the first act would be a sequence that causes Mom to take on the problem of saving her family. Each of these sequence beats would consist of bits and scenes. For example, if the second sequence—introducing the world of the middle-aged sports fanatic—were to be teased out into bits and scenes, it might include the following:

- Mom is driving the kids to the game. Incident shows how important sports are to Dad and how his concerns dominate the family. This would play as a minute or so of dialogue.
- The softball game would show how passionately Dad and his gang play the game. Dad could suffer a minor injury and need taping. Mom has not yet arrived. This would probably be an action scene that plays for two minutes or so.
- Mom arrives with the kids, and the plot thickens when she is criticized for being late. Undercurrents of a nasty family situation surface. This would probably be an action and dialogue scene that plays for a minute or so.

- Joe Jet and his lady friend arrive and create a stir. A minute or so may be sufficient for this incident of plot.
- There is more game action, which ends when Mom goes home and Dad goes off to the local pub for beer and companionship. This would probably take a minute or so of action and dialogue.

This sequence could play for six to eight minutes and would probably begin one or more of the subplots, which means introducing some of the secondary characters. Even so, the sequence shows little detail or interest at this stage, which is a bare-bones listing of the order of incidents and what generally happens in each. We must have faith that the beats will come alive during scripting, when characters and the details of the situations are imagined.

The third sequence, which deals with the family at home, has appeared in countless films; such beats are usually popular because audiences are curious about characters who are written with passion, love, and thoughtfulness. These writing tasks are made easier when we know that our goal is a first-act setup that causes Mom to take on the problem of saving her family. Such a setup requires Dad and others to abuse Mom until she reaches her breaking point. If the story were to go this way, the need would be for a dramatic incident that precipitates this crisis. The problem could begin after Dad makes an error at the ball game and takes out his frustration on his wife, chewing her out for arriving late at the game. Their dispute could worsen at home and lead to Mom's decision to take action to save her family. Considerably more work than can be briefly described is needed to complete the setup, but the discussion indicates how this work proceeds.

Note that we have not yet discussed how to make our characters complex, how to work out a backstory for Mom and Dad, and how their backstories indicate what is bothering them. All we know now is that we are dealing with an unhappy family, a Mom who is abnormally strong, a Dad who is a sports fanatic, and two children who have yet to be defined. Although this is not much, even these beginnings suggest possible story beats that will become much more specific when they are imagined and dramatized. For example, we could dramatize Mom's strength by having her sling a bat bag into her van. A woman nearby—Joe Jet's female companion—notices and is impressed at how easily Mom tosses the eighty-pound load. The woman (call her Vera) reacts to the bat-bag incident and Mom's unhappiness by inviting her to visit the woman's health club. Vera could be motivated by her desire to marry Joe Jet; she hopes that Mom and Dad are a means to this end. This suggests a Joe-Vera subplot that could be sustained throughout the story.

BLOCKING THE STORY FOR A SHORT FILM AND EXPANDING IT TO FEATURE LENGTH

If a two-hour story is intimidating, you might wish to write your idea as a half-hour or one-hour piece. Some writers find that the short-film approach makes it easier to hold an overview of the story. Later, when the short version is completed, it can be expanded to feature-length by adding subplots. Short films launch quickly, in the first page if possible; they track the dramatic problem with a minimum of distraction or subplotting. The aim during this is a story that can be told on one double-spaced page. Most of the plotting and blocking strategies outlined so far apply to the short film as surely as they do to features. (In Appendix A you will find references to short films that are models for this approach to plotting a story.)

As you become familiar with structure, you will recognize that there are patterns and similarities to plots. You will also understand that most plots have been done many times over and that most of them are quite simple. Screenplays become complex when interesting characters and unusual locations are tied to simple plots. Failure to grasp this trait of movie stories leads some writers to extend their plots until they are too complicated. Thus, *simplicity* is a key plotting perspective.

Another plotting insight is learning to value and to trust your original story notion. This is pointed out because some writers feel that their story idea will not be interesting unless it is stuffed, like a Strasbourg goose, with action and spectacle. As a teacher and editor who has dealt with thousands of stories, I would say that at least a third of the ideas from new writers that I deal with have commercial potential—a figure that puts them at about the same level as professionals. Many student ideas have rich connections to family and relationship stories, to parents and children recovering and making a new life, to growing up, to finding love, to achieving a sense of self, to bonding as a family or with a partner, as well as to many other contemporary topics. Such ideas show up on the big screen as *King of the Hill, Forrest Gump,* and *The 400 Blows.* The point here is to trust your idea and keep it simple and focused on the characters as they struggle with the problem.

WRITING A FEATURE STORY FROM A SCENE

The final strategy for blocking a feature story is to select an emotionally rich incident from the unformed plot. The beat selected is then written into a feature-length scene that plays for three to five minutes. For example, the sports widow might be distraught when she throws the bat bag, so if Vera were to step forward to comfort her at this moment, an emotional scene could result. Cast the scene with your favorite actors; locate the action anywhere you wish; give yourself an unlimited budget. Writing a scene requires shifting from the rational mode, which tends to be used during blocking, to the imaginative side of the brain, which can suggest specific details and dramatic incidents of story. This happens because writing from the unconscious calls forth the characters who can help drive the story. Scripting asks writers to think about motivation, reactions to conflict, action incidents, and dialogue that leads to confrontation and character revelation. If you try this approach, think about what led up to the moment, the reaction that follows, and how it relates to the event of the story. It should take three days to a week to write (and to rewrite) such a scene.

The short-film and scene exercises are part of writing the story, which usually takes weeks of intense work, so (again) give yourself enough time to learn this work. You should also know that it can take six months or so of full-time screenwriting (15–20 hours per week) to extend a plot idea into a feature script. Richard Walter and Lew Hunter, esteemed colleagues who co-chair the Graduate Screenwriting Program at UCLA, feel that new writers usually must complete five feature screenplays to acquire the hands-on experience needed to understand the basic craft skills of screenwriting. I agree with their judgment.

MULTIPLE STORYLINES

Though seldom used, one of the most effective story types is the multiple-storyline film. Also called *ensemble* or *gang* stories, they include such works as *The Big Chill, Hannah and Her Sisters, Pulp Fiction, Dinner at Eight, The Right Stuff, Nashville, Ship of Fools, Parenthood, California Suite,* and *The Gods Must Be Crazy.* Television makes more frequent use of multiple storylines, with such shows as *L.A. Law, Barney Miller, China Beach, NYPD Blue,* and *Twin Peaks* having achieved considerable success with this type of plot. Disaster movies occasionally use multiple storylines so that a group of disparate characters can endure a horrific experience of some sort, as in *The Poseidon Adventure, Towering Inferno, Titanic,* and similar films.

For a time I used an episode of *Hill Street Blues* to discuss how multiple-storyline shows are written. The study film, David Milch's award-winning "Trial by Fury," examines what happens in the fictional Hill Street police station. The "Trial by Fury" episode devotes one of its storylines to tracking how a young hustler is befriended by one of the continuing police characters. Another storyline involves two of the continuing characters with a domestic dispute; a third storyline concerns a woman whose storekeeper husband is murdered in a robbery; a fourth is about a cop who must face an IRS audit. All of these storylines are subsumed by the main storyline, which deals with the murder of a nun. All five storylines are introduced, interwoven, and concluded in the 48-minute playing time of the episode.

Unlike this *Hill Street Blues* episode, traditional TV shows (*Murder, She Wrote; Frasier; X-Files; Dr. Quinn, Medicine Woman*) focus on a single storyline that is resolved during the show. In most cases, the secondary characters orbit around the hero and villain in ways that help the lead character deal with the problem of the week.

Because of time constraints, multiple-storyline shows are able to develop only brief and simple plots. This means that the characters in each storyline do not have time to develop as fully as do those in a monoplot. The advantage of multiple storylines is that they allow more characters into the spotlight, where they can pursue their individual problems, whereas single storylines center action on a hero who solves the main dramatic problem. Multiple storylines also mean that the dramatic problems can be much simpler because the audience is diverted by the pace of what happens in the various storylines.

One of the interesting traits of a multiple-storyline show is the way the storylines intersect, overlap, and/or interact with each other in ways that energize the story. This shows in the *Hill Street Blues* episode cited, where the murder of a nun pulls officers away from their original cases so that the entire station can become involved with finding the killers of the nun.

The downside of multiple storylines is that they seem difficult to plot because there are so many characters in motion and so many problems that must be activated and resolved. However, writers who work with this form feel that these stories are easier to plot because the individual storylines are so simple. The secret to writing multiple-storyline plots is learning how to keep track of the various plot lines and how they relate to each other, as well as learning how to make the all-important transitions that shift the work from one plot line to another. A first step in learning these skills is to reduce the multiple storylines to an outline made up of sentence summaries of each beat.

Hannah and Her Sisters is a useful study for figuring out how multiple storylines organize. In this case what shows up is a classic romantic triangle in which Hannah (Mia Farrow) and her sister (Barbara Hershey) become involved with the same man (Michael Caine). The triangle becomes obvious when Woody Allen's comic relief storyline is stripped away, revealing the main problem—how to repair family bonds that are being ripped apart by a sexual crisis. Everything comes together in the end when the main couple reunite and Barbara Hershey's character, the third leg of the triangle, ends up marrying a professor. Allen emerges from his imaginary brain tumor and marries Hannah's other sister (Diane Wiest), which ties up the loose ends of the plot.

Styles of Multiple-Storyline Plots

Outlining also reveals how multiple storylines can be divided into three distinct categories. The first uses *intersecting storylines* that occasionally cross each other in ways that energize the plot lines, as in *Pulp Fiction* and *The Gods Must Be Crazy*. *Pulp Fiction* uses three storylines: John Travolta and Samuel L. Jackson as a pair of assassins, Bruce Willis as a boxer, and a gangster and his wife. These storylines are bookended by a framing device: Amanda Plummer and Tim Roth as robbers who hold up a diner where the two assassins are eating. Each time two of these plot lines intersect, it results in a surge in dramatic energy, as when Travolta's character is shot when he runs into Willis, who has returned to his apartment to retrieve a family heirloom.

A second variety of multiple storyline uses *converging plots,* as in *Dinner at Eight, California Suite, Murder on the Orient Express,* and *Nashville.* These films often begin as characters prepare for a gathering that will occur later in the story. As the characters get ready for their grand coming together, they reveal themselves as troubled people struggling with various problems. Later, the characters assemble wearing their public faces that often only show traces of the inner problems revealed earlier. However, the audience knows what lies beneath the exterior masks and expects the problems raised to be addressed and/or resolved during the public appearance.

A third variety uses *tangential storylines* that connect to an unusual circumstance that causes the characters to interact and play out their stories. Examples: *The Poseidon Adventure, M.A.S.H., The Big Chill, The Right Stuff,* and such TV miniseries as *Winds of War.*

Certain stories seem like multiple storylines, but they are really puffed up single-storyline narratives in which the secondary characters are captured in the service of a dominant star hero and his or her goal, which often is to solve everyone else's problem. Multiple storylines, by comparison, assign a protagonist and unique problem to each plot line. The difference between the two forms shows in *The Great Escape* (a multiple-storyline movie) and *Von Ryan's Express,* another World War II POW story. The latter is a single-storyline narrative that places Frank Sinatra as the leader of a prisoner escape plan. *The Great Escape* gives a number of characters distinct and separate storylines that contribute to the overall escape attempt; in *Von Ryan's Express,* the secondary characters orbit the hero, reflecting his star status, which means that the secondary storylines are not given time to develop.

Transitions in Multiple Storylines

Another way to understand multiple-storyline plots is to appreciate how they shift from one storyline to another. To learn how these transitions are accomplished, study the edit points where the storylines shift from one to the other in a few of the films cited. Again, *Hannah and Her Sisters* is a useful study for learning how transitions work in multiple-storyline films.

Hill Street Blues, an innovative TV show of the 1980s, shifted storylines by camera moves that refocused attention from one set of characters to another. Thus the episode might frame on two cops arguing in a hallway of the station house until it became time to move on to a new set of characters, whereupon the camera would shift slightly and frame on new characters, who present a different storyline. As soon as the newcomers enter the frame, they become the center of attention until this transition process occurs again. The *Hill Street Blues* transitions suited the leitmotif of turmoil and nervous energy that surged through the station house during each episode.

Hannah and Her Sisters illustrates a second transition strategy, this one based on verbal references to a character not in the scene. *Hannah and Her Sisters* opens with a Thanksgiving Day family gathering; this proceeds until someone asks Hannah if her ex-husband is still worried about his health. That dialogue cue sets up the transition to Woody Allen's character as he experiences his latest health crisis.

A "clock" can serve as a transition device, as when people hurry to arrive for dinner at eight or for a rendezvous or engagement of some sort. These strategies seem to work best when the audience is aware of what the characters in the different storylines have in common—usually they are going somewhere, are part of a group, are equally beset or endangered, and so on.

Transitions can also involve a physical location (*Grand Hotel*), object (*Twenty Dollars*), or vehicle (*The Yellow Rolls-Royce*) that inspires moves from one storyline to another. We see this in *The Gods Must Be Crazy* when the Bushman's storyline crosses that of the romantic leads when he comes upon their Land Rover after it has winched itself high into a tall tree. Transitions can also be keyed to sound effects, music, weather, eating, working, holidays, and many other commonly shared experiences.

Additional Narrative Techniques

Although multiple storylines are a familiar genre, there are variants that are less well known despite their narrative interest. I would place *The Singing Detective* at the top of my personal list in terms of narrative potential. This multiple-storyline film played as a miniseries on PBS in 1986. Written by Dennis Potter, it is an intriguing mix of flashbacks, several types of fantasies, a parallel fictional story that the novelist-hero is writing, along with the main storyline, which concerns the writer's hospital recovery from a severe skin condition. The storylines converge in the end, allowing the hero to understand his life and the basis of his unhappiness. I recommend *The Singing Detective* to those interested in innovative motion picture narrative technique.

Inventing new storytelling methods is a perennial topic among film schools, critics, and the avant-garde. Many filmmakers feel the same way, but they continue to use the three-act structure that movies took from the theater a century ago. They persist with traditional structure because it has proven itself to be more successful than any new narrative form that has been tried. Over the years, there have been many attempts to reinvent narrative, but aside from multiple storylines, audiences have rejected these innovations. That is the rub with reinventing movie narrative: *The movie-going public must approve of the new technique.* Daunting as this is, it has not prevented experimentation. One attempt at innovation was *Lady in the Lake* (1946), which presented a detective story entirely from the hero's point of view. However, the film is now viewed as an oddity, and the strategy has not been tried again.

Steve Martin's *Dead Men Don't Wear Plaid* (1982) presented moments when the hero interacted with clips from old movies. Although this technique has not caught on, a cable TV series *(Dream On)* occasionally uses it. Some of Woody Allen's films have displayed highly innovative touches *(Play It Again Sam, Zelig, The Purple Rose of Cairo)*, but his films follow traditional structure.

The movie industry has also attempted some "real time" movies, in which the plot incidents play continuously and the span of the story on screen equals the amount of time that the movie plays on screen. *High Noon* (1952) was done this way. In the movie (which plays for 85 minutes), the action begins at about 10:30 in the morning and ends shortly after noon, which is also approximately 85 minutes in the life of Marshall Will Caine (Gary Cooper). TV shows occasionally use this technique, but it flies in the face of film's ability to move about in time and space. However, stories that use real-time strategies to compress the clock of their narrative are often dramatic, and this technique can add energy and focus to a story.

Another experiment was Alfred Hitchcock's *Rope* (1948), which was shot with long takes that played for ten minutes or so. Hitchcock hoped to create a seamless and claustrophobic story. Although the venture was fairly successful, the style of this film, which mainly played in a single set, did not inspire imitation.

Like many writers and teachers, I am interested in discovering new ways to tell motion picture stories. The list of innovative narrative films that have been produced over the years is, however, not long; of these, *Rashomon, Toto le Heros, The Mystery of Rampo, Day for Night, Repulsion, Pulp Fiction,* and *The Singing Detective* were found to have the most appeal. The common thread in these films is the subjective way they tell their stories and how they shift about in time and levels of reality.

I hope that this brief discussion of narrative technique will not discourage writers from seeking new ways to tell stories, but clearly the task is not easy; otherwise, wouldn't something new have been invented by now? While waiting for the Godot of the new narrative form, filmmakers watch experimental and avant-garde films and wonder whether CD-ROM, computers, digital imaging, and interactive video will at last offer new ways to tell stories. Until then, traditional story forms are exploited for all they are worth.

SUMMARY

Blocking involves creating a list of incidents that arrange into a plot. This work begins after the writer has thought about the basic idea and the frame of the story, as well as the story's concept, theme, conflict, backstory, problem, emotional style, and audience. Professional writers often spend hundreds of hours thinking about these values as they work out their stories. Because it is easy to lose the thread of the story during such ruminations, many writers maintain an overview that encapsulates what should be happening in the story. Awareness of the event, the story concept, and the problem can help this overview. It sometimes helps to type these values on a card that is posted nearby as a reminder. A few days spent working out a story armature that expands the story concept with the twists that end the first and second acts is also recommended.

Some writers use the story template and the outline of traditional scenes noted in Figure 3-1 as they block the story. In a general way, the template indicates what happens in each of the three acts and the two twists. The outline of traditional scenes presents at least half of the beats found in most stories. Of course, the details of each beat must be written in the very best way possible.

The plot beats can be written as a prose treatment or as an outline (beat sheet). Either way, the list of plot incidents should provide a beginning-middle-end progression of what generally happens in each of the three acts of the story. Many of the beats outlined will be sequence beats that play for five to fifteen minutes each. Most feature plots contain ten or so sequences. The sequence outline serves as a road map that can spare you from becoming lost in the details of incident, which accumulate with confusing rapidity when the plot is written as bits and scenes.

Three or four sequences are enough to create the strong first-act setup that is essential to drive the story. Unless the first-act setup is cranked with dramatic potential, it is unlikely that the story will survive the long span of Act II.

The hour or so of the second act is less intimidating when you appreciate the role of subplots and the simplicity of most movie stories. Avoid the temptation to fill what may seem like a skimpy plot with action and spectacle. Instead, trust that your characters will develop the subplots and take up the slack. (Subsequent chapters will explain how to make this happen.)

Subplots connect the main characters to secondary players and to thematic concerns that branch off the main storyline. Subplots supply psychological content as they explore the problem and the interior lives of the characters from different perspectives, giving the story emotional and dramatic variation. The love-interest subplot is a useful outlet for thematic concerns. Subplots have a structure that intensifies dramatically as the story plays out. Subplots usually conclude at story's end and are not left dangling.

Most third acts contain one main beat, that being the climactic scene or sequence in which the problem of the story is solved. In most cases, what happens in the climax is synonymous with the event of the story.

The incidents of plot should be logical, motivated, and connected. This linkage, called *continuity,* creates a throughline that builds dramatic intensity and momentum as the story heads toward the climax.

Working out the plot beats can be done with an action-and-reaction approach that is based on how the characters react to verbal or physical provocation. Speed-writing possible incidents of story is another plotting strategy. A third strategy is to cast your story with your favorite actors, who must then be persuaded to accept their roles. Some writers like to back into a story by writing the idea as a half-hour film or as a scene. Writing a short film can provide an overview of the story; writing a scene can tap into the unconscious mind and unleash the energy of characters who dramatize the story. Do not rush through this work, because if your story is flawed, chances are that your script will be flawed as well.

Exercises

Select a feature film to use to answer the questions in this exercise set.

1. Jot down a beat-by-beat summary of the film studied. Note how the action-reaction dynamic develops the beats of the story.
2. How does the film deal with subplots and continuity? Analyze how the subplots are used to fill out the span of the second act.
3. What strategies of time, logic, editing, sound, music, dialogue, and action link the scenes into a story? How much story time passes between the scenes? How does the film create momentum?
4. Work out the story armature that organizes the film.
5. Summarize the first-act setup in the film. How does the setup invest the story with dramatic potential?

(For media that illustrate the points made in this chapter, see Appendix A.)

CHAPTER 4

Scene Structure and the Basic Dramatic Units

The building blocks of a screenplay are sequences, scenes, and bits. Understanding the structures and the dynamics of these units is essential to writing dramatic scripts.

So far we have discussed story, three-act structure, and the dramatic values that expand an idea into a story concept and a plot. This chapter examines how incidents of action and character (called *beats*) form the three basic dramatic units found in all screenplays, namely, the *bit*, the *scene*, and the *sequence*.

Of the three units, bits are the shortest, playing for a minute or so. Next in length are scenes, which generally play for three or four minutes. Finally, bits and scenes combine with each other to form sequences, which are the longest of the three basic dramatic units; they play for five to fifteen minutes in most cases. An act is usually made up of two to four sequences. Typical playing times for all of the dramatic units are depicted in Figure 4-1.[1] The eggs-within-eggs relationship of the various dramatic units is depicted in Figure 4-2. It shows how bits and scenes combine into sequences, which in turn combine into the three acts of a script. Before discussing how the three dramatic units organize and how they accomplish different dramatic tasks, let us first examine the bit, which is the smallest of the three basic dramatic units.

THE BIT AS A DRAMATIC UNIT

A bit can reveal character, communicate theme, establish relationships, and/or advance the plot. Because bits only play for a minute or so, they are more likely to advance the plot than to reveal character, which usually requires more

---

[1]Interestingly, movies are playing longer, according to a survey by *Entertainment Weekly* that was cited in *The Los Angeles Times* (February 19, 1995). For example, the *EW* survey found that in 1932 the average feature played for about 90 minutes. In 1952 average playing time increased to 109 minutes; in 1972 a typical film played for 113 minutes; in 1992, the figure grew to 121 minutes.

THREE-ACT FEATURE	90 TO 120 MINUTES OR SO
Act I	20 to 30 minutes or so
Act II	50 to 60 minutes or so
Act III	20 to 30 minutes or so
Sequence	5 to 15 minutes or so
Scene	3 to 4 minutes or so
Bit	1 minute or so

FIGURE 4-1. Feature film playing times for various dramatic units.

time. The brief playing time of a bit means that it requires little internal structure, other than to begin late and end when it makes its point.

Bits are adaptable to almost any dramatic situation; they can also relate a considerable amount of story in a short time. We see this in *The Verdict* (Shot 37), when Galvin selects potential jurors. This beat could have been written as a scene, but it would have ended up making an obvious point, which is that Galvin is out of shape as a lawyer and out of his league against Ed Concannon. Written as a thirty-five-second bit, the incident as scripted makes this point without slowing the pace of the narrative.

THE SEQUENCE AS A DRAMATIC UNIT

The first thing to note regarding sequences is that each one makes its individual point of plot, relationship, theme, and/or character. As discussed in Chapter 3, a sequence might introduce the problem, the hero, the villain, or some other important aspect of the story. Additionally, each bit and/or scene in the sequence also makes its individual story point. The "double-duty" nature of the three basic dramatic units is clearly shown in *The Verdict*'s opening sequence, which is composed of seven bits that play for a total of seven minutes. As each bit makes its individual story point, they combine to make the overall point of the sequence, which is to introduce Frank Galvin. The seven bits in this sequence also establish the somber tone that sustains throughout the movie, as follows:

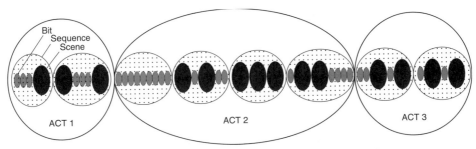

FIGURE 4-2. How three-act screenplays organize into bits, scenes, and sequences.

1. The first bit (under the opening credits) shows Galvin playing pinball. The story point here is to arouse curiosity about why a professional man is wasting his time on a trivial game. (1:22)
2. The second bit shows Galvin hustling a widow in a funeral parlor. The bit presents the Boston frame of the story and shows how Galvin secures clients. (1:09)
3. In the third bit, Galvin circles obituary notices as he washes down a morning doughnut with a jigger of whiskey. The beat advances the plot and reveals more of Galvin's ghoulish law practice. (:40)
4. In the fourth bit, Galvin is expelled from a funeral home for pretending to be a friend of the deceased. (1:35)
5. The fifth bit takes place in Galvin's saloon, where he drinks to blot out the pain of being expelled. (:37)
6. The sixth bit shows Galvin wrecking his office. The beat reveals him to be an alcoholic who is tormented by inner demons. (:45)
7. The final bit in the sequence begins the next morning when Mickey arrives and finds Galvin passed out on the floor. Mickey drags Galvin into the next room and props him up on the couch. The bit ends when the music ends, whereupon Mickey tells Galvin to shape up. The second sequence, which introduces the problem, begins immediately thereafter. (1:10)

As with most sequences, *The Verdict* sequence above builds to a climax that occurs near the end of the beat, when Galvin's torment causes him to wreck his office. Analyzing screenplays in this fashion shows how most of them lay out in an orderly array, with only an occasional "orphan" beat not tucking into one sequence or another. Analyzing a script by breaking it down into a beat-sheet outline provides an overview of how the bits, sequences, and scenes tell the story. Without such a perspective, the writer may be pulled into the narrative or may speed through the read and lose the thread of the analysis. Breaking down a movie or a script this way takes three or four hours, but only a dozen or so works need to be analyzed over time. I recommend using this scheme because it is a sure way to understand how scripts are structured. (Whenever possible, read along with the script as the film plays on video.)

To ensure that you understand how a sequence can be made up entirely of bits, note this example from *Witness* (Shot 73). The eight-minute sequence is mainly plot exposition that explains how Book is taken in by the Amish and how he is nursed by Rachel. The twelve bits have been timed, which is how many writers analyze films and what happens in them. Additionally, to give you a sense of how quickly and easily outlining can be done, the beat summaries are presented exactly as jotted down while I analyzed the script and the movie:

1. Eli drives wagon to Book's car. (:15)
2. Book loaded into the wagon. (:36)
3. Book tended by an Amish healer. Bit reveals the communal nature of the Amish, establishes relationships, addresses thematic value of cooperation, advances plot. (1:37)

4. As healer leaves, he tells Eli that the elders must decide whether Book can stay. The bit advances the plot by setting up a second visit to Book and further reveals the communal nature of the Amish.   (:20)
5. Rachel and Eli roll Book's Volkswagen into the barn so it is hidden from Schaeffer. The bit serves the plot by signaling that the Lapps have committed to hiding Book.   (:20)
6.–9. Four bits of Rachel ministering to Book. They reveal her caring nature and Book's inner torment. They also advance their relationship and touch on the theme.   (2:15)
10. Schaeffer telephones the local sheriff, who is unable to locate Book because the Amish do not use phones. Exposition bit dealing with the plot.   (1:00)
11. Book is visited by the Amish Elders. Reveals character, theme, and relationships, and advances the plot. This bit, which climaxes the sequence, allows Book to remain in Rachel's house.   (1:25)
12. The Amish Elders mutter as they leave the house. Point of the bit: they are uneasy about the fact that Book is hiding among them.   (:25)

Overall, *Witness* employs nine sequences that are made up of a total of seventy bits and scenes to tell its 112-minute story. There will be times when you are unclear about whether a dramatic unit is a bit or a scene (although timing the beat will usually identify whether it is a bit, a scene, or a sequence). You may also be uncertain about which sequence a particular bit or scene serves or where some of the sequences begin and end. Do not fret over this, for what matters is developing a sense of what each beat accomplishes in the story, how it is structured, and how it combines to make the larger point of the sequence.

THE SCENE AS A DRAMATIC UNIT

Scenes, which play longer than bits, run three to four minutes (or longer). Scenes also have internal structure, and they are more likely to deal with emotion. Like bits, scenes combine into sequences. For example, the third sequence of *The Verdict* deals with Galvin's decision to turn down the bishop's settlement offer. This eight-minute sequence is composed of two bits (Shots 24 and 25) and a four-minute scene (Shot 26).[2] The two opening bits set up the scene by first showing Galvin on the phone with his client, Sally Doneghy; in the second bit he visits his client in the hospital, where he takes Polaroid photos that he plans to show to Bishop Brophy. These two bits are followed by a scene in which Galvin refuses the bishop's settlement offer. That rejection climaxes a sequence that tracks the growth of Galvin's conscience until it causes him to turn down the bishop's offer.

Another point to be taken from this sequence is how it illustrates the stinginess of movies when it comes to revealing plot information. Movies

---

[2]This scene has a clearly defined three-part structure, as can be seen in Appendix C (Sequence 3), which briefly analyzes this beat and how it segments.

hoard plot information and release it in small increments needed to sustain interest in the narrative. Movie stories usually do not tip off or discuss what will happen next; appreciating this tightfisted dynamic is essential to writing simple plots with complex characters. Hoarding plot revelations presents a difficult lesson for writers who have yet to learn how much time movies spend developing their characters.

Later, this chapter will present an analysis of a scene, but first we shall discuss working from a plot outline or a treatment that lists the incidents of the narrative. Each of these moments presents a writing task that begins when the writer decides whether a beat should be written as a scene, a bit, or a sequence. Often, the deciding factor is whether the beat will stir the characters emotionally. When this seems to be the case, the beat is usually written as a scene or as a sequence. On the other hand, when a beat seems to deal mainly with plot mechanics and exposition, it is usually written as a bit because such information is less emotional and dramatic. For this reason, bits tend to be kept as brief as possible so that more time can be spent on scenes that create emotion.

Writing bits and scenes is one of the joys of screenwriting. They allow us to clamber out of the trench of thinking out the story and to imagine our characters and settings. Writers slip into their fictive dreams for however long it takes to write the beat—an hour, a day, a week, or more. There is no norm for this; the work takes as long as it takes. Some writers ride an emotional wave when they write a scene; others work with one eye cocked to structure and the internal dynamics that organize and drive a scene. Whichever approach is taken, things happen in scenes that drive them and that create drama.

DYNAMICS OF THE SCENE: CONTENT, STRUCTURE, AND CONFLICT

It is easy enough to say that scenes are driven by conflict and by characters, or that scenes should be dramatic, or that scenes should have shape and substance. When it comes to the fine print of implementing these goals, explanations often end up as a brave injunction that says, "Be creative!" Because it takes more than pluck to write scenes, you will be given specific strategies for developing conflict and emotion, and for creating their mood, style, and structure. These insights are like the wrenches in a mechanic's tool chest: individually, they are modest, and a few of them are downright peculiar. Used together, however, these strategies can help you to create scenes with structure and drama.

Please note that you will be confronting these strategies en masse, which may make them seem daunting. They are not. All except one can be worked out in a few minutes. The single item that must be worked out carefully is the one that determines the point of the scene. Take your time with that task. There is no particular order in which these tools should be used. As often happens, screenwriters reach out for whatever helps to solve the task at hand and to answer the main question that devils writers throughout: What do I want to say in this scene—and am I saying it in the best way?

This is a wide-ranging discussion because scenes are complex, variable, and essential to the success of a script. Scenes also demonstrate the screenwriter's ability to create characters, to put words in their mouths, and to create drama. To guide you through these discussions, scene study is viewed from three perspectives: *scene content, scene structure,* and *scene conflict.* All points noted in the discussion will be illustrated later in this chapter by an analysis of a scene from *The Verdict.*

Scene Content

This scene perspective looks at scenes from four angles: point of the scene, subtext, emotional hits, and the circumstances and details (the "box") of the scene.

Point of the Scene

As noted, stories are made up of a series of beats, each making a dramatic point. Thus, if the first beat of the plot is to introduce General Custer, then the writing task has been defined: find a dramatic way to introduce Custer. Although this point may seem too obvious to mention, *a primary cause of weak scripts is the failure of scenes to make their dramatic point in an unequivocal manner.* When the point of a scene is unclear, the thread of the story can be frayed or broken, causing confusion. This can happen when the writer worries about seeming too "obvious," an attitude which often leads to scenes that are fuzzy and confused. The cure for this is to analyze various films with their scripts in hand. Then, when you hear how actors deliver seemingly "obvious" lines, you should be cured of this worry. "Obvious" scenes work when the writer invests drama and conflict in a beat that clearly makes the dramatic point intended and that moves the story toward its climax. If drama and emotion are present in the writing, trust the actors and other filmmakers to make the scene play.

Scenes go wrong when the thrust of the story and the nature of the characters change, causing the writer to become unsure of what the scene should accomplish. Sometimes the writer is led astray by a character who takes over a scene in a way that does not address the point that should be made. Other scenes drift away from the throughline of the plot because the writer is vague on the purpose of the scene or unsure of how the characters should behave. The intensity demanded of movie stories argues in the strongest possible terms against allowing this to happen. The script should retain dramatic focus from fade-in to fade-out.

When changes occur during scripting, make sure that the plot is reexamined and adjusted carefully. Make sure that the scenes make their intended story points, as stated on the beat sheet. This plot outline is the writer's road map. It aims the story that has been carefully worked out. Therefore, do not write the scene until you are satisfied with the plot and the story point that must be made in the beat. When irresistible ideas pop up, squeeze them hard to see if they truly add to the story. If the notion seems worthwhile, adjust and rethink the entire plot, because such changes can be extremely risky and damaging.

Subtext

Subtext refers to the unspoken meaning of the scene. Subtext is meaning and content that is implied rather than stated directly through dialogue. This content should be worked into every moment of your script. Subtextual content can be indicated by a look, a gesture, a silence, or a vocal tone that conveys sarcasm, contempt, coldness, or any other emotion. Scene study is a good way to learn this value. (Subtext is discussed more fully in Chapter 6, which deals with dialogue and character.)

Emotional Hits

The content of scenes is enriched when characters experience strong emotions. Such "emotional hits" are among the most dramatic moments in films. A typical movie may have only one or two moments of high emotion, or none at all. Spotting opportunities for emotional hits requires tuning in on what the characters are feeling, especially when the dialogue or action swerves toward a painful personal experience. A strong emotional hit occurs in *The Verdict* (Shot 61), when Galvin whines to Laura that he's going to lose the case. She angrily tells him that she cannot invest in failure again. The exchange so unnerves Galvin that he must take refuge in the bathroom to catch his breath, indicating that he has suffered a strong emotional hit. As in this example, the emotional hit should be earned by the ordeal of the drama; otherwise, it may come off as sentimental manipulation that undermines the drama.

Having said this, let me now backtrack and say that there are times when the emotional hit should *not* be expressed, when that emotive force should be retained within the character and *not* released. When a surge of feeling remains bottled up this way, it allows the audience to share the ordeal of the character as he or she silently suffers the emotional burden. For an example of this, see *The Verdict* when the insurance company calls Galvin at his office to reject his settlement offer (Shot 51). Our hero is so distraught by this development that he is again unable to breathe. Here Mamet treats Galvin as a complex human being instead of a robot who has been wound up to do the writer's bidding. Characters who respond as human beings have an inner life and memories. They are tense and emotional because they have been caught up in a major life crisis. Such characters are able to set off emotional sparks.

The "Box" of the Scene

Our final value concerning scene content involves the contents that the screenwriter puts into a scene. If a setting is bland, it is the writer's job to fix it. If the decor is not helping the drama, something better should be imagined. If a character is dozing and inactive, energize this person. Such matters seemed so obvious that I never gave them much thought until Bo Goldman raised this point at a gathering of writers in 1976. He was discussing a writing problem in his script for *One Flew Over the Cuckoo's Nest*. A key scene takes place in the recreation room where Nurse Ratched (Louise Fletcher) holds her group meetings. The location had been used several times earlier, and Goldman's problem was to reuse it for the scene that would send McMurphy (Jack Nicholson) to electroshock. As the filmmakers discussed the scene, director Milos Forman recalled an incident he had seen in a Prague train station when a cigarette dropped into a cuff of a traveler's pants, scorching the man's ankle. The filmmakers devised a similar piece of business in *Cuckoo's Nest* that sent Christopher Lloyd's character screaming out of the room. Lloyd's outburst sets off a chain reaction among the other patients that ends when McMurphy punches one of the guards. This attack prompts the authorities to send McMurphy to electroshock, which fries his brain.

Goldman used the incident to advise the writers in his audience to think of their scenes as a "box" into which they can put whatever makes the scene work—as long as it is real and truthful. Ask whether the setting for your scene is dramatically useful. Could the time of day or night affect the scene? Could the weather be a factor? Are the characters in an emotional state that could create drama? Could something be added to the "box" that might dramatize the scene? That "something" might involve furniture, clothing, lighting, a view, a prop, a machine, an animal, equipment, or whatever jacks up the drama.

Goldman's "box" idea advises writers to create simple, available props and situations that energize the drama and open up writing opportunities. In the hotdog scene from *Witness* (Shot 52B), for example, Book immediately begins to scarf down his food, unaware that Rachel and Samuel have paused to say grace. He must wait awkwardly, his mouth full of food, as they bow their heads to pray. Thus the "box" of the scene is expanded by the rush of the fast-food joint and by the prayer in a manner that creates drama. In *The Terminator* (Shot 232), the truck that runs over the cyborg could have been a bread truck; instead, it was a huge oil tanker that added drama to the story. These two examples present useful advice: when a character, setting, prop, or piece of business is in the way, inactive, or somehow not working for the scene, eliminate or change it. The scene is the writer's box, and it is the writer's task to make sure it contains items that add to the drama.

Scene Structure

This discussion deals with how the scene elements are assembled and how long they play. It also deals with certain moments that occur in most scenes. Naturally, our standard generality applies: The following is true in most but not all cases. After learning the traditional approaches to screenwriting, feel free to break the mold and invent something new. In the meantime, the following notions, which have worked for the past century or so, are available.

Organization

Most scenes can be divided into three segments that are analogous to the beginning, middle, and ending of the overall story. The point of the scene is usually made at the end of the third segment.

Scenes segment when a line of dialogue or an action enlivens or diverts the narrative with a surge of conflict or energy that may be barely noticeable. For example, *When Harry Met Sally* contains a scene between Carrie Fisher and Meg Ryan (Sally) that takes place in a bookstore. Fisher tells Ryan that a man is watching her. Ryan recognizes the man (Billy Crystal, as Harry) from their college days, but doubts if he would remember her. Her words are barely out of her mouth when Crystal enters the frame and says, "Sally Albright!" Harry *does* remember Sally, and the surprise recognition intensifies the scene and bounces it in a new direction. This moment is the first of two twists in the scene. The second segment of the scene, in a restaurant where Harry and Sally reminisce about their lives, ends when Sally recalls playing a game of "I spy" with a friend's child. The child noticed a young family on an outing and said, "I spy a family." For inexplicable reasons, this remark struck a painful chord in Sally, causing her to realize that her marriage was an empty, loveless sham. Not long afterward, her marriage ends. This moment of revelation opens the third segment of the scene, in which Harry and Sally's love affair begins.

Please note that the preceding scene plays in two locations (the bookstore and the restaurant), demonstrating how a single scene can play out in multiple locations. The coming together of Michael Douglas and Glenn Close in *Fatal Attraction* is a scene that plays in three locations: (1) the business conference where they meet; (2) the rain-drenched sidewalk outside the office building; (3) a restaurant, where their affair is launched.

The structure of a scene can be complicated by intercutting it with another scene or with other bits. Such mixing can create suspense and visual stimulation and/or present parallel action that conveys conflict, irony, humor, and so on. Example from *The Verdict* (Shot 47): as Mickey and Laura talk about what happened in the Lillibridge case, the story intercuts bits that show Galvin meeting with the judge and, later, phoning the insurance company to avoid a trial.

The Make-Point Moment

The make-point moment occurs when the point of the scene is made. In Shot 26 of *The Verdict*, the point of the scene is made when Galvin turns down Bishop Brophy's settlement offer. The make-point moment is crucial, for, as previously noted, *the scene must make the dramatic point listed in the plot outline.* When scenes fail in that task, the story becomes vague and loses drama. In most cases, momentum and intensity benefit when the make-point moment occurs at the end of the scene. The make-point moment also signals that the scene is over and that it is time to move on to the next beat. *Inability to follow this advice is a major cause of script failure.*

Length of the Scene

Scenes should begin late and end early. Most feature scenes play for three to four minutes, although occasionally they may play twice as long as that. One of the study scenes used in my class is the father-daughter reunion from *Running on Empty*, which spends seven minutes with the two characters as they talk in a restaurant.

As noted earlier, scenes play longer than bits because they present the feelings of the characters. As a result, scenes must be given enough time to bring the characters up to speed emotionally. Learning to cut through or to minimize this emotional "warm-up" is one of the keys to starting a scene late and ending it early. For an example of how this is done, see *The Verdict* (Shot 60), when Mickey grills Dr. Thompson (Galvin's expert witness). Harsh questioning is already underway when the scene begins. Although television scenes generally play for two minutes or so, they also follow the internal structure and dynamics found in feature scenes.

The "Button" of the Scene

Some scenes begin with a line or two of chit-chatty dialogue or physical business (feeding the cat, mixing a drink) that allows the audience to tune in on what is happening in the scene. This is followed by a moment, often referred to as the "button," where the substance of the scene is addressed. In most cases this moment occurs within the first few seconds of the scene. An example of a button moment that starts a scene can be found in *The Verdict* (Shot 30), when Concannon meets with his legal team. The scene begins with Concannon's line about "For want of a shoe a horse was lost." This bantering continues for a few more lines before Concannon informs everyone that their case comes to trial on January twelfth. This announcement is the button that fires up the legal juggernaut that Concannon plans to use against Galvin. The button also tells the writer when the scene has begun.

Sometimes a scene is concluded with a flare that adds a dramatic fillip. This can be a line of dialogue, or it can be an action, such as snapping a pencil or slamming a door. See *Sleepless in Seattle* (Shot 70) when Annie bursts into her brother's office to vent her confusion over Sam. After serving as her sounding board, brother Dennis (*Frasier's* David Hyde Pierce) tight-lips his final line ("Any time") in a way that puts a comic kicker on the end of the scene. There is a comic button in (surprisingly) *The Terminator* (Shot 158), when the cyborg smoothes its hair after completing Exacto-knife surgery on its damaged eyeball.

Scene Conflict

Conflict drives scenes and gives them shape and dramatic interest. Conflict feeds off the situation and the characters. Weak characters who lack motivation and who are emotionally limp generate weak conflict. Writing dynamic characters is discussed in the next chapter, but let it be noted here that characters are energized by making them comical, sexy, egotistical, unpleasant, aggressive, eccentric, or whatever will intensify their internal life and motivation. If characters lack passion or interest, bring in replacements who are more dramatic and energetic. When scenes contain situations and characters that are dynamic, the strategies and perspectives examined below can be useful.

The Chase-and-Escape, Chase-and-Capture Dynamic

Scenes often involve one character pressuring another to do something that he or she does not want to do. For example, a scene might involve pressuring a character to leave town, to give up a love interest, or to sell the farm. If the character refuses to yield on the point, the scene is said to follow a chase-and-*escape* dynamic. This is because the character "escapes" doing what the other character wishes. If the character is persuaded or coerced into accepting an action or relationship, then the scene follows a chase-and-*capture* dynamic. In the *Fatal Attraction* scene noted above in conjunction with scene structure and organization, Close chases and captures Douglas, and he ends up spending the night with her. If he had resisted her and gone home instead, the scene would have followed a chase-and-escape dynamic. Although this may appear to be a minor perspective on how scenes operate, it is a small confidence-builder that takes but a minute or so to work out.

Polarity of the Scene

Another aid for figuring out what happens in a scene is to determine whether it should begin on a positive note and end on a negative note, or whether it should begin negatively and end positively. Determining the polarity of a scene can help you to figure out its emotional direction. For a positive-to-negative scene, check out *The Terminator* (Shot 204) when we realize that Sarah is not talking to her mother. Instead, she is speaking to the cyborg, who is imitating the voice of the now-dead mother. The scene follows a positive-to-negative direction because it seems to begin on a relatively pleasant note and ends badly because of the death of Sarah's mother.

A negative-to-positive scene occurs in *Sleepless in Seattle* (Shot 27), when Sam first talks to the radio psychologist. The polarity shift occurs because Annie's attitude changes from cynicism (negative) to tearful interest in Sam as she listens to him over her car radio (positive).

Clearly, positive and negative are relative terms. For example, the scene from *Sleepless in Seattle* noted above is not especially upbeat, yet it ends on a note that is more positive than when it began. For this reason the scene has a negative-to-positive dynamic.

A polarity shift can occur when the mood of the scene changes from friendly to loving, reserved to accepting, unpleasant to cruel, or tense to angry—the polarity shift is *relative*. During most scenes, conflict is responsible for the polarity shift, because contention changes the beat's energy, attitude, or emotion. When you have a sense of which way your scene will shift polarity, it is easier to intensify the conflict and the scene's emotional direction.

ANALYSIS OF A SCENE FROM THE VERDICT

The scene tools presented above are not academic busywork; they are strategies for figuring out and dramatizing a scene. Keep in mind that scenes can be analyzed in many ways. Producers might think about story, cost, and audience appeal. Cinematographers might be concerned with how to tell the story through images. Directors might think about how to dramatize the beat, how it fits the rest of the story, and the like. Actors study scenes for what the characters want and how they relate to the other characters.

Because writers must imagine the entire movie, we think about all the above. To help organize our thinking, we develop a reviewing posture of some kind, so that we can evaluate and understand our work and that of other writers. *The Verdict* scene that follows (Shot 38) presents one such analyzing scheme that uses polarity, structure, "box," and other values discussed in this chapter. These points have been applied to the Galvin-Sweeney-Concannon scene that follows, which occurs shortly after Galvin turns down Bishop Brophy's settlement. The meeting is called so the judge in the case (Judge Sweeney) and the opposing lawyer (Ed Concannon) can talk Galvin out of taking the case to trial.

The scene is set up by a preceding bit. As scripted, Shot 37 has Galvin watching the courthouse from a nearby bar, deliberately killing time so he will be late for his meeting with Concannon and the judge. This bit was revised during shooting so that Galvin is seen not as a crafty lawyer with a plan but as a fool who behaves carelessly. To dramatize this, Galvin is shown playing pinball with such glee that he loses track of time. As in the script, Galvin is drinking whiskey—hardly the nourishment needed to confront Ed Concannon. When Galvin realizes the hour, he hurries off. Rewriting the bit in this manner presents an unpromising beginning for Galvin's meeting.

The pinball game is augmented by a nonscripted transitional bit that shows Galvin ascending the stair of the courthouse to the judge's chambers. After a squirt of breath freshener, Galvin enters and the scene begins. The pinball game and the transition to the judge's office play for about one minute, long enough to set up the scene and to prepare the audience for Galvin's poor behavior:

```
38 INT. JUDGE SWEENEY'S CHAMBERS - DAY

JUDGE SWEENEY, a florid man in his sixties, sitting in
shirtsleeves eating bacon and eggs off of a hotel service
on a tray, talking conspiratorially with Ed Concannon, who
is drinking coffee, seated across the desk.  The two are
obviously old friends.  The sound of a door opening.  They
turn their heads to the door.

ANGLE - P.O.V.

Galvin standing in the door.

                    JUDGE (voice over)
            You're late, Mr. Galvin.
```

He enters the room.   CAMERA FOLLOWS him as he sits next to
Concannon.

                        GALVIN
           Yessir.   I'm sorry.

                         JUDGE
           Why is that?

                        GALVIN
           I was held up.

Concannon smiles and extends his hand.

                       CONCANNON
               Ed Concannon.

                        GALVIN
           Frank Galvin. We've met before.

As the Judge starts to speak Galvin cannot help looking at
Concannon out of the corner of his eye.

                         JUDGE
              Let's do some business.

ANGLE - P.O.V. GALVIN

Concannon, brisk, expensive-looking, tanned, huge gold
watch, custom-made suit.

                    JUDGE (voice over)
              They tell me that no bargain ever
              was completed other than quickly
              when both parties really cared to
              make a deal.

Concannon feels Galvin's eye on him.

ANGLE - THE JUDGE, CONCANNON, GALVIN

                         JUDGE
              Now, have you boys tried to resolve your
              little difficulty because that certainly
              would save the Commonwealth a lot of time
              and bother.

                              GALVIN
                    This is a complicated case,
                    your Honor. . . .

                              JUDGE
                    I'm sure it is, Frank: and let
                    me tell you something. If we
                    find it so complex, how in the
                    hell you think you're going to
                    make a jury understand it?
                    (smiles at Galvin)
                    See my point? Let's talk a
                    minute. Frank: what will you
                    and your client take right now
                    this very minute to walk out
                    of here and let this damn
                    thing drop?

                              GALVIN
                    My client can't walk, your
                    Honor.

Comment: The meeting opens on a negative note because Sweeney and Concannon are annoyed at Galvin for arriving late. Judge Sweeney is the dominant character in the scene, for he must broker the settlement; he also experiences the most emotion. The film includes Sweeney's opening ad lib ("I met him at the club the other night"); the line suggests that Sweeney and Concannon are insider cronies who have been chatting as they wait for Galvin to show up. The line also smoothes the continuity of Galvin's late entrance and makes him appear like an outsider to be finessed by Sweeney and Concannon.

The "button" that begins the scene occurs when the judge says, "Let's do some business." The scene quickly assumes its chase-and-escape dynamic when the judge and Concannon pressure Galvin to settle the case.

The logic of the first part of the scene sees Galvin live up to his shabby reputation when he makes a tactless remark about his client's inability to walk. There is a five-second silent reaction to Galvin's remark, which is the twist that bounces the scene into its second segment.

                              JUDGE
                    I know full well she can't,
                    Joe. You see the Padre on
                    your way out and he'll punch
                    your ticket. You follow me?
                    I'm trying to help you.

```
              CONCANNON
     Your Honor, Bishop Brophy and
     the Archdiocese have offered
     plaintiff two hundred and ten
     thousand dollars.


                    JUDGE
     Huh!


                 CONCANNON
     My doctors didn't want a
     settlement at any price.  They
     wanted this cleared up in
     court.  They want their
     vindication.  I agree with
     them.  But for today the offer
     stands.  Before we begin the
     publicity of a trial. For
     today only.
                 (beat)
     When I walk out that door the
     offer is withdrawn.
                 (turns to Galvin)
     As long as you understand
     that.
                 (beat)
     It's got to be that way.


                 GALVIN
     We are going to try the case.
A beat.
Galvin fumbles for a cigarette. The three sit in silence.
```

Comment: Galvin's last line ("We are going to try the case") registers powerfully with Concannon and Sweeney, causing another five-second silent reaction. Mamet notes the importance of the moment with the stage directions ("The three sit in silence") that follow Galvin's decision. The moment creates the second twist in the scene by shifting the story toward contention. To forestall this negative drift, Sweeney swings into action:

```
              JUDGE (incredulous)
     That's it . . . ?
                 (beat)
     Come on, guys . . . life is
     too short. . . .
                 (beat)
                 (MORE)
```

                    JUDGE (CONT'D)
          You tell me if you're playing
          'chicken,' or you mean it.
                    (beat; turns to
                    Galvin)
          Frank: I don't think I'm
          talking out of school, but I
          just heard someone offer you
          two hundred grand . . . and
          that's a lot of money . . .
          and if I may say, you haven't
          got the best of records.

                    GALVIN
          . . . things change.

                    JUDGE
          . . . that's true. Sometimes
          they change, sometimes they
          don't. Now, I remember back to
          when you were disbarred . . .

                    GALVIN
          I wasn't disbarred, they
          dropped the pro . . .

                    JUDGE
          And it seems to me, a fella's
          trying to come back, he'd take
          this settlement, and get a
          record for himself.
                    (beat)
          I myself would take it and run
          like a thief.

                    GALVIN
          I'm sure you would.

The Judge turns, unbelieving that Galvin has patronized
and insulted him. He controls himself.

                    JUDGE
          Hm.
               (beat; checking book)
          We have the date set? Next
          Thursday. Good.

> (smiles)
> See you boys in court.

The Verdict, written by David Mamet, 1982
Playing time: 4:16

Comment: Galvin's line "I'm sure you would [take the money and run like a thief]" makes the point of the scene because it represents Galvin's rejection of the final settlement offer. By implying that Sweeney is a thief, Galvin adds to the conflict, for now he must contend with the most powerful lawyer in town and a hostile judge as well. So that the magnitude of what Galvin has done registers on the audience, the final shot lingers on Galvin as he sits alone in the judge's chambers.

CRITIQUE OF THE GALVIN-SWEENEY-CONCANNON SCENE

The scene requires Galvin to make an "or else" decision. This moment of choice occurs when Concannon warns Galvin to settle before he walks out the door, *or else* the case will go to trial. Dramatic writing often forces characters to make difficult choices such as this. As is typical of many scripted scenes, this beat might not be appreciated unless the reader senses the dramatic tension that the writer has pumped into it. As discussed later in this book, in Chapter 7, tension often raises a powerful dramatic question—will Sarah and Reese destroy the cyborg? Will Galvin win the case? Tension also shows within each scene through conflict that inflames the character relationships and the dramatic circumstances of the scene.

The dramatic tension in *The Verdict* springs from the backstory and Galvin's bitterness about his betrayal during the Lillibridge scandal. This experience causes Galvin to reject Bishop Brophy's settlement offer and puts him on a collision course with Ed Concannon. Galvin's rejection neatly and inextricably entwines the inner and outer problems of the story in a way that causes the audience to worry whether the hero will survive his ordeal. There is also tension within the scene because of Galvin's decision to try the case. Initially, the judge and Concannon look at this as an empty threat because they know of Galvin's lowly status as a lawyer and his scandalous past. As a result of this backstory, the judge and Concannon have no intention of letting Galvin shake them down for a larger settlement. Their plan is to nudge Galvin into avoiding a trial, but if he refuses, they will skin him in court and he will get nothing. Although Galvin needs the money, he follows his instincts, believing that he can defeat Concannon and regain his life by standing up for his client. Because Concannon and Sweeney are unaware of this agenda, they are unprepared for Galvin's intransigence.

The tension caused by these dynamics is exacerbated by Galvin's late arrival, which annoys the judge and Concannon because they are important men who do not appreciate being kept waiting by a boozy lawyer. The script ratchets down the dramatic tension in a way that convinces the audience that Frank Galvin is a fool to defy the Catholic archdiocese, the insurance company, the judge, and Ed Concannon. The David-and-Goliath incongruity of this conflict reflects solid dramatizing that sums up our advice on creating a strong setup: *Match the hero against an opponent who is so powerful that there seems to be no way for the protagonist to win.*

Throughout, the tone of the meeting is controlled and swift—exactly what one expects of skillful lawyers. Although there is no shouting or histrionics, there is cunning and menace hidden beneath the smooth talk. To detect this content, imagine how David Mamet might have created this scene, perhaps recalling a personal experience in which he saw smooth operators finesse a sucker. Such a memory would give the writer a sense of how such meetings operate. The dialogue in the scene has an almost casual tone that seems to lack emotional wallop. However, when the text is examined closely and imagined, which is how scripts that are green-lighted for production are studied, nuances of contention squeeze the characters and create drama. Galvin's backstory bitterness surfaces and turns the scene into a pressure vessel of conflict when Sweeney mentions Galvin's near-disbarment. The remark, perhaps meant to intimidate, backfires when the hero snaps back that he was not disbarred. This is the only time in the story that Galvin directly refers to the Lillibridge case. His terse retort dramatically understates the depth of his feeling on this matter. For his part, Galvin never mentions being the fall guy in Lillibridge, for to do so would make him sound whiny. To spare the hero such diminishment, other characters comment on Galvin's connection to Lillibridge. This is a crafty writing strategy that is worth remembering.

The scene not only makes its point, but it does so in a way that alienates the judge, a development that will make Galvin's task more difficult. Galvin's line implying Sweeney is a thief is so abrasive that it was not necessary to hype the moment by having Sweeney smile as he exits his chambers, as called for in the stage direction. Even so, the instruction tips the reader that Sweeney will have his shot at Galvin when they meet in court. (This is an example of writing slightly "fat" stage directions to ensure that the reader does not miss the intent of the scene.)

Character Points Made in the Scene

The scene logically combines plot and character because the judge acts like the insider he is, the "Prince of Darkness" (Concannon) stays above the fray, and Galvin behaves in a manner that befits his shoddy reputation. This sets up Sweeney and Concannon as they behave like charter members of the establishment's old boy network. Their smug coziness annoys Galvin, who sees the two men as the personification of the establishment that he resents because of Lillibridge. Galvin's lingering pain over this incident simmers deep within his unconscious, bubbling up as anger during the scene.

The legacy of Lillibridge causes Galvin to behave like a man seeking what he *wants* rather than what he *needs* to deal with his pain. From this perspective,

Galvin's *need* is to regain trust in the law and to believe in himself. Galvin's *want* is to get even with the establishment for betraying him. By pursuing what he wants, Galvin follows the wisdom of his heart rather than his brain, instinct instead of reason. This is a common tack in movies that (somewhat miraculously) always seems to work out for the best. It is not until the third act, when all seems lost, that Galvin combines thought and passion to realize his potential as a lawyer. This happens after he refuses to quit, locates the admitting nurse, masterfully presents her testimony, and wins the case. During the drama, the hero suffers bitterly, fights the lonely fight, and earns a sweet victory by solving both the internal and the external problems of the story. The drama thus tracks the struggle of Galvin's return to grace. The hero's rebirth is what the story is really about. It is a perspective that makes *The Verdict* a portrayal of human redemption and not just another court case à la Perry Mason.

Content of the Scene: Unzipping the Characters

Although it contains exposition and backstory, the scene mainly deals with *emotion* and *conflict*, as when the judge tells Galvin, ". . . and if I may say, you haven't got the best of records." Although the remark is annoying, Galvin controls his feelings. Another emotional hit occurs when Galvin tells the judge, "I'm sure you would [take the money and run like a thief]." To ensure that the reader notices this moment, Mamet's stage direction states: "The judge turns, unbelieving that Galvin has patronized and insulted him. He controls himself." Although these two examples keep a lid on emotional display, scenes can be more effusive, as in Shot 159 of *The Terminator*, when Reese expresses rage while being interrogated by a police psychologist.

These examples show characters who have been emotionally "unzipped" in ways that expose their inner feelings. Often characters can be primed for an emotional reaction when they have experienced painful life experiences. Juliette Lewis's character in *Natural Born Killers* illustrates the type when she encourages men to flirt with her so she can attack them. Her twisted pathology, based on childhood molestation memories, makes Lewis's character a potent source of drama and conflict.

Movie scenes, like moments in real life, can suddenly turn emotional when a casual remark, a silence, a gesture, or an action causes characters to react. This happened during a recent script conference when I asked a writer about her research on SIDS (crib death), the topic of her story. The question blundered into a painful memory because, as the writer tearfully explained, her baby brother died of this syndrome. Although embarrassed by her outburst, the writer drew comfort from Robert Frost's observation: "No tears in the writer, no tears in the reader. No surprise for the writer, no surprise for the reader."

To create scenes with dramatic content, writers often become so involved with their stories that they share the emotional ordeal of the characters. Such empathetic responses enable writers to relive the scene and to locate an emotional thread that can be pulled until it unravels the characters. Once inside, we explore, reveal, and invent as we wish. Interestingly, even when our explorations discover truths about the characters, this backstory is usually stated briefly, to avoid slowing the momentum of the story.

A skillful example of how writers slip in emotion can be found in *Witness* (Shot 93K), when Eli Lapp instructs the hero on how to milk a cow. When the lesson goes poorly, Eli chides Book by asking if he has ever "had his hands on a teat before." Book responds (grimly), "Not one this big." The remark causes Eli to laugh, which sets the two men at ease and lets us glimpse each one's inner being. Small, human moments such as these enable audiences to form positive or negative attitudes toward the characters.

Juicing scenes with emotion and conflict is not the only way to add content to scenes, for it can also be done with *thoughtfulness,* as in Shot 65 of *The Verdict.* In this courtroom scene, Concannon discredits kindly old Dr. Thompson in an especially nasty manner. This cruelty clearly marks Concannon as the villain, which was part of what Mamet had in mind when he wrote this scene.

Scene content can also be fired up by presenting a dramatic *context* that adds interest, as in the opening of *The Verdict,* when Mickey discovers Galvin passed out on the floor. The drunken spectacle presents a context that causes Mickey to denounce Galvin. In *My Family, Mi Familia,* a naked child suddenly presents himself to the WASPy future in-laws whose daughter is marrying into a Hispanic family. The moment is both comical and dramatic because, as the two families are attempting to get together, the boy's father (recently released from prison) is attempting to bond with his son. The double richness of the context creates drama in what could have been a cliché scene.

In addition to emotion, conflict, thoughtfulness, and context, writers use *exposition* to enrich scenes. This approach is evident in *The Verdict* scene analyzed above, when Judge Sweeney's line goads Galvin: "Now, I remember back to when you were disbarred. . . ." Galvin reacts angrily to this provocation because it touches the raw nerve that dominates his backstory.

Although most stories require expositional scenes, tread lightly on this point, because when too much time is spent installing the girders of plot, the story may detach from the characters and become plot-heavy. Plotty stories spend so much time setting up and justifying what happens that the characters lose focus and lack emotion. Part of story sense is knowing how to simplify scripts that are clanky with plot contrivances and explanations that labor to sell a yarn that is too complicated and/or lacks credibility. *Total Recall, The Firm, Backdraft, Crimson Tide, Lock Up,* and *Far and Away* illustrate. Of course, here again, I am making a judgment call, for what seems like an elegant plot to one person might seem messy or weak to another.

To sharpen your views on this topic, write one-page summaries of a dozen successful movies that have employed complicated plots and then study the summaries. *Paths of Glory, The Shawshank Redemption, The Guns of Navarone, Bullitt, The Professionals, Paper Moon, Moonstruck, Widow's Peak, The African Queen, The Sting,* and *The Day of the Jackal* illustrate splendid plots that are worth considering. To repeat earlier advice: There is often a clear action-reaction connection between major incidents that causes the characters to interact. This dynamic shows in *Witness* (Shot 34), when Book informs Schaeffer that an Amish boy saw the murder in the train station. Book's revelation leads to an attempt on his life that connects the story to renegade cops. Although this plotting is easily followed, it is also unpredictable as it bounces the story in a menacing direction that creates tension and drama.

Scenes also acquire content when they are charged with *action,* which can range from two people settling into a picnic in the park to showing the destruction of a village by a tank. *Sleepless in Seattle* (Shot 18) added action content by giving Walter (Bill Pullman) an allergy; there is an action scene in *Unforgiven* when Gene Hackman's sheriff dares Saul Rubinek's journalist to play gunfighter; in Shot 91 of *The Terminator,* the cyborg destroys a disco in one of the bloodiest scenes that I can recall. In each example, varying degrees of action add dramatic content to the scenes.

Finally, it should be noted that scenes should not build content with false emotion and sentimentality. Good writing wrings *earned emotion* from the characters by setting up dramatic moments that are logical, yet unexpected. Earned emotion puts the characters through an emotional ordeal, places them in conflict, exposes their secrets, or in some way makes them earn whatever emotion occurs in the scene. This happens in *The Verdict* (Shot 40), when Dick Doneghy (portrayed by James Handy) confronts Galvin in the courthouse. Doneghy, angry because Galvin did not consult with him before turning down the bishop's settlement offer, delivers an impassioned aria that is based on a lifetime of betrayal by bosses and politicians.

These strategies for beefing up scene content echo advice that writer-producer William Blinn (*Brian's Song, Roots*) once offered to my class. Blinn mentioned that when scripts are submitted to the shows he supervises, he sometimes marks them with an "MTBH" notation. MTBH is Blinn's way of telling the writer that there is "more to be had" from story and script. MTBH is a handy admonition that asks the writer to rewrite the scene using conflict, humor, action, thoughtfulness, business, emotion, or whatever might add drama to the beat. Writers use their sense of story to invest scenes with the values discussed above. These strategies are pursued until the beat is as perfect as possible, so there is no MTBH.

Conflict

The conflict in the study scene is primed by having Galvin show up late, which annoys Sweeney and Concannon. They feel, with justification, that Galvin is using cheap tactics to increase his settlement. They do not realize that he has a deeper agenda. There is a subtext to the scene because Sweeney and Concannon are not overjoyed about dealing with a man of Galvin's sorry reputation. Galvin senses their attitude, and the irritation it produces in him leads him to make clumsy remarks about his client's inability to walk and the judge's character.

The conflict causes the scene to follow a positive-to-negative flow as the three men fail to agree on a settlement. This is tied to the chase-and-escape dynamic that occurs because Concannon and Sweeney are unable to pressure Galvin into a settlement.

Directorial Influences

Director Sidney Lumet did a splendid job with this scene, relying on a good script and gifted actors who were allowed to tell the story through their characters (the subtle hand of the director was all but invisible throughout the movie). The camera was unobtrusive but was in place to record emotions. Lumet added the long silence at the end of the scene, when Sweeney dons his judicial robes before exiting; otherwise, he shot the scene more or less as Mamet wrote it.

The script does not explain how Concannon will exit, but this is a simple staging problem, which Lumet solved by having Concannon pause at the door and look back at Galvin in a way that says, "A nobody such as yourself should have taken our offer." Most actors and directors realize that some sort of a kicker can be invented during shooting that will put a concluding flourish on the end of the scene, if needed. For such reasons it is not always necessary to include these ending moments in the stage directions if the dramatic point is strongly made.

Finally, Lumet handled the Galvin-Sweeney-Concannon scene (and all others in the film) cleanly. The beat made its point and combined with others into a movie that holds up under intense scrutiny. I have used this movie as a model of mainstream filmmaking that tells a complex story of the law and personal redemption without theatrical excess or false emotion.

BLOCKING: ANOTHER DEFINITION

So far we have used the term *blocking* to describe how the various dramatic beats are set forth in an outline or treatment. *Blocking* also has a second meaning that refers to *the movement of the actors and the action within the scene.* Blocking in this context refers to how the filmmakers work out how the actors and the camera will move and how the movement helps to tell the story. Gaffer's tape is affixed to the stage floor to mark the exact spot where each actor is to stand to produce a particular moment. When they "hit their mark" this way, the actors will be in the correct spots for prepositioned camera, lighting, and sound equipment to record the moment. Long before this happens, however, writers imagine how their characters move about in every beat of the story and how they interact with the room and the other characters. In this way, blocking the scene in imagination moves our work beyond conjuring characters who enter a room in a master shot and then turn to stone. If the scene imagined by the writer has visual possibilities, this vision has a chance to show up in the script and to inspire the actors and other filmmakers.

The Verdict scene we have been discussing illustrates how blocking and cinematography (by Andrzej Bartkowiak) work together. The scene opens with a wide-angle establishing shot that shows the audience the layout of Sweeney's office as well as the two characters who are in it. A few seconds later, Galvin arrives and is immediately scolded by Sweeney for being late. Then Concannon stands and extends his hand, catching Galvin at an awkward moment as he is removing his overcoat and juggling his briefcase. Galvin's unease continues when Sweeney launches the settlement discussion without offering to store Galvin's things or get him coffee. This blocking requires Galvin to stack his overcoat and briefcase on his lap. The hero does not respond well to these slights, which will contribute to his poor behavior at key moments later in the scene. Except for one brief close-up that shows Galvin's discomfort, the first segment of the scene is done in a wide-angle shot that frames the three characters.

The first major camera move occurs on Galvin's remark about his client's being unable to walk, which triggers a cut from the three-shot to close-ups of Sweeney and Concannon that register their negative reaction to Galvin's remark.

The second segment of the scene consists of medium shots of Galvin and Concannon. Note that Galvin is filmed at a slightly down angle, which diminishes him and encourages the audience to feel that he is weak. The down angle on Galvin has been used before (Shots 5, 6, 24, and elsewhere) to suggest that God is looking down on Galvin, judging his behavior. It is through subtle camera work such as this that filmmakers draw audiences into a story.

The twist that ends the second segment of the scene occurs when Galvin announces that he intends to fight the case. The moment is signaled by another round of close-ups and stone silence. The image then cuts to a wide-angle three-shot that favors Sweeney as he stands and moves to the front of his desk. This camera move and the blocking suggest a change of energy in the scene as Sweeney tries a new tactic—false bonhomie in which Galvin is suddenly "one of the guys." The chortling Sweeney asks if Galvin is playing chicken or if he intends to fight the case. The question causes another five-second silence that confirms Galvin's hard-nosed attitude. At this point the coffee business pays off when the Judge steps close to Galvin to pour him a cup. Almost with a wink, Sweeney confides that if someone offered him a fat settlement, he'd "take the money and run like a thief." Galvin's response ("I'm sure you would") makes the point of the scene because it represents a rejection of Concannon's final settlement offer. Note that the tightest angle in the scene belongs to a full-frontal head shot of Galvin when he speaks his "thief" line; the close-up of his eyes communicates the depth of Galvin's feeling.

After a final round of close-ups while this news sinks in, the scene reverts to the original wide-angle shot that shows first the judge and then Concannon as they exit, leaving Galvin alone in the room. The final image is a wide-angle shot that down-angles on Galvin as he mutters, "Dumb! Dumb! Dumb!" This moment gives the scene a concluding kicker that suggests the gravity of Galvin's decision.

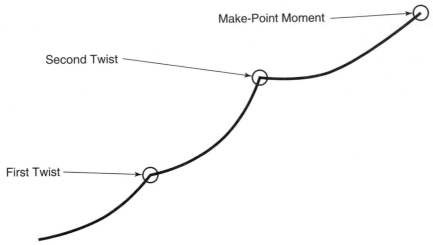

FIGURE 4-3. Structure of a typical scene.

Scene Structure

The four-minute scene from *The Verdict* discussed above follows standard structure. As shown in Figure 4-3, the diagram presents two twists and the moment when the point of the scene is made. As mentioned, the two twists form a three-part scene structure that is analogous to how most stories divide into three acts. The structural plan in Figure 4-3 asks you to rough out the two segmentation points and the story point made by the scene you are writing. Just as the story armature can be used to rough out the twists that end the first and second acts, you can easily work out the twists that segment your scene into its parts, whatever their number. Working out the twists can be done quickly, usually in five or ten minutes. There are usually changes and adjustments during writing, or you may decide to scrap the original scene and write something different. Even so, the diagram provides a work plan that can clarify what happens in the scene and what needs to be written. Although this approach to scene construction may seem overly complicated, it falls into place easily and offers a pattern and a game plan for writing scenes.

Also, as mentioned, not all scenes will follow this pattern—some may have two parts, and some may even have four or more. Whatever the number of segments, the diagram and the other strategies mentioned above conserve energy and reaffirm the point to be made in the scene.

Applying the Scene Plan to the Sport Widow Story

To demonstrate how the diagram and the strategies work, let us apply them to one of the plot incidents in the sports widow idea. Say, for example, the scene to be written involves Mom's decision to visit the health club. In such a case, our first task might involve whether to write this beat as a scene or as a bit. Because Mom's decision is important—it is when she begins to take charge of her life—the incident deals with a major emotional moment that probably should be written as a scene. Why? Experience. Intuition, and my sense of story. Fifty writers would develop the beat in at least as many ways, or they might skip over the incident and invent something different. Here, however, a decision is needed and the scene diagram helps to make it. Common sense suggests that because of her personal history and because of her desperate family situation, Mom's decision would be emotionally charged, which also suggests that this beat be written as a scene.

Imagine that Mom is talking to Vera, the woman who invited her to the health club. If our instinct is that the scene will shift from negative to positive, we might begin the beat by having the two women argue (negative). Because Mom will decide to visit the club, we would dramatize the scene in a positive direction. This could mean brightening the conflict with humor. If, on the other hand, we went from positive to negative on this beat, the exchange could begin with flattering awe on Vera's part over Mom's strength, then the tone of the scene could shift to talk about the urgency of getting Mom into shape and having her take charge of her life if she wishes to save her marriage.

Working from these simple beginnings, the next step would be to try out possibilities that segment the scene. For example, the first twist could occur when Vera gets Mom to drop her "happy" mask and to talk honestly about her life. The second twist could be Vera asking Mom if she wants to do something about her life. The question could cause fear and spluttering that ends up with Mom saying that she is afraid. The make-point moment of the scene occurs when Vera tells Mom to put up or shut up: she can go to the gym and make life happen *for* her or she can continue her present course, where life is happening *to* her. It is not necessary for Mom to announce that she will visit the gym—that may be the result of another run-in with her husband. The point of this beat could involve how Mom deals with a major fork in the road of her life, a confrontation that requires her to make a choice, to "escape" or to be "captured," depending on whether she goes along with or rejects Vera's health club blandishment.

As seen in the preceding discussion, the values we have been discussing help to rough out the structural needs of a scene. Once you have done this, you have a clearer shot at dramatizing the beat and developing the characters, which can be done in any way you wish, as long as the point of the scene is clearly made. Beyond that, the diagram merely sets up a few markers that are easily obtained and just as easily changed or discarded. The proof of the diagram is whether it works for you. Try it; if it hangs you up or feels contrived or mechanical, try another strategy. The scene strategy, which takes only a few minutes to implement, allows you to be as freewheeling as you wish.

THE MONTAGE

Although this final dramatic beat, the **montage,** is not found in all movies, its ability to compress story time, exposition, and backstory gives screenwriters another handy tool, should they need it. A montage usually consists of overlapping images, music, and sound that can encapsulate time or experience. A montage might show overlapping images of a boy leaving the farm, riding the rails, arriving in the city, and fighting his way to the championship. In older films, this montage might have included elements such as pages of a calendar blowing off (time passing), piles of money accumulating or tumbling over (economic success or failure), locomotive pistons driving (traveling), and the like. Montages usually do not contain dialogue, although some use voice-over narration. The screenwriter indicates what should go into the montage. If you make your wishes known, trust the filmmakers to deliver your vision.

Although most montages play for a minute or so, there are exceptions. One of these is certainly the irrigation sequence that concludes *Our Daily Bread*, which was filmed in 1934, when montages were more popular. The movie, about dispossessed people who cooperate to build an irrigation project, climaxes with a twelve-minute montage that shows the water rushing into parched fields. Other films that use montages include *The Natural, Searching for Bobby Fischer,* and *Out of Africa.*

Today's movies use a new form of montage made up of beautiful images and music that convey a sense of such things as characters in love, the glory of nature, or patriotic fervor. Usually, screenwriters present a general description of what happens in the montage, trusting the filmmakers to capture the moment. An example of how montages are written can be found in Chapter 10 of this book, as well as in the following excerpt from *Out of Africa*. This montage plays for three minutes as it shows Meryl Streep's character taking her first airplane ride. Buoyed by John Barry's music, the montage (as filmed) presents pink clouds of flamingoes, shimmering lakes, and the green glory of Africa. The montage as scripted:

```
The plane accelerates across the meadow, lifts into the
sky.
FLYING

Africa from air.  The possibilities are endless but would
include a herd of elephants moving through the high
forest, a soda lake ringed by flamingoes, the Susw
volcano, all sorts of game on the plain.  Karen is
ecstatic.  As a pilot, Denys is more bold than expert:
once, they'll exchange a look, then a laugh, when he cuts
it too close.

The mood is one of exhilaration, all concern put aside.
Toward the end, Karen will grow quiet.  Heading home,
she'll turn in her seat, hair streaming, to look at Denys,
her carefree warrior, reach back to him but fail to touch.
She will live to be seventy-seven years old, and remember
these as the finest moments of her life.
```

Out of Africa, written by Kurt Luedtke, 1985

The basic dramatic units that screenwriters use to tell a story are like parts of a symphony that convey varying moods and emotional colors and energies. We imagine beats that manipulate sound, images, and emotions that move audiences emotionally. We create language, passionate characters, and dramatic situations that seem alive on the page. When a scene is good enough, and when the filmmakers do their job, it captures the heart of the audience. This is no easy task. It requires truthful and dramatic scenes that pull audiences into moments such as Paul Winfield returning to his family after being in prison in *Sounder;* Alec Guinness realizing he has unwittingly exposed a secret commando raid in *The Bridge on the River Kwai;* or French troops recognizing their kinship with the frightened German woman who sings to them in the final scene of *Paths of Glory.* Such scenes can touch audiences with profound emotion. Every word of this book intends to move you in this direction. Ultimately, such guidance, whatever the source, reaches its boundaries and the writer is alone, staring at a blank sheet of paper. Dancing about in the writer's mind are fears, dreams, and a story and characters struggling to be born. Strong scenes are the vertebrae that combine into the spine of the story; they organize the chaos of the writer's imagination, capturing a view of the world as it is or as it could be.

The strategies and craft insights that have accumulated so far present a tangle of choices—which value, which audience, which dramatic unit, and dozens of others decisions. The swarming choices sometimes block out our vision, but this is also part of screenwriting. Often our only guide during the writing is a sense of the story we wish to tell and the characters we intend to bring to life. The advice in this book, though extensive and drawn from many sources, offers a personal perspective on how this work is done. Use it, adapt it, and/or invent your own ways to write your scripts. The lessons in *Story Sense* are exacting and they take time to learn. I do not believe that this can be done by merely reading this book—or any book. The lessons must be pondered, practiced, adapted to your style, and put to work as you write. When you lose your way, look up what you need to know or call a friend. These two options are about all that are available as we dig our way out of writing problems that crop up every day and every hour. When this happens, recall that screenwriters earn their living by creating and solving dramatic problems. It's what we do, and no one who knows anything about the movies ever said this work would be easy.

SUMMARY

The two main building blocks in filmwriting are the *bit* and the *scene*. These units are dramatized with dialogue, action, music, and sound effects in ways that advance the plot, reveal the characters, establish relationships, and/or communicate thematic values.

Bits and scenes combine into larger units called *sequences*. These are longer dramatic units that play for five to fifteen minutes or so to make major story points, such as introducing the problem, the main characters, or the climax. I recommend blocking the story with ten or so sequence beats, rather than trying to organize the unwieldy number of bits and scenes (perhaps sixty or seventy) found in most features.

Bits tend to deal with plot and exposition rather than with what the characters are feeling. Most bits play for a minute or so and are useful for passing on exposition and for showing small but essential actions. Because they tend to be expositional rather than emotional, bits should be brief.

Scenes can be analyzed by how they deal with *content*, with *structure*, and with *conflict*. The content of a scene involves moments when the story point is made and when the characters experience emotional hits. The writer encourages such moments by enriching the setting and situation. In this view, the scene is like a box that the writer fills with whatever adds to the scene. Scenes, which mainly deal with the emotional life of the characters, make their points through physical action and through dialogue.

Subtext refers to what the characters think and feel but do not express through dialogue. Subtextual content is indicated by how the actors infuse their lines with emotion and meaning.

Structurally, most (but not all) scenes organize into three parts. Feature scenes usually play for three or four minutes; TV scenes usually play for one to three minutes. Scenes begin at a certain point (the button) and they end when the point of the scene is made. This make-point moment usually occurs at the end of the scene. *The most common scene weakness is failure to clearly make the dramatic point intended.*

The *conflict* of a scene usually follows a chase-and-capture or a chase-and-escape dynamic. As they play, scenes shift polarity as the action moves from a positive to a negative tone or from a negative to a positive tone.

The final dramatic unit is the *montage,* a beat that compresses time and/or shows the development of a character, a relationship, or a situation. Usually montages are done without dialogue, although music or voice-overs are frequently included. Most montages play for a minute or so.

Exercises

Use the following questions to analyze a scene of your choice. You should have both the taped excerpt and the script of the scene selected.

1. What story point is made in the scene analyzed? Locate the scene's make-point moment. What changes occur in the story or in the characters because of the scene?
2. What is the mood of the scene? How is the mood indicated? What roles do the settings, the camera work, and the music play in creating the mood?
3. What do the main characters want? What are their needs? Why is it difficult for the characters to get what they need? How does their need relate to the conflict in the scene?
4. Locate the scene's "button," the moment when the scene engages dramatically. Is there a closing kicker on the scene?

5. Cite examples of backstory in the scene. Note how this information is marbled into the scene through dialogue and visuals.
6. What is the subtext of the scene? How is it evidenced through dialogue, action, visuals, or mood? What are the characters really saying, i.e., what feelings underlie the dialogue?
7. Summarize the character relationships. Do the characters change emotionally during the scene? What causes the change? How does it add to the drama and conflict?
8. Are there moments when a character is unzipped (opened emotionally)? Describe the motivation for the emotional hit.
9. How does the scene use moments of silence and reaction?
10. What is the logic of the scene in terms of story and character?
11. Does the scene work off a chase-and-capture or a chase-and-escape dynamic? Explain.
12. Describe the polarity shift that occurs in the scene. What causes the shift?
13. Indicate the twists that divide the scene into segments. What causes the twists? How do they alter the energy and direction of the scene?
14. What have the writer and the filmmakers put into the box of the scene that adds to its drama and to our understanding of the story and its characters?
15. Examine the tape of the scene and note how it is staged. Storyboard the scene and indicate the camera positions and how they combined with blocking and movement during filming. How does the staging relate to the content of the scene? Is there an overall visual pattern? When and why does the camera use close-ups? When and why does the scene revert to wider angles? Finally, compare the script with how the movie was filmed.

(*For media that illustrate the points made in this chapter, see Appendix A.*)

PART TWO

Writing the Script

As the discussion shifts from writing the story to writing the script, think of this latter task in terms of *eye control.* The first step in the scripting process begins when you learn to control the third eye of your imagination, so you not only see your characters in action but hear what they say as well.

When you learn this level of eye control, you will be able to envision the scenes and characters that appear on the stage of your mind. This opens the second instance of eye control, which occurs when you learn to control the eyes of the characters who appear in imagination so they reflect whatever thoughts and feelings you have invested in them. For this eye control to happen, you must *become* the characters and fill them with felt emotion so they come alive on the page.

The third phase of eye control occurs when the script persuades the reader to see the same movie that you saw during scripting. Furthermore, when the script is taken up by the director, the actors, and the other filmmakers, they should also see the story that you envisioned.

Finally, the movie made from the script should control the eyes of the audience, so they see the story that the writer, the director, the cinematographer, and the other filmmakers want them to see. From this perspective, the following chapters of *Story Sense* deal with controlling eyes so that the incidents of plot and story come to life in imagination and on the page. As you will discover, there are strategies and traditions for doing this, and they can be learned.

CHAPTER 5

Creating Emotionally Dimensional Characters

This chapter discusses how to create characters that have the emotional complexity needed to make simple stories entertaining.

The preceding chapters deal with creating a plot that follows a problem until it is resolved in the climactic scene. Values such as emotional slant, frame, event, conflict, story concept, dramatic problem, structure, and the like were proposed as tools for enriching the story idea and expanding it into a plot. Also discussed were ways to work out the beats of the plot, which are usually done in a rational manner. However, once the plot feels right, most writers shift from the rational mode to a more imaginative mode to begin the second phase of screenwriting—writing the script.

Writing a script involves refining ordinary daydreaming until it conjures characters and settings that come to life in the writer's imagination. If the incident to be written shows on the outline as "Mom decides to enter the Iron Woman contest," then the specifics of that incident must be imagined. These might include imagining music and mood, settings, costumes, characters, dialogue, weather, machinery, action, and the history of whatever is at stake in the story. Once dramatic moments are imagined, they can be written into the script. To describe this imagination process, we can borrow the computer term WYSIWYG. Pronounced "whizywig," it means What You See is What You Get. For screenwriters, WYSIWYG means that what is seen in the mind's eye determines the quality of the script, because what we imagine is usually what we write.

Our discussion of scripting is therefore dependent on this notion of WYSIWYG because we must imagine interesting characters before we can write them into our scripts. Imagining at this level of intensity is the second master skill of screenwriting (the first is knowing how to work out a viable story). Because it is so important to writing characters, let us examine how the imagining process usually works.

IMAGINATION

Although there are various theories on how creative imagination works, many psychologists feel that it takes place mainly in the dreaminess of the unconscious mind. This is where we store experiences, secrets, hopes, and fears, in a mysterious domain that is populated with enough characters and surprises to write a hundred movies. Imagination is the lamp we use to explore the inner space of our unconscious mind; what we find is used to create characters, dialogue, and scenes.

Perhaps it is because screenwriters spend so much time imagining that some of us have become rather expert at describing how the process works. Screenwriter Gene Fowler felt that imagining was a fairly simple process: "All you do is sit staring at a blank sheet of paper until the drops of blood form on your forehead." Sportswriter Red Smith said more or less the same thing: "There's nothing to writing. All you do is sit down at a typewriter and open a vein." The wisdom in these wisecracks sums up screenwriting: the unconscious puts words on paper when the writer concentrates until interesting things appear in imagination. If you are unhappy with what you imagine, you can use your power of will to change what is playing inside your head. Novelist John Gardner had an interesting take on all this:

> All writing requires at least a degree of being in a trance-like state. The writer must summon out of nonexistence some character, some scene, and he must create that imaginary scene in his mind until he sees it as vividly as, in another state, he would see the typewriter and cluttered desk in front of him, or last year's calendar on his wall. But at times—for most of us, all too occasionally— something happens, a demon takes over, or a nightmare swings in, and the imaginary becomes the real. . . . When I come out of these trance moments . . . I seem to have been taken over by some muse. Insofar as I'm able to remember what happened, it seems to me that it was this: for a moment the real process of our dreams has been harnessed. The magic key goes in, all the tumblers fall at once and the door swings open.[1]

Here Gardner is referring to the writer's creative essence—the energy that gives life to the scenes and characters that we experience in imagination. Oftentimes we imagine with such intensity that we drift out of normal consciousness and into the fictive dream state. When our concentration flags, the stream of energy slackens, the images in our mind's eye disappear, and the stage of our imagination is suddenly empty. It remains so until the scene is reenergized and everything reappears. Scenes can be imagined with such intensity that characters come alive, break free from the author, and take over the story for a time. Imagining at this level is one of the joys of screenwriting.

However, the unconscious rarely swings open at a touch, and most new writers must work for a year or so to access the imaginative domain. Initially, you may see your imagined scenes as brief flashes or as darkness that is

---

[1] John Gardner, *On Becoming a Novelist*, Harper & Row, New York, 1983, pp. 57–61.

devoid of images or sound. This is normal and does not mean that you lack "talent," for imagination is like a muscle that strengthens with exercise. And the exercising cliché applies: *No pain, no gain.* In this case, the gain occurs when your imagination becomes stronger, allowing you to sustain what is seen in the mind's eye for longer periods. (The pain, such as it is, comes from the time spent trying to imagine scenes that refuse to appear in the mind's eye.) The goal of this work is the ability to switch on the lamp of imagination and to sustain the images. Imagining also means knowing when an image or a scene is not useful, so it can be tossed out and replaced with something new. Imagining this way is so exhausting that three or four hours a day is all that most screenwriters can manage.

When the imagining is going well, we scribble down what the characters say and what they do as they move about on the stage of the mind. Sometimes nothing happens and the stage remains empty and dark. This may happen many times each day, so do not fret, because your characters remain in your unconscious, waiting to be energized so they can play and replay moments of the story.

IMAGINING THE SETTINGS

To help you ease into imagining, you might wish to try the following meditative plan, which begins when you focus on the setting of the scene. Once you can imagine the location, it is usually easier to conjure the characters. If, for example, Mom decides to join the health club, a decision must be made about where the scene will play, whether in the back of a van, in the corner of a stadium, in a restaurant, or wherever feels right. We might try ten or twenty possible locations before settling on one that appeals. Some writers find it easier to imagine after drawing a layout plan of the location, including doors and windows and what lies beyond.

Research often comes in here, as discussed in Chapter 2, when writers take field trips to visit their settings or to visualize them through illustrations and library readings. Tom Rickman, for example, noted that a key scene in his script for *Coal Miner's Daughter* occurs when Sissy Spacek's Loretta Lynn tells her father that she is in love. As he was deciding where to stage this scene, Rickman remembered the small caves he observed while visiting Lynn's hometown. Called "coal holes," the caves had been cut into hillsides behind the miners' Appalachian homes to provide household coal. The coal holes were enlarged over time until they became small rooms. Intrigued by their authenticity, Rickman decided to use one of the family coal holes as the setting where Loretta tells her father of her marriage plans.[2]

Your story setting should be imagined in as much detail as you need to see its dramatic possibilities. This advice holds even though most settings are

---

[2]Video interview with Tom Rickman by Cristina Venegas and Roger S. Christiansen, The Sundance Institute, July 1989.

scripted briefly, especially when the location is generic. Thus, a posh apartment can be suggested quickly, as in, *Lilly's apartment is expensive yet under-
stated, much like its owner.* Such a description is enough to clue the filmmakers
about the look and style of the setting. (In case you are wondering why you
should bother to imagine the settings if they are sketched in just a few words,
it is so you can use the details imagined to encourage your characters to react
to their surroundings and to each other. This character interaction should
show up in the script.)

There are times, of course, when writers wish the reader to see the location
clearly, so they write in more detail, as in this example:

```
36  INT.  BOOK'S CAR  (MOVING)  PHILADELPHIA NIGHT

Book drives around 13th Street, a ravaged corridor
between neon-lit restaurants, bars, porno shops and
darkened storefronts.  Carter sits beside him, Rachel and
her son in the back seat looking out at the assorted
array of desperate characters huddled in doorways or
wandering aimlessly about.  On the POLICE RADIO a
description of the cop killing is BROADCAST EVERY FEW
MINUTES.
```

> *Witness,* written by Pamela and Earl W. Wallace and
> William Kelley, 1984

Imagining the setting can ease you into a psychological state similar to
that obtained using guided imagery. This psychotherapy technique might ask
a patient to imagine a setting such as a forest or a placid lake that will be used
as the starting place for a journey of psychological discovery. After the setting
is imagined, the patient is eased into a waking dream in which the unconscious mind is encouraged to take over. This journey is assisted by the thera-
pist, who may introduce universal symbols such as a meadow, which represents the patient's inner space, or a deer, which is a spiritual symbol that may
lead the patient deeper into the unconscious. Interestingly, psychologists feel
that the conscious mind sees the unconscious in terms of images, which makes
the imagining process sound like the "magic key" that Gardner feels opens the
unconscious. Although creativity theories are plentiful, at this time we need
only think about imagining settings as a first step toward imagining characters and scenes.

IMAGINING THE CHARACTERS

Imagining characters is done partly through perspiration and partly through
inspiration. Writing through perspiration means assigning a backstory (history) to the main characters, as will be discussed shortly. Writing from inspiration requires being alert to whatever our characters say, do, feel, and think

as we imagine them. This approach is used by many writers, among them Alice Walker, who recalled hearing voices from her unconscious that told her, "We don't want to be written in New York. We want to be written where it's pretty."

Such entreaties persuaded Walker to move to a cabin in Mendocino, where throughout the writing of her book she felt that she served as a medium for her characters in *The Color Purple:*

> The people in the book were willing to visit me, but only after I stopped inter-rupting with poetry readings and lectures. If you're silent for a long time, people just arrive in your mind. It's all a matter of hearing. I just waited and listened very intently and their voices became clearer and clearer to me so that if I started to think the way one of my characters would think it, if I didn't think it in his language I would immediately realize that it was false.[3]

Pursuing this notion, let us assume that the task is to create a character—the hero's best friend, for example. When the writer initially attempts this role, no one may come to mind, or a dozen characters might appear, in which case the writer must sort through the hopefuls and cast the best person for the role. Although there are as many ways to create characters as there are writers, you might wish to try this approach: Find a quiet place and sit very still. After you are relaxed, imagine until you have created and sustained the setting, as noted above. As you do so, listen to whatever ambient noise attaches to the loca-tion—sounds of traffic, machinery, wind, or birds, for example. In time, a wraithlike figure may begin to move about, just beyond the range of your imagination. If you are patient, the figure may step into view, at which time you can study this person and decide if he or she belongs in your story. Take your time; there are often many characters available for each role. Think of the process as a casting session in which characters audition for the roles. If the characters imagined do not fit the part, ease them away and conjure others until you are satisfied.

If this approach does not work, try casting someone you know, such as a relative or your neighbor. Or use famous actors, dead or alive, as described on pages 22 and 99. No one need know who the star models are because they will become unrecognizable by the time the script is written. Sometimes, a com-plete stranger may step out of your imagination and take over a role. Feel free to imagine anyone in any manner that you wish, in whatever setting seems right.

As each figure becomes familiar, ask questions that coax forth a face, a physique, a way of walking, or whatever adds definition to the character being imagined. Play with your characters; encourage them to experiment with dif-ferent accents and voices as you ease them into their roles. As you invest energy in your characters, they should become stronger, more visible, and eas-ier to image each day. Care about your creations, appreciate their problems and their humanity, and before long, you will accumulate information on who

[3]*The Los Angeles Times,* June 8, 1983.

they are and what they can contribute to the story. Sometimes we are able to control how the characters develop; other times (if luck is with us) they break away and behave with brazen independence. Imagining this way may only yield pages of doodles at first, but stay with the work until the characters begin to develop psychologically.

CREATING CHARACTERS WITH PSYCHOLOGICAL DIMENSION

The temp characters described on page 29 are usually temporary figures who lack psychology and history. Scripted characters, by comparison, are imagined until they seem real, replete with motivating life experiences (called *backstory*) that can generate the emotional baggage that makes characters interesting; actors use this dimension to build their performances. An actor's interpretation of a role is based on his or her understanding of human nature, on how this experience applies to the actor's concept of the role, on what the characters say and do, and on how the characters interact in the story.

The actor's sense of story tells him or her whether the writer has created a character with inner life or a role that is empty and shallow. What actors seek are characters who seem to have a history and emotional content, who have principles that they are willing to defend. They prefer characters who are flawed and variable, characters who show moodiness, humor, and other quirky traits. Such roles allow actors to energize characters with thought, emotion, and human content that make certain movie characters unforgettable.

Joan Plowright touched on this point when she discussed her decision to play the antagonist in *Widow's Peak*:

> Half the time I turn them down, especially the ones where the male characters have last names and a history and the female is simply identified by her first name. You know instantly that the lady's not going to have much of a history or identity. Who is this woman? I don't respond because I don't know her history. The producers say things like, "We thought you could make something from it" or, "There are four wonderful scenes with all of the great gentlemen stars." It's nice to be able to choose a role where I have a last name. It's not that I'm a kind of militant feminist, but I prefer scripts presenting women in the light of being active participants in life and really moving things along.[4]

In this delightfully daffy period film, Plowright plays a dowager who dresses in black, drives a Rolls-Royce, and rules her Irish village. These are the externals of the character; more interesting are the motives, history, and inner being that Plowright uses to energize this cleverly plotted story in which the widow must contend with her nitwit son while keeping the locals in line.

---

[4]*The Los Angeles Times,* May 1, 1994.

Creating interesting characters such as the widow described above is easier when writers have a sense of how the human mind works. Although the vast literature of psychology is available for study, most of us acquire our psychological views through experience and popular readings as opposed to formal study of the topic. Practical though it is, casual psychological insight may not give new writers the sharp tool needed to create and motivate movie characters. To deal with this, teachers sometimes cobble together psychological lessons and readings to encourage students to create complex, motivated characters.

A brief excursion into psychology as it relates to screenwriting can begin by acknowledging that real-life problems seldom resolve in a neat three-act structure. In movies, however, this is how problems are almost always resolved, whether completely or partly. To make this happen, movie scripts give their characters a problem that seems impossible, yet which in the end turns out to have a solution—or at least the beginning of a solution. Furthermore, many movie problems connect to four basic human needs: (1) the need to survive and reproduce; (2) the need to belong, to love, to share, and to cooperate; (3) the need to have power (which often conflicts with the desire to belong, especially through marriage); (4) the need to have freedom and options in life, especially to have fun. These four basic needs can be used as starting points for examining the problem of a story and how it affects the characters. In *The Verdict,* for example, Galvin's betrayal during the Lillibridge case created a psychological problem that causes him to turn down Bishop Brophy's settlement offer and battle the establishment in court. Galvin does this because he wants to even scores with those who ruined his life. In terms of the four basic drives, Galvin is influenced by the need for power that attaches to being respected as a lawyer. The characters in *Witness* and *The Terminator* have a need to survive. The need in *Sleepless in Seattle* is to belong. Acquiring a fix on a main character's basic need can be done quickly, allowing the writer to figure out motives of the characters and how they respond to incidents in the story.

In real life, individuals deal with the four basic needs according to the complex tangle of genetic factors and life conditions that are the nature and nurture influences that affect all aspects of our being, including personality, intelligence, and aptitude. Appreciating how various nature and nurture influences shape personality is another insight for understanding not only real psychology but the psychology of movie characters as well.

Genetic Influences (Nature)

Genetics determines physical characteristics and, to a degree still being debated, influences personality and intelligence as well. If, for example, genetic inheritance inclines a particular person to grow up to be strong and athletic, he or she will probably have a life that is different from that of someone whose genetic inheritance has given him or her a weak, unathletic physique. Of course, genetics can also give physically weak people a willfulness that allows them to overcome disabilities and to earn success. It is also known that people inherit various abilities and personality traits that encourage them to be introverted, extroverted, aggressive, passive, and the like. Such physical, intellectual, and attitudinal traits often have profound influences on personality.

Although screenwriting and genetics form an unlikely alliance, the relationship allows writers to make decisions about the sex, age, appearance, and other traits that shape their characters. *The Elephant Man, Mask, Rainman,* and *Rudy* present characters who are genetically distinctive in terms of intelligence, appearance, and physical attributes; they illustrate how assigned traits can dramatize a story. The titular character in *Forrest Gump* was saddled with a genetic problem (low intelligence) that was used to organize the story. The intelligence of Tim Robbins's character in *The Shawshank Redemption* was used to organize that story as well. Similarly, *Amadeus* is organized around Mozart's musical genius. In the sports widow idea presented in previous chapters, we have given Mom exceptional strength, which allows us to use this trait and its attendant psychological baggage to develop the story.

Conditioning Influences (Nurture)

Characters are also shaped by social, economic, and family conditions. When social deprivation, drugs, alcoholism, war, natural disasters, and the like occur, they can affect the neighborhood, the family, and the psychological development of those involved. Factors such as these register most strongly during the first five to ten years of life, when we are most vulnerable to positive and negative influences. So, when the title character in *Arthur* shows up, we recognize a poor little rich boy who has been spoiled rotten and has become a loveless lush who is filled with self-loathing. The problem of the story is to make Arthur feel better about himself. Similarly, years of police work have turned *Witness*'s John Book into a lonely warrior. Long- and short-term conditioning can be summed up by the adage "As the twig is bent, so grows the tree." This aphorism restates the nature-nurture influences by asking the writer to identify the forces that bent the twig and what kind of wood is involved. Simple as they are, such considerations can invest characters with internal drives that affect motives, interests, and emotions, as we shall discuss next.

PSYCHOLOGICAL IMPERATIVES

Screenwriters use nature-nurture influences to create psychological drives, needs, or fears that motivate characters. Based on backstory and genetic influences, this content can be sharpened into a **psychological imperative** that inclines a character to behave or think in a certain way. For example, the hero of *The Fugitive* has a psychological imperative to find his wife's murderer. Tom Cruise's Ron Kovic in *Born on the Fourth of July* operates under the influence of several psychological imperatives. One is based on the conservative values that Kovic took on as a boy and which led him to volunteer for hazardous duty in Vietnam. After his spine is shattered in the war, Kovic is motivated by a different psychological imperative because he feels betrayed by the gung-ho values that put him in harm's way. The movie deals with Kovic's evolution from patriotic high school wrestler to wounded wreck to the antiwar activist who takes charge of his life. To reveal these psychological depths, the character was "unzipped" emotionally, so that intensely personal human moments could be captured on screen.

The Verdict presents a number of psychological moments. One occurs in Shot 2 when Galvin pauses as he hoists his morning whiskey and for a few searing seconds, we see a man watching his life going down the drain. An insightful moment that occurs in *Witness* is when Book comes upon Rachel as she bathes (Shot 114). Actors spot such moments and use them to reveal the complexity of their characters. Few actors appreciate such moments more than Meryl Streep:

> Everyone spends so much time on the script—the big picture—but it's always those intangible things that you discover in the moment—those things that are so transporting. It's what you live for. It's what makes you feel good at the end of the day. You've discovered something there that nobody knew was there and there it was to be had. Ohhhh, that's sooo seductive.[5]

As noted, backstory is often the source of these special moments. Interestingly, *The Terminator* presents a useful study of backstory because the cyborg's backstory is based on a computer program that compels it to kill the heroine. Characters can be programmed, as well, through community and family pressure, natural inclinations, and the events of life. We see this in *Witness* (Shot 100A) when the family patriarch (Jan Rubes's Eli Lapp) discovers Book and Rachel as they dance in the barn. Angered, Eli criticizes Rachel for defying Amish traditions and for bringing Book into their home: "You bring fear to this house. Fear of English with guns coming after. You bring blood and whispers of more blood. Now English music . . . and you are *dancing* to English music!"

Eli's outburst causes Rachel to refute the old man's accusations, which reveals the psychological imperatives of the two characters. Eli's is to enforce the rules of the Amish; Rachel's is to enjoy a moment of freedom and fun. Their conflict points up the gap between Book's world and that of the Amish.

Psychological imperatives are based on life experiences that are invented by screenwriters. The *Witness* screenwriters, to illustrate, numbed John Book with police work to make him vulnerable for his sojourn among the Amish. Part of the history of the hero of *In the Line of Fire* involved the assassination of President Kennedy, which motivates the character. In such ways, psychological imperatives influence behavior through experiences that accumulate over time (long-term conditioning) and/or experiences that occur suddenly (short-term trauma).

[5]*Venice Magazine,* September 1994, p. 30.

Short-term Trauma

When someone is severely injured in a war or accident or when a person is betrayed or humiliated or cheated, the experience can cause lasting psychological effects. Screenwriters create such trauma to influence the psychology and motivation of their characters. In *The Verdict*, Galvin's betrayal during the Lillibridge case causes him to suffer a short-term trauma that motivates his character and helps to organize the plot, for without this betrayal, Galvin might have taken Bishop Brophy's settlement offer. In *Witness*, Rachel suffers short-term trauma when her spouse dies, as does Sam in *Sleepless in Seattle*. Similarly, the personalities of the hero of *In the Line of Fire* and Juliette Binoche's character in *Blue* are shaped by short-term trauma caused by the sudden death of people that they are close to. These incidents indelibly mark each character and motivate his or her behavior.

Long-term Conditioning

An abusive childhood, homelessness, chronic illness, poverty, a bullying family, and a destructive neighborhood are among the long-term conditioning factors that create psychological influences. Writers create these problems to develop their characters through the B-storyline, which deals with the inner struggle of the main characters. Thus, if experience or inclination has made a character timid or unassertive (as in *The Heiress* or *Forrest Gump*), the drama can be used to overcome or moderate that problem.

This process is at work in Carrie Fisher's script for *Postcards from the Edge*, which uses long-term conditioning to shape Meryl Streep's character (Suzanne). Although Suzanne's problem is addressed obliquely, it drives the story. Fisher does this by flagging the audience's attention with Suzanne's cocaine problem. Then, as the story unfolds, the audience realizes that the character is caught up in a deeper problem that binds her to a dysfunctional matriarchy that extends back to her domineering grandmother (played by Mary Wickes). The grandmother, in turn, has prevented her daughter (Shirley MacLaine's Doris) from growing up. Once the daughter-mother-grandmother pattern is revealed, the audience senses the psychological imperative that Suzanne must overcome and the story organizes around this point.

Suzanne's problem is one of individuation, a serviceable strategy that has been employed in countless films. It asks the protagonist to become independent and free of controlling relatives, friends, or organizations. *What's Love Got to Do with It, The Graduate, Moonstruck,* and *Breaking Away* illustrate the archetype. Such stories usually have endings that are positive enough to please the audience. This is important, for unless positive change occurs in the main character, the audience may feel that there is no point to the movie. This change, however slight it may be, can be the difference between a downer story that audiences shun and a story that offers a positive ending that attracts viewers. *Midnight Cowboy* and *Bonnie and Clyde* illustrate stories with positive endings; *A Perfect World* illustrates a story with a negative ending that audiences did not flock to see, even though it starred Clint Eastwood and Kevin Costner.

Finally, short-term trauma and long-term conditioning should be worked deeply into the story; otherwise, the audience may become aware of the psychological strings that the writer is using to manipulate the characters. Fortunately, psychological imperatives are easily hidden in the emotional rush of a story. This is mainly done by oblique references to backstory experiences that intimate but do not reveal outright the psychological imperative that drives the main characters; anything that might explain away the mystery of the characters should be avoided.

BACKSTORY AND THE PSYCHOLOGY OF CHARACTER

Because backstory deals with what happened to the characters before the story began, it asks the writer to invent the nature-nurture influences that have shaped the personalities and the values of the characters. If a character is written to be aggressive, passive, cruel, playful, or whatever, the writer should have a sense of what is responsible for the trait or attitude. Even when the causes of behavior are not stated directly, they should be understood by the writer so they can bleed into the script, allowing the audience to intuit what motivates the characters. For example, *The Verdict* reveals almost nothing about Mickey's backstory, yet because of how the character is written and portrayed, Mickey comes across as a survivor of a thousand courtroom battles. Mickey's sly counterpart is Judge Sweeney.

Even a scant backstory can enrich the lead characters. For example, we know little about Reese in *The Terminator,* other than that he is from a ruined, post-apocalypse world that is controlled by machines. Flashbacks of this world suggest Reese's grim childhood, which makes him susceptible to Sarah's tenderness. The hero of *In the Line of Fire* is also marked by violence, in his case the JFK assassination in Dallas. That backstory incident haunts Horrigan's life and his dealings with the new assassin.

Backstory can connect to a value system that organizes the plot, as in *The Verdict*, when Galvin rediscovers his belief in the law and in himself. Concannon's values, by comparison, are those of an insider who manipulates rather than serves the justice system. The difference between the two men creates the thematic basis of the movie; it also provides the hero's margin of victory, because Galvin is empowered by a moral force. Concannon, on the other hand, is stuck on the low road that he took when he hired Laura as a spy.

Creating Backstory

This ongoing discussion of backstory is meant as general advice, and it may not suit writers who prefer to let their characters develop during the writing, without preplanning. Either way you approach characterization, if your characters seem shallow and uninteresting, you might wish to try a simple question-and-answer strategy to create or add depth to the backstories of your main characters.

You should be as curious about your characters as you would be about someone in life. In the case of the sports widow mentioned earlier, we might ask the following: How old is she? How did her parents earn their living? When did Mom become aware of her strength? How did her family and school chums react to her strength? Did Mom conceal her physical prowess from others? What was her romantic experience before marriage? How did she meet her husband? What does she do for fun? After a sufficient number of questions concerning each of the main characters, backstory histories should accumulate. There need be no orderliness to these questions—merely write out whatever questions and answers come to mind. During the Q&A, you should be able to nudge the characters in whatever direction feels appropriate. The goal of the Q&A is to come up with life experiences that make the characters seem dramatic and alive.

Quirkiness

Certain characters, like certain people, are unpredictable, offbeat, independent, and original. These quirky types often go their own way and refuse to be categorized or quantified. Quirky characters grow out of dialogue and action, as in *Forrest Gump*, when Gary Sinise's legless soldier behaves in ways that are angry and eccentric, yet appropriate for a man in his situation. Other examples of quirkiness: when Kevin Costner dances around a fire at night in *Dances with Wolves*; when Shirley MacLaine mixes herself a vodka health-food breakfast in *Postcards from the Edge*; when Jack Nicholson plays the piano from the back of a truck as it drives down the road in *Five Easy Pieces*.

Quirky, active characters such as these are often charged and intense; they are not afraid to reach out, to initiate, to take chances. Such characters are imperfect and unpredictable because they are involved with the drama of their lives. For example, Sarah Tillane (Mildred Natwick), the strong-minded widow in *The Quiet Man*, has a backstory that explains her powerful energy. Frank Nugent's script describes her as being a handsome woman in her forties, "A woman of breeding, with a slightly bitter humor, great practicality and a severe manner that is for the most part superficial." Although Sarah Tillane is not as beautiful as the heroine, the script nonetheless notes that she is "a highly sexed woman and her four years of widowhood have set her teeth on edge." This mention of the widow's backstory creates psychological currents that energize her so she becomes an active player in the story instead of a stereotypical grand dame.

Contrast this character with one who behaves in a wistful, sad, or pained manner, while waiting for someone or something to come along and bring him or her to life. While a small amount of moping may be permissible, active characters usually do more for the story. This advice applies to shy, likable characters, for they need not be passive either. The hero of *Rocky* illustrates the type, for although Mr. Balboa is a humble, inarticulate lug, he courts Adrian, takes her ice-skating, counsels a street kid, invents a training regimen, and modestly fashions a life for himself. As a result, Rocky is an active character who initiates, who reaches out, and above all, who is alive on every page of Sylvester Stallone's script and alive on the screen as well.

When quirky traits are mentioned in the stage directions, they should be presented skillfully; otherwise, the actors and other filmmakers may dismiss them as silly contrivances or clumsy attempts to create character through superficialities. *Sleepless in Seattle* skillfully presents quirkiness when the writers note the braying laughter of Victoria (Barbara Garrick) in the stage directions: "Victoria laughs far too enthusiastically" (Shot 92); "Victoria almost dies laughing" (Shot 99). The dialogue also refers to her disconcerting habit of tossing her hair (Shot 125). These simple but odd traits help to make Victoria a quirky and memorable character.

BACKSTORY AND "LIFE ON THE PAGE"

One of the key questions of screenwriting: *Why is one character said to be "alive," while another ends up as a cardboard figure who lacks life?* To answer this we must distinguish between script and screen, for what ends up on celluloid depends on the budget, the director-actor relationship, the chemistry between the actors, and factors that are beyond the writer's control. Also, the "aliveness" of characters in the script is not the result of glorious character descriptions. For example, *The Terminator*'s hero is described simply: "KYLE REESE is 26, his face hard, eyes grim." There is also a moment when Reese removes his shirt and reveals his battle scars, but otherwise he looks like the standard Hollywood tough guy from hell. What makes Reese "alive" and interesting is the way screenwriter James Cameron stokes this character with inner life and an unbending commitment to protecting Sarah. We care about this fellow because we sense his harsh life, which makes his tender feelings for Sarah more poignant. These traits are demonstrated through action, as when Reese escapes from the police who chase him through a store, shortly after he drops out of time (Shot 12). Later, we witness Reese's intensity when the police scoff at his warnings about the cyborg (Shot 154). Thus Kyle Reese's "aliveness" and survival instincts, honed through painful backstory experiences, persuade the audience that the character is willing to die for his cause.

Witness's John Book is also described minimally: "He is about 40, with a rangy, athletic body." Book draws our attention by the force of Harrison Ford's performance and by how the script gives the actor opportunities to demonstrate Book's character. When he questions Samuel in the train station, Book is gentle with the boy (Shot 30). We see Book as a man of action when he rousts the suspect known as Coalmine from a saloon (Shot 36C). During lunch at a hot-dog stand, Book is bemused when Rachel intrudes on his privacy by relating what his sister said about him (Shot 52B). Moments such as these reveal a solitary man whose life is so tied up in police work that his main contact with normal life seems to be as a watchful uncle for his sister's children. There is no mention of a romantic partner, where he lives, or what he does for fun, and other than a few friends on the job, Book is a loner. The only time that Book reveals the stress that he carries within occurs when Rachel overhears his delirious mutterings as he recovers from a bullet wound (Shot 80).

Both Reese and Book (and countless other movie heroes) display vulnerabilities that connect to the audience's instinctive wish to see these needful men paired with a love interest. However, because the audience has seen this pattern so many times and because it is such an obvious dramatic ploy, the writer must be inventive before this dynamic will be accepted. The most promising strategy for doing this is to be truthful and thoughtful as you develop the story and the specialness of its characters. Ask what could reasonably (or unreasonably) happen within the situation of your story. Be patient during this, for good work takes as long as it takes.

Character traits can be revealed gradually, as they are in the people that we meet in life. Well-written characters are seldom self-absorbed, contrived, or sticky with goodness. They often have a flaw that humanizes them to the audiences—for example, Galvin's alcoholism in *The Verdict*, or Loretta's (Cher's) cheerless practicality in *Moonstruck*. Despite their imperfections, interesting characters not only possess a humanity that is worth saving but are often responsible for the absurd and unpredictable moments that spice up stories. This applies to both heroes and villains, for the latter may also have charm, courage, energy, and intelligence; however, their tragic flaw is that their good traits are overridden by base instincts that they are unable to overcome. Kevin Bacon's outlaw in *The River Wild* illustrates such a character, as does Linda Fiorentino's character in *The Last Seduction*. In these cases and countless others, the characters are alive on the page because they are emotionally *dimensional*. They have values, needs, intelligence, and tensions that send off emotional sparks that create moments of drama.

In sum, dramatic characters are imperfect but human, like the interesting people we meet in real life. They have a sense of self, even when their view is negative or distorted; they do not back away from challenge; they may be flawed, dangerous, or eccentric. For most characters, such behavioral patterns, attitudes, and personality traits usually grow out of their backstories.

Marbling Backstory into the Script

Backstory and exposition should be slipped into the story in ways that do not slow the forward momentum of the drama. One of the primary strategies for doing this is to marble (or "freight") the dialogue with backstory information that reveals the characters. *The Verdict* (Shot 47) illustrates how this is done, when Mickey tells Laura what really happened in the Lillibridge affair. In the course of this, Mickey mentions that Galvin is the sort who believes that anyone who "knows what a 'spinnaker' is got to be a saint." The remark demonstrates marbling because it reveals Galvin's naïveté with a joke that adds interest and exposition without slowing the story. In much the same way, *Sleepless in Seattle*

(Shot 150) uses humor to freight the dialogue with exposition and backstory when Becky tells Annie that "verbal ability is a highly overrated thing in a guy, and our pathetic need for it is what gets us into so much trouble."

Good screenwriting reveals backstory not only by what the characters say but also by what they do and by what others say and do. For example, *The Verdict*'s drunken hero reveals his backstory by his actions: scrounging business in a funeral home (Shot 1), wrecking his office in a drunken rage (Shot 7), and pilfering Nurse Rooney's mailbox to get at her telephone bill (Shot 81). Throughout, the script uses such moments to track Galvin's ascension from legal scavenger to principled legal-eagle. As this positive arc of character plays out, the audience is persuaded to care about Galvin and his struggle. (For more on how backstory is marbled into dialogue, refer to Chapter 6.)

Backstory can also be revealed by how characters dress, live, work, and behave. Brando's tough dockhand in *On the Waterfront* looks and acts very differently from James Spader's yuppie hero in *White Palace*. Spader's character is defined by the actor's grooming, style, and manner of speaking; even his Volvo is the preferred yuppie-mobile of the era. Brief visual moments are used to suggest the character's fussiness, as when Spader pauses to smooth the fringe of his Persian carpet. Later, with his credentials established, Spader meets an older woman (Susan Sarandon) who works as a waitress in a hamburger joint. The contrasting backstories of the two characters clearly establish that they have little in common, yet the movie bucks expectation and launches their affair.

Backstory and plot information can also be conveyed through voice-over narration that is recited off-screen by one of the characters in the movie, as in *The Shawshank Redemption*, or by an off-screen narrator, as in *Barry Lyndon*. Voice-over narration can be read by a character in the story who has matured and who is looking back on what happened earlier, as in *Stand by Me* and *The Wonder Years* TV show. Another approach is for a character to recite backstory dialogue while looking directly into the camera, as in *Shirley Valentine* and *Annie Hall*.

Backstory can be presented as a printed graphic *(The Terminator)*, as family photographs *(Five Easy Pieces)*, or as voices from the past *(Twelve o'Clock High)*. Other backstory strategies: messages from computers *(Sleepless in Seattle)*, home movies *(Starman)*, a job summary, old letters, mementos and clothing, a nostalgic visit to a childhood home. *Apocalypse Now* uses newspaper clippings and Martin Sheen's voice-over to sketch Brando's character.

How Much Backstory Is Enough?

Now that you know a bit about backstory and psychological profiling, you should also know that very little of this work shows up in the script, because audiences are more interested in what the characters do than in why they do it. Also, psychological complexity can become tedious and uncinematic, which is why screenwriters avoid stuffing their scripts with backstory. This is important advice for writers who are inclined to load their scripts with the inner workings of their characters. As we have already noted, good screenwriting slips backstory into the drama so subtly that viewers hardly realize how much they are learning about the characters. Following this advice will seem impossible at first, but stick with it and you will shift from writing speeches to writing movies. The difference between these two writing styles is, to borrow from Mark Twain, like the difference between lightning and lightning bug.

A few brief references to a character's backstory can suggest his or her psychological roots and prepare the audience for whatever happens. As noted earlier, a single backstory experience can explain the main character's motivation. This can often be explained with minimal probing of the characters, as was the case with the male leads in *The Verdict* and *Sleepless in Seattle*. In many cases, backstory can be suggested by dialogue references that take up but a few minutes of the drama.

In most cases, the hero's backstory experiences should be raised quietly and only when necessary—unless the character is a braggart, bully, or misfit. Often it is more dramatic for the character to bear his or her pain in silence than to speak openly of it. Audiences admire such courage, especially when they sense the character's vulnerability. Real life is the model here, for most of us have probably met a stranger who suddenly unloads his or her life history. At such times our instinct may be to avoid this person, especially when the stranger's history is discomforting. In real life there is a social code that dictates how people release information: questions lead to answers, which lead to more questions, until we acquire a sense of the other person.

Do movies really follow this pattern? Usually, but not always, for occasionally a character bursts out with a huge backstory aria that can be entertaining. In *Jaws*, for example, Robert Shaw's character (Quint) has an extended speech that recounts the sinking of his ship during World War II. In the ocean for days, Quint had to watch helplessly as his shipmates were devoured by sharks. The story looks backward on this experience because it motivates Quint's obsession, which is to kill sharks. This is important because Quint's psychological imperative has a profound impact on the story.

Flashbacks As Backstory

Flashbacks are bits, scenes, or montages that review a character's life experiences. Movies are as inventive here as they are with everything else, as can be seen in the flashbacks in *Waterland*. This story plays with time to reveal backstory in original and surprising ways, not the least of which is having the hero of the film travel back in time to become an observer of incidents as they happened to his grandparents several generations earlier. Like most flashbacks, these have a subjective quality that presents experience as personal memory. Flashbacks can be initiated by a sound or an image that recalls a memory, as in *The Terminator* (Shot 46), when Reese sees a construction machine that triggers memories of the killer machines he once battled. *Sleepless in Seattle* (Shots 7, 54D) features two brief flashbacks as Sam remembers his dead wife. The opening of *Midnight Cowboy* contains a number of flashbacks that review the sad early years of the main character. Flashbacks also can be cued by ghostly music or voices from the past, a memento, an artifact, or a visit to a location. Minor characters are seldom given flashbacks, unless the purpose is to reveal one of the main characters.

The transition to a flashback often occurs when the camera angle tightens to a close-up of the character experiencing the flashback. Then the image dissolves or cuts to the flashback. This approach was used in *The Terminator* (Shots 45, 183FX). Transitions to flashbacks can also occur when the image shimmers on screen and dissolves to an earlier time, or the image can fade to white, use a cut, or slow-dissolve to the flashback. Screenwriters usually skip over the mechanics of the transition by writing brief stage directions that describe what happens: "This is John's flashback (or memory) of that wonderful night in Paris."

Although flashbacks can be interesting, they are like a musical number— entertaining at the time, but when the song is over, the story must be restarted. In most cases it is risky to break story momentum, especially when the flashback information can be carried by dialogue. Movies are not reality; they are a kind of superreality that catches the audience up in emotional tension. Because of their need for story momentum and dramatic intensity, movies have a low tolerance for treading water while the author unloads backstory and flashbacks.

Although this advice usually applies, there are (again) exceptions to this cautionary note on flashbacks, because certain movie moments are so interesting and/or so essential that they deserve presentation. *Breaker Morant*, which concerns a military trial that takes place during the Boer War, requires considerable backstory exposition to explain the unique conditions of the story, which is why this exposition is presented mainly through flashbacks. Similarly, flashbacks are often used in courtroom dramas to explain the plot. Ultimately, the writer's sense of story must decide when a flashback is essential, but usually *less is enough*.

WRITERLY PERSPECTIVES ON CHARACTER

Human nature might well be humankind's most discussed and most interesting subject. Even so, the topic always seems just beyond understanding, which is perhaps why there are so many opinions on what makes us human. Among the interesting screenwriting perspectives on this topic is Waldo Salt's, who saw his characters as having a need to be healed. Salt made that journey difficult by creating characters who are unable to recognize their problem or to grasp a solution that would remedy their inner weakness. As a result, his characters make destructive choices, often at the worst possible moment. In Salt's *Midnight Cowboy*, Jon Voight plays such a type. His name is Joe Buck, a lonely, neglected young man who desperately needs to be close to someone. Instead of pursuing what he *needs* (to be loved), Joe Buck chooses what he *wants* (to become a rich gigolo in New York City). Joe Buck thus chooses the wrong path, the pursuit of money rather than a search for someone with whom he could be close. It is not until he befriends Ratso Rizzo (Dustin Hoffman) that Joe receives the emotional trust he needs to become more complete. Salt's *want vs. need* strategy is an effective approach to creating a character's inner problem.

A somewhat different angle on character is taken by Robert Towne:

> The single most important question, I think, that one must ask one's self about a character is what are they really afraid of? *What are they really afraid of?* And if you ask that question, it's probably for me the single best way of getting into a character. And that finally is where stories are told . . . with a character that's real. Jake Gittes, in *Chinatown,* was afraid of being a fool. . . . And he would overreact: "I won't let anybody put this over on me." He would overreact, and that would become a self-fulfilling prophecy, and it did. He ended up in the very place where he didn't want to be. He was so afraid of being a fool that he brought it on himself. He wasn't going to let anybody push him around.[6]

Here Towne is describing the psychological imperative that is Jake Gittes's character flaw. There is no explanation for why Jake behaves this way. Perhaps he was born with the characteristic and it is his nature; or he could have been raised by strict parents who demanded a standard of behavior that little Jake could not deliver, and so the boy was punished for his purported failings.

Although Gittes's secret fear was created by Towne, neither its origins nor its existence was mentioned or explained, for to do so might demystify the character. This strategy allows Towne to tease the audience by presenting Gittes as a character who acts in unpredictable and troublesome ways, for reasons that are never made clear. All that shows up on screen is Gittes's headstrong behavior; we do not see the psychological strings that Towne uses to motivate Jake. This allows Gittes's psychological imperative to operate like a shadow puppet: audiences see the shadow of behavior that the puppet causes, but they do not see the puppet itself, which is the psychological imperative (the fear of losing control) that grew out of Gittes's backstory. In the end, Gittes's fear of being outsmarted causes him to become an unwitting participant in his lover's death.

Jake Gittes and Joe Buck are characters who repeatedly work against their best interests because they are unaware of the inner drives that motivate their behavior. Furthermore, like many characters and real people, Jack and Joe are blind to what causes them to behave as they do. We see similar traits in the lonely kid who tries too hard to make friends and ends up being shunned or in people mired in debt because they are paying off the trappings meant to impress others. In these and so many other ways, people struggle to break free of negative patterns and to realize their human potential. Reaching that goal requires a wrenching shift away from what we *want* to what we

---

[6]"Robert Towne," in Terry Sanders and Freida Lee Mock (eds.), *Word into Image: Writers on Screenwriting: Transcripts of the Award-Winning Film Series,* by American Film Foundation, Los Angeles, 1981, p. 3.

need to be whole and healthy. Skillful screenwriting invests characters with these needs and devises ways to solve them. Accomplishing that shift provides the psychological drive that dimensionalizes characters as it powers stories.

The Blind Spot

I recommend that you study how Salt and Towne include a blind spot that prevents their protagonists from seeing the error of their ways. In real life, removing such a blind spot—and almost everyone has at least one of them—may take years of therapy and/or self-repair.

Greek classical drama frequently afflicted the hero with a blind spot that prevented that character from seeing the error of his or her ways. This strategy still shows in films that range from character studies *(What's Love Got to Do with It)*, to epics *(The Bridge on the River Kwai)*, to action stories *(Jurassic Park)*. In the latter film, characters must rid themselves of their blind spot before they can see the dangers of tampering with nature.

Shadowlands works this way, too. The film chronicles the struggle of C. S. Lewis (Anthony Hopkins) to remove his blind spot (a shrunken worldview and a limited appreciation of life). Lewis's problem traces back to the loss of his mother when he was a boy. The trauma caused Lewis to take refuge in academia, which is where American writer Joy Gresham (Debra Winger) finds him—a timid celibate dozing his life away. When Lewis falls in love with Gresham, he realizes what an academic dustball he has become, abandons his ivory tower, and embraces life. In this example, removing the blind spot involves casting away an attitude that blinds Lewis to truths that could lead him to a fuller life.

Other Psychological Models

Psychologists are fond of personality models that help them to understand their patients. My wife, for example, is a psychotherapist who follows the Family Systems theory of psychology, which contends that family problems often repeat from generation to generation. Thus, if a child is abused, there is a better-than-average chance that he or she will eventually become an abuser as well. There are too many psychological approaches to even list, but I have selected a few of them that suggest the usefulness of this thinking to screenwriters.

One perspective comes from UCLA psychologist Jack Katz, who has studied a character type who shows up in many stories: the recidivist criminal. Katz's findings indicate that many criminals are so committed to a tough-guy image that they are undeterred by threats of prison. Additionally, many of these people are part of a social caste that expects them to behave like criminals. This helps to explain why recidivists often fritter away their stolen gain: it is done to show their public that they do not steal for the money's sake but rather because of their contempt for society and its rules. It is, in essence, a form of bragging. Katz quotes one such individual:

Straight people don't understand. I mean, they think dudes is after the things straight people got. It ain't that at all. People in the life ain't looking for no home and grass in the yard and shit like that. We the show people. The glamour people. Come on the set with the finest car, the finest woman. Hear people talking about you. Hear the bar get quiet when you walk in the door.[7]

A life of crime gives these people, many of them from deprived, abusive homes, a sense of self and importance. This point, well known to social workers who deal with inner-city gangs, shows up in *American Me*, a film about the Mexican Mafia. Although status as a nonperson may be a criminal's greatest fear, his or her actions often lead to death or prison. Incarcerated, these people not only lose many of their human rights, but even their names are taken away and replaced by prison numbers. In this way, the criminal's psychological imperative—to seek status by defying society—drives him (or her) away from what he needs (to be whole and human) and toward the anonymity he sought to escape through crime.

As criminals play their outlaw roles, a related phenomenon can affect non-outlaws too. This was pointed out by University of Southern California psychoanalyst Jay Martin, who has studied the way people assume fictive personalities.[8] Martin contends that certain people consciously or unconsciously take on aspects of a favorite character from fiction, movies, or television. For example, a man might unconsciously imitate John Wayne's rolling gait or Hugh Grant's shy charm; a woman might adopt the brazen style of a rock star or use Katharine Hepburn as a model of independence. Although many healthy people build their public persona from bits and pieces of real and fictional characters, a few are taken over by fictive personalities. William Faulkner, for one, so identified with the aristocratic English flyers of World War I that for years he walked with a limp that he attributed to a plane crash. Faulkner was a great writer who trained as a pilot in Canada, but as far as his biographers know, he did not suffer a plane crash. Even so, Faulkner clung to his fictive personality because it created an image that he found appealing.

Screenwriters use psychological insights such as these to create and to motivate their characters. The fictive personality idea, for example, could influence where a character lives and also his or her dress style, socializing habits, occupation, and recreational activities. Annie of *Sleepless in Seattle* could be such a character, attracted as she is to movie romance, highly verbal men, true love, and destiny. Nicholas Cage's character in *Moonstruck* seems to have formed his persona from the operas that he adores. If we decide that Mom in the sports widow story will transform herself into the amazon she has always feared she would become, then that decision would influence the direction of the story.

---

[7]Jack Katz, *Seductions of Crime: Moral and Sensual Attractions in Doing Evil*, Basic Books, New York, 1988, p. 315.
[8]Jay Martin, *Who Am I This Time: Uncovering the Fictive Personality*, W. W. Norton, New York, 1988.

THE "EMPTY CHAIR" EXERCISE

Writers often go to great lengths to understand their characters and to improve their stories. One strategy, the "empty chair" exercise, pursues this goal by asking the writer to imagine that one of his or her main characters is sitting in a nearby empty chair. The writer then barrages the character with personal questions that can be angry, intimate, or whatever comes to mind. We might wish to place Mom in the empty chair and ask her about the secret self that she has been hiding, or Dad or any other character could be questioned. This exercise can be emotionally freeing as the questions reveal the character. Tape the sessions so you can review what is said during the exercise.

The empty chair exercise can be varied if you play the part of the character in the empty chair, so that instead of asking questions, you must answer them. Or use two people who have a question-and-answer session about a particular issue or problem; one person becomes the character in the chair while the other interrogates. After five minutes or so, take a break and switch roles. The questions can be accusatory or gentle. They can be about money, favoritism, suffering, sex, professional situations, why the person was a good or bad son (or daughter or parent), and so on.

As with speed-writing and other exercises mentioned in this text, the empty chair exercise can be a loud, messy, and at times unnerving experience that pries open the writer's unconscious and reveals useful character and story insights. A typical empty chair exercise can be completed in a half hour or so.

Although the empty chair exercise is often liberating, it is so potent that I am reluctant to use it in class because some students are upset by the emotions unleashed. When I do use the exercise, I prepare for it by turning off the lights for ten minutes or so while the class watches a relaxation video. The empty chair is placed in the center of the room with everyone gathered around in a circle. When the music ends, a small spotlight, pre-aimed at the empty chair, is turned on and the questioning begins. All of this is quite theatrical, but it can help unleash interesting currents from the unconscious.

WRITING INTERESTING MINOR CHARACTERS

Certain films *(Ruthless People, Midnight Run, Moonstruck)* allow minor characters to demonstrate their needs and personalities. Scripts are usually improved when the minor roles are allowed to sparkle. Although the narrative must be kept moving, moments given to the supporting roles can add dimension and interest to the story. Usually a minor character can be revealed quickly and in ways that enrich the story without slowing momentum.

To illustrate how minor characters add to a story, compare two scenes from *The Terminator* films. The actor who plays the police officer staffing the desk in Shot 160 of *The Terminator* has little to do except to say his line before the cyborg drives a truck through the front of the police station, killing him. By comparison, the character who runs the biker bar in *Terminator 2: Judgment Day* is given a chance to reveal his inner being when he points his shotgun at the cyborg and warns the critter to step away from the motorcycles. The cyborg, who has been programmed to be more kindly in this sequel, snatches the gun away, removes a pair of sunglasses from the man's shirt pocket, and drives off. Although the incident only plays for ten seconds or so, it allows the character (portrayed by Pete Schrum) to display the grit expected from someone who runs a saloon for outlaw bikers. As a result, a minor character's moment in the spotlight adds credibility to the entire scene.

Writing minor roles is easier when the writer appreciates how much an actor can do in a few seconds. For example, Edward Mason, who plays the son in the funeral home in Shot 3 of *The Verdict*, needs but two lines to expose Galvin's ghoulish lie about being a friend of the deceased. Other memorable minor roles include George Murdock's dying father in *Shoot the Moon*, Julie Bovasso's loyal Nurse Rooney in *The Verdict*, Cicely Tyson's dangerously quiet helpmate in *Fried Green Tomatoes*, and many, many other supporting players who, when given even a small chance to demonstrate their talent, add glory to the movies. Well-written television shows (e.g., *Cheers, Frasier, China Beach, NYPD Blue, Roseanne*) are built around outstanding supporting players. The only hazard in this area is taking so much attention away from the main characters that the story lacks focus. Movies avoid this by being judicious in the time and attention given to minor roles; also, the director may decide that the minor role is unbalancing a scene or the story, which usually means the role will be eviscerated and the writer's work to develop the secondary characters will be chucked out. When this happens, it usually means that outstanding actors will be again reduced to roles in which they are used as human furniture or carriers of exposition.

SUMMARY

People are born with certain talents, physical traits, and inclinations that intertwine with family, social, and other factors to shape personality. Screenwriters use such nature and nurture influences to write emotionally dimensional characters. Reading and observation can help writers develop psychological insights useful for figuring out what characters are thinking, what motivates them, and what they are struggling to overcome or achieve.

Much of a character's psychology is based on backstory—what happened before the story begins. Backstory involves the experience of the characters, the history of the dramatic situation, and whatever has bearing on the drama. When the location and the characters are alive in imagination, it is possible for a writer to capture that life on paper. Remember WYSIWYG (what you see is what you get).

It is easier to imagine at this intense level when the characters can be understood psychologically and socially. Characters who express emotions and the drama of their lives—who seem alive on the page—are appreciated by actors, directors, producers, and those who buy literary material.

Writers create backstories that supply characters with psychological imperatives that are based on short-term trauma or long-term conditioning. The imperatives drive the characters and generate internal stresses and emotional energy that make the story and the characters interesting. When a story is dull and not working, the characters may need to be energized with backstory experiences and quirkiness. Coming up with these traits is easier when the writer routinely observes people that he or she meets in everyday life. The empty chair exercise is one way to reveal characters and their motivations.

Finally, this reminder: The points made in the text aim to acquaint you with the values that go into writing characters so you will notice them in the movies you watch and in the scripts that you read and write. However, to fully absorb these lessons, you must practice them; otherwise, it is unlikely that they will become useful to you.

Exercises

Select a male and a female character from one of the main study films and work out psychological imperatives that you feel fit each. Your analysis should include answers to the questions below.

1. What created the psychological imperatives that drive the two characters? What is the nature of each character's short-term trauma or long-term conditioning?
2. How is the imperative displayed by the character?
3. Assign sociological influences and life experiences that might have affected the characters.
4. What are the characters most afraid of? How does the psychological imperative create needs in the characters?
5. Are the characters pursuing what they need or what they want? Explain.

(For media that illustrate the points made in this chapter, see Appendix A.)

CHAPTER 6

Dialogue and Character

This chapter examines how dialogue advances the story, reveals character, and presents strategies for revealing backstory and exposition.

WRITING DIALOGUE

Dialogue can be written either as straight talk (called *on-the-nose*) or as dialogue with subtext that contains unspoken but implied meaning. This chapter discusses how to freight these two types of dialogue with content that reveals the characters and their backstories while passing on essential plot information without slowing the forward momentum of the story. The chapter also discusses how to write "actable" dialogue that has emotional subtext as well as dialogue that speaks with dramatic silences and pauses. There are strategies for managing these tasks so that your characters and their stories can come to life.

We can open this topic with a valuable dialogue lesson that I learned many years ago when my agent (Mel Bloom) returned one of my scripts and asked me to fan the pages. When Mel asked whether I noticed anything unusual, I told him that the pages contained long speeches that showed as brick-sized masses of typing. Mel then handed me an award-winning script and I saw that its pages were white and airy because the speeches used but a line or two of dialogue. That lesson from the fanning incident suggests the most important advice in this chapter: *Use as little dialogue as possible,* because audiences pay to see moving pictures, not to listen to illustrated radio or to watch "talking heads."

This is not an easy lesson for screenwriters, we who spend our days alone in a room talking to and for our characters. We may play with voice-over narration, internal voices, subtitles, talking billboards, animals and machines that talk, voices from another time or dimension, and so on. Some of us may mutter to our computers or our pets, or say lines and make faces at ourselves as we try material out while staring into a mirror! With all of this buzzing going on in our heads, it is understandable that we write characters whose endless babble must be cut. Cutting often requires removing large chunks of dialogue initially, and then refining what is left by snipping a little here and a little there until all that is left is effective, pared-down dialogue.

New writers should also know that buyers often read a script by skimming the stage directions and following the story by reading the dialogue that tells the reader about the characters and their dramatic ordeal. Let this be your second dialogue lesson: *Invest in what your characters say, not the stage directions,* because regardless of how brilliantly this "black stuff" is written, it will not sell the script.

WYSIWYG (see Chapter 5) applies to this topic, for when your characters are alive in your imagination, they should say things that advance the story while revealing who they are. The dialogue also indicates whether the screenwriter has an ear for dialogue, i.e., did the author write empty speeches or did he or she use enriched speech that reveals the characters? This aspect of screenwriting was discussed with screenwriter Julius Epstein *(Casablanca)* during a WGA interview.[1] Epstein said that the ability to create effective dialogue depends on whether the writer has "an ear for dialogue." When I asked which ear he meant—the external ear used for everyday speech, or the internal ear that hears what characters say to us in imagination—Epstein replied that both the inner ear and the outer ear are needed.

Epstein's observation on how writers perceive dialogue organizes this chapter, because as screenwriters we must not only hear what our fictional characters say but also what people in everyday life say—and how they say it. This means being alert to accents, emotional content, tension, rhythms, and especially the unspoken subtext behind spoken words. It also means that screenwriters must listen *hard,* reading the speaker's eyes to discern if the words spoken match what the person seems to be thinking and feeling. We also observe body language, gestures, facial expressions, vocal quality, quavers in the voice, and the choice of words, because these elements are components of dialogue and speech.

Although screenwriters are not the only people who listen this way, we may be among the few who visualize spoken language as printout on an imaginary page. The purpose of this trick is to help us judge whether the words that we hear are laden with the emotional content of what was said. We then use the lessons of this study to write dialogue that reveals the characters' inner being. I look at this aspect of the work as writing characters rather than dialogue, so that if a character is not saying interesting things in a particular speech, I ask him or her to say the speech again—and to make it better this time!

During this work, we can be so close to the imagined characters that we see them tremble with passion and experience the emotion in their eyes. We feel what they feel and sense what motivates them. Our goal as we write is to become the characters, to slip into their skins so we can lend them our energy or even let them take possession of us. In such a state, we become our creations, experiencing what the characters feel and think. We become their medium, their outlet to the world—but only up to a point, for no matter how intense the writing session, there is always a piece of the writer that sits in the corner, scribbling down everything that happens. Without such intimacy with the characters, we cannot experience the passion that inspires the dialogue.

---

[1]Writers Guild of America (WGA) interview, May 1994.

Screenwriter Paddy Chayefsky's version of the creative delirium sounds very much like John Gardner's fictive dream (mentioned in the preceding chapter):

> Dialogue comes because I know what I want my characters to say. I envision the scene; I can imagine them up there on the screen; I try to imagine what they would be saying and how they would be saying it, and I keep it in character. And the dialogue comes out of that. I think that goes for every writer in the world. Then I rewrite it. Then I cut it. Then I refine it until I get the scene as precise as I can get it.[2]

Writing dialogue during a fictive dream requires endurance and force of will as we cajole our characters to repeat speeches until the words come from *their* hearts, not our own. For this to happen we must step back and give our characters opportunities to come alive in imagination.

Writers have many ways of writing dialogue. Some do it gradually, carefully completing each beat of the outline; others go into overdrive and write the entire first draft in a week or so. Blasting out a first draft this way requires enormous energy, and whether craft skills are used during this work depends on the state of the writer's frenzy. Often during a first-draft sprint the writer is only interested in finishing, to see if the story that has been gestating can be captured on paper. Usually the story is there, but it will probably have fragmentary scenes, gaps, dopey characters who say dopey things, scenes that make no sense, actions that are sappy, and other problems that can be fixed. All that really matters at this stage is whether the writer has written a story that has some passion and fire; everything else can be cleaned up during later drafts. We know we are on to a good thing when the first draft presents characters who have gone through an ordeal and who have expressed heartfelt, honest emotion in their dialogue. If the emotion felt by the characters seems real and alive, the screenwriter will remember the moment so it can be used to refine the dialogue and the scenes.

REEL DIALOGUE VERSUS REAL SPEECH

By the time dialogue shows up in a movie, it has been sanded and smoothed until it sounds so natural and so easy that it seems as though anyone could write it— or act it. This is one of the deceptions of good movie dialogue, for screenwriters know that the words are invested with content that creates conflict and drama as they build tension and make the point of the scene. Because it has work to do, movie dialogue is "invisible," that is, it is stripped of flowery language, wise sayings, word plays, puns, metaphors, and anything else that might call attention to its cleverness or take the audience out of the story. Joining these items in the scrap heap are repetitions, clichés, stale language, and fatty babble such as *Your hair is the most beautiful flame-red color I've ever seen.* This line could be edited to *Nice hair* or replaced with a tousling gesture that the actors can improvise.

[2]John Brady, *The Craft of the Screenwriter*, Simon & Schuster, New York, 1981, p. 61.

Whether profanity needs to be cut depends on the writer's temperament. Some writers feel that cussing adds realism to their work, and it can. However, I advise cutting as many cuss words as you can, because foul language usually adds little to a story, and too much of it can bloat a story with ugliness. The TV version of *The Verdict*, to take one case, edited out the original's cussing, and the movie did not suffer at all.[3] Even *Heartbreak Ridge*, which must be in someone's book of records for "most swear words in a single movie," was scoured of vulgarity without losing its machismo swagger. Also see *On the Waterfront*, which depicts thuggish gangsters who make it through this very realistic movie without cussing. Screenwriter Budd Schulberg made up a few ersatz terms for this film ("cheese-eater" for *stool pigeon* was one of them), which illustrates how thoughtful insults can add importance to the characters, the dialogue, and the movie.

Movie dialogue simulates real speech by assuming a conversational tone. It does so without droppin' letters from words or employing unique wayzuv spellin'. However, it is advisable to use contractions. Thus, *I won't go if they're coming* is usually preferable to *I will not go if they are coming*. As a general rule, dialogue should be grammatically correct, unless the mistake is to reveal something about a character.

Movie dialogue seldom underlines or bold-prints words for emphasis; such an approach is usually a sign that the screenwriter is trying to direct the movie with the script. Most dialogue is unadorned except by exclamation points (to indicate emphasis or emotional heat) and question marks. Not all writers follow this advice, but most do, because the intent and emphasis of good dialogue are difficult to miss. It is also cadenced and structured in ways that indicate the style and energy of how the speeches should performed.

Because motion pictures are intensely focused, characters do not speak unless there is a reason. Their words are spare and carefully chosen. They make the point of the scene and then they shut up. Unlike real speech, movie dialogue is seldom repetitive or vague (unless there is a reason).

Some characters speak with a foreign or regional accent. It is usually not necessary to write dialogue in either dialect or a foreign language. For example, some of the Amish in *Witness* speak German and also English with a German accent, but the scripted dialogue is in English; it does not say how the dialect should be spoken. The funeral eulogy (Shot 9) is said in German, but the scripted speech is in English. The stage directions note that "the preacher begins to speak in a formal German dialect. SUBTITLES OVER." The filmmaker decided not to use subtitles, and the solemnity of the ceremony proved to be sufficient.

---

[3]Some films are dubbed by the performers during production, so that the cursing used for theatrical release can be replaced when the movie is aired on broadcast television. If this is not done, the network or individual stations may make the cuts; when done poorly, such editing can mangle a movie. To prevent this from happening, some writers protect their work by placing profanity at the beginning or at the end of a speech, so the cussing will be easier to edit and the cuts will be less noticeable.

One of my TV movies was about North Carolina mountain people who speak in a regional dialect, which I indicated with a single stage direction: "The mountain dialect is twangy and muscular, with a courtliness that is almost Elizabethan." Whatever the language, it can be set up with stage directions: *Ch'ang immigrated from China ten years ago; he continues to struggle with English.* This is enough to tell the reader that the character has an accent; there is no need to write the dialogue in broken English. If the dialect or accent is a factor, use stage directions to set it up, as in *struggling to express herself, garbling the sentence,* or *a confused mix of languages.*

Movie dialogue is not radio dialogue that must describe what the home audience cannot see. On a radio show, a character might say, "Why are you taking that pistol out of the drawer and pointing it at me?" Because movie audiences can see what is happening on screen, the dialogue should supply fresh information.

Movie dialogue often makes its points by playing against expectation. For example, when a scene is explosively dramatic—say, parents learn their child has been injured in an accident—the expectation is for a major emotional upheaval. Such a scene could be written against expectations by having the couple putter in their garden, containing their anguish with small talk, until one of them finds the child's ball, which causes their facade of control to collapse. Such a moment can be found in *The Verdict* (Shot 6) when Galvin jokes with his cronies after being ejected from the funeral home. Rather than showing anger about his humiliation, Galvin makes light of the incident. Only later, alone and drunk in his office, does he express his anguish.

Movie dialogue does not sound like a progression of speeches; it sounds like people talking so that one side of dialogue leads to another in a way that maintains continuity. The language is simple, direct, and easily understood. Because movie dialogue uses fewer words, the actors enunciate them with clarity and emphasis. Unlike real life, movie dialogue is stripped of conversational chaff such as *ah, y'know, well,* and *ummm.* Write straight dialogue and trust the actors to embellish it, if needed. In sum, movie dialogue is as different from everyday speech as a Seeing Eye dog is from the family pooch. Like a Seeing Eye dog, movie dialogue has a mission. It is disciplined. It is lean and precise, and it works.

HOW DIALOGUE IS CONSTRUCTED

There is an organized build to movie dialogue that is uncommon in everyday speech. There may be three or four small dialogue peaks within a scene. Example: In Shot 65 of *The Verdict,* when Concannon humbles Dr. Thompson, Galvin's expert witness, the dialogue contains four small dramatic rises that increase tension and conflict. The first sees Concannon demean Thompson for being Galvin's hired mouth. The next peak occurs when Concannon impugns Thompson's medical credentials. The third peak has Concannon all but accuse Thompson of abusing the legal system by testifying against other doctors. The fourth peak occurs when Concannon implies that Thompson's actions are prompted by racial antipathy.

As the dialogue in this scene intensifies, it does so by arranging for the most important point—the punch line—to occur at the end of the speech. In the following exchange from *The Verdict* scene that we have been discussing, Dr. Thompson tries to explain his qualifications, but Concannon cuts him off:

CONCANNON

```
Yes, we've heard that.
Doctor: you testify quite a
bit against other physicians?
Isn't that right?  You, you're
available for that?  When
you're paid to be there?
```

DR. THOMPSON

```
Sir.  Yes.  When a thing is
wrong . . . as in this case, I
am available.  I am seventy-
four years old, I am not
board-certified.  I have been
practicing medicine for forty-
six years and I know when an
injustice has been done.
```

CONCANNON

```
Do you, indeed.  I'll bet you
do.  Fine.  Fine.  We'll save
the court the time.  We will
admit the Doctor as an 'expert
witness,' fine.
```

The Verdict, written by David Mamet, 1982

Although the elegance of this exchange is best appreciated by viewing the scene, note how the dialogue in the first Concannon speech peaks where he remarks that Dr. Thompson has been "paid to be there." Because it is the strongest line (the punch line), it comes at the end of the speech.

Thompson's speech is also organized dramatically: note when he asserts that what happened to Galvin's client was wrong. Thompson continues, admitting that he is an old physician of modest accomplishment, but he knows "when an injustice has been done." This is the punch line of his speech. Concannon tops it when he turns the "injustice" line around so that the elderly African-American is made to sound like a racist who testifies against white doctors. This occurs on Concannon's line "I'll bet you do [know when an injustice has been done]." As a parting slap at Thompson, the quotes tell the actor to impart a sneering quality when referring to Thompson as an "expert witness."

When Concannon voices no objection to having Dr. Thompson testify, it is only after he has discredited him. The dialogue of this scene is thus able to discredit Galvin's expert witness so the hero is alone when he faces a hostile judge and Concannon. In this way, the story makes the audience worry about the hero's ability to solve the problem of the story (how to win the case).

EXPOSITION AND DIALOGUE

Expositional dialogue reveals information about the plot and the characters. In *The Verdict*, expositional dialogue tells us that a case is coming to trial, that Galvin is a lush, that his clients need legal help, and other information that fills in the details of the plot. Exposition can deal with the history of a situation, as in *Witness* (Shot 34) when Book tells Schaeffer why the officer was murdered in the train station. Although writers are driven to explain their stories with dialogue exposition, resist the urge and remember the main rule of exposition and dialogue: *less is more*. Too much information can slow the story and dilutes the intensity of the drama.

It is difficult to generalize how much exposition should be freighted into the dialogue, because it depends on the nature of the story and the interests of the writer. Yarns such as *Jurassic Park* and *Clear and Present Danger* require considerable explanation; *Moonstruck* and *Ruby in Paradise* deal with ordinary situations that do not require much explanation. Script and film study is the most practical way to learn how much exposition is needed to tell a story. Such study will teach you to resist dumping loads of exposition on the audience. Although it is sometimes necessary to fill in important plot or character information, long expository speeches slow the story, they often lack strong imagery, and extended exposition can have an undesirable effect on the audience. This happens because movies conspire to put viewers into an emotional state; exposition undermines this condition by asking them to process names, dates, facts, and comings and goings. To keep the audience enthralled emotionally, it is therefore advisable (in most cases) to use minimal dialogue that focuses on what the characters are experiencing emotionally rather than to pound the audience with exposition that deals with plot and backstory.

Ask if the story will suffer if the expositional dialogue is cut. If not, the information may not be needed. When the exposition is important, ask if the information can be inserted elsewhere in the script. Also think about how plot and character information can be communicated with images rather than dialogue. For example, in *The Terminator* Sarah and Reese could have drawn up a diagram as they discussed the damage suffered by the cyborg and how this might affect their chances of defeating the creature. Instead, the movie presented three minutes of the cyborg silently repairing itself (Shots 152, 158). In *The Verdict* there was no talk of Galvin's drinking problem; instead, we see it in action when he wrecks his office during the opening sequence. These examples illustrate another prime (and demanding) bit of dialogue advice: *Showing is usually better than telling.*

FREIGHTING DIALOGUE WITH EXPOSITION

There is no mystery as to how speech is loaded with exposition; we do it every day, as in, "Dad, can I use the car tonight? I'm taking Sis to the game and we'll be home early." This dialogue conveys the request to use the car; that the person is taking Sis to a game; and that the couple will return home at a reasonable hour. Additionally, the tone of the request (arrogant, tentative, nervous) could provide subtext that affects the dramatic moment. Thus, marbling dialogue with exposition means salting the speeches with information that tells about character, plot, relationships, theme, and/or backstory.

As mentioned in Chapter 5, when exposition must be worked into the story, trickle it in—a point here, a reference there, and an inference, intimation, or attitude wherever possible. Marbling this way keeps the story moving and gives viewers enough time to absorb the dialogue without realizing they are being fed information. Example: In *Witness* (Shot 93C), when Rachel tells Book about the rude tourists who ridicule the Amish way of dressing, her dialogue conveys exposition about herself and about her sect, as well as plot information. At the same time, the subtext of the dialogue is furthering the couple's relationship, for Rachel is watching Book to see whether he will react like a rude tourist or like someone that she can trust.

Exposition can be freighted into dialogue through conflict, when tempers flare and angry words are spoken, as in this excerpt from *The Quiet Man*. It is early in the movie, when Sean Thornton (John Wayne) returns to Ireland to buy his family cottage from the current owner, the iron-willed Mrs. Tillane:

```
          MRS. TILLANE
My own family, Mr. Thornton,
has been in Ireland since the
Norman invasion . . . but we
have seen no reason to
establish monuments or
memorials to that fact. . . .


          SEAN
Look, I didn't say anything
about monuments or memorials!
It's just that ever since I
was a kid living in a shack
near the slag-heaps, my mother
used to talk to me about
Inisfree and White o'Morn.
With me, Inisfree's always
been another word for heaven
. . . so, when I quit the
ri . . . (he catches himself)
```

```
. . . when I quit, I came
here--just one thought in my
mind.
```

The Quiet Man, written by Frank Nugent, 1951

This exchange tells us that the widow's family is of ancient Norman origin and that Sean grew up midst slag-heaps and steel mills. The dialogue also suggests that Sean was close to his mother and that their hard life was eased by dreams of White o'Morn, the family cottage in Ireland. Additionally, Sean almost reveals that he was a professional boxer, a fact he wishes to conceal.

Note how the conflict allows Mrs. Tillane to take the measure of the Yank newcomer. Their discord sparks when she accuses him of "monument building." Although this is a manufactured little spat, it creates conflict that drives the scene. At the same time, the beat remains true to the logic of the story and its characters.

Expository dialogue can be loaded into the desperation of an action scene, as when Reese tells Sarah about the cyborg in *The Terminator* (Shot 116). His long speech—pure exposition and backstory—plays off the excitement of a wild car chase. Similarly, key information can be blurted out during moments of extreme anger, passion, or peril, as in *The Verdict* (Shot 61) when Laura angrily tells Galvin that she will not invest her life in another failure. When using disputation to reveal exposition, the conflict should be motivated and necessary; otherwise, it may show as a shrill plot contrivance.

Key plot exposition can also occur during a *reveal,* when the audience is told hitherto concealed information. We see this in the climactic scene of *The Verdict* (Shot 92), when Kaitlin reveals that Dr. Towler forced her to change the admitting form. Her testimony enables Galvin to win his case.

Exposition and backstory can be worked into dialogue by **torquing** the scene. As will be discussed in Chapter 7, torquing presents a diversion or context that entertains the audience while the story pumps out needed exposition and backstory. We see torquing during the engagement party in *Sleepless in Seattle* (Shot 18) because Walter's allergies and Annie's daffy relatives entertain the audience while the dialogue delivers exposition concerning the couple's marriage plans.

Exposition Through Images

Whenever possible, convey exposition through images. *The Verdict* opens this way when the hero enters the funeral home and takes a squirt of breath freshener to hide his whiskey breath. The action asks viewers to figure out why he did this; the answer appears when they see him having whiskey and doughnuts for breakfast in the next beat and they realize that Galvin has a drinking problem.

Often the ambiance of a scene can be created without dialogue. *Jaws,* for example, opens with a beach party: night, music, young people, a bonfire, good times. The setting instantly explains itself, and throughout the four-minute establishing scene the dialogue consists of little more than throwaway lines.[4] Also see *Sleepless in Seattle* (Shots 81–84), when Annie and Sam are sitting alone on opposite coasts, brooding over their lives and their sense of incompleteness. There is no dialogue, yet the film communicates their unhappiness through music, expressions, gestures, and body language.

ON-THE-NOSE DIALOGUE

When expositional dialogue passes on information in a direct, unembroidered fashion, the author is using **on-the-nose dialogue.** "They went thatta way!" is straight exposition that states the obvious. On-the-nose dialogue lacks subtext and implied meaning; instead, it clearly states its meaning. Most of the dialogue for youth films is written on-the-nose because such stories generally do not probe character. Instead, on-the-nose dialogue quickly explains backstory and plot information that the young audience must have to track the story.

On-the-nose dialogue shows up in action stories and in character stories as well. *The Verdict* (Shots 8, 14, 21, 26, 53, 57, 65, 92) uses on-the-nose dialogue to explain legal and medical issues that the audience must understand. Just as writers develop a sense of how much exposition is appropriate, they also sense how much on-the-nose dialogue is appropriate. Too much exposition or on-the-nose dialogue can overexplain the story; too little and the story may be confusing.

Expository dialogue can be made more palatable to the audience if it is glazed with irony (*Reversal of Fortune*), humor (*Under Siege*), menace (*Misery*), and the like. The overlay tone may be due to an attitude that the writer assumes toward a character. Some writers do this by pretending that a famous actor is delivering the speech; for example, dialogue written for George Saunders or Flora Robson might have a sophisticated or snide tone. When the dialogue must be cranky, Mary Wickes or Eugene Pallette might be imagined. Pick a few of your favorite actors, put their faces on your characters, and use the resulting energy to invest your dialogue with emotion and style.

DIALOGUE AND SUBTEXT

The opposite of on-the-nose dialogue is dialogue with subtext, which a student once defined as being "talk that's pregnant with meaning." The definition makes its point: subtext goes beyond the surface meaning and intimates what the characters are thinking and feeling but not saying directly. For example, in Shot 38 of *The Verdict*, the judge remarks that if offered a fat set-

---

[4]**Throwaway lines** seem ad-libbed or unimportant, although this may not be the case. There is an indirectness to throwaway lines, as if they were an afterthought or something that did not require close attention. The cutting edge of a joke can be deemphasized by delivering it with a throwaway quality.

tlement, he would take the money and run like a thief. Galvin's response ("I'm sure you would") contains a hostile subtext that connects to the hero's bitterness over the Lillibridge case.

Just as people load exposition into everyday speech, they also infuse subtextual attitudes into conversation: "He's not doing too well—but that's typical of his kind." "Jack's a generous guy . . . surprisingly!" "I hear she's doing better, but you know Mary!" Similarly, movie dialogue uses subtext to imply feelings, tension, and energy that are not stated outright by the characters. In *Sleepless in Seattle* (Shot 21) we learn that Annie and Walter do not have the most exciting relationship. The point is made subtextually, when Annie cheerily tells her mother that Walter is wonderful and their love life is working like "clockwork"—i.e., it is mechanical and lacks excitement.

Screenwriting is more than wordsmithing and clever dialogue. It means, above all, writing a story with situations that are charged with drama, as in *It Could Happen to You,* when the hero enters a grocery store, unaware that it is being robbed. Although everyone in the store tries to act as though nothing is wrong, the context of the robbery imposes a subtext of tension on the dialogue.

The dramatic context can be the result of personal chemistry, as when two people are attracted (Cher and Nicholas Cage in *Moonstruck*; Tom Hanks and Mykelti Williamson's Bubba in *Forrest Gump*). Context can also be caused by negative chemistry (Melanie Griffith and Sigourney Weaver in *Working Girl*). This strategy requires giving the characters an attitude—one person is trying to dominate the other, or one person is snide, insinuating, teasing, nasty, or whatever. Example: In *The Terminator* (Shot 153), the attitude of the smug police psychologist who scoffs at Reese's story about a cyborg from the future provokes a tirade that intensifies the drama.

Subtext can be generated by the energy of a situation, as in *Sleepless in Seattle* (Shot 196), when Sam reunites with his son on top of the Empire State Building. Movies have used this strategy from the earliest days. On a simplistic level it may be a haunted house or some such Oh-my-gawd-don't-go-there! situation or location that a character must enter. As a result, the tensions of the setting and the circumstances create a context that affects the dialogue. This happens in *The Shawshank Redemption* when the young convict is lured to a secret location and shot when the warden learns that the convict is willing to testify for the hero. The opening action scene of *In the Line of Fire* presents a tense situation when, to prove that he is not a cop, the hero is ordered by the criminals that he is trying to capture to execute a helpless man.

Subtext can be influenced by the pressures of time or circumstances, as when something must be accomplished within a given period of time. *In the Line of Fire*'s hero guards against an assassin. This knowledge imposes a subtext of urgency and danger on the plot and its dialogue. *Speed* uses a speed-controlled bomb on a bus to energize the dialogue with urgency.

Music can create a powerful context that energizes dialogue, particularly if the audience recognizes the piece as a signature cue. The music in *Jaws* and *Klute* signals the presence of the menace and shades the dialogue with urgency and meaning. In most cases, the audience needs to hear a signature theme only once to associate it with a character or situation. Sometimes writers need a confidence booster before taking on a risky scene; knowing that supportive music is available can provide that lift. Usually, the musical cue is not stated in the script, but the writer imagines it while writing the dialogue. If the music cannot be imagined, play a tape or CD containing appropriate music. We know that intense movie moments are often punched up this way, so use music that floats you into the desired mental state.

A sound effect can create context for dialogue if the audience understands its significance. *The Man in the White Suit* uses an odd gurgling sound to indicate that the scientific genius of the hero is percolating; thus, the sound effect creates a context for the dialogue. In some cases, sound effects can replace dialogue, as in *The Terminator* (Shot 46), which uses battle sounds and music instead of dialogue during Reese's first flashback.

A mood can create a context, as in *Moonstruck,* when the magic of a full moon generates subtext for dialogue. In *Like Water for Chocolate,* the heroine's passion affects her cooking, driving those who partake of it to emotional extremes. Thus the food supplies a context that affects dialogue and action. Context can charge a scene and its dialogue with humor and emotion, as in *Sleepless in Seattle* (Shot 139B), when Annie rehearses what she plans to say to Sam when she meets him. Her anxiety energizes her private moment with humorous subtext.

SUBTEXT AND "ACTABLE" DIALOGUE

When actors step before cameras, they are armed only with their craft and the fig leaf that is the script. They must combine these elements with grease paint, costumes, sets, and shadow and light in a way that entertains people all over this planet. In their quest to entertain, actors search scripts for dramatic content that will enthrall audiences. If the writer of a script has created such content, the actors will discover it. If the script lacks content, the actors will discover this too. What the actors are looking for are moments that connect to backstory experiences and personality traits of their characters, so their humanity and emotional life can be revealed. For example, the characters played by Clint Eastwood in *Unforgiven* and *In the Line of Fire* are haunted by memories that shape their personalities and affect how they react to the incidents of the plot. The audience sees emotional flashes from these men—nightmares, crankiness, vulnerability—that connect to their backstories. Such moments clue actors about the emotional state of the characters so they can use that energy to build the characters and to drive the story.

An actor's analysis of a role begins with a reading of the script and a determination of the character's contribution to the story. The actor analyzes what the character wants, how much emotional juice is spilled, and how much of it belongs to that character. This work usually finds actors going over the script as if it were a treasure map. Dialogue, stage directions, plot, and even marks of punctuation are studied to learn what motivates the characters and how they relate to each other. The purpose of this analysis is to discover moments in the story that are actable.

Actable dialogue gives performers a chance to play beyond the mere meaning of the words so they can indicate the deep-felt thoughts, longings, feelings, and memories that are part of the characters' backstories. Usually, this emotional and thoughtful content is expressed obliquely, without using dialogue, as in *Sleepless in Seattle* (Shot 200), when Annie returns Walter's ring and calls off their marriage plans. In this exchange, unspoken relief, sadness, rejection, and selfhood are expressed by the actors because the screenwriters invested those values in their script.

Silences and the Actability of Dialogue

There are even more profound levels of actability, where the performers act out the silences in the dialogue. Most films have times when there are intensely silent moments as the characters react to what has been said or to an action. At such times, just a few words can play for a minute or so as the characters, usually filmed in close-ups, reveal the intense emotional activity that rages within. Often this passion is not expressed with dialogue or action; it is expressed through unspoken feelings and thoughts that are communicated through gesture, body language, and vocal inflection, and especially by what shows in the eyes of the actors. The ability of gifted actors to *show thought* can draw audiences into the story by making them aware of what is going on within the minds of the characters. Even though the silence lasts but a few seconds, it is enough time for audiences to intuit the unspoken thoughts of the characters and to empathize with the characters and share the drama of the story, which is one of the main goals of the movie.

Although the importance of silences seems like an obvious point, it is ignored by many writers who fear that their stories will sag because nothing seems to be happening. So, instead of trusting the power of their images and dramatic situations, they opt for overall "busy-ness" in which someone is constantly talking or doing something to entertain the audience. You can overcome such fearfulness by studying and learning to appreciate the eloquence of silences and how they are set up to make key story points. (It also helps when you trust that the people who read your script will imagine and appreciate the silences that you write.) You should also appreciate that the silences being referred to are not dead time, as when someone walks across the room to answer the phone; instead, the silences being described are usually tied to emotional hits that befall characters, and they are therefore major moments of the story that have been carefully set up. There are examples of dramatic silences in the scene from *The Verdict* (Shot 38) in which Galvin refuses the final settlement offer from Concannon and Judge Sweeney; you might wish to review the scene to see how it sets up and exploits three or four powerful emotional hits and the resulting silences (see page 120).

Emotional Levels in Dialogue

In the same way that people in real life shift between emotional levels when they speak, actable dialogue also can play on more than one emotional level. In a real situation, a person might be smiling upon entering a party, despite being worried over how he or she is dressed and nervous about being among strangers. At the same time this person might notice someone attractive at the party and feel guilty about the attraction if he or she came with someone else. Lurking behind these attitudes might be a desire to meet someone for professional reasons. *Sleepless in Seattle* contains numerous examples of dialogue written on more than one level: Shot 33 finds Sam on the phone with the radio psychologist on Christmas Eve. Although he makes light of how he is being used by the program, Sam's feelings show on several levels:

<pre>
                           SAM
              Look, it's Christmas --
                  (as the two of them sit
                down together on the bench)
              Maggie -- my wife . . . always
              did it big, she loved . . .
              she made things beautiful.
              It's just tough, this time of
              year.
                  (puts his arm around Jonah)
              Any kid needs a mother.
</pre>

> *Sleepless in Seattle*, written by Nora Ephron, David Ward, and Jeff Arch, 1993

This speech allows Tom Hanks to act tough on the outside and sad on the inside. While balancing these two feelings, he must be brave and fatherly to his son, Jonah. To these levels add the loneliness that is teased from him by the talk show host. Finally, the speech touches on the dramatic problem being tracked in the story, which is how to find a wife and mother for Sam and Jonah. The excerpt is typical of good dialogue: it flashes through several emotional colors; it is heavy with emotion; it reveals the character. Actors are quick to recognize acting opportunities where feelings are implied but not directly expressed.

Subtextual dialogue does not explain everything; it creates shadows that suggest mysteries of personality. Such dialogue drips with emotional juice that the screenwriter can choose either to unleash or to retain within the character. Both approaches work, but often the most effective strategy is to keep the emotion bottled up in the character, for when that force is unleashed, its energy dissipates. When the emotive force remains inside the character, instead of being released by tears or cathartic[5] dialogue, the moment invites the audience to share whatever emotion the character is feeling.

Richard Brooks addressed this subtle topic during a discussion of the climactic scene of *In Cold Blood*. Robert Blake's character is about to be hanged,
but first he delivers an aria about his wasted life. Brooks wanted the audience
to empathize with the character as he stands next to a window at night, looking down through the rain on the gallows. Brooks's aim was to use this scene
to convey a broken man whose final moments are consumed by remorse and
pain that cannot be shared and that will die with him. Some filmmakers might
have encouraged the actor to weep, but Brooks mistrusted tears, feeling that
they would compromise his story's integrity. As they discussed this matter,
cinematographer Conrad Hall noticed shadows of the rain as it reflected
through the window onto Blake's face. The filmmakers used the odd lighting
effect to suggest the young killer's ruined life and that of his victims. The
shadowy raindrops comment eloquently on the sadness of the moment, while
at the same time the character's inner pain is retained.[6]

DEEPER LEVELS OF DIALOGUE

Much of what people talk about comes from the conscious level, as when we
enter a shop and ask if our dry cleaning is ready. Conscious-level dialogue is
primarily on-the-nose as it deals with the ordinary business of life. Less predictable is dialogue that bubbles up from the unconscious, for at this level,
characters may not realize the significance of what they are saying. For example, in *The Verdict* (Shot 58), when Galvin visits Nurse Rooney for the first time,
she is speaking from the unconscious when she expresses loyalty to Kaitlin
and contempt for Galvin, whom she feels is as unscrupulous as the doctors
who drove her friend out of nursing. Later, Galvin realizes the importance of
Rooney's unconscious remarks, and he uses them to locate Kaitlin (the admitting nurse) and win the case.

Profound life experiences often create psychological scars that can shape
dialogue, as in *The Verdict*, in which Galvin is so bitter over being betrayed by
his in-laws that he chooses to fight an impossible battle with the most powerful lawyer in town. Even *The Terminator* (Shot 211) uses this tack when Reese
reveals that he is conditioned to think of women as soldiers, not as romantic
partners. Reese must move beyond this unconscious attitude to express his
love for Sarah.

Emotion and Thoughtfulness in Dialogue

Many scenes have moments when writers must choose whether to slant the
dialogue toward emotion or toward the thoughtfulness of philosophical or

---

[5]**Cathartic dialogue** purges the character's emotion and pain. Such dialogue is often loud and passionate. For an example of cathartic dialogue, see the climactic scene of *The Verdict* (Shot 92), when
Kaitlin accuses Dr. Towler of forcing her to alter the figures on the admitting form.
[6]In *Visions of Light* Conrad Hall discusses how this shot was devised. *Visions of Light*, a retrospec-
tive of the cinematographer's art, is available at video rental stores. The Richard Brooks lecture
was taped by the author at the Writers Guild of America (WGA) in November 1969.

moral content. Here again, this is a judgment call, because most speeches can be interpreted toward either emotion or thoughtfulness. Even so, certain films are noteworthy for their thoughtfulness—*The Bridge on the River Kwai, All the President's Men, The Verdict,* and *The Remains of the Day* illustrate. The thoughtfulness of movies is often based on a moral or ethical point that is wrapped in a potent emotional package. As a result, a scene or a speech can have considerable thematic impact, even when its point is quite simple.

The Verdict seems to be the most thoughtful of our four main study films because of speeches by Galvin to Laura that express his views on justice and juries (Shot 33). Similarly, his summation speech (Shot 94) presents Galvin's views on what the law and juries mean to society. Thoughtful scenes or speeches provide intellectual substance to stories that might otherwise be frothy with emotion or action. For example, the love scene in *The Terminator* (Shot 211) is passionate and thoughtful, which provides a respite from the story's high-octane action. (Interestingly, many of the thoughtful speeches in Cameron's script did not make it to the screen, perhaps because he felt they would slow the story.) Other thoughtful moments from classic films: the farewell speech by the hero (Henry Fonda's Tom Joad) to his mother (played by Jane Darwell) in *The Grapes of Wrath;* the hero's speech to the heroine in *Out of Africa* about why he cannot give her the closeness that she desires.

Like many topics in this book, this one—thoughtful versus emotional dialogue—blurs, because speeches and scenes can be slanted toward either emotion or thoughtfulness during production; the decision depends on what feels right to the actors and the director as they are shooting the scene. Also, there are dialogue scenes that blend thoughtfulness and emotion, as when Brando confronts Steiger in the back of the taxicab in the "I could've been a contender" scene from *On the Waterfront.* Other examples are when Eli lectures his grandson about avoiding the modern world and its violence in *Witness* (Shot 93) and when Sam talks to the radio psychologist in *Sleepless in Seattle* (Shot 33).

Writers choose between dialogue that is thoughtful, dialogue that strikes for emotional content, and dialogue that combines these two values. Your sense of story, based on experience, appreciation of work from films, and the needs of your story, is your guide toward what feels right.

How Levels of Dialogue Reveal Character

Movies reveal character as people in real life are revealed: by what the character says, by what others say about the character, by what the character does, and by the character's appearance. A particular way of speaking—bragging, arguing, complaining, speaking timidly, and so on—quickly suggests a personality type, but before audiences can understand why a character behaves in a certain way, they must experience dialogue and action that digs deeper. Usually this means that the writer must understand the character's backstory and demonstrate at least some of this content through the character's behavior. We sense who *Witness*'s John Book is when he eats hot dogs with Rachel and Samuel and we hear what his sister said about him (Shot 52B). In *The Terminator* we see Reese's character in action in flashbacks, which loads his dialogue with backstory content that is revealing. The death of Sam's wife in *Sleepless in Seattle* makes viewers aware of his grief; this backstory content shows up in Sam's behavior and in his dialogue in ways that reveal his character. As a result, Sam Baldwin, because of casting, performance, direction, camera, and how the character was written, comes across as an intelligent, decent man who deserves what he gets in the movie.

Some characters are written at a theatrical pitch that adds weight to their dialogue, so it is more revealing. Clint Eastwood in *Heartbreak Ridge* and Geraldine Page in *The Pope of Greenwich Village* are given salty lines that reveal their characters. The refinement of Winona Rider and Eric Stoltz in *Little Women* shades their dialogue so the audience can understand two characters from an earlier century. Deeper levels of character can be revealed during emotional hits when characters express their life experiences in powerful dramatic moments. In *Braveheart*, the hero (Mel Gibson) is being tortured to death when the assembled mob hears him cry out the final word of his life. That word, *freedom*, validates his character and the entire movie. These examples (and those in Chapter 5) illustrate how characters are revealed by what they say and how they say it, by life experiences that are revealed through action and dialogue, and by values that are expressed through action as the characters meet the challenges of the plot. All of these elements can be packed into a single scene, as in *Sleepless in Seattle* (Shot 125), when Sam tells his son, Jonah, that he is merely dating Victoria, not marrying her. This is done in a way that reveals Sam's respect for Victoria and Jonah and also displays Sam's innate decency.

Finally, the screenwriter should appreciate the physical appearance of the character and how he or she is dressed, for this too can affect dialogue. The heroine in *Working Girl* (Melanie Griffith), for example, presents a tacky contrast to her Ivy League boss (Sigourney Weaver), at least regarding how the two women dress. Griffith, with her squeaky voice and lush physique, is further disadvantaged by being spangled with costume jewelry that accentuates her garish taste for cheap clothes and excessive hairstyles. Weaver, by contrast, is perfectly groomed for success. When they first meet, the contrasting appearance of the two women makes them aware of their superior-inferior relationship, which affects their dialogue and the story. Other examples of how appearance, dress, and grooming suggest characters and influence dialogue: Reese (Michael Biehn) in *The Terminator* looks like a derelict because the clothing he is wearing was taken from a derelict; Godfrey (William Powell) in *My Man Godfrey* is a highly cultured man who also looks like a derelict, a condition that gives poignancy and bite to the character's dialogue; Eastwood's Bill Munny in *Unforgiven* looks so much like a pig farmer going broke that his appearance makes it easy to forget that there is a deadly side to this man.

Dialogue That Reflects a Life Stage

Another level of dialogue is that based on how characters view themselves at a particular stage in life. Have they realized their potential? How do they compare with their friends and colleagues? Such questions ask whether the characters are measuring up to their potential. Life questions show up, for example, in *The Unbearable Lightness of Being, My Life,* and *It's a Wonderful Life.*

A stage-of-life example occurs in *Sleepless in Seattle* (Shot 79), when Jonah awakens from a bad dream and reveals that he is forgetting his mother:

                         JONAH
          I miss her.

                         (BEAT)
          What do you think happens to
          someone after they die?

                         SAM
          I don't know.

                         JONAH
          Like do you believe in heaven?

                         SAM
          I never did. Or the whole
          idea of an afterlife. But I
          don't know any more. I have
          these dreams about . . . your
          mom . . . and we have long
          talks about . . . about you,
          and how you are, which she
          sort of knows but I tell her
          anyway. So what is that?
          It's sort of an afterlife,
          isn't it?

                         JONAH
          I'm starting to forget her.

                         SAM
          She could peel an apple in one
          long curly strip.

Hold on the two of them as Jonah cuddles closer and music begins. Bye Bye Blackbird.

                         Sleepless in Seattle, written by Nora Ephron, David Ward,
                                          and Jeff Arch, 1993

The dialogue in this excerpt reveals that Sam and his son are a loving pair and that Jonah thinks of his mother, although she is fading from memory. The exchange also tells us that Sam remembers his dead wife and he wants Jonah to remember her too. This is why Sam reminds Jonah how Maggie could pare an apple in a single strip—a detail that suits a child's view of what is important. At a deeper level, the exchange indicates that Sam continues to grieve. At an unconscious level, Sam senses that he and Jonah are alone. Finally, at the stage-of-life level, Sam realizes that the void caused by Maggie's death should be filled, especially for Jonah's sake.

It would be difficult (if not impossible) to write dialogue such as the above by squeezing it out with craft strategies of the sort listed in this book; however, this advice is not meant for such use. Instead, the strategies are meant as path markers for getting through the mulling process, when writers zigzag through every strategy they know to find the truth of their characters. When we make that connection—when our characters seem alive in imagination—multilevel dialogue happens spontaneously because the words come spontaneously from the characters and reflect their feelings more than the writer's.

Good dialogue is based on a few simple craft strategies: know your characters and their history, and work out how they relate to the problem of the story and to each other. Good dialogue also means knowing how to crank energy into the situation and into the characters so that the scene's story point is made dramatically. When these values are at work, imagination takes over as the writer watches, listens, and records what the characters say and do on the stage of the mind. Once recorded, the dialogue is polished and refined by the writer until it feels perfect.

DIALOGUE AND NARRATIVE DRIVE

The first thing cut from a script is repetitive dialogue, especially when it announces what has happened or what may happen. Repetitive dialogue can be rewritten when the writer has a standard of professional dialogue (this too can be acquired through reading scripts and studying their films). This standard makes speeches such as the following easy targets:

```
              CAPTAIN BROWN
      Tom?  Do you trust him to do a
      job like that?  He's a
      weakling.  I wouldn't bet a
      nickel on the bum.  I know him
      too well.
```

The thirty words of this speech say that Tom is incompetent in four ways. If the speech said more about Tom, it might earn its keep, but it does not. It also excludes the audience because it overexplains Tom, albeit superficially. The dialogue does not persuade the audience to create a personal vision of Tom. Additionally, the speech slows the story's momentum. These problems can be rewritten so that one word conveys the content of the original speech:

CAPTAIN BROWN
(contemptuously)

Tom!

The single word also asks the audience to supply the reasons for Brown's negative attitude toward Tom. Even though viewers may not realize that they are collaborating, their contribution pulls them into the story, however slightly. This is why professional dialogue knows what not to say and what can be implied with a look or a silence. Minimalist dialogue reaches out to the audience through silences and underwritten lines. Movies use small, crafty strategies such as these to hook their audiences and to entertain.[7]

Underwritten Dialogue

Writers often skimp on the amount of exposition in their dialogue to make the audience curious about what is happening in the story. For example, there is no explanation of how the cyborg and Reese manage to drop out of the sky in *The Terminator* until Shot 114, which is thirty minutes into the film. Only then does Reese tell Sarah (and the audience) about his mission and the cyborg. The example shows how audiences will accept a certain amount of ambiguity if the story holds their interest and eventually explains the confusion.

In many cases, audiences enjoy being teased by vagueness because it makes them curious and draws them into the story. Note how *Sleepless in Seattle* (Shot 173) reveals Jonah's secret trip to New York: Sam calls to him when the baby-sitter arrives but there is no answer. Next, Sam searches the house and the deck and panics when he is unable to locate his son. The scene makes the audience curious about Jonah's whereabouts, which sets up the shift to Jessica's house, the trip to New York, and the happy ending on top of the Empire State Building. The point to be taken from this: dialogue that leads the audience and makes them curious can be dramatic. To write this way, you should appreciate the intensity of movies and how this enables audiences to follow and anticipate what is happening on-screen.

Overwritten Dialogue

The reverse of underwritten dialogue is talk that sounds as though it were written by Morris the Explainer. Morris is the creation of a University of Southern California screenwriting colleague who feels that Morris encourages

---

[7]Even for scripts that are shot more or less as written *(Thelma and Louise, The Shawshank Redemption, The Verdict)*, 10 percent or so of the dialogue is often cut during production, as can be seen by comparing scripts and movies of the four main study films.

new writers to explain, report, elucidate, and clarify to such a degree that readers doze off, as in the following:

```
                    FRANK
          You bought a new car, I see.
          Not bad!  Straight eight,
          automatic, air conditioning --
          impressive.

                    DONNA
          Fuel-injected with dual air
          bags too.  I wanted the
          leather seats but I got a deal
          on this -- do you like the
          wheel covers?  They're real
          spokes.

                    FRANK
          They gave this puppy a good
          write-up in the car magazines.
          Top car of the year according
          to one of 'em!  It kinda makes
          my heap look old!

                    DONNA
          It's not so bad!  How many
          years have you had that?  If
          you get the dents knocked out
          and a paint job, and maybe a
          new bumper from a junkyard,
          it'll look good!
```

This is standard Morris the Explainer dialogue. It slows the story with exposition that is unimportant. A limited amount of this dialogue is tolerable, but too much can be deadly, for Morris not only overexplains; he also takes too long to say things:

```
                    JACK
          We should get moving if we
          want to catch the ferry.

                    VELMA
          Yeah, the last boat leaves at
          sunset.
```

```
              BILL
    It's almost five now!


              VELMA
    My watch is slow then!   It
    says . . . four-thirty!


              BILL
    My goodness, you're right!
    We'd better get going because
    the next boat isn't for three
    hours!
```

This sluggish dialogue stops the story as it dawdles over petty details and does not present conflict, subtext, or drama that connects to the characters emotionally. Instead, the dialogue presents exposition that deals with plot, which quickly becomes boring. The four sides of dialogue could be summarized by having the characters rush to the boat when they hear the ferryboat's whistle. This could trigger a spat that reveals the characters or other aspects of the story.

TELEPHONE DIALOGUE

As noted in the discussion of continuity (Chapter 3), telephones, especially cellular models, can connect the characters in a story. Because writers use telephones as a continuity device, these devices can influence dialogue in ways that are worth mentioning.

First, telephones are intrusive and capable of instantly ringing their way into our lives—or into a scene—with good or bad news. We also know that when a phone call interrupts, it invariably signals important news, and for this reason telephone dialogue can energize a scene or unhinge a character. This implies our first advice regarding telephone dialogue: *Make the call worth the interruption.*

When only one person is shown using a phone, the audience must fill in the missing half of the conversation; done properly, this can arouse curiosity and suspense. The four study films use phone calls this way. In *The Verdict*, Galvin telephones his client to report on their case (Shot 24); in Shot 50 Galvin calls the insurance company to settle the case; in Shot 51 he calls Dr. Thompson; in Shots 77, 78, and 83 he calls New York to locate his missing witness; in Shot 85 he calls Laura and tells her that he is flying to New York. In some of these calls we hear what both parties are saying, while in others only one person is heard.

Telephone conversations tend to be more dramatic when other people in the room tune in on what is being said. There is a splendid example of this in the French film *Love After Love,* which shows Isabelle Huppert's character having lunch with Lover No. 1. They are settling into their food when Lover

No. 2 telephones. Huppert moves as far away from the first fellow as the phone cord will allow, but it is not far enough to prevent him from hearing what she is saying. The master image in this scene is the shot of the stretched phone line that binds the three lovers together.

During Huppert's phone scene, the camera was on her alone. Films may also ping-pong the images between the characters on both ends of the conversation, as in Shot 119A of *Witness*, when Book calls Schaeffer and swears vengeance over the murder of Officer Carter, his police partner. In some stories, the party uses a speaker phone; in others *(When Harry Met Sally)*, the phone parties are split-screened, allowing both characters to appear on-screen together. The use of a cellular phone in an open convertible takes advantage of the outreach of phone service, while at the same time giving the audience a top-down driving experience that can present visuals of passing scenery.

Some people have odd telephone habits that can be exploited. For example, people may assume a different personality or change their style of speaking when they are on the telephone. A person's voice may become deeper, more formal, or in some other way unnatural or forced. People can turn cold, seductive, or domineering on the phone. There may be a contrast between what the person is saying and the situation in the room. Some people primp before a mirror or perform odd movements or exercises while they talk on the phone. Others untangle the phone cable, tidy their desk, eat, make faces, and the like.

The person on the phone may try to sound calm in the midst of a passionate, tense, or dangerous situation. See the telephone calls to husband Darryl (Chris McDonald) in *Thelma and Louise* as the FBI swarms through his house. *Clear and Present Danger* and *In the Line of Fire* also make good use of telephones. Thrillers often involve a villain who uses the phone to taunt the police or to deliver messages. In such films, there may be a high-tech race to trace the phone call, as in *The Fugitive*.

Useful as they are, telephone calls have a major disadvantage because they tend to be visually static. Regardless of how cleverly the scene is done, a person speaking into a telephone is a talking head that disallows face-to-face confrontation between the two parties. It is generally advisable, therefore, to keep telephone calls brief and to use them only when necessary. Naturally, there are exceptions, and few movie moments are any finer than the telephone scene in *It's a Wonderful Life*. It happens as Donna Reed and James Stewart share a phone call from a loud-mouth classmate who offers Stewart a job. Reed and Stewart, inches apart as they share the earphone, are overwhelmed by their closeness and end up kissing.

SUMMARY

Most important, use as little dialogue as possible. Movie dialogue advances the plot; it creates character relationships; it reveals the characters; it comments on the theme; it deals with backstory and exposition. Good dialogue can address each of these points in a single speech. Dialogue can be enriched with subtext, or it can be written on-the-nose (without subtext). On-the-nose dialogue is useful for passing on information directly and quickly. Although both on-the-nose and subtextual dialogue are valid, a script with too much on-the-nose dialogue may not explore the interior life of the characters.

Movie dialogue is usually stripped of the repetitions, civilities, and warm-up chitchat of everyday speech. Movie dialogue is effective because it is dramatized by sound, camera, and actors who charge the lines with emotional content and nuance. Movie dialogue knows when to step aside so that a look, a gesture, a silence, or an image can make the point. This dialogue skill can be learned from film study and writing scripts, but the beginning of wisdom on this point is to examine every line of your dialogue and to ask if the moment will play without dialogue. If you feel it will, think about cutting the dialogue.

To prevent exposition from slowing the story, writers marble essential information into the dialogue. The technique of freighting dialogue with exposition and backstory can also be learned by studying scripts and the movies made from them and by listening to how people reveal themselves as they speak.

Subtext suggests the inner life and backstory of the characters. Subtextual dialogue asks the viewer to intuit what the characters are thinking and feeling but are not saying directly in the dialogue. This is a prime goal of dialogue because it draws the audience into the inner being of the characters so the audience can share the drama.

Actable dialogue contains subtext that asks the actors to communicate levels of emotions and thought that are not expressed directly in the dialogue.

Dialogue spoken over the telephone can be dramatic and useful for continuity purposes. However, telephone scenes are often weak visually, so they are usually brief.

Exercises

Because dialogue is so important, here are three exercises for improving your understanding of the topic. Each one will take a few hours, but they reinforce key lessons in the chapter.

1. Screen the first act of one of the main study films and study it for its dialogue. Note when and how the dialogue reveals backstory, theme, character, and relationship while at the same time advancing the plot. Also note when the dialogue is on-the-nose and when it contains subtext. What is the nature of the subtext? Is the subtext based on backstory of the characters, the situation, the relationships, the theme, or the plot? Notice how the on-screen dialogue is augmented by inflection, gesture, facial expressions, subtext, and body language. Observe how the actors convey subtext.

2. Select your favorite movie scene and hand-copy it to experience the author's language and the emotional state of the characters. (See *Film Scenes for Actors,* edited by Joshua Karton, Bantam Books, New York, 1983. The book presents seventy scenes from American films.)

After you have hand-copied the scene, type it up and silently read and study the lines. Listen as if the speeches were being performed by actors. Visualize the actors in the scene setting; imagine how the dialogue might sound in a movie theater.

Next, act out the scene, aloud this time. (This works best when the lines are memorized.) Add whatever pauses and dramatic touches feel appropriate. Stand up and move around doing this. Perform the scene with a friend if possible, or play all of the roles yourself. If you have a camcorder, videotape the reading and review the tape with the text in hand. Finally, review the tape of the scene, following along with script in hand. Use the questions noted in exercise 1, above, to further analyze the scene.

3. Write a two- or three-minute dialogue scene based on the following situation. A man or woman becomes tired of waiting for his or her lover to propose marriage, and in this scene an ultimatum is delivered: "Marry me or I'll marry my friend in Texas!" The person receiving the ultimatum is shaken but refuses to be pushed. When you finish writing your scene, act it out, as described in exercise 2, above. Finally, compare your scene with the professional version given in Appendix D.

(For media that illustrate the points made in this chapter, see Appendix A.)

CHAPTER 7

Dramatization

The simple stories that organize most motion pictures become grand theatrical experiences when writers employ ancient dramatizing strategies. This chapter presents how these strategies work and how to use them.

Dramatic   Having vivid, emotional, conflicting, or striking interest or results.

Although this dictionary definition summarizes our topic, I would add one word: *intensify*—to worsen; to enhance; to make more dangerous, more romantic, more desperate, more hopeless, more, *more*, MORE! This chapter presents many insights that attach to the main topic, but before getting into them I shall review how dramatization relates to the emotional slant of the story. As discussed on page 11, one of your first decisions should be whether the story will make audiences laugh, make them sad, or make them fearful in some way. At all times, the writer should be working to dramatize one or more of these basic emotional slants. *Sleepless in Seattle* makes the audience laugh, weep, and worry about whether Sam and Annie will get together. Throughout, the movie is dramatized so that these emotional values are at work on the audience. *The Terminator* is an action picture meant to frighten the audience, and its dramatic strategies address that dynamic, because throughout the film the audience is fearful that the heroes will be defeated by the seemingly indestructible cyborg.

Dramatizing means creating situations and moments that seize and hold the attention of viewers so tightly that they are transported to the world of the story. Often, this process is the result of conflict. We see moments that are dramatized through physical conflict in *Witness*, as in Shot 60, when McFee tries to murder Book in a parking structure, and in Shot 122C, when Book punches out the three hoodlums. For an example of a dramatic moment caused by verbal conflict, see *The Verdict* (Shot 66), when Galvin finishes his first day of trial and threatens to ask for a mistrial because of the way Judge Sweeney is handling the case. For an example of a dramatic moment that is both verbal and physical, check out the murder scene in *In the Line of Fire*, when the assassin tests his new plastic pistol by shooting two hunters.

Dramatizing means making life difficult for the hero. It means making mountains out of molehills. It means convincing an audience that there is no way that a nobody such as Rocky Balboa would be given a title shot for the heavyweight championship of the world—and almost win. Dramatizing often means stretching, bending, or folding the circumstances to enhance the tale. For example, a cyborg from the future did not destroy one of the LAPD's police stations, yet *The Terminator* presents a sequence in which this happens. *The Verdict* is a more realistic film, yet it too stretches reality by placing Ed Concannon in a situation where he jeopardizes his firm's reputation and, in the same swipe, besmirches that of his client, the Catholic Church. This happens when he hires Laura to prostitute herself so she can spy on a lowly ambulance-chaser, Frank Galvin. Clearly, Laura is trotted into the story not for legal reasons but for dramatic reasons, so she can serve as the love interest who betrays the hero and thereby arouses sympathy for him. This is the way dramatization works—by making situations more desperate, more dangerous, more impossible. Through such machinations, movie stories stir emotions and entertain audiences. The process works even when the story is based on fact, as in *Silkwood, All the President's Men,* and *Quiz Show.*

Writers create difficulties and skillfully present them to persuade audiences to accept what is happening on-screen. If the hero is endangered when a bear rips off the door and invades his cabin, the incident can be dramatized by making the bear gigantic. And ferocious. We might ease the bear into the story by showing that it is bleeding from a bullet wound. We see it tear apart a Volkswagen camper—its strength is unbelievable! Then the monster bear scents smoke and turns its murderous eyes toward the hero's cabin as thunder and lightning crash.

In sum, dramatization means pumping up the incidents of story. If the hero's task is difficult, dramatize it until it seems impossibly difficult. Skillful dramatization and movie magic can convince audiences of almost anything— that dinosaurs can be brought back to life, or that someone with the intelligence of a chipmunk could become an all-American football player and a millionaire war hero. Dramatizing means skewering characters in the worst way in the worst place at the worst possible time. It means elevating injustice, passion, suffering, danger, and whatever seems appropriate to the story. If our efforts create melodrama, the dramatic heat can be lowered.

CREDIBILITY

Movies must make us believe that Superman can fly, that The Shadow, Batman, Darkman, and other comic-book heroes live unseen among us and emerge to punish evildoers. As noted, audiences will accept almost any assumption imaginable, but from that point onward, the story should stay within the bounds established and not ask for further dispensation. *Frankenstein* adhered to this advice and convinced the audience that a giant could be pieced together from body parts. Werewolf and vampire movies have seemed real enough to haunt our dreams for decades. However, accomplishing this is no small task, and credibility is a major concern of filmmakers. During a 1983 interview, for example, screenwriter Philip Dunne recalled John Ford's pleased reaction after reading his script for *How Green Was My Valley*. The great director was praising the great screenwriter while at the same time pointing out the task facing the film crew when he said, "Well Phil, maybe I can keep this piece of crap afloat for two hours." Sustaining a motion picture story for two hours—or five minutes!—is not an easy task.

Much of the work of plotting involves making the audience accept the story that is playing on-screen, regardless of how preposterous it is. *The Terminator, Jurassic Park,* and *Forrest Gump* show how this is done. Even when the story seems to be anchored in reality *(The Verdict, Braveheart, On the Waterfront)*, the incidents of plot and the characters must be carefully introduced, logically sequenced, and thoroughly believable or the audience will see through the artifice. It is not overstating to say that *unless viewers believe (at least temporarily) what is playing on-screen, they will not be drawn into the story.* This urgent advice applies to all of the strategies cited below, which must be presented so the audience finds them believable.

Achieving this degree of credibility can present major plotting chores that require complicated "engineering" in which the incidents of plot are carefully eased into place. For example, *Sleepless in Seattle* went to considerable lengths to justify how Sam and Annie became connected through the call-in radio show. We also needed to understand the emptiness in their otherwise ideal professional lives and their need for romance and closeness. Additionally, the screenwriters needed to plot believable ways for Sam and Annie to learn about each other; their solution was to invent the private eye, the computer search, and coast-to-coast travel. Piece by piece, the story added plot elements until everyone and everything came together.

Credibility might seem impossible in stories about werewolves, or messengers with computer brains, or other preposterous concepts. Writers get around this by enlisting the audience's willingness to accept an unlikely or impossible story concept. They then construct a story universe that can accommodate the improbable concept so that the yarn plays out within those boundaries.

The real, unreal, or surreal nature of a story determines how tightly the straps of logic and probability should cinched. In realistic stories, logic is usually tighter than in whimsical fare such as *Big* or *Back to the Future*. Accordingly, you should double-check whether your story is real, unreal, or surreal, for this slant has a major bearing on the way you approach the issue of credibility.

For an example of how credibility works, check out *Jurassic Park*, which spends considerable time making us believe what happens on dinosaur island. *The Terminator* fudges its improbabilities with Reese's vague line (Shot 126) about cyborgs and nuclear death "being one possible future. I don't know the tech stuff." That clever line explains away the Mobius loopiness of time travel and illustrates how a small amount of artful mumbo jumbo can plaster over rough spots in a story's believability.

The conflict should seem believable as well, which can be a chore because many stories border on the ridiculous or the impossible. In spite of this, as writers we must make the audience believe our yarns. This task, over the millennia, has led to the dramatizing strategies presented below. Most will be familiar, but labeling the strategies may help you to remember them when you spot them in movies and when you apply them to your own work. As with many topics in this book, the dramatizing strategies are briefly discussed. To absorb them, you will need to think about each value and practice it in the exercises and in your writing. The first dramatizing tool—and the most powerful—is the *dramatic engine.*

THE DRAMATIC ENGINE

Most movie stories are (1) visual, (2) based on simple plots, (3) intensely focused and structured, and (4) energized by something that propels the story and gives it intensity, tension, and forward momentum. The "something" that drives most movie stories toward the climactic moment is usually connected to the dramatic problem that organizes the plot. The problem, in turn, can spin off a character, a force, a goal, a force of nature, a task, or a situation that drives the story. Each of these elements can be described as a *dramatic engine* that dramatizes the story and creates tension and momentum, as will be discussed below. The value of this concept is that it can be identified and beefed up so it energizes the story. For this reason alone, the engine is the most potent of all dramatizing strategies because it can motivate the characters, determine the action, dictate the momentum and intensity of the story, and focus the drama.

The Problem As the Engine

Most stories are driven by a dramatic problem that pulls opposing forces into conflict over how the issue will resolve. This dynamic shows clearly in *The Verdict*, in which the problem is winning the malpractice suit. Other films that are organized by the problem include *The Guns of Navarone, The Andromeda Strain, The Fugitive, Breaking Away,* and *On the Waterfront.* As noted in Chapter 2, most feature stories are built around a problem that is life-threatening and/or life-shaping. In most cases, the problem draws characters into the drama, stirring up their lives. In *Witness*, police officers and members of the Amish community are drawn into the problem that organizes the story, which is the hero's need to apprehend Schaeffer and his gang.

In most instances a strong dramatic problem is enough to drive the story, but not always. Sometimes the problem is diffused, as in *Forrest Gump, Lawrence of Arabia, Citizen Kane,* and *The Grapes of Wrath.* In such films, other means are employed to bolster the problem and to drive the story. The strategies for accomplishing this are presented below, but you should appreciate that they frequently overlap, so that a powerful story may employ three or four dramatizing engines.

The Villain As the Engine

One of the most effective dramatic engines is a powerful antagonist who creates desperate conflict. For an example of a classic antagonist, consider the dogged police official, Inspector Javert, who drives the action in *Les Misérables*. Javert's quarry is ex-convict Jean Valjean, who spent nineteen years in prison for stealing a loaf of bread. Victor Hugo's grand old story, which has been made into movies, stage plays, and musicals, spends considerable time justifying the incongruity of Valjean's small crime, his enormous punishment, and Javert's obsession with Valjean. The dramatic problem of the original story— Valjean's criminal past—is overwhelmed by the monomaniacal pursuit of the antagonist, which initiates plot incidents that drive the story.

When it was adapted into a TV series, *Les Misérables* became *The Fugitive*. In 1994 the TV series metamorphosed into a feature film in which Tommy Lee Jones's Sam Gerard reincarnates the mythic pursuer who harries his prey through the centuries and through various forms of media. In all his guises, Javert/Gerard drives the story by pursuing the hero. Motivating such a character is essential for credibility, and Javert's motivation stems from his psychological imperative, which was summarized by Trevor Nunn, director of the London production of *Les Misérables*:

> Javert's credo is that if you were born criminal, it is part of God's plan. You cannot be saved, there can be nothing in your nature that can ever save you. And if it looks as if there's something in your nature that would redeem you from that state, it's play-acting, it's hypocrisy. Javert constantly says to Valjean, I know you. I know who you are. The story dealt with that obsessive theme, of one man who perceives life in a very simplistic way: that those who cannot be redeemed must be hunted down and rooted out. Javert's personal obsession takes him over to the point where he dedicates his life to finding one man because it represents to him what his life is about, what society is about. Javert's behavior, from his own perspective, is the behavior of an utterly righteous and inspired man. . . . He doesn't behave in a malign way, doesn't wake up in the morning and say, "How can I torment the world today?" He says, "How can I make a better world?"[1]

The cyborg is the engine that drives *The Terminator* because the creature has been programmed to kill Sarah Connor; it goes about this task by destroying whatever interferes with its mission. Throughout, the cyborg initiates actions that threaten the heroes. This is typical of an engine—it is the instigator, the troublemaker, the person or force that energizes the story and disrupts the status quo. Such a villainous engine must be menacing and clever enough to create dramatic contrast: Ulysses against the Cyclops, David against Goliath, Cool Hand Luke against the prison, a huge shark against a big-city cop.

The confrontation must be carefully set up, with one small believable incident leading to the next. Rocky Balboa and Apollo Creed illustrate an unlikely

[1] *The New York Times*, March 8, 1987.

pairing, yet the setup of *Rocky* persuades the audience that such a battle could occur. As discussed in Chapter 3, pitting a relatively weak hero against a stronger opponent is one of the most valuable of all the dramatizing strategies, as can be appreciated by studying films such as *The Verdict* and *The Fugitive*.

Additional examples of villains who drive their stories: In *Manhunter* the engine is the serial killer known as "Dollarhide" (skillfully played by Tom Noonan). In *High Noon* the engine is the three outlaws who ride into town to kill the marshal. The villain can be a creature or force that drives the story, as in *Dracula*, *Alien*, *Frankenstein*, *Jurassic Park*, and the crazy quilt of types found in mad-scientist/monster movies. More conventional examples of strong villains who drive their stories include Glenn Close's lover from hell in *Fatal Attraction*, Michael Douglas's wheeler-dealer in *Wall Street*, and Linda Fiorentino in *The Last Seduction*.

The Hero As the Engine

The hero can be the engine that drives the story, as in *The African Queen*, *Lorenzo's Oil*, *The Man Who Would Be King*, *Crocodile Dundee*, and *What About Bob?* These protagonists are given a need, a task, or a situation that energizes them or forces them to take action. Often that need or task connects to the main problem of the story. In *The Shawshank Redemption*, Tim Robbins's Andy Dufresne is the hero who drives the action, which concerns how he escapes from prison.

Television series are usually driven by their heroes. Tim Allen drives *Home Improvement*. Roseanne Barr drives *Roseanne*. Ted Danson's bartender character drives *Cheers*. The engine in *The Incredible Hulk*, *Superman*, *I Dream of Jeannie*, *Mork and Mindy*, and similar shows is the character who possesses a magical power of some sort.

The System As the Engine

An engine can be an organization or a group that serves a corporate or institutional agenda. In *Three Days of the Condor*, the engine is a renegade intelligence unit. *McCabe and Mrs. Miller* is energized by the thugs sent by a mining company. In *The Parallax View* the engine is a shadowy organization that arranges assassinations and sets up fall guys. As in *Quiz Show*, *The Firm*, and *The Client*, "system" stories often follow the Faust archetype in which the hero (by choice or by accident) becomes ensnared by a sinister organization. The story problem concerns how the hero disengages, exposes, and/or defeats the villainous system.

A Force of Nature As the Engine

Disaster and science fiction movies are often driven by an extraordinary natural force. In *Them* the engine is the giant ants. In *The Andromeda Strain* it is the virus. In *The Poseidon Adventure* the engine is the capsized ocean liner. The shark in *Jaws* is a force of nature that drives that story. The model for this film, *Moby Dick*, on the other hand, is driven by the obsessive character of Captain Ahab.

A Task or Quest As the Engine

A movie can be driven by a plot that challenges the hero or heroes to achieve a difficult goal or to complete an impossible task. In *The French Connection* the task that confronts the hero (Gene Hackman) is to foil drug smugglers. In some stories the task is a super-crime that must be committed or solved (*The Great Train Robbery, Rififi, The Killing, Topkapi*). In war stories the task that drives the story is often conquering or destroying an objective (*The Guns of Navarone, A Bridge Too Far*) or proving that the troops are worthy (*Glory*). In most cases, engines such as these are closely bound to the dramatic problem as well; knowing this can make dramatizing easier because it encourages the writer to aggravate the problem so that it drives the story. In the sports widow story we have been building, for example, if we decide that turning Mom into a competitive athlete is the problem, we must set up that goal and then make accomplishing it as difficult as possible.

Many quest stories deal with a goal, often mystical or noble, that a hero or a team must accomplish. Quest stories are often set in exotic locations, which encourage the yarn to be told on an epic scale, as was the case in *Braveheart, Lawrence of Arabia, King Solomon's Mines,* and others. High-adventure, crime, and caper films frequently are driven by situations that are dense with intrigue, danger, and ingenuity (*Romancing the Stone, The Professionals, Escape from Alcatraz,* and *The Wages of Fear*).

The Conventions and Circumstances of the Story As an Engine

Certain genres come equipped with a built-in engine. For example, courtroom dramas are usually driven by the engine of the trial. In romantic comedies, the engine is often getting the couple together and sorting out romantic entanglements. Crime stories are driven by the need to find out "whodunnit." Science fiction and monster movies are usually driven by the need to eliminate or contain the creature or the threatening force. Most biographical stories are driven by a main character who struggles to deal with a challenge that is personal or professional, as in *Sunrise at Campobello, Pride of the Yankees, Gandhi, Amadeus,* and the like.

Again, the purpose of an engine is to energize the story, to generate incidents of plot, and to add dramatic tension. Therefore, if your story seems soft and tepid, if it does not seem dramatic, if things are not happening, you may need to develop an engine that raises the stakes, initiates action, and generally cranks things up. This is best done early in the writing, so the plot can be organized around the circumstances of the engine, as in *Witness, Cool Hand Luke,* or *Sleepless in Seattle*. The least desirable approach is to install an engine during rewriting, after the script has been written. Writers (or producers) sometimes attempt such a fix when a script seems dead in the water. Often this is like attempting a last-minute heart-lung-and-liver transplant, that is, it's a radical procedure with a dubious prognosis, but it may be the only way to save the patient.

INVENTIVENESS

The effectiveness of the dramatic engine and the strategies listed below depend on how skillfully screenwriters create twists of plot, incidents of action, dialogue, character, settings, and other effects that come under the general title of *inventiveness*. Inventive stories are cranked with dramatic potential because the characters are intense and committed to a course of action. Inventive stories are unpredictable; they take unexpected plot and character turns that surprise us, as in *Pulp Fiction* when two of the characters put their war aside when they end up in a ghastly dungeon run by two depraved men. Although it is difficult to offer advice on how to be inventive (other than to say *be creative*), you should know that this level of work is expected of writers, for we are the ones that executives turn to when a script needs an idea, a twist, or some sort of "fix."

As noted on page 20, the definition of creativity that applies to screenwriting is *the ability to perceive relationships*. This means combining disparate elements to create something that is greater than the sum of its parts. Often those parts are scattered about, waiting for an industrious writer to appreciate them and to use them in the story. For example, the inventiveness of *Jurassic Park* is based on Michael Crichton's readings in biogenetics and paleozoology. Many of Crichton's stories—*Coma, The Andromeda Strain, Terminal Man*—are also based on technical articles that are available to all. Writers do not need a medical degree from Harvard (which Crichton has) to tap into the popular literature of technology that can be found in *Nature, National Geographic,* and *Scientific American*. Story ideas can be found in such sources, which is why many screenwriters read them.

Writers use research and whatever useful information they have ferreted away to solve story problems. The writer's secret weapon during this time is patience: we must be willing to work until we find a solution. For example, some years ago while working on a script for *The Fugitive* television series, I was unable to figure out how to rescue Kimble from the underground trap I had concocted for him. Waiting for him at ground level is his nemesis, Inspector Gerard. The experience, grueling as it was, taught me the lesson that I have been passing on to you: *Any problem, regardless of how intractable, can be solved—if you keep working on it*.

The solution may require ingenuity, research, and thinking, but it can be done. My breakthrough on *The Fugitive* story came when I visited a construction company and inspected the heavy cranes. While there I noticed the clamshell attachment that was used to dredge harbors and dig foundations. This proved to be the missing element that I needed, for it gave me a place to hide Kimble—within the jaws of the clamshell. I positioned three grimy men on top of the device when it rises to ground level after digging out a deep vertical shaft. At this point, the trio dashes off in different directions, which causes Gerard's men to take off after them. No one notices the crane when it lifts high overhead and lowers the clamshell (with Kimble inside) behind a concealing mound of debris where a truck is waiting. Kimble drives away and escapes for another week. A number of incidents were plugged into the escape, but the key was the clamshell. Until I saw that big rusty bucket, I was totally depressed and convinced that ten days of thinking about nothing except how to get Kimble out of that damned hole was in vain and that the story would defeat me. It did not and no story has since. You too must learn this lesson

The example points out that invention often comes down to brute thinking. For the longest time nothing may happen, but gradually (or, sometimes, suddenly) you will find a way to solve the problem. The solution may require a certain amount of **engineering,** which refers to elements that the writer puts into the story to justify what happens. The movie *Speed* presents a solid example of engineering and inventiveness because it challenges the hero with a problem—a big clunky city bus has been rigged to explode if it slows below fifty miles per hour. Aside from bashing whatever gets in its way, the bus must leap a gap in an unfinished freeway, speed along while the hero is lowered underneath, become a mobile prison for the hostages aboard, and serve as an information source for the diabolical bomber who rigged this problem. Such elements illustrate how writers engineer incidents and contraptions that make stories work. Remember: *It's your "box" to fill as you wish.*

Inventing details can begin by refining the dramatic situation: does it operate from action or from character? After this simple determination, the next step is to figure out how to escalate the stakes so the difficulties of the problem are heightened. For example, *Speed* would have been less suspenseful if the bus had been able to unload its passengers, but this was engineered out of the story because a videocamera, hidden over the driver's seat, enabled the mad bomber to monitor what went on in the bus.

Speed is typical of thrillers that ask writers to make the problem dangerous and seemingly impossible for the hero to solve. Stories such as this have been done before, except that in earlier incarnations the problem was a bomb on an airplane that would explode if the plane descended to less than five thousand feet. In another film the menace came from an ocean liner in the Atlantic that had been rigged with bombs. In these situations writers make the hero's task seem hopeless and then invent a solution. In the case of *Speed*, the screenwriter (Graham Yost) presented ideas that were fresh, and the movie earned several hundred million dollars.

ADDITIONAL DRAMATIC STRATEGIES

The dramatic engine is our first strategy for dramatizing and enlivening stories, for solving problems, and for making the audience eager to learn what happens next. Additional dramatizing strategies are presented below. Even though some of these conventions overlap, they all work, they all can be found in countless movies and television shows, and they all are tools that can help dramatize your stories.

Obstacles

Obstacles, the simplest and most enduring dramatic convention, occur when a character attempts something and is blocked or defeated by circumstances or by other characters. An obstacle adds interest to the story when it deflects the plot in a new direction and makes things more difficult for the hero. In most cases, the hero or villain reacts to the attempt to overcome the obstacle by inventing another obstacle or another way to deal with the problem. In *The Verdict,* for example, Galvin confronts an obstacle when his star witness (Dr. Gruber) abandons the case (Shot 44). The defection causes the hero to react by locating a new expert witness (Dr. Thompson). When Thompson proves unsatisfactory, the hero reacts by devising a new strategy that leads him to the admitting nurse. She helps the hero win the case, but not before he overcomes the obstacle of locating her in New York City. Tom Cruise in *A Few Good Men* is repeatedly confronted by obstacles (marines who will not cooperate, superiors who want the case concluded, and so on), but in the end he prevails.

In many cases, much of the overall plot and the dramatic ordeal are involved with presenting and overcoming obstacles that try to prevent the hero from defeating the villain and solving the problem. Sometimes this is doubly dramatized by placing the hero in a hellish situation where he or she must confront an implacable villain under impossible conditions. *The Shawshank Redemption, The Terminator,* and the *Die Hard* movies work this way.

The Power Tool

The power tool energizes a story with a character, a device, or a situation that causes a spike of interest to register with the audience. Unlike an engine, which exerts pressure on the entire story, a power tool usually appears but once or twice in the movie and is gone. The power tool in *Repo Man* is the car containing radioactive space aliens. In *Star Wars* "The Force" is a power tool. In *Excalibur* the magical sword is a power tool. In *Indiana Jones and the Last Crusade* the power tool is the notebook compiled by the hero's father. In the *Wizard of Oz* the power tool is Dorothy's ruby slippers, as is the carnival machine in *Big.*

In episodic television, the power tool is often the hero's special skill, magic power, or talent. *Kung Fu's* hero has martial arts skills; *I Dream of Jeannie* and *Bewitched* featured women with magical powers; and *The Incredible Hulk* was about an ordinary fellow who turned into a green muscle-man.

Undeserved Suffering

Undeserved suffering is a strategy for making the audience care about a character or a group that is unjustly abused. The four main study films use undeserved suffering to ingratiate the hero to the audience. In *The Verdict* we empathize with the hero because he was framed in the Lillibridge case, which ruined his life. In *The Shawshank Redemption* we empathize with the hero because he is an innocent man who has been sentenced to a double life sentence. In *The Terminator*, Reese's difficult life and his impossible mission imbue him with undeserved suffering. In *Sleepless in Seattle*, Jonah and Sam suffer because of Maggie's death. In *Witness*, both Book and Rachel are so emotionally needful that they also draw feelings of undeserved suffering.

The strategy also works for difficult characters, like those found in *Unforgiven, City Slickers,* and *The Piano.* Undeserved suffering humanizes prickly characters and allows the audience to glimpse their needs or weaknesses. Rosie Perez in *It Could Happen to You* and Jeff Bridges in *The Fabulous Baker Boys* and *American Heart* are also of this type, as are the killers in *Bonnie and Clyde, White Heat, Natural Born Killers,* and other tales that focus on outlaws.

Although highly effective when skillfully done, the strategy of undeserved suffering becomes cloying, weepy, and manipulative when it is mishandled. Movie characters who overdo their suffering come across like the people we meet occasionally who try to elicit sympathy with stories of their suffering and pain. Instead of finding such characters sympathetic, we often find them whiny and unattractive.

Undeserved suffering becomes poignant when a weak, defenseless character is abused or made to suffer. In *Dominick and Eugene* we learn that Tom Hulce's character is brain-damaged because he was beaten as a child, but it is not until they are adults that his brother (Ray Liotta) learns about the abuse. This revelation occurs when Dominick prevents a child from suffering physical abuse. In this way, undeserved suffering is woven into the plot and is used in the climactic moment of the movie to prove that Dominick can take care of himself.

Undeserved suffering is often more effective (and less saccharine) when someone other than the sufferer reveals the backstory. If the protagonist tells how he lost his ranch because his wife died and his cattle ran off a cliff and—blah-blah-blah-poor-me!—he will lack the ennobling style expected of a hero. The heroine of *Working Girl* does not tell about her difficult life, but we sense it as she tries to improve herself. Countless films have used undeserved suffering to good effect: *The Grapes of Wrath, Ruby in Paradise, My Life, Pelle the Conqueror, A Dog of Flanders, The Waterdance, Rambling Rose, The Men,* and *Born on the Fourth of July,* to name a few.

Torquing

Torquing involves using a situation, a moment of character, or a contrasting element to divert and entertain the audience. Torquing focuses the audience on the shotgun pressed against the hero's jaw or the man trying to propose while wearing a gorilla suit. While cringing, laughing, or otherwise being entertained by the context, the audience soaks up exposition and backstory that might otherwise make for a dull, talky scene.

The scene between Reese and the police psychologist in *The Terminator* (Shot 153) is torqued because the audience knows that the cyborg is nearby and will be coming after Sarah. The torquing context is intensified by the psychologist's sniggering disbelief of Reese's warnings. These elements divert the audience while Reese relates exposition about his mission.

Writers torque scenes by putting characters in awkward situations such as getting drunk, eating strange food, riding horseback for the first time, dressing in strange clothing, undergoing a medical examination, and so on. There is an example of torquing in *Green Card* when Gerard Depardieu entertains a pompously proper dinner party with his wild piano playing. The contrast between the untamed composer and his stuffy audience presents a humorous context that torques the scene.

A scene can be torqued when something that only the audience sees threatens a character. *Arachnophobia* presents such a moment when it shows a deadly spider crawling toward the exposed arm of an unsuspecting woman as she sits on a sofa. A character can be so bizarre that his or her appearance is enough to torque the scene. Steve Martin as the strange brother in *Dirty Rotten Scoundrels* illustrates. Dressing men in women's clothing *(Some Like It Hot)* or in costumes *(Dumb and Dumber, Stir Crazy)* is another torquing strategy.

Before leaving torquing, it is important to note that this is a powerful dramatizing strategy; consider it carefully, because if it is misused, torquing can unbalance the script.

Reversals

A reversal occurs when good news turns to bad news or when bad news turns to good news. Some of the most effective reversals occur in the complication scenes that end the first and second acts. Note the reversal that ends the first act of *Witness* (Shot 72): first, Book returns Rachel to her farm (good news), but when he drives off, Book faints from a gunshot wound (bad news), which forces him to stay with the Amish. This reversal turns the story away from cops-and-robbers and toward the romance between Book and the Amish widow. There is a dramatic reversal in *The Verdict* (Shot 54) when Galvin awaits the arrival of his expert witness (good news). This good news becomes bad news when Dr. Thompson turns out to be an unimpressive elderly man who cannot help Galvin.

Reversals are dramatic. They surprise the audience and bounce the story in new, unexpected directions. Reversals are most effective when one reversal follows another within the same scene. A stellar example of multiple reversals occurs in the climax of *The Verdict* (Shot 92), when Galvin calls in his surprise witness. The first reversal occurs when Kaitlin (Lindsay Crouse) testifies that the doctors made her alter the admitting form. The second reversal occurs moments later when the flustered Concannon asks how she could remember such a detail after so many years. Kaitlin's answer is to produce a photocopy of the original form. The third reversal occurs when Concannon carelessly asks why she kept the photocopy. This prompts Kaitlin to launch her aria, in which she reveals that she kept it for self-protection because the doctors threatened to drive her out of nursing should she reveal that they ordered her to change the time written on the admitting form. This triple reversal is the climactic moment that enables the hero to win his case.

Coincidence

Coincidence occurs when something unexpected intrudes and turns the story in a new direction. Example: In Shot 80 of *The Verdict* the hero sees his telephone bill slide through the mail slot just as he seems ready to stop looking for his missing witness. The delivery of his phone bill prompts Galvin to look through Nurse Rooney's mailbox, which contains her monthly bill and the New York telephone number of his missing witness. Magical coincidence (synchronicity) occurs in *Sleepless in Seattle* (Shot 125) when Sam notices Annie at the airport. Coincidence occurs in *Working Girl* when Melanie Griffith begins an affair with Harrison Ford's character, unaware that he is involved with her boss.

Discovery, Shock, and Surprise

These three strategies are enough alike for them to be lumped together. The first, **discovery,** occurs when a movie character notices or stumbles upon something (a weapon, a diary, a clue, or the like) that advances the story or reveals the characters. Discovery occurs in *The Verdict* (Shot 85) when Jack Warden rummages for cigarettes in Laura's purse and notices an envelope from Concannon's law firm. Discovery occurs in *Witness* (Shot 57) when Samuel spots a news photo that identifies the killer in the train station. Discovery occurs in *The Color Purple* when letters to the heroine from her sister in Africa are found under floorboards.

Discovery can be overused, making the story plotty, difficult to follow, and unbelievable. This seemed to be the case in *Shattered, Big Trouble in Little China,* and *Presumed Innocent.* Misuse of a simple strategy such as discovery points up the importance of studying good works for how their dramatic strategies grow out of the story naturally, so they do not appear as stick-ons intended to goose the narrative.

Shock refers to something sudden and surprising that happens in a film: a door is opened and a body tumbles forth; a character is suddenly assaulted; an incident occurs that startles the audience. The human head that suddenly floats into view as Richard Dreyfus explores a sunken boat in *Jaws* is a shock effect. One of the most shocking moments in *Psycho* occurs when the figure we think is Norman Bates's mother turns out to be mummified. Shock effects often show up in suspense films, when the audience is primed for a frightful reaction.

Surprise involves an unexpected discovery, revelation, or plot twist. Examples: In *The Terminator* (Shot 204) the audience experiences surprise when it learns that the heroine is not talking to her mother but to the cyborg who is imitating the mother's voice. Surprise occurs in *Toys* when we learn that Joan Cusack's character is a robot. Ditto in *Alien*, when Ian Holm's character turns out to be an android. Surprise occurs in *The Verdict* (Shot 72) when we learn that Laura is Concannon's spy.

Surprise, shock, and discovery are similar, but they vary in their degree of impact.

A Catalyst

A catalyst is an incident, dramatic character, or emotional state that speeds up the plot or a relationship. We see it when characters get drunk, injured, drugged, or hurt, or experience a state that causes them to say or do something that accelerates the action. In *Witness* (Shot 80), delirium gives Rachel sudden insight into the hero's tormented inner state. Liquor is the catalyst that turns William Munny into a killer in *Unforgiven*. A catalyst turns Dr. Jekyll into Mr. Hyde and Jack Nicholson into a werewolf in *Wolf*. The sensuality of the artist's colony is the catalyst that loosens up the young couple in *Sirens*. Love or friendship, as in *Four Weddings and a Funeral* and *The Secret Garden*, can serve as a catalyst that causes dramatic change and conflict. A gift, an animal, sudden wealth, new clothing, or anything that breaks down inhibitions and causes an emotional response that speeds up the plot can serve as a catalyst. Mistaken identity can be a catalyst. We see it when the snob shows his or her true colors by behaving badly toward the person raking leaves, not realizing that this is not the gardener but the owner of the estate.

Contrast

Contrast between characters and/or their settings can create drama, as when a ragged beggar is brought before the rich lord and is whipped for making off with a sack of fallen apples. There is dramatic contrast when the shabby hero of *The Verdict* appears in the regal chambers of Bishop Brophy (Shot 26). In *On the Waterfront* there is contrast in the unlikely pairing of Marlon Brando's dockworker and Eva Marie Saint's convent girl. Tim Robbins's character in *The Shawshank Redemption* possesses a quiet sophistication that contrasts with the prison's guards and inmates. *Unforgiven* uses dramatic contrast by playing up the difference between the hero's gruesome reputation and his bumbling demeanor. The contrast between the rough-and-ready hero and the sophisticated villain in *Die Hard* is dramatic. *Rocky*'s mighty champion (Carl Weathers) contrasts dramatically with Sylvester Stallone's humble character. In *Working Girl*, Melanie Griffith's working-class secretary contrasts with Sigourney Weaver's elegant boss. As these examples show, contrast involves inequality of

status, emotion, intelligence, strength, courage, and other values that dramatize the story.

Repetition

Repetition of sounds, dialogue, action, location, or natural phenomena can be
dramatic. Repeatedly, *Sleepless in Seattle* uses a map of the United States to
point out the intercontinental gap separating Sam and Annie. Each time the
audience sees the strange clouds in *Close Encounters of the Third Kind*, it braces
for something new from the aliens. Repeated use of the eerie musical theme
and the tape recorder in *Klute* dramatically announces the presence of the
killer. Repetition is used in *Ruthless People* as ransom requests are phoned in
and are repeatedly turned down by Danny DeVito. Repeatedly, in *The Outlaw
Josey Wales,* various villains get the drop on the hero, only to be outgunned.
Horror movies often use a signature sound, music, or camera effect to
announce the presence of the menace. A musical theme can develop into a
motif that repeats throughout the movie, as in *Jaws* when sinister music
announces the presence of the shark.

A McGuffin

A McGuffin is a strategy for getting the story going. Even though the McGuffin may be something that the audience cares little about, the object becomes
the prize that the characters in the story are desperately seeking, which drives
them to extremes of emotion and daring. The giant diamond everyone wants
can be a McGuffin. The title art object in *The Maltese Falcon* is a McGuffin that
drives the story. The same is true for fire in *Quest for Fire,* the jewel in *Romancing the Stone,* and the gold in *The Treasure of the Sierra Madre.* The McGuffin is
usually sought by both the protagonist and the antagonist, which can lead to
deadly conflict. Many of the James Bond films are based on some sort of
death-ray/super-weapon McGuffin.

McGuffins were a favorite of Alfred Hitchcock, who heard of the notion
from a friend, Angus MacPhail, a fellow member of the London Film Society
in the 1920s. MacPhail's tale concerned two men who are traveling by train to
Edinburgh when one of them notices a parcel on the luggage rack overhead
and asks what it is. "Oh," says his friend, "it's a McGuffin for trapping lions in
the Highlands." The other fellow is puzzled momentarily, but then announces
that there are no lions in Scotland. "Well, then," says his friend, "I suppose that
it's not a McGuffin."

Although MacPhail's anecdote seems to have lost some of its sparkle over
time, the McGuffin has endured for more than a half century (with various
spellings). In essence, the McGuffin is the mysterious objective that sets the
story in motion. It can also provide a modest perspective on stories that use
this device, whether they involve a secret virus, bomb, treasure, atomic code,

or the like. Thus films like *Outbreak, Crimson Tide,* and *Dr. Strangelove* employ a form of McGuffin; knowing that your story addresses this device can help you to understand and dramatize its mystery or menace.

The Secret Plan

The secret plan is an ancient strategy that shows up when a character pulls someone aside and announces, "I know how to take care of that!" Then the person whispers a plan that the audience does not hear but which it knows will unfold shortly. Often the secret plan involves a trap or an embarrassment for the hero or the villain. The plan may be successful or it may lead to a reversal in which an unintended result occurs. The secret plan in *Die Hard* is the villain's strategy to trick the FBI into cutting electrical power to the office building, thus opening the time vault. Two troublemakers have a secret plan in *It's a Wonderful Life.* We realize what it is when they open the dance floor of the gym, allowing everyone to jump into the swimming pool below.

Misunderstanding

Misunderstanding occurs when characters misinterpret or fail to comprehend the problem being confronted. It is often used in comedies, as in *Ruthless People,* when a dim-bulb conspirator misunderstands the sex tryst that he is videotaping and believes he is taping a murder. In *What About Bob?* Bill Murray believes that his psychiatrist (Richard Dreyfuss) is fitting him with a vest of dynamite as part of shock therapy. He is unaware that Dreyfuss plans to detonate the explosives to be rid of his bothersome patient.

Curiosity

Curiosity is a simple strategy for adding drama to a story. It often combines with surprise or discovery, as in *The Verdict* (Shot 72) when Concannon delivers a monologue to someone off camera. This goes on for several minutes as he writes out a check, mixes drinks, and finally sits down beside . . . Laura! At this point our curiosity is rewarded when we discover that Laura is Concannon's spy. Curiosity is at work in *The Terminator* as we wonder how the cyborg can withstand shotgun blasts. In *Sleepless in Seattle* we become curious about how Sam and Annie will bridge the continent that stands between them. *The Fugitive* uses curiosity when the hero comes upon medical testing data that he must connect to the murder of his wife. The story teases the audience by extending the hero's follow-up of this information until it is finally connected to the villain.

Foreshadowing

Foreshadowing indicates the imminence of death or a major moment that will occur later in the story. There is foreshadowing throughout *Of Mice and Men:*

when Lennie must get rid of the dead mouse he has killed by petting and when George shows Lennie where to hide if he gets in trouble. The key foreshadowing incident of the film (when Curly's ancient dog is put out of its misery by gunshot) foreshadows what George must do to Lennie at the end of the movie. *My Girl* uses foreshadowing to warn of the death of Macaulay Culkin's character. The picnic in *Bonnie and Clyde*, when Bonnie's mother bids her daughter good-bye for what everyone knows will be the last time, foreshadows the death of the titular couple.

The Verdict (Shot 21) uses foreshadowing when Dr. Gruber tells the hero he will testify against his fellow doctors "to do the right thing, isn't that why you're doing it?" This remark foreshadows the hero's decision to fight the case because Galvin also feels that it is the right thing to do. Foreshadowing is a quick, effective way to add dramatic texture to a story. However, it must be done subtly, in a way that does not tip off the plot.

Superior Position

Superior position occurs when the audience and/or the characters in a story know something that the hero and/or the villain does not know. This knowledge often gives one side in the drama an advantage, as in *Dave*, when the audience knows that the hero is being manipulated by crafty higher-ups. Later, when Dave realizes this, he takes corrective action. In *The Terminator* (Shot 153), the audience has superior position over the police officers who do not believe the hero's ravings about a monster from the future. In *The Verdict* (Shot 15), the audience acquires superior position when Alito (the insurance agent) tells Bishop Brophy about Galvin's shoddy record. Later, in Shot 47, Mickey presents Galvin's side of the Lillibridge incident, which shames the audience for believing Alito's version of what happened.

False Alarm

The false alarm is a modest and effective strategy in which one of the main characters seems to be in jeopardy, but the threat turns out to be empty. There is a false alarm in the feature version of *The Fugitive* when a SWAT team attacks the tenement where Kimble is staying. The hero is trapped and sure to be captured, but at the last moment we realize that the SWAT team is after the drug-dealing son of the landlady. A false alarm occurs in *Witness* (Shot 69) when Carter runs into two officers immediately after he removes Rachel's folder from police files. At the time, the audience is unsure of the extent of the police conspiracy, which causes fear that Carter (skillfully portrayed by Brent Jennings) may be assassinated.

Secret Experience

Secret experience involves a private, personal happening that is memorable and in some way dramatic. In *Close Encounters of the Third Kind, Poltergeist,* and

E.T.—The Extraterrestrial, children have mysterious solitary encounters with strange life-forms. A tribal shaman in *The Power of One* enables the young hero to have a secret experience. A film can usually only tolerate one or two secret experiences, which should relate to the main storyline. The secret experience can be a moment of revelation or terror or an occurrence that physically or psychologically affects the character. The hero's escape in *The Shawshank Redemption* is a secret experience, as is Morgan Freeman's discovery of the money that the hero left for him.

The secret experience can combine with other conventions, such as discovery to dramatize the story. For example, in *Witness* (Shot 25) the Amish boy has a secret experience when he discovers a murder taking place.

A Red Herring

A red herring is a false lead that the heroes or villains pursue as they attempt to solve the problem. The red herring may be a clue, a suspicious character, an incident, or a circumstance that seems promising. The convention often appears in crime shows and romantic comedies. Kurt Russell, the hero of *Backdraft*, serves as the red herring when circumstances point to him as being the pyromaniac that the authorities are hunting. A false lead can act like a red herring, as in *The Silence of the Lambs* when the FBI descends on a man they believe to be the killer. This action leaves the heroine alone when she confronts the true killer. Be careful when using the red herring strategy, because audiences do not enjoy being misled unless there is a payoff that makes the dead-end diversion worthwhile. For such reasons, the red herring is often employed to turn up a clue that leads to a larger payoff. There is an example of this in *The Verdict* (Shot 58) when Galvin is rebuffed by Nurse Rooney. Later, he remembers what she said and uses the information to find the admitting nurse (Kaitlin) who helps him win the case.

A Reveal

A reveal occurs when the audience learns something important about a character or the plot. Reveals usually deal with major plot or character information, as when Luke Skywalker learns that Darth Vader is his father. The dramatizing force of a reveal shows in *In the Line of Fire* when the hero learns that the CIA has withheld information on the man who is trying to kill the president because the assassin once worked for the agency.

A story can have a half dozen or so reveals, each causing a moment of surprise and drama, as in *Speed*, *Paths of Glory*, and other well-plotted stories. A mighty reveal occurs in *Manon of the Spring*, when Yves Montand's character learns the identity of the man that he has hounded to death. There is bitter dramatic irony in this moment as well, for Montand's character cared about the land and his family more than life itself. In the end, his greed causes the death of everyone in his family, and he dies knowing that his line will disappear with him. At the same time, the land he struggled to win ends up being sold for taxes. To appreciate *Manon of the Spring,* you should see *Jean de Florette* first because they are two parts of the same story.

Not surprisingly, there is often overlap between a reveal, a discovery, and a surprise. *Alien,* for example, presents three such moments: when the creature bursts from John Hurt's chest; when we discover that one of the crew is an android; and when Sigourney Weaver discovers that the alien has stowed away on her escape vessel. It is of minor consequence that one person might consider these moments to be surprise, while others might view them as reveal or discovery. More important than the label is inventing such incidents and using them to dramatize.

The "Or Else" Moment of Choice

This moment confronts a character with a decision of some sort. In many films heroes (and sometimes villains) must make critical choices—whether to continue on a dangerous path, whether to fight the case, whether to assume an impossible task, and so on. These choices are often characterized by an "or else" quality: the character must do something *or else* the monster will escape, love will be lost, dignity will be destroyed, or whatever.

"Or else" moments can be major turning points in stories when they are tied to a main character's psychological needs. An "or else" moment occurs in *The Verdict* (Shot 26) when Galvin tells Bishop Brophy that he cannot accept the settlement money [or else] "I'm going to be a rich ambulance chaser."

Some moments of decision allow the hero to agonize over values. At other times the character's choice is based on intuition and the wisdom of the heart, rather than hard thinking. However it happens, the moment of choice moves the protagonist toward the difficulties that are found on the moral high ground where he or she will be defined through heroic action.

A Force of Nature, Act of God, or Happenstance

Such events as hurricanes, disease, fire, drought, plagues, tidal waves, blizzards, floods, or a chance happening or an accident can dramatize a story. *The River* involves a flood that heightens the drama. In *Bound for Glory* the act of nature involves drought and dust storms. In *Hud* it is the disease that destroys a herd of cattle. *Fearless* organizes around a plane crash, which might be caused by a force of nature. Anything reasonable that adds to the drama is fair game. Such incidents often lead to a major sequence, so prepare the audience for what happens and for the consequences. (Also see the discussion of hero-versus-nature conflict in Chapter 2.)

Planting and Payoff

Planting and payoff occurs when the story introduces a character, a location, an animal, or anything else that will later influence what happens in the story. The clue, the weapon, the secret, the tool, or whatever, should be planted so it is noticed but does not call attention to itself. *The Verdict* (Shot 72) uses planting when Concannon slips an envelope containing Laura's salary into her purse. The payoff on this plant occurs in Shot 85, when Mickey discovers the incriminating envelope while rummaging for a cigarette in Laura's purse. The incident has logic and credibility because Laura is busy on the phone with Galvin, she is groggy after having spent the night in the office, and she is not paying attention to what Mickey is doing.

Another example of planting comes to light when the audience realizes that the assassin in *In the Line of Fire* has been practicing no-look blind-assembly of a plastic gun because it is part of his plan to kill the president. In the climactic scene of *The Terminator*, Reese presses buttons that start the machinery of a factory (Shot 256). The logic of Reese's doing this, which is actually a plant, is explained by his line about how the machinery will confuse the cyborg. The machinery pays off shortly thereafter, when Sarah presses a button that causes a giant press to crush the cyborg's skull. Planting and payoff can be used to create the lifeline found in some stories.

Lifelines

As discussed on page 87, a lifeline can come into play when the hero seems about to be defeated in the climactic scene. Then, when all seems lost, the hero uses, seizes, or discovers an action, a tool, a device, or information that solves the problem. In *Witness* (Shot 152), the lifeline is the bell that Samuel rings to summon the neighbors. The lifeline in *My Cousin Vinny* is the heroine's knowledge of automobiles. In *Clear and Present Danger* the lifeline is the Special Forces sniper who shoots the villain.

Dramatic Irony

Dramatic irony is a powerful convention that occurs when the hero or the villain is thwarted or rewarded in a painful or unexpected manner. In *All My Sons*, the father is so desperate to earn money for his family that he cheats on the equipment that his firm supplies to the Air Force. Later, his son dies while flying in one of the defective airplanes. The dramatic irony is that the father sinned to help his family, only to see his sins return and destroy his family.

War stories respond well to dramatic irony, as in *All Quiet on the Western Front*, which ends when the hero (Lew Ayres) reaches for a butterfly and is killed by a sniper. The war is about to end, the innocent hero makes a peaceful gesture, and the anonymous bullet ends his life, creating an exquisite moment of dramatic irony. In *The Bridge on the River Kwai*, Alec Guinness's Colonel Nicholson exhibits dramatic irony when his blinkered sense of duty almost foils the commandos who are attempting to blow up the bridge.

Parallelism

Parallelism involves the use of two similar actions that are intercut to make a single story point. In *The Color Purple* the heroine (Whoopie Goldberg's Celie) prepares to slit the throat of her abusive husband (Danny Glover's Mister). As Celie sharpens the razor, the film intercuts to Africa, where her sister is witnessing a ritual scarification ceremony. The scene intensifies as the heroine's friend races to prevent Celie from cutting her husband. The story point dramatized through this parallel action is that as the children in Africa are coming of age, so is Celie, who rebels against her brutish husband.

The Godfather uses life and death parallelism when it intercuts the baptism of a Corleone infant with contrasting images of the godfather's assassins murdering a rival gangster. There is a stunning parallel metaphor in *Apocalypse Now,* when Martin Sheen's character hacks Marlon Brando's Colonel Kurtz to death, while at the same time jungle tribesmen ceremonially behead a water buffalo.

Combination Moments

As already noted, story moments can include a combination of several of the dramatic conventions cited. Often combination moments are used to hinge (twist) the story in a new and surprising direction. For example, when the computer expert (Wayne Knight) in *Jurassic Park* is killed by a dinosaur, it required coincidence and an act of nature (the storm) to cause his demise. At the same time, the grandchildren of the park owner are trapped in a Jeep when the electric fences shut down, freeing the dinosaurs. This combination of events concludes a first-act setup that is tight with the dramatic potential that sustains Act II.

All the President's Men uses a shadowy informant who passes on information whenever the investigation bogs down. Donald Sutherland's mysterious character fulfills the same role in *JFK.* In both cases, these "mouthpiece" characters are power tools that dramatize the plot by revealing information. They also act as catalysts who speed up the story and create surprise and discovery. Various combinations of dramatic conventions can be created. For example, a character can be tipsy and have an affair with a stranger, who turns out to be the boss's lover. This combination of using a catalyst and coincidence can be found in *Working Girl.* Contrast, undeserved suffering, irony, superior position, and foreshadowing combine to dramatize moments in *Schindler's List.* Film study will reveal that many of the most powerful moments in a story result when two or more of the dramatic strategies noted above come together in a single scene.

SENTIMENTALITY AND EMPATHY

Sentimentality

The dramatization strategies discussed in the preceding section can invest energy, emotion, and excitement into a story. You should also know that, when misused, they can create false emotions that render a story shallow and manipulative. These sentimental stories contain emotion that is not earned by the drama. Although a judicious amount is okay, it should not come at the expense of logic and credibility. The dictionary definition that applies to *sentimentality* is "affected or extravagant emotion." The dictionary synonyms for *sentimental* also define what to avoid: "bathetic, maudlin, mawkish, mushy, schmaltzy, slushy."

Writers fall into the trap of sentimentality when their stories lack drama and substance and when the work is lathered with unearned emotion. Sentimentality oozes in when the characters are deliberately abused, regardless of justification or credibility. On-screen, this is often accompanied by syrupy music and unreasonable situations aimed at wringing unearned emotion from the audience. For example, in *For the Boys,* the characters played by Bette Midler and James Caan are entertainers performing in a war zone. Coincidentally, their soldier son is in the audience during a field performance when the enemy attacks; one of the casualties is their son, who is killed before their eyes. Could such a catastrophe happen? Possibly. Did the incident give Caan and Midler a chance to simulate a major emotional hit? It did, but the sequence left a saccharine aftertaste because it felt like a contrivance to draw sympathy for two characters who are not very likable. The incident aimed at pathos, which connects to emotions of sadness, tenderness, and sympathy. Such a response is admirable, if it is earned by the ordeal of the main characters. Here is where our sense of story can either betray us or lead us to glory. In this case, the filmmakers' judgment seemed off.

Except for stories for children, who have an innocent capacity for sentimentality, avoid the easy story fix that this value promises. This can be challenging because writers can convince themselves that the dreariest drivel is heartfelt and real. Our main defense against such tendencies is to ask whether the incident feels truthful. Is it logical? Is it motivated? Is it something that could happen in a reasonable story universe? Does the incident tie into the event being dramatized and relate to the characters? Does the incident connect to the hero-villain conflict, or is it only a cheap thrill that is tacked onto the story? Is there another way to make the point so the emotion seems honestly earned and unsentimental? The reward for such thinking is a story that generates *empathy.*

Empathy

An empathetic story persuades the audience to identify with a person or a cause. When the motives are understood, the audience can embrace the humanity of the characters and share the ordeal of the story. **Empathy** means sharing and understanding another person's situation, feelings, and motives. Audiences move into this state when the truth and integrity of the drama pull them into the story where they share the earned emotions of the on-screen characters.

Empathy persuades viewers to open their hearts to the movie and its characters; films that can manage this are among the profession's finest achievements. Writing at this level means distinguishing between what is sentimental and what is empathetic, a distinction that can be difficult to make. Some see films such as *Sleepless in Seattle, Paradise, Man in the Moon, My Girl,* and *Kramer vs. Kramer* as sentimental claptrap; others see them as honest stories that arouse empathy. When we develop an idea that seems to be moving over the thin ice of sentimentality, the least we can do is do is skate swiftly, i.e., keep the story moving. There is an example of this in *The Shawshank Redemption* when the hero gives his friend (Morgan Freeman's Red) a harmonica. Red is grateful but does not play it until he is alone in his cell. Only then does he cradle the instrument briefly, then play a single, quiet chord. The incident immediately ends, which steps away from a sugary excursion into harmonica music sounding into the cells of attentive convicts. Besides, such a moment is done more effectively when the hero plays the opera duet over the prison loudspeaker system. The harmonica incident might have been momentarily affective, but later the audience might have felt conned by the mushiness of that moment. If this happened, viewers might become resistant to the rest of the story. Choosing how to write these moments is clearly a judgment call that depends on what each writer feels will pull on the audience's heartstrings. In most cases, this happens when our characters experience a dramatic ordeal that makes them stronger.

Because this topic has such a strong bearing on dramatization, let me present another example, from *Awakenings,* the story of a man (Robert De Niro) who is reduced to a vegetative state by a virus. His mother (Ruth Nelson) has been visiting him for years, until one day a wonder drug enables De Niro to regain consciousness. When he embraces his mother for the first time in decades, the audience is deeply touched. Tears flow again when the drug loses effectiveness and De Niro's illness begins to return. Then, as other doomed patients watch, he slow-dances with the young woman who has been visiting him at the hospital. Although *Awakenings* punches the pathos button hard, the film works because the ordeal of the characters is cruelly unjust and their victory, however fleeting, seems earned. The screenwriter (Steven Zaillian) dramatized this true but grim story in a way that drew an empathetic response from viewers and connected them to the characters.

Empathy can be extended to villains and negative characters when their motives and humanity are understood. Examples: Jack Nicholson in *Witches of Eastwick,* Danny DeVito in *Other People's Money,* Glenn Close in *Fatal Attraction,* Michael Douglas in *Falling Down.* The strategy here is to appreciate the psychological imperative that drives the antagonist and use it to develop the character's inner life. So, instead of merely assigning vicious motives to a character, think about why the person behaves in that way and give reasons for how he or she thinks. Demi Moore's character in *Disclosure* is presented this way. Although we do not understand why she is so aggressive, we sense that she is powerfully motivated in ways that make her life difficult.

DRAMATIZING WITH MOMENTUM

One of the most important contributors to drama is story *momentum.* This value supplies the narrative rush of the story, a feeling that something is happening and that events and characters are being propelled toward a climactic moment. In most cases, story momentum begins within the first few minutes of a feature story; it happens even sooner for most TV shows. These beginnings often involve a sense of story takeoff, a feel that something has started, that a narrative is underway. This is the case in *The Terminator*, when two naked beings drop from the sky and immediately proceed to execute a mission of some sort. Even though we are unsure of their intentions, both parties have an agenda that gives the film its sense of story takeoff.

In most cases, the driving force behind story momentum is the story problem and the willfulness of the main characters. As a story approaches the climax, the rush of events creates a sense of dramatic urgency that makes the audience worry about the conflict: Will the boy win the chess tournament in *Searching for Bobby Fischer*? Will Kimble escape Gerard and be vindicated in *The Fugitive*? Momentum is the confluence of character, time, and logic, as when the assassin tries to kill the president in *In the Line of Fire*. Momentum is controlled by the characters and by the logic of the story, which ultimately ask for an unexpected, inevitable, and satisfying climax that solves the story's external and internal problems.

Audiences have little difficulty following the swift pace of today's films, thanks to television and modern movies that have familiarized viewers with cinematic grammar and how motion picture stories are told. For example, a character in a movie made before the 1960s might announce that she is leaving on a trip to a foreign city. The movie might then show travel preparations, boarding the plane or ship, arrival, and the like. Modern films are likely to cut from first mention of a trip directly to the foreign city. This eliminates the need for travel continuity and adds to the momentum of the story. Obviously, occasions arise when traveling is essential to the story, but when this is not the case, it can be abbreviated without causing the audience to lose the thread of the narrative.

Story momentum is not a movie constant, because there are "fast" stories and slow-paced stories, and everything in between. *Speed* is a "fast" story that generates frantic energy, whereas the momentum is deliberately slow and stately in *The Remains of the Day*. As will be explained in Chapter 9 ("Writing Stage Directions"), screenwriters indicate not only the style and mood of stories but the pace as well. Although the director can speed up or slow down the pace, by the time most scripts go into production, they have been timed and paced by the production team. There may be timing changes involving individual beats—some will be speeded up, others played out—but overall, the pace of the story as scripted is what usually shows up on-screen.

Story Momentum and the "Clock"

Many adventure stories can be dramatized by adding a time factor—a "ticking clock"—as in *High Noon*, when the train carrying the outlaws arrives at a certain hour. In *Dr. Strangelove*, the time factor connects to stopping a jet bomber before it triggers nuclear annihilation. The ticking clock that helps to dramatize *Speed* is a bus rigged to explode if driven below a certain speed.

Dramatizing within a time frame begins when the writer approximates how much time will elapse from the beginning of the story to the end. That span places an overall "clock" on the story. Most movies have a clock that is either implied or stated. For example, the clock on one-hour television shows often involves less than one week of story time. Television sitcoms usually play out in a day or less.

Most feature stories span a few weeks to a few months. The clock in *The Verdict* is a bit confused, but it seems to extend for about two weeks, beginning when Mickey tells Galvin that the trial starts in ten days (Shot 8). The clock is at work when Concannon informs his staff that they will face Galvin in court on February 19 (Shot 30) and then when Judge Sweeney tells Concannon and Galvin that the trial will begin "next Thursday" (Shot 38). Using Thursday as the trial start date serves logic and continuity because it gives Galvin enough time to fly to New York over the weekend, where he locates his mystery witness. This time arrangement allows Kaitlin to show up in court when the trial resumes on the following Monday.

Throughout, the pressure of time prods the hero and adds to the drama of the story. We see this when Galvin realizes that he needs more time to get himself back into fighting trim, but there is none (Shot 39). Later, Galvin asks the judge for more time to locate a witness and his request is denied (Shot 49). Later still, Galvin must locate a missing witness, but he seems to have run out of time (Shot 77).

In *Witness*, the clock extends for a month or so (assuming that it would take that long for Book to recover from his wound). Although *The Terminator* does not mention time, the rush of incidents and of days turning into nights indicates that the story spans two or three days. Not counting the eighteen months of mourning that took place at the beginning of the story, the clock in *Sleepless in Seattle* extends from Christmas to Valentine's Day. As general advice, keep the clock brief by beginning the story as close to the climactic scene as possible.

Certain genres—thrillers, crime and sports stories, science fiction, whodunnits—tend to employ a "clock" that adds to story momentum. Most courtroom dramas are time-restricted because they require the litigants to show up and to present testimony. In such a rigid setting, when time, procedures, and language are precise, the protocol of the trial can create momentum.

Movies that deal with a mission (*Juggernaut*), a deadline (*Bullets over Broadway*), a contest (*Hoosiers*), and the like often use time to intensify the drama. If it is important for the audience to know how much time is left before the bomb explodes, there may be cutaways to the numbers that tick off the seconds remaining. *WarGames, Dr. Strangelove*, and *The Andromeda Strain* use time to dramatize the urgency of preventing disaster.

Different time strategies are used for stories that span long periods (*Malcolm X, Driving Miss Daisy, The Shawshank Redemption, What's Love Got to Do with It*). Audiences can become lost in a sprawling story unless given a sense of time passing. Among the many ways of doing this, aging the main characters is a very popular strategy. Time awareness is also managed through dialogue, by superimposing a date, by television news reports of the period, by voice-over narration, and so on. *A League of Their Own* uses an older look-alike to show how Geena Davis's character might appear in later years. The illusion was heightened by looping Davis's voice so it replaced that of the older woman.

How Movies Indicate Time

Time can be noted quickly and obliquely by a snatch of music, a radio or TV show, a glimpse of a period newspaper headline, or a product that typifies an era. *My Favorite Year* opens with many of these conventions: newspaper headlines marking the fall of Senator Joseph McCarthy, Les Paul and Mary Ford playing one of their hit tunes, and cars and fashions of the time (1954).

Time can be tracked by visuals: a sapling transforming into a mature tree, a child growing older, the completion of a construction project, and so forth. Throughout the four-year clock in *Rudy*, periodic letters and interviews apprise the audience of time passing. This dramatizes the story by making the audience worry whether the hero will be given an opportunity to play football for Notre Dame before he graduates. The entire movie builds toward this goal, so it is important that the audience know about the story's ticking clock. Finally, at the end of the film, when Notre Dame lines up for the final play of its final game, the coach sends Rudy into the game; thus, he achieves his goal and solves the dramatic problem of the story.

Dislocations in Time and Place

Films create temporal discontinuities by shifting back and forth in time through flashbacks, as in *The Terminator*, when we see Reese's nightmare world of the future (Shots 46 and 183FX). If the story is deliberately discontinuous (*Performance, Petulia, The Stunt Man*), explain what is happening in the script's stage directions; otherwise, the reader may lose the thread.

Think carefully before dating your script with references to a specific year or to events, songs, movies, and the like. Movies will be played on home screens for decades, and in some cases, a reference can take viewers out of the story if they do not remember the thing being referenced or understand its significance. For example, I assume that audiences in 2009 will not remember Mr. and Mrs. Bobbitt, Tonya Harding, Amy Fisher, or similar tabloid personalities of the 1990s; they will mean even less to audiences overseas.

Of course there are exceptions to this, especially in stories when specific time references are unavoidable. Films such as *1942, The Unbearable Lightness of Being,* and *Fat Man and Little Boy* are tied to specific historical events. Exceptions aside, think carefully before including anything that dates a story. This includes objects, devices, or references that are out of time or out of place in your story universe. There were several anachronisms in *The Shadow*, which seems to take place in the 1930s. The movie opens with what appears to be a 1935 Buick driving through Tibet or Mongolia in what should have been the late 1920s or early 1930s. Seven years later, cars of the same era are shown in New York. The bomb that ticks off time in that film uses an LED display, although LED technology was not invented until decades later. The film also used expressions not appropriate for the 1930s. These are minor items, yet they eroded the film's continuity and credibility.

Movie Conventions That Indicate Time and Continuity

The three principal time strategies in movies are the cut, the dissolve, and the fade-in/fade-out. Each is discussed briefly so that you can use them to imagine transitions.

A *cut* occurs when two pieces of film[2] are joined together, without overlapping footage. Cuts that occur within a beat indicate continuous action. The Galvin-Sweeney-Concannon scene (Shot 38) discussed in Chapter 4 illustrates.

When a cut connects footage from different locations, it indicates action that may *not* be continuous, and a span of seconds or even days might separate the two pieces of film. In *The Verdict* (Shots 71 and 72), the action cuts from Galvin's office, where he discusses the case with Mickey, to Concannon's office, where we discover that Laura is a spy. A second, an hour, or a day might separate the action of the two incidents.

The cut is the most widely used continuity device, especially in modern films, where it often replaces the dissolve and the fade-in/fade-out convention. When in doubt about how to move from one beat to another, imagine them joined by a cut, so you can get on with writing the next beat.

A *dissolve* occurs when two or more images from different locations overlap. The dissolve transition means that time has elapsed between beats. The dissolve is often decided on by the director or the editor, who tells the processing lab how long the overlap should last. The lab will overlap images from the end of beat A with the first images from beat B. Most dissolves sustain for a few seconds.

When the dissolve is accompanied by a close-up of a character, it can signal that the story is moving from an objective view of the action to a subjective view. This use of the dissolve indicates that the action is moving into a flashback or a fantasy scene. (See *The Terminator* [Shot 45] for an example of this transition.) Dissolves are also used in montages, which are discussed in Chapter 4.

Fade-in/fade-out occurs when the picture dims to black (or white) for a few seconds and then fades into the first image of the next beat. This strategy, the movie equivalent of a chapter break in a book, usually indicates that a

---

[2]Although references here are to film, the editing conventions cited also apply to videotape, which is edited electronically, without physically cutting the tape. A number of production companies now transfer their film footage to videotape and use computerized electronic editing to prepare an edit decision list that locates the IN and OUT points needed to edit the film.

major phase of the story, a sequence, or a character's development has concluded and a new phase is beginning.

TENSION

Tension joins its twin, *momentum,* as another goal of the dramatizing strategies noted above. Dramatic tension shows in two ways: as an overriding concern for whether the hero will solve the problem that organizes the story and as tension within each bit and scene. In *The Verdict,* the overarching story makes the audience worry about Galvin's ability to win the court case. Additionally, there is tension within the various scenes, as when Judge Sweeney and Concannon pressure Galvin to settle the case (Shot 38); when Concannon humiliates Dr. Thompson while accepting him as an expert witness; when Laura castigates Galvin for quitting the case before the trial has even begun (Shot 61). In each instance, these scenes create tension because they generate conflict that challenges the hero.

Tension can also result from how the characters respond to the circumstances of the scene, as well as the attitudes that the characters bring to the scene. For example, in *Witness* (Shot 100A), Eli comes upon Book and Rachel as they dance to music from the car radio in the barn. This beat has sexual tension because of the attraction between Book and Rachel. Additional tension flares from Eli, who is outraged to find his daughter-in-law dancing to "English" music, something not done by the Amish. Finally, there is tension between Book and Eli as to which man Rachel will ally herself with. These threads bind the characters in a tense dramatic relationship that connects to the larger circumstances of the story, the tension of possibly being found by Schaeffer and his gang.

Overall story tension often occurs when a threat of some sort is imposed on the good guys and gains on them despite their best efforts. Tension takes hold when the hero is presented with a challenge or a problem that must be solved, as in *The Terminator,* in which survival of the heroes and of humanity itself depends on defeating an indestructible cyborg. In *Witness,* tension connects a solitary hero and an Amish family to a murderous police conspiracy that must be stopped. The tension is ratcheted up a few notches by the hero's being weakened by a gunshot wound and by his deeply felt concern for Rachel and her family.

Tension involves strategies that I recall from the 1960s and 1970s, when various story editors would ask me, "Where's the menace? What causes the jeopardy? Who's gunning for the hero?" In one way or another, today's stories work the same way because most of them require the audience to worry about whether the hero will survive the menace. We see tension connect to the menacing problem in *Unforgiven,* when William Munny and his two mates ride into the hell town run by Gene Hackman's sheriff. So that there is no doubt that Hackman is a menace, we see him cruelly beat and humiliate Richard Harris. Later, the same sheriff almost kicks Munny's guts out. After Hackman's menace has been established, he becomes the formidable enemy that the hero must kill to avenge the murder of his friend. Munny rises to this challenge when he stokes up on bourbon, rides into town, and shows why his name once sent a chill through the West. Throughout the story, the inevitability of the showdown—Munny against the sheriff and his gunmen—dramatizes the story with tension because there seems to be no way that the hero will triumph, but he does.

There is tension in *Alien* when Sigourney Weaver's Ripley ends up as the sole survivor of a spaceship. To destroy the horror that killed her crew, she rigs the spaceship to explode, grabs her cat, and slips into the escape ship. Then, just as she is about to doze off, Ripley discovers that the alien is sharing the long ride to earth—and will begin to snack on her when it feels hungry! Throughout this film the menace of the alien creates suspense and tension. Similar values dramatize *The Fugitive*, because Gerard and his team are tireless hunters who menace the hero.

The Verdict, Moonstruck, and *Sleepless in Seattle* are gentler stories, but they also employ a degree of menace to create tension. In *The Verdict*, tension stems from the hero's problem, which is to defeat a powerful lawyer and his establishment cohorts. In *Moonstruck* and *Sleepless in Seattle*, the tension involves the difficulties of getting the lovers together. In these and in so many stories, tension grows out of conflict that is connected to the problem being tracked. When stories drift off the problem, they lose tension, focus, and dramatic rush.

"HINGING" THE PLOT WITH TWISTS

This final dramatizing strategy—and also one of the most potent—asks the writer to create plot twists that surprise the audience regarding what they thought would happen in the story. In most cases the complication involves making the hero's situation more desperate. The complication (or twist) also "thickens the plot," as in *The Verdict* (Shot 25), when the hero visits his brain-dead client to take photographs and has an attack of conscience. The plot thickens again when Galvin experiences another attack of conscience that causes him to turn down Bishop Brophy's settlement offer. Galvin's decision is a major twist that swings the plot in a new and unexpected direction—toward conflict with the most feared lawyer in town.

In *The Shawshank Redemption*, the hero (Andy) overhears the head guard griping about the taxes he owes on an inheritance. To dramatize the scene, Andy is uncharacteristically clumsy when proposing to help the guard with his taxes, which almost causes him to toss Andy off the roof. At the last moment, Andy explains his offer and a deal is struck with the guard. This twist brings Andy's financial skills into play, and before long he is transferred to duties that are more suited to what a former bank officer like Andy might do. In this way, the roof incident hinges the story (swings it in a new direction) by bringing Andy's banking skills to the attention of the other guards. The incident also obligates the guards to Andy and they return the favor by beating the "sisters" so badly that they no longer assault him. The final ripple in this incident is to call Andy to the attention of the warden, who allows him to renovate the prison library.

The Shawshank Redemption is unusual for the number of twists that hinge the story. They include the incident in which Andy becomes friends with Red; when the "sisters" brutalize Andy; when the warden takes kickbacks for convict labor and uses Andy to hide the money; and when the young convict tells of a former cellmate who claims to have committed the murders that sent Andy to prison. The twists continue when the head guard murders the young convict so his story will not free Andy and jeopardize the fortune that the warden has been skimming. The plot hinges again when Andy escapes; when he implicates the prison hierarchy; when he makes off with the warden's money; when Red is released; when Red finds Andy's message; and when the two men are reunited in Mexico. These twists indicate skillful storytelling by Stephen King (for his novella) and by Frank Darabont for his adaptation and direction. Their techniques are worth careful study. (The novella from which this screenplay was adapted [*Rita Hayworth and the Shawshank Redemption*] is part of King's *Different Seasons*, Signet Classics, New York, 1983.)

Most stories contain one or two twists in each act; their nature depends on the intensity and style of the story. I can offer only general advice on inventing twists, since the topic has so many variables. High-energy stories with strong life-or-death conflicts (*Speed, Jaws, Alien*) often present a plot twist, however minor, at the end of each sequence. The resulting twists hinge the plot and surprise the audience, keeping moviegoers on the edge of their seats.

In *Witness*, the lives of Rachel and her son swing toward danger when the boy witnesses a murder. The story hinges in a new direction when Schaeffer turns out to be the leader of a group of renegade cops, which we realize when one of his gang tries to kill Book. Although bleeding from his wound, Book rescues Rachel and Samuel before Schaeffer has a chance to kill them. The story hinges again when Book collapses and is tended by Rachel and the Amish. The story hinges again when the antique life-style of the Amish prevents Schaeffer and his men from locating Book and the Lapp family. This gives Book time to recover, and when he does, he gets in a fight with hoodlums, Schaeffer learns of his whereabouts, and the plot hinges toward the final showdown.

A useful piece of advice on plotting came from Billy Wilder during a Writers Guild of America interview in October 1994. When I asked him how he might advise young writers on their plots, Wilder replied that the plot incidents "must be logical. You must make the audience believe in the logic of the characters and what is happening." Wilder went on to explain how he and his writing partner (I.A.L. Diamond) often spent several months working out their plots. Part of their work involved concealing the machinations of the plot so the audience would believe the story. For example, *Some Like It Hot* is based on an obscure European film about a saxophone player who dresses as a woman to escape his enemies. The Wilder-Diamond version of the story involves two men who escape their enemies by dressing as women and hiding among an all-girl band that travels from New York to Miami by train. During the trip, the two men (Jack Lemmon and Tony Curtis) develop attachments to women in the band, identities become confused, and the gangsters pick up their trail. In the end, the story turns out happily, but only because the screenwriters had carefully plotted this intricate yarn.

A certain amount of this work involves logic, which is fairly easy to point out, since this is what inspired invention often looks like in hindsight. For example, the Lemmon-Curtis characters needed a reason to put on women's clothes and take refuge in an all-girl band, which is what these groups were once called. The screenwriters took care of that problem by having the two heroes blunder upon a gangland massacre, where one gang of criminals slaughters another. When the two heroes are recognized as musicians who had performed for the gangsters, Lemmon and Curtis have a reason for fleeing. This incident supplies the wacky logic for Lemmon and Curtis to take refuge among female musicians. Throughout this farce, the hinges and twists of the plot are justified, and the masterful storytellers and an inspired cast and crew offer an impossibly wonderful ride that everyone is invited to enjoy.

Sleepless in Seattle is another story that is dramatized with interesting plot twists. From the start, Bill Pullman's Walter is presented as unappealing, yet Annie seems to be stuck with him. Then the plot hinges when a call-in radio show connects Sam and Jonah to Annie, and before long she checks out the call-in show (and Sam) on company time. Throughout the story, incidents occur to justify behavior, motives, chance meetings, and long-distance connections. This is done persuasively, without making the audience notice how the incidents are planted and how successive beats in the story are set up. *Skillful screenwriting hides its machinations and persuades the audience that what is on-screen is credible.* To make this happen, the writer must constantly justify the logic of the plot, of the incidents, and of the characters. The incidents that were roughed out in the beat sheet must be written into bits, scenes, and sequences that build the story and entertain the audience.

For example, one of the beats outlined in *Sleepless in Seattle* might have presented a general instruction: "Annie learns more about Sam." Writing such a beat would require devising logical, believable ways for this to happen. Since Annie works for a newspaper that has a computer service, this presented a logical, believable strategy for locating Sam and for finding out that he is an architect and a widower, as stated on the call-in show. This information validates Sam and justifies a woman of Annie's education and social background launching her improbable manhunt. To plot this way requires asking what is truthful, what is logical in terms of the story situation and the characters, and what could happen that is dramatic, believable, and useful to the story. There is no easy way around this phase of the work, which is done both by solid thinking and by diving into the unconscious and swimming around until something dramatic turns up. This work takes time, so be patient.

Dramatizing with plot hinges sometimes requires bringing in a character who can swing the story in a new direction. Wilder and Diamond did this in

Some Like It Hot when they introduced Marilyn Monroe as the singer in the band and Joe E. Brown as the wealthy playboy. Alexander Godunov's Amish suitor in *Witness* hinges that story because he competes with Book for Rachel's attention. His presence adds heat to the love story that takes up most of the second act. Nurse Rooney in *The Verdict* and the hospital workers that the hero of *The Fugitive* encounters also present fresh characters who create credible, logical incidents of plot that swing those stories in new directions.

Before leaving the topic, you should know that stories become dramatized when the writer invests his or her energy and life force in the work. This involves thinking through the story until you feel that your brain will burst with the effort; it means imagining with an intensity that seems to be frying something deep inside your skull; it means never accepting work that is "good enough," because good enough is never good enough. Dramatizing requires passion, focus, a sense of story, and the determination needed to stay with the script until it is as good as you can make it. Then send it out for review from friends, read their comments, and see if any of them suggest ways to improve the script. This is how movie stories and screenplays get written, and unless the writing is supercharged with the writer's energy, experience, intelligence, and spirit, the work may not be good enough. There can be no faking this, and writers must deliver the full measure of their craft to be noticed.

SUMMARY

Dramatization makes a situation more desperate, more poignant, more wonderful, more romantic, more entertaining. Dramatizing means writing scenes that may feel outrageously over-the-top. Put this attitude aside and remind yourself that nothing is too wonderful or too terrible not to be true. If your impossibly dramatic notion suits the story, use it—but make it logical and believable. When the dramatizing strategy seems too extreme, it can be toned down, but scripts are more likely to fail for being too polite, too proper, too reasonable, and too dull rather than for being too over-the-top.

If the dramatizing strategies outlined in this chapter seem like tricks and contrivances, it is because that's what they are—theatrical tricks and contrivances! Even so, as you spot them in films, especially the strategy of the dramatic engine, you will appreciate that what may seem overblown on paper usually shows up as dramatically effective and appropriate on a movie screen. The message here is simple: *It is easier to tone things down than to energize a script that is dull and undramatic.*

Be truthful and tough-minded whenever you are tempted to become sugary and sentimental, which can dilute the dramatic content. Make the characters earn whatever kindness or release they receive. The goal is to persuade the audience to empathize with characters by having those characters display courage and humanity in the face of adversity.

The strategies described in this chapter are not magic bullets that will automatically dramatize the story and create plot twists, but each item has utility. For example, torquing can create a spin or energy that diverts and entertains the audience so it does not notice a scene's talkiness, exposition, or lack of drama. At the least, the strategies cited should add to your under- standing of how films dramatize, how they use twists that hinge the story so that it swings in new and dramatically useful directions, and how the strate- gies play on paper and on the screen.

Exercises

1. Select a feature film and analyze it in terms of the dramatizing strategies discussed in this chapter. Note when each convention appears and briefly describe its nature and purpose.
2. Time the speeches and scenes in the film analyzed in question 1. Note whether the speeches end abruptly or linger. Note whether they use transitional visuals that show characters traveling from one location to another or whether the action cuts directly from scene to scene.
3. Examine how the film uses conflict to dramatize the story. What causes and intensi- fies the conflict? How does the conflict relate to the problem? How are the problem and the conflict resolved?

(For media that illustrate the points made in this chapter, see Appendix A.)

CHAPTER 8

Writing for the Camera: Visual Storytelling

Screenwriters create dramatic images that advance the story and reveal character. This chapter discusses those strategies and how you can use them to tell your story with motion pictures as well as dialogue.

The eye has been called the thief of the senses because vision overrides our other senses and demands that it be fed first—and continuously. For filmwriters, this means telling stories that have visual content. Accordingly this chapter discusses how to supply the visual content that audiences expect to see when they go to a motion picture show.

The visualization strategies in this chapter add another layer to the story sense that began to accumulate with our discussion of how to locate a movie idea and how to expand it into a plot. Additional layers came from chapters on blocking the story, creating basic dramatic units, writing complex characters, writing dialogue, and dramatizing a script. This chapter examines writing for the camera from three angles:

- Cinematography for screenwriters
- The visual design of a film and how screenwriters use their understanding of cinematography to write stories told through images rather than through dialogue
- Strategies for adding visual content to stories

These three aspects of visual storytelling can overcome a common tendency which is to tell stories with dialogue and stage directions rather than with images. Much of the discussion that follows deals with writing scripts that give the audience things to look at. On one level these "things" are visual details that connect to what the characters do, where they do it, how the characters are dressed, and how the images are lighted, as well as the colors and textures of the costumes, the sets, and the physical locations.

There is also a grander design for visual content that depends on the writer's overall conception of the story. For example, some stories insist on being told through dialogue (*The Verdict, Sleepless in Seattle*); when this is the case, the writing often slants toward dialogue and away from action visuals. When the writer conceptualizes a story with physical action, as in *Braveheart* and *The Terminator,* then that decision will swing the story toward action visuals. *Full Metal Jacket* illustrates this key point: The final sequence involves a squad of marines who are pinned down and picked off by an unseen sniper. In time, the marines manage to get into a maze of ruined buildings, where they hunt down and kill the sniper, who is a fierce young woman. That remarkable location (a gasworks in London that was to be torn down) was dressed with palm trees, debris, and assorted fires until it became a unique battleground for this forty-minute action sequence whose visual content was unavoidable once the writers (Stanley Kubrick, Michael Herr, and Gustav Hasford) conceptualized the climax of the movie as a hunt for a sniper in a ruined city. Their concept set up incidents of sudden death and rage as the marines are being killed during the nightmarish cat-and-mouse game. The sequence allows for personal moments in which the horror of the experience registers on the men in the squad.

Full Metal Jacket presents a sterling example of how action stories are told with images, and it also exemplifies a point that should not be missed: Triple-check and triple-check again to determine if your story will support the visual content of an action or visual scene. This advice applies as well to stories that are not in the action category, since in most cases they must also support visual content, as in *Witness*. Although basically a character story, this movie is visually enriched with physical action scenes (the murder in the train station, the assassination attempt, the barn raising, and the final shootout). Each of these plot incidents lends itself to strong visuals. Note that action beats need not involve violence, as evidenced in the eight-minute barn raising sequence.

To ease you into writing images rather than static, talky scenes, we shall discuss how cinematographers approach their work. This will not be a discourse in cinematography, any more than our discussion of "reel psychology" was a treatise on the workings of the mind. Instead, we shall examine the camera and visual content from a screenwriter's perspective to give you a sense of how visual potential is worked into stories. The fine points of cinematography—and there are many—will become obvious to those who pursue the references cited in this chapter[1] and in the bibliography. What follows is merely a simplified overview of how cinematography works and how screenwriters can use this information to write visual content.

CINEMATOGRAPHY FOR SCREENWRITERS

This first part of the discussion aims to familiarize you with such basics of visual grammar as shot selection, camera moves that tell a story through

---

[1]See Dennis Schaefer and Larry Salvato, *Master of Light: Conversations with Contemporary Cinematographers,* University of California Press, Berkeley, 1984. Also see Nestor Almendros, *A Man with a Camera,* Farrar, Straus, Giroux, New York, 1984. Also recommended for their discussions of how the camera tells a story are the periodicals *American Cinematographer* and *Film and Video: The Production Magazine.*

images, and how to add visual interest and texture to your script. As you study this topic, you will realize that visual awareness is not something to be switched to ON when sitting down to write. Rather, a screenwriter's visual awareness, like that of other filmmakers, is *always* on. Such awareness will make you more alert to ideas, locations, character moments, physical business, and whatever has visual interest. Screenwriters observe. We study. We use our eyes to scrutinize the world and its inhabitants. We note specific images: a child dashing through a lawn sprinkler, a cat snoozing in a patch of sunlight, trees swaying in the wind, parents cheering their child at a Little League game. In this way we sharpen our visual awareness, which is essential to creating motion pictures.

Because filmmakers are good at their work, movies have become the dominant communication form of our century. The public is so conditioned by them that even children can understand cinematic content, whether in music videos, TV commercials, TV shows, or feature films. As the public's ability to comprehend motion picture narrative has expanded, viewers demand more spectacle, action, stunts, and exciting special effects.

Much of this content is experienced in movie theaters, a dreamy environment where audiences gather anonymously in a semidarkened room. As they wait for the movie to begin, audiences experience a degree of sensory deprivation that visually primes them for the movie that lies coiled in cans of film in the projection booth. Just before the movie begins, there is a ritual rising of the stage curtain, which symbolically wipes away the concerns of the outside world. Thus prepared, the audience settles into a movie that will play from beginning to end, without commercial breaks and (it is hoped) without audience commentary on what is on-screen.

These factors are part of what psychologist Hugo Mauerhofer calls the "cinema situation,"[2] where viewers are lulled into a relaxed state. Some call this a "waking dream," where reality is slightly out of kilter and the viewer's attention is focused by invisible but controlling forces (the camera and editing) that use brilliant images to pull the audience into the story on-screen.

Audiences are receptive to visual content because the projected images are perfectly framed and lighted in ways that best tell a story whose narrative rush makes the audience eager to see what happens next. Technological advances make today's movie theater experience more affective than that of the past. Movie screens today are brighter; film stocks are sharper, more light-sensitive, and more colorful; and projection systems are smoother and more efficient. Visual excitement is encouraged by big sound, for when characters speak, when a bomb explodes, when music enhances the story, super-real sound booms forth over theater sound systems that have become so powerful that we can feel the physical impact of the audio waves. Furthermore, filmmakers have become so skillful that there is almost nothing that they cannot create through computer animation, composite imaging, digital and special

[2]Hugo Mauerhofer, "Psychology of Film Experience," in Richard Dyer MacCann (ed.), *Film: A Montage of Theories*, E. P. Dutton, New York, 1966, p. 229.

effects, model work, and other technical feats. The result is that the world's standard for movie entertainment is very high, and audiences expect considerable visual content when they buy their tickets. If the movie does not deliver the anticipated visual "fix," viewers may become bored.

This observation applies equally to character-driven and to plot-driven stories. The images projected onto the screen must satisfy the eye's appetite for visual stimuli. To illustrate this key point: If two people are filmed as they sit at a table that is surrounded by four blank walls, the audience will quickly consume whatever visual details are contained in the frame, leaving viewers hungry for something new to look at. Unless the movie supplies it, the audience may become restless and bored. Thus, *writing motion pictures requires an understanding of how quickly the eye absorbs and processes visual information.* For screenwriters this tells us to write stories that supply a constant flow of images that have visual potential. Shortly, you will be given advice on how to write scenes with visual content, even in dialogue scenes that might seem visually static.

A second important point is that the eye of the viewer is drawn to movement. If a scene shows a cat walking across the living room where two people are reading a book, the audience will usually shift its attention from the people to the cat, particularly if the shot frames on the cat. If the cat chases a mouse across the floor, attention will be more focused because the action of the chase contains conflict and drama.

These two points—the audience's need for visuals and the audience's attraction to movement—are simple perspectives on visual storytelling. The two points came to me one sunny afternoon in Dublin, where I was researching pubs and noticed the similarities between saloons and movies. In both establishments, the patrons are kept visually busy. In a theater the focus is on the screen; in a pub the focus wanders. To keep patrons from becoming visually bored, pubs give customers a variety of things to look at. First, a large mirror is often positioned behind the bar so patrons can see what happens in the room. They may also be given bric-a-brac, mementos, posters, stuffed animals, sports trophies, framed photographs, model boats, and antique musical instruments to inspect. Holding everything together are soldierly ranks of liquor bottles, glasses, condiments, and snacks. The purpose of these props is to give patrons something to look at, no matter how glazed or baleful the stare.

Movies follow a similar plan. Regardless of the setting on-screen, the images should give patrons something to browse through visually, for whether responding to saloon, salon, or cinematheque, the human eye is swift and insatiable in its absorption of visual information. Because moviemakers understand this, they devote considerable effort to lighting, interior decoration, fabrics, furniture, art objects, textured doors and moldings, and whatever else transforms an ordinary setting into one that has visual interest. Additionally, the camera angles shift to present the audience with changeable visual perspectives of the scene.

As mentioned previously, the visual literacy of movie audiences has been heightened by MTV and TV commercials, and filmmakers must step lively to keep apace. For example, the opening credits on *NYPD Blue* present fifty-four snapshots during its sixty-three-second playing time. The message here suggests that if TV shows fail to serve up a steady flow of visual details, the audience may switch to another channel. When TV viewers attend a movie theater, they bring their visual expectations with them. Because audiences place visual demands on filmmakers, we shall now examine how filmmakers use four elements of cinematography to realize the visual potential of a script.

THE FOUR ELEMENTS OF VISUAL CONTENT

Directors are familiar with the work of the cinematographers they use. Often the same people are hired picture after picture because they form into a skilled team that knows how to work effectively without confusion or dispute. The director, working with the producer, cinematographer, and production designer,[3] sets the visual design of the movie. To make sure the desired look is being achieved and that the dramatic moments are captured on film or tape, the filmmakers view an hour or so of "dailies" (aka "rushes") that show the unedited footage that was exposed during the previous day of production. Monitoring this way ensures that the desired style, energy, and look are being recorded on film. The skills of the cinematographer and production designer allow the director to concentrate on working with the actors so they can deliver the performances needed to tell the story.

The alchemy of how cinematographers translate pages of script into individual frames of film organizes around four values that shape the visual content of a film: *lighting, movement, color,* and *space.*

Lighting

Cinematographers describe their work as "painting with light." Good lighting shows clearly in films and can be appreciated by screenwriters even if they do not understand how the lighting effects are achieved. However, with a bit of film study, you can familiarize yourself with the main lighting effects and cinematic styles.[4] If you have neither the time nor the opportunity for such study, select a dozen or so lighting effects from films you admire and define them in your own terms. Then, when writing a scene that has, say, a horrific setting, simply describe it as imagined (*The crypt is creepy and slimy, with drippy walls*

---

[3]The **production designer** determines the overall look of a film's sets, decoration, costumes, colors, locations, and props. The production designer works closely with the art director and the set designer, as well as the director and cinematographer. Patrizia von Brandenstein feels that her job as production designer (*Ragtime, Postcards from the Edge*) is to "provide a visual focus in both a general, conceptual way and a practical one." (*Metropolitan Home,* January 1982, p. 18).

[4]*Visions of Light,* a documentary sponsored by the American Society of Cinematographers, presents outstanding examples of cinematographers at work and how they solve visual problems. As noted in Chapter 6, a videotape of this program is available at video rental stores.

and menacing shadows.). The filmmakers will understand your intent and construct and light the scene accordingly. If the setting is a birthday party that has a soft-focus looks, as if the images are seen through a gauzy haze, describe your vision briefly (*Jeannie enters the room and everything is magical and golden, as in a dream.*). Here again, the filmmakers will understand the visual effect that you imagine. They may choose to ignore your idea for something that they feel will work better, but they invariably consider the visuals proposed in the script. The lighting effects applied to modern films are meticulously (and expensively) worked out and go far beyond the all-night-market school of lighting that uses one overall wash of featureless floodlighting, as one might find in amateurish productions. Professional cinematography is done carefully because audiences are too demanding to accept movies that lack visual texture, shadows, and lighting effects that subtly feed the eye.

Screenwriters do *not* call for specific lighting effects; instead, we briefly describe the look and the mood of the setting, as in this example from *Single White Female*, when screenwriter Don Roos suggests the basement storeroom, where the "lights flick on in this ominous room full of cobwebs and chain-link cages numbered by apartment." Although the script does not mention lighting or camera cues directly, it presents a verbal snapshot of the setting that visualizes the look and mood of the location; this was enough for the crew to understand what was needed. Throughout their work, filmmakers refer to the movie that the writer has summarized in the script. The director and cinematographer discuss each scene and each shot; they may go with the script or they may invent a location or lighting effect that they believe will work better. In most cases, however, the filmmakers are guided by the script.

Light and shadow create visual details, nuance, mood, and focus points in a scene. The light may be diffused with a fog machine that creates interesting effects. A small light on a picture or an odd shadow might call attention to a dark corner. Curtains or venetian blinds can cast interesting shadows on the wall. A tiny pinspot might call attention to a specific object or feature. In the end, cinematography manipulates shadow and light to feed the eye with visual details that induce the audience to "look at this!"

Movement

When the camera records characters walking through a room, it reveals how they move and why they move, as well as recording other parts of the setting and the adjacent space. This movement presents visual information that feeds the eye. Visual detail also accrues when characters remain stationary and the camera moves, or when both the camera and the characters move simultaneously. For such reasons, canny screenwriters stage their action in locations that contain visual details that can be recorded through movement of camera and/ or characters, machinery, animals, and other items of visual interest.

This is all easy enough when the setting is grand, but how do writers invest visual details in a modest interior setting, as in *The Verdict* (Shot 72), which presents a ninety-second scene in Concannon's office? The room is his inner sanctum—a small paneled space reeking of wealth and conspiracy. The scene opens with Concannon at his antique rolltop desk, filling out a check. He speaks to someone off camera and we become curious about this person's identity. Throughout the scene, the sound is so intimate that it too conspires to pull us into the drama. Concannon mixes a drink and crosses the room again, extending one of the tinkling glasses to—of all people!— Laura. Concannon steps behind her, slips the envelope containing the check into her purse, and sits beside her. Finally, he raises his glass and offers an ironic toast, welcoming Laura back to the world. At this point we realize that Laura is Concannon's spy and that she has slept with Galvin so she could betray him.

Although the movement in this scene is limited, it was precisely performed in a small room that looked like the lair of a consummate insider. There was no need to describe the room, since a lawyer such as Concannon would have first-class digs that the production designer could "dress" with appropriate props, furniture, and art. Concannon's movements allowed the camera to reveal that visual content in a way that dramatized his speech to Laura. Mamet's stage directions here are minimal, noting only that the lights are soft and dim and there is a sofa. The writer's contribution was making Laura a spy, concealing this fact from the audience for most of the movie, and then dramatically revealing her duplicity in a visually interesting location.

Shot 204 of *The Terminator* works similarly, but instead of panning the room, the camera dollies through the mother's house while Sarah talks to her mom on the phone. After a moment, we realize that the house has been wrecked . . . and that it is not mom who is speaking but the cyborg, imitating the mother's voice. In both of these examples, movement and lighting create dramatic reveals that are enriched visually by the settings.

Modern camerawork is more fluid than in earlier times, especially when the first sound cameras were encased in heavy soundproof booths and the actors were required to huddle close to microphones hidden in flowerpots and similar camouflage. Today's cameras and sound gear are light and portable. Whereas early camera operators had to manage cameras that weighed up to 165 pounds, modern cameras weigh a fifth as much. These lighter cameras can be mounted on stabilizers that permit steady footage to be filmed from helicopters, speeding vehicles, rockets, or horses. An early use of gyro-stabilizers was in *Funny Girl*, which features a shot of Barbra Streisand singing from the bow of a tugboat. The shot begins with a close-up of the star singing; as her song sustains, the shot pulls back . . . and up . . . and away . . . until the tugboat looks like a toy in the middle of New York harbor. Only then do we realize that this continuous shot has been filmed with a stabilized camera mounted on a helicopter. The opening shots in *Touch of Evil, The Player, Thief,* and *The Shining* also present outstanding examples of camera movement. In most cases, specific shots are not the work of the screenwriter. Even so, if you imagine a unique image, write it into the script (briefly) and trust that the production team will consider its visual potential. Most likely, the team will extract visual moments from the script that you overlooked.

Color

The overall look of the settings—the design, paints, and fabrics and other materials employed by the production designer—sustains a color scheme that may be followed through even by costumes and makeup. Color (or lack of it) is influenced by filters that fit over the camera lens and lights, by the film stock, and even by the chemicals and methods used to process the film. Although none of this color concern goes directly into the stage directions, skillful writers imagine the overall visual potential of their stories. Often that thinking works its way into the script and suggests the emotional mood, historicity, time, weather, energy level, and/or a character's personality. The warmth or coldness of the light and the way the set is decorated can suggest danger, decay, sexiness, emotional energy, or whatever quality the script indicates.

For example, *Dead Ringers,* about twin brothers who descend into madness and death, features chilly green and blue images that hint at the emotional sickness of the brothers. *Schindler's List* was shot in black and white because the director felt it suited the time period of a Holocaust story. *The Verdict* is shot in golden browns and earth tones that are appropriate to its wintry Boston setting. The farcical *Ruthless People* uses bright cartoon colors that suit its comic book characters and style. The sepia tints used in *Butch Cassidy and the Sundance Kid* and *Bonnie and Clyde* suggest the antique settings of these films.

Skillful writing enables readers to "see" the same movie imagined by the screenwriter. Such skillful writing is evident in *The Silence of the Lambs,* which employs strange green images in the climactic scene, when the heroine (Jody Foster's Clarice Starling) and the killer (Ted Levine's Mr. Gumb) play deadly cat and mouse in a darkened basement. The location permits the killer to wear infrared goggles that enable him to see in the dark, while the heroine sees very little. Terrifying music and the greenish images combine into a nightmare experience that works effectively. The infrared diversion illustrates how a change in the visual content of a scene can create a major effect. Here is how Ted Tally imagined the heroine's chilling confrontation with the homicidal Mr. Gumb. The shot favors Clarice, who is shocked to see a "corpse's withered hand protruding from a bathtub":

```
CLARICE

is reacting with horror to this sight, to be replaced a
split second later, by the eerie green glow of Mr. Gumb's
infra-red system.  Clarice cries out, turns blindly,
reaching for the door, can't find it, free hand clawing
desperately into what is, for her, utter darkness.  SOUND
of Catherine KEENING again, in the far distance.  Clarice
stumbles, goes to her knees, rights herself, finally
clutches the door frame.
```

CUT TO:

INT. MR. GUMB'S WORKROOM - DAY (GREEN LIGHT)

Clarice emerges from the bathroom in a half-crouch, arms
out, both hands on the gun, extended just below the level
of her unseeing eyes. She stops, listens. In her raw-
nerved darkness, every SOUND is unnaturally magnified -
the HUM of the refrigerator . . . the TRICKLE of water
. . . her own terrified BREATHING, and Catherine's
faraway, echoing SOBS . . . Moths smack against her face
and arms. She eases forward, then stops again, listens . . .
She eases forward again, following her gun, and creeps
directly in front of, and then <u>past</u> - MR. GUMB

who has flattened himself against a wall, arms spread,
Colt in one hand. He wears his goggles and a wig, and
below that, over just a jockstrap, his hideous, half-
completed suit of human skins. He smiles at Clarice as,
completely unaware, she moves beyond him, exposing her
back. Very slowly and quietly he steps out behind her,
taking his gun in both hands, lowering it towards her. . . .

The Silence of the Lambs, written by Ted Tally, 1989

Tally expertly guides the reader into the spooky scene he has imagined. When Clarice reacts to the hand in the bathtub, the script is suggesting a close shot—otherwise, the hand would not be seen and Clarice's shocked reaction would not be motivated. Similarly, a close shot would probably be needed to show Mr. Gumb's smile. The lighting effect allows Clarice to pass unknowingly within inches of the lunatic killer, who grins wickedly as he prepares to shoot her in the back. Even though the scene was not shot exactly as written, Tally's script clearly visualizes what happens, which allows the filmmakers to do their job.

Space

Most feature films and TV shows are shot (on 35mm film stock) with three prime lenses: medium, telephoto, and wide-angle. The most common shot in movies is made from a stationary camera fitted with a lens with a medium (35–50mm) focal length. The view presented is most like the way we see reality, with minimal spatial distortion. Shot 93 of *Witness,* when Eli warns Samuel about the dangers of firearms and violence, illustrates.

Telephoto lenses are longer (75mm or more). Their optics create the illusion of compressing distances and flattening space, as when characters move directly into or away from the camera and appear to be walking or running in place. *The Graduate* contains such a shot: as the hero runs toward the church, he heads directly toward a long lens, which records his run and makes it seem that he is standing still, unable to rescue his love. *Lawrence of Arabia* uses a long lens to show a spectral shape riding out of the desert and toward the camera. As it draws closer, the shape defines into Omar Sharif riding a camel. Long lenses also indicate when a character or setting is being "observed." For example, in Shot 60 in *The Terminator,* Sarah enters the garage to motor-scooter to the disco; made using a long lens, this shot (augmented by creepy music) suggests that someone is watching her—and someone is. Fortunately, it turns out to be Reese. The telephoto shot presents Reese's point of view as he watches Sarah.

Short-focal-length lenses (25mm or less) present a wide-angle view of a scene; they are useful for filming in cramped spaces and for creating a sense of "neurotic space." This type of shot shows up in certain TV commercials that distort a person's face so that it appears egg-shaped, with an oversized nose. This lens was used in some of the intense moments in *Death and the Maiden* because it created a nightmarish, trapped quality that suited the intensity of the story.

A screenwriter's ability to imagine cinematic space can be enhanced by an understanding of how the camera uses the three prime lenses during shooting. A *panning* shot, for example, occurs when the camera pivots left and right on a horizontal plane to follow movement. We see this in Shot 54 of *The Verdict,* when Galvin moves to a telephone after meeting Dr. Thompson at the train station. As the shot pans, it reveals visual information that ties the location, the characters, and the story together.

A circular dolly shot (or *arcing* shot) requires the camera to move circularly around the subject. (Shot 68 of *The Verdict,* when Dr. Towler seems to doom Galvin's case at the end of Act II, illustrates.)

A *dolly* shot (also called a *trucking, tracking,* or *moving* shot) uses a dolly-mounted camera that rolls alongside the characters as they move or walk. (Shots 19 and 20A of *The Verdict,* when Galvin first meets Dr. Gruber, illustrate.) Some dolly shots use a track that allows the camera to roll faster and more smoothly. Moving shots can also be done with a SteadiCam, which is a stabilizing body mount that allows the operator to walk (or run) with the camera while filming steady images of the subject. Shot 33 of *The Terminator,* when the cyborg exits his car and walks to the front door of his first female victim, illustrates a SteadiCam shot.

Moving shots can be filmed from a chase vehicle as characters drive, or as they ride a bicycle, ski, skateboard, run, or whatever. Shot 108 of *The Terminator,* in which Reese and Sarah drive away from the disco, illustrates one such moving shot.

When mounted on a crane, the camera can be elevated to look down on a scene and present a panorama that orients the audience to a setting. **Crane shots** were used in the courtroom scenes in *The Verdict* to both elevate the camera and swing it horizontally, over the heads of the jury and into the center of the action (see Shots 63, 65, 68, 92). And, as mentioned earlier, the camera can be mounted on a helicopter that has been fitted with a stabilizing mount, as in

The Shawshank Redemption, when the camera looks down on the exterior of the prison.

When the camera is tipped five or ten degrees to the left or right from the mount's vertical axis, the result is a **dutch angle** that presents a tilted horizon line. Such a shot creates a sense of disorientation or lack of control.

Dutch angles should not be confused with tilt shots, in which the camera presents a level horizon but is aimed up or down five or ten degrees on the camera's vertical axis. Depending on which lens is used, when the camera is tilted up, it tends to make space (or a character) seem larger and/or more imposing; when the camera angle tilts down, the space (or a character) seems smaller and/or less imposing. Shot 14 of *The Verdict,* when Galvin first meets with the Doneghys, illustrates both up and down tilt angles. A tilt angle can be used in combination with a Dutch angle to create an even more out-of-control, spooky, or disoriented effect.

The camera can manipulate space by focusing on something in the background or something in the foreground—or on something in between. Whatever is in focus tends to attract attention. For an example of how this works, note Shot 72 of *The Verdict,* when Concannon slips a check into Laura's purse. The shot has Laura in focus in a foreground close-up, while Concannon stands behind her in a medium shot that is defocused. The composition and focus of the shot direct attention to Laura's pain and away from Concannon as he gives her the check. By deemphasizing the planting of the check, the story is able to deliver a larger surprise when Mickey discovers it later, while he rummages through Laura's purse looking for a cigarette (Shot 85).

None of the examples used above call for a specific shot in the stage direction. Instead, the writers briefly describe the movie as they imagined it, trusting the filmmakers to understand the visual cues as scripted. Stage directions that suggest visual content are done this way because writers trust that their script will enable filmmakers to imagine the same movie, and the filmmakers trust that the writers have written a drama that will sustain and suggest interesting visuals and colorful locations. For example, in *Witness* (Shot 93) the screenwriters imagined what the Lapp kitchen looked like, but they did not describe it beyond the slugline that said, "INT.   KITCHEN—LAPP FARM-HOUSE—NIGHT." Instead of describing the kerosene lamp or the office chair that Eli uses to scoot himself about the kitchen, the writers focus on Eli as he lectures to Samuel on the dangers of guns and outsiders. This is as it should be, because the other filmmakers are expert at recreating any location imaginable. Additionally, the writers realized that the kitchen might be built on a movie set, or it might be a farmhouse kitchen shot on location in Amish country. These are concerns that writers need not bother with—as long as they create drama that takes place in interesting settings. Note how the *Witness* writers did their job by using minimal stage directions to set this important scene:

```
Book's holstered gun and bullets at center table.   Eli
sits on one side, a chastened Samuel on the other.   Rachel
looks on from the b.g.
```

Eli knows that this is as important a dialogue as he will
ever have with his grandson: at issue is one of the
central pillars of the Amish way.

Witness, written by William Kelley and
Pamela and Earl W. Wallace, 1984

As filmed, the scene was done without Rachel; instead, Eli and Samuel were shot in tight two-shots and in close-ups, with occasional cutaways to the gun on the table. The power of the scene draws from the concerns of the characters, for there is something elemental and important about Eli's lecture to the boy; that content gives weight to the visuals. This was the intent of the writers, who made sure that the stage directions at the end of the scene nailed this point: "His intensity tinged with righteous anger, he [Eli] is hugely impressive."

One of the curious things about the curious business of making movies is that it is populated with egotistical people whose work is most successful when it is anonymous; in other words, the audience should not notice the work of the actors or the other filmmakers. When a camera effect is noticeable, it calls attention to the nifty camerawork and takes the audience out of the story. When an actor is too actorish, the story suffers. When the music contains "too many notes," the story suffers. When the dialogue is too clever for words, the story suffers. When the decor attracts too much attention to itself, the story suffers. In all cases, *the audience should be focused on what is happening with the characters on the movie screen.*

Motion picture camerawork should be invisible, i.e., the audience should be unaware of the shot. The conventions presented in this chapter are described to help you to imagine your scenes and to write scripts that read easily and dramatically. To make this happen, do not junk up your script with camera instructions and tech-head mumbo jumbo. To repeat another mantra of this text: *Do not slow or confuse the read in any way,* especially with camera instructions. The script should flow through the mind as easily as film flows through a projector.

THE THREE PRIME CAMERA ANGLES

A *shot* is a single "take" or photographic run of a scene: the camera is turned on when the director says ACTION and it stops when the director says CUT. The film exposed between ACTION and CUT is a **take.** Bits and scenes from various takes are edited together to make the dramatic point of the beat. Occasionally, an entire scene can be done in a single shot. *The Verdict* (Shot 51) uses a stationary camera to film its three-and-a-half minute scene that shows Galvin in his office as he calls a last-minute replacement for Dr. Gruber.

Most movies are filmed using three main camera shots: the close-up, the medium shot, and the long shot. Each has a specific storytelling function that writers should know about, because envisioning a script in terms of close-ups, medium shots, and long shots can make writing easier.

The close-up fills the frame with a character's face. The closeness of the shot has an ability to convey the emotions and inner feelings of the characters. This occurs because many movie actors have a remarkable ability to communicate inner feelings through their eyes. (See the Galvin-Sweeney-Concannon scene from *The Verdict* [Shot 38] for examples of how this works.)

Because medium and long shots distance the characters from the audience, these shots are less able to show the actors' eyes, and thus the emotions they project. For such reasons, medium and long shots are often concerned with action and with moments that are less emotionally intense than those filmed in close-up. Although there are endless exceptions to all of this advice, normally, long shots and medium shots lead into the close-ups. This prime lens pattern is evidenced in the Galvin-Sweeney-Concannon scene from *The Verdict* (Shot 38). The scene opens, in traditional fashion, with a wide-angle shot that orients the viewer to the setting and to the characters in it. As the emotional intensity of the scene heats up, the camera angle narrows from a wide-angle shot, to medium shots, and then to close-ups. That plan—from wide-angle, to medium shot, to close-up—is commonly used to film dialogue scenes. As it moves closer to the characters, the camera gives the audience a progressively stronger sense of what the characters are experiencing emotionally. You can see this for yourself by viewing a few scenes and noting how the three shots combine to make the dramatic point of the scene. If possible, still-frame a shot and observe how it is staged, lighted, and photographed.[5] Awareness of the three shots and how they progress from wide-angle to medium shot to close-up as emotions flare is sufficient to enable the writer to visualize most scenes.

During production, scenes are filmed from various directions and distances. Each shot is tape-measured so that exact distances between the subject and the lens are calibrated. Bits of tape (called "marks") are then affixed to the floor so the actors know exactly where to stand and where to move to be in focus and framed in the shot. It is not unusual for a crew to spend an hour or more preparing, testing, and rehearsing one shot. The cinematography crew takes care of lighting, shadows, extraneous details, composition, and setting. The exacting pace of this work means that features typically spend one day shooting one to three pages of script. In television, five or so pages can be shot in a day. Many of the half-hour sitcoms are shot in one day, with three or four cameras being used simultaneously.

Throughout this volume you have been advised not to use the script to tell filmmakers how to do their job. However, even David Mamet could not resist (perhaps savoring the time when he would direct his scripts), as shown in the Galvin-Sweeney-Concannon scene. Many of the script's visual ideas were ignored by the director and cinematographer. For example, at the beginning of the scene the script calls for a point-of-view shot when Galvin enters

---

[5]A dozen or more crew members may be required to light and prepare a shot. Filmmakers refer to each shot as a camera "setup" (yet another term with a double meaning). A scene may be shot many times, with each take marked (slated) according to a "Shot" and "Take" number. Thus, an individual shot might be identified as SHOT 15/TAKE 5.

Sweeney's office. This shot would show Galvin as seen by either Concannon or Sweeney (the script does not indicate which). This visual idea was not used because the filmmakers had a more elaborate image agenda. Their design for the film was based on the script's religious implications, in which Galvin is seen as a fallen angel who needed redemption. This is why he is so often seen ascending and descending stairs, which symbolize his attempt to regain the life he had before his fall and expulsion from the inner circle of lawyers. It was in this context that the filmmakers decided to make Galvin seem like an outsider who makes a clumsy entrance (as noted in Chapter 4). This raises an interesting topic, which concerns how filmmakers work out the overall style and look of a film.

THE VISUAL DESIGN OF THE FILM

Someone must decide where the movie will be filmed, and someone must decide the look and the style of the sets. Such matters are the responsibility of the filmmakers who read and research the script, consult with production managers and producers on what can be done with the budget, and float choices concerning who will act in the movie. Often, the writer, producer, director, cinematographer, and production designer will visit locations, study films with similar locations, and shoot test footage so that there is agreement on the overall look of the film. Preproduction activity may include research into costumes and makeup, storyboards,[6] and models of the sets, as well as consultations with historians, computer and special-effects companies, teachers, wranglers, animal trainers, and whatever other experts are needed.[7] The production team also selects china and silver patterns, furniture, fabrics, hairstyles, automobiles, clothing (especially hats, which show in close-ups), and whatever props tell the story. During this time the screenwriter may be consulted; the extent of cooperation depends on how well the writer gets along with the other filmmakers and what the writer can contribute.

Elaborate films may spend a year or more on preproduction before shooting begins. Not long ago, for example, I researched a film that required a full-

---

[6]*Storyboards* are sketches that help the filmmakers figure out how they will shoot a scene. Storyboards are especially important when the action is complicated or when the location is available only briefly. Shooting on big-city streets, for example, is often scheduled for Sunday mornings, when there is minimal traffic. Because the time available for such shooting is limited, the scene may be shot with several cameras, each with its own set of storyboards. Such organization allows the scene to be shot before the city wakes up. Documents describing how movies are designed can be studied at the Margaret Herrick Library of the Academy of Motion Picture Arts and Sciences in Los Angeles. They include scripts, still photos, storyboards, designer drawings of costumes, props, location sketches, visual effects, production notes, and the like. The Writers Guild of America's (WGA's) James R. Webb Memorial Library, which is also open to the public, maintains an extensive collection of award-winning scripts, as well as videos of the WGA seminars cited in this volume.

[7]Even with the best counsel, movie gaffes occur. Bill Givens has gathered some of them into a book called *Film Flubs* (Carol Publishing, Secaucus, New Jersey, 1990). One of my favorites, from *Camelot,* shows King Arthur with a modern bandage strip on his neck.

scale, operational pirate ship. Because 200-foot pirate ships cannot be ordered from a catalogue, the production was delayed for the several years it took to build the ship. In such ways, the visual design of a movie is worked out by many individuals who imagine the script and translate it into a movie that maximizes the visual bang that can be realized from the budget bucks.

Organizing this activity is the script, which should challenge the filmmakers and put visual content on the movie screen. The production team will respond to that content by doing what it takes: tons of artificial snow or straw and dirt may be spread to conceal modern pavement, leaves may be painted or stripped to indicate a particular season, special trees may be trucked in or manufactured. In *Breaking Away,* an abandoned stone quarry was sandblasted to make it look more like an ideal swimming hole. Very little escapes the eagle eyes of directors, cinematographers, and production designers. For example, if a key meeting takes place in an elevator, there are various ways to write this. Although elevator settings are usually less interesting than scenes played in gambling casinos or on warships, a claustrophobic elevator may be right for a particular scene in a particular story. When he wrote *Fatal Attraction,* James Dearden set a scene in an elevator, which he did not describe. The filmmakers, who could have chosen any number of elevators, decided that Glenn Close's character would live in an industrial loft equipped with a big clunky freight elevator because they felt it was visually more interesting, and it provided a sturdy launch pad for Close's affair with Michael Douglas.

The screenwriter has the first shot at imagining the visual design of the movie and then suggesting this vision in the script. Even though the screenwriter may not see the settings and decorations as thoroughly as the production designer or as precisely as the cinematographer, he or she imagines a mass of details and works them into the script in a shorthand fashion. Because the script contains the hidden structure that supports the entire venture, filmmakers are cautious when making the nips and tucks that usually occur when a script is being fine-tuned for production.

Finally, writers should appreciate the visual potential of their scenes and the lengths that filmmakers will go to realize a script's visual opportunities; in many cases the filmmakers create visuals that go far beyond what the writers imagined. *Witness* presents a grand example of this in Shot 106, which begins the barn-raising sequence. As written, this eight-minute beat focused on the macho rivalry between Book and Hochstetler (Alexander Godunov) as much as it did on the barn raising. As shot by director Peter Weir and cinematographer John Seale, the beat addressed the larger, more subtle issue of community spirit as embodied by the Amish. In refocusing the script this way, the movie touched upon the theme of the story, which concerns community and cooperation rather than competition.

There is almost no dialogue in the sequence, which relies on Maurice Jarre's soaring music and on stunning images to communicate the significance of the barn raising. Although the beat illustrates how the other filmmakers add to the work of the screenwriters, the shift in tone took off from the vision of the writers, which is clearly expressed in the stage directions that open this sequence:

106 EXT. ZOOK FARM - LANCASTER COUNTY - DAY

BIG SHOT . . . it's early morning as the Amish buggies are
arriving at the Zook farm for a barn raising.

In the b.g. we can see big stacks of lumber all around the
construction site where a couple of dozen men have begun
raising the main supports on the already laid foundation.

Elsewhere, long tables have been set up and women are
spreading them with cloths, setting out big tanks of hot
coffee and cold lemonade for the men.

Witness, written by William Kelley and
Pamela and Earl W. Wallace, 1984

VISUALIZING ACTION SCENES AND CHARACTER SCENES

As noted in earlier chapters, movies can be divided into those driven by action
and those driven by the characters. *Speed, The Terminator,* and *Alien* are action-
driven stories that are told visually, with minimal dialogue. *The Verdict, Sleepless in Seattle,* and *Little Women* are character-driven stories that rely on dialogue to reveal the characters and the plot.

Action stories require visual sequences that show the characters performing physical action, especially when they organize around escapes, searches,
battles, quests, physical ordeals, and adventures that are based on a physical
conflict between hero and villain. As with silent films, action movies have little need for dialogue. Few films show this better than *Quest for Fire* and *Naked
Prey*. In the latter, the hero (Cornel Wilde) is given a head start and then is pursued by a band of warriors in colonial Africa. Throughout, Wilde must devise
strategies to escape his relentless pursuers; there is almost no dialogue in the
movie. *Quest for Fire* works similarly as it follows three Neolithic tribesmen as
they hunt for a source of fire. Aside from a few guttural sounds, they have no
language, there are no subtitles, and the entire film relies on visuals to tell the
story. It does this by repeatedly confronting the tribesmen with physical challenges as they battle toward their goal.

Action films favor wide-angle shots and spacious settings that show the
spectacle of what is happening in their stories, which is why action stories are
usually more effective when staged in exterior locations rather than interior
settings. However, the keys to writing these stories are their dramatic situations and how they challenge the main characters with problems that are usually more physical than intellectual. Much of the work of writing this type of
story involves inventing the basic dramatic problem and staging it in interest-

ing locations. Once this has been accomplished, the incidents of plot can be worked out. *Alien, Full Metal Jacket, The Guns of Navarone, Speed,* and *Die Hard* are good examples of action stories.

Visualizing Talking-Heads Scenes

Stories that lack visual content are more likely to occur in character-driven works. Such films (*The Verdict, Sleepless in Seattle, My Family, Vanya on 42nd Street*) use a more intimate visual focus to register the thoughts and feelings of the characters. For this to happen, the actors must experience heartfelt moments of emotion that can be expressed through dialogue, gesture, facial expression, and inner feelings that are revealed in camera close-ups of their eyes.[8] One of the writing tasks in these stories is to enrich the dialogue scenes with visual content. Even a cursory understanding of the basic camera moves and conventions noted above is a step toward inventing visual content for talky scenes that might otherwise be visually static. These so-called talking-heads scenes—two people sharing coffee on a back porch or talking in the front seat of a car—are difficult to avoid, but there are ways to avoid making them seem stagy and visually starved.

One of the most effective ways to visualize a talking-heads scene is to rewrite it so the characters can demonstrate who they are with action rather than with talk. For example, if a character is assigned a distinctive personality trait—cowardice, a gambling habit, an athletic skill—the writer should be able to find a way to reveal the trait through visuals and action. Example: Laura Dern's title character in *Rambling Rose* is a sensual but naive young woman from the country. Her persona could have been established by having her employers discuss her nature and how to rein it in. This might have led to a talking-heads scene in the kitchen over coffee. Instead, screenwriter Calder Willingham visualized Rose's nature by giving her a day off so she could go to town. The beat begins when the writer dresses Rose for her trip to town:

```
CUT TO a shot of Rose in the doorway of the kitchen.  She
is quite an apparition.  She wears bright red lipstick,
pink rouge on her cheeks, mascara, and her hair is coifed
up in some outlandish manner, but her clothes are the most
remarkable of all.  The skirt is of strange, pink, semi-
shiny and very thin material and has about a dozen tiny
little flowers that could be rosebuds sewed on it.  It
fits extremely snugly to say the least.  The blouse seems
a composite: it has frilly white sleeves that are opaque
and otherwise is made of filmy white material that is
```

---

[8]In 1988, Michael Caine conducted a workshop on acting for the camera. This instructive session, which illustrates some of the points of this chapter, is available on videotape. Caine also wrote a book based on this workshop (*Acting in Film: An Actor's Take on Moviemaking,* Applause Theater Books, New York, 1990).

hardly opaque at all. She has no bra and her breasts are half visible, the nipples denting the material. It is pretty wild for 1935. She seems to have on no underwear of any kind; the skirt, which clings to her like a bathing suit, shows no panty seams. She is carrying a shiny black patent leather pocketbook and has on high heel black patent leather shoes and no stockings. An ingenuous little smile is on her face.

Rambling Rose, written by Calder Willingham, 1990

When Rose wears this gaudy outfit in town, men follow her down the street in ways that objectify her sexuality. The scene is staged in a small Southern town that was prepped with period cars and costumed extras to simulate the 1930s setting of the story. As Rose strolls through the town, Louis Armstrong sings "Dixie" in a style that underscores the allure of this strapping young woman. The scene plays for five minutes or so and creates a major visual moment of the movie.

The character of Clint Eastwood's William Munny in *Unforgiven* is revealed through visuals as well, for the dialogue does not inform us that Munny is too old for bounty hunting; instead, the character demonstrates his age and rustiness through action: he is unable to ride the family horse, he needs a shotgun to hit a nearby target, and he appears generally unfit for the job offered by the twitchy Schofield Kid.

Devising visual alternatives to dialogue begins when writers set aside enough time to come up with a visual solution that recasts a talking-heads scene into action. The strategy here is to inventory the scenes and select two or three that seem amenable to visualization.

A second fix for talking-heads scenes is based on recognizing when one is coming and filling the scene with emotional content rather than exposition. Also, do not allow your characters to turn into cement and become rooted in place, unmoving except for their mouths. Additionally, beats can be made more appealing by staging them in visually interesting locations. Remember, the scene is your "box" and you are free to put whatever you wish into it. You can make a scene more visual by staging it in a crowded restaurant (Shot 92 of *Sleepless in Seattle* with Sam and Victoria), a busy saloon (Shot 23 of *The Verdict,* when Galvin first meets Laura), or whatever location promises visual detail.

Visual content can be added by reconceptualizing some of the scenes. This does not mean turning a sensitive character story into an adventure, but it does mean rethinking the story so it has more visual action. This perspective can be acquired by studying talky movies that are strong in action. *My Favorite Year* presents such a story because screenwriters Dennis Palumbo and Norman Steinberg energized the story's witty talkiness with action that gives life and dimension to the hero (Peter O'Toole's Alan Swann). The action visuals begin during the introduction to the hero, a fading movie swashbuckler, who we see interacting (drunkenly) with clips from his old movies before collapsing on a screening table. There are additional bits of Swann being wheeled into his hotel while strapped to a cart and wearing his breakaway "drunk suit." Once the audience has met this outrageous character, the story unspools four action scenes that require Swann to steal a policeman's horse in Central Park; to separate a beautiful woman in a nightclub from her loutish escort; to swing into a penthouse party on the end of a firehose; and to engage in a donnybrook during a live TV show. The action from these scenes, most of which are modest and nonviolent, "opens" the film visually, showing off the unique main character through action that adds spice to the dialogue.

Although reconceptualizing can be an effective way to add visual drama to a story, it asks the screenwriter to think of the story in radically different terms. Consultations with a friend and comparisons with study films can both be useful during this work.

If a talky scene does not lend itself to action, perhaps it can be made more visually active. Shot 124 of *Witness* presents a talking-heads scene between Rachel and Book that takes place in the barn, shortly after the hero's assault on the hoodlums in town. As scripted, Book and Rachel discuss his decision to leave the Amish. This talking-heads scene (Shot 124) was cut and replaced with visuals that begin when Rachel enters the kitchen and notices the wooden toy that Book has made for her son Samuel. She puzzles over it for a moment, not sure of its significance. Then Rachel looks outside and sees Eli and Book repositioning the birdhouse that the hero's car knocked over when he arrived. This business makes her realize that Book plans to leave. An expectant musical theme sounds as Eli enters the house and confirms that Book is leaving. Rachel thinks about this for a moment, trims the lamp, removes her Amish bonnet, and goes outside to be with Book. The music rises to the moment and they embrace. This handling of the beat has more visual interest than the talkier scripted version that was replaced.

This plea for visual content is not meant as an attack on intimate character moments, for the movies are at their best when characters reveal their inner beings. For example, few scenes are more visually static than when Brando accuses his brother (Rod Steiger) of betraying his chances to be a "contender" in *On the Waterfront*. The scene takes place in the back of a taxicab, where there is nothing to look at except the two characters. Even so, this quintessential talking-heads scene is one of the great movie moments because of close-ups that reveal a lifetime of loss between the two brothers.

Movies also do very well with poignant moments that are revealed through imagery and action, as in the second flashback of *The Terminator* (Shot 186). It concerns a cyborg attack on a band of humans who are surviving in the ruins. When Reese is wounded, the last thing he looks at is his most precious possession—the Polaroid of Sarah—as it burns. Visual storytelling is at work in *The Piano* when the husband discovers his wife's adultery. This does not inspire the cuckold to discuss their marriage over tea. Instead, he drags her home, clamps her hand onto a tree stump, grabs an ax, and chops off her finger. This shocking action caps a dramatically visual scene. Similarly, *Witness* does not discuss the cooperative customs of the Amish. Instead, it makes the point visually by showing the Brethren as they come together for a funeral

(Shot 9). Other shots show them conferring about Book (Shot 86), building a barn (Shot 106), and converging as neighbors to save Book (Shot 154). In this way, the idea of community is made visually, by the actions of the Amish, rather than by talking-heads scenes.

HOW SOUND AND IMAGES WORK TOGETHER TO TELL THE STORY

Movies communicate because sound and images work together. As you study movies, notice how dialogue dominates in some, especially when characters become emotionally lathered. When this is done effectively, the audience can be so taken up with the story that there is little need for visual content. The taxi scene from *On the Waterfront,* noted above, illustrates.

At other times, extraordinary sound effects can overwhelm the need for visuals, as in submarine pictures when the camera focuses on the sub's hull as it groans under crushing ocean pressure. Although its visual details may be limited, the moment works because the sound makes the audience worry that the hull will rupture and drown the crew. Sound effects enhance the visuals in *Jurassic Park,* as when the massive footsteps of the approaching *Tyrannosaurus rex* are heard. The roar of racing cars, jet planes, and other machines can add to the energy of a scene, as in the steel mill sequence that opens *The Deerhunter,* the scene with jets landing on the aircraft carrier in *Top Gun,* and the combat scene in *Forrest Gump.* Strange breathing, an unusual hissing or scraping, or sound effects that signal the approach of a dramatic presence can make scenes with modest visual content more dramatic.

Audiences quickly recognize sound effects that warn of the approaching monster, menace, love interest, or nosy neighbor. Whatever the sound effect, a mention in the script will call it to the attention of the production team. The sound designers may recognize the effect's potential and opt to include it, or they may elect to use silence, knowing that a lack of sound can also send a signal. For example, if the crickets suddenly cease their nightly chorus, the silence could be taken as a warning. Silence is used dramatically in *Apocalypse Now* when casual talk between two soldiers ceases when they sense danger. On full combat alert, the men probe the jungle—and are startled out of their wits when a tiger bursts from the bush.

As noted on page 174, music is a powerful dramatizer because of its ability to create an emotional landscape that enhances the visuals. This is easily verified by turning off the sound of the TV, whereupon you will notice how rapidly the lack of music can drain dramatic energy from the movie. Music can create an ominous subtext to otherwise benign visuals, as in *Jaws,* when a signature piece of music warns that the shark is close by. Horror films often have a "monster" theme that alerts the audience to whatever danger is afoot.

Because movie music can keep stories and scenes afloat, it is important that screenwriters appreciate how to imagine the music that may be added to their story, and for this reason the topic deserves attention. You will find, for example, that music cues are usually not written into the script unless performance or business is involved. There are also certain scripts that are so dependent on music (*Footloose, All That Jazz*) that writers suggest styles of music (salsa, reggae, rock, etc.) or even specific titles, whether performed on camera or as part of the sound track that will support the visuals.

There are two main types of movie music: incidental background music, which is played over the images to establish mood, and so-called *source* music, which is the result of either on-camera performance or music that is heard from a radio, live performance, or similar source that is part of the scene.

For an example of incidental music that enhances the mood of a scene, see *Witness* (Shot 124), where Rachel removes her Amish bonnet and embraces Book; also check out *Sleepless in Seattle,* in which pop music is used to punch up the story and its visuals.

Source music takes many forms, from a character's singing on-camera (for example, the singing of Sissy Spacek as Loretta Lynn in *Coal Miner's Daughter*) to a radio playing dance music, as in *Witness* (Shot 100A), when Book and Rachel dance to a tune sounding on the radio of the hero's Volkswagen. Characters also perform music on-camera, as Dooley Wilson did when he played piano for Bogart in *Casablanca.*

An example of source music from a recording is the operatic aria that is played over the prison public-address system in *The Shawshank Redemption,* which shows how an entire scene can be anchored by music. The incident is part of a larger sequence that deals with the importance of hope; this point is communicated through visuals showing the inmates as they listen to the broadcast music. The incident pays off in key dialogue that occurs at the end of the sequence when Andy and Red talk about hope, which is the theme of the story. The music cue used in this sequence is scripted as follows:

```
134  INT - GUARD STATION/OUTER OFFICE - DAY (1955)

Andy wrestles the phonograph player onto the guard's desk,
sweeping things onto the floor in his haste.  He plugs the
machine in.  A red light warms up.  The platter starts
spinning.

He slides the Mozart album from its sleeve, lays it on the
platter, and lowers the tone arm to his favorite cut.  The
needle HISSES in the groove . . . and the MUSIC begins,
lilting and gorgeous.  Andy sinks into Wiley's chair,
overcome by its beauty.  It is "Deutino: Che soave
zefferetto," a duet sung by Susanna and the contessa.
```

The Shawshank Redemption, written by
Frank Darabont, 1993

Films frequently use music to signal the inner state of a character or a dramatic highlight, as in the final scene in *Postcards from the Edge.* The climax of that film occurs on a movie sound stage as the heroine (Meryl Streep) sings. Her ballad ("I'm Checking Out") begins slowly and builds until the extras and the stagehands are swept up in Streep's performance. The lyrics of the song make the climactic point of the movie—that the heroine has broken away from her controlling mother and grandmother, thus solving the problem that has organized the story. Interestingly, Streep continues to sing on-camera as the closing credits roll, which adds to the film's strong ending.

STRATEGIES FOR ENHANCING VISUAL CONTENT

The following are additional strategies for investing your script with visual content:

- Visuals from action
- Grand images
- Visual metaphors
- Symbols
- Continuity visuals
- Mood and setup visuals
- Wallpapering
- Walk-and-talk scenes
- Business
- Settings
- Image systems
- Visual triggers

Keep in mind as you read about these strategies, discussed below, that they are not miracle cures. If story and script are flawed, enhancing the visuals will be like putting powder and rouge on a corpse.

Visuals from Action

The action scene has always been one of the glories of cinema. Whether it involves the acrobatic escapades of Douglas Fairbanks, the chariot races in *Ben Hur,* or countless battle scenes, train wrecks, brawls, parties, and natural disasters, audiences everywhere respond to action. Even when the film is less than perfect, great action draws an audience. This was the case with *Cliffhanger,* a film that is not memorable, yet it grossed $255 million world-wide. The success of such films is often based on nothing more than John Ford's advice that "movies shouldn't talk too much, shouldn't put too many ideas into one scene, and they should have plenty of action."

In the script, an action visual should be described quickly, as in this next example, from *Working Girl*. The heroine (Melanie Griffith's Tess) untangles herself from an unwelcome sexual encounter with a colleague (Bob); then, just as Tess exits from the limo:

She takes the champagne bottle and puts her thumb over the
top and shakes it vigorously and puts it in Bob's lap,
holding it point up. . . . She takes her thumb off. The
champagne shoots out, showering him.

Working Girl, written by Kevin Wade, 1986

Action scenes are often the put-up-or-shut-up moment for hero and villain, when they earn victory or suffer defeat. Action requires the characters to
stretch physically and emotionally and to commit to a stressful course of
action. The physicality and desperation of action scenes create visual content,
as in *The Terminator*. This film is a bullet train of action and narrative drive, but
when it is analyzed, the plot turns out to be nothing more than a sustained
chase containing three action spikes—the disco attack, the police station
attack, and the final sequence. The three sequences demonstrate the relentless
mission of the cyborg that organizes the movie: Can Sarah and Reese stop an
unstoppable being? In all, the three sequences play for about a half hour. The
remainder of the movie deals with setting up the characters and their relationships and showing how the characters recover and prepare for the next action
sequence.

If the action dynamic were applied to the sports widow story we have
been developing throughout this text, the script would take on a more physical and less talky quality, which may not be the best way to handle this notion.
But if we were to pursue this tack, the story would organize as most action
pieces do, around an escape, a chase, a journey, a competition, a battle, a
quest, and/or self-actualization. This suggests that the sports widow story
could be tied to a race or a contest. Conceptualizing the story this way would
challenge Mom and her family in ways that were more physical than emotional. If the idea were written as an escape story (say, *Sleeping with the Enemy*
with kids), the material would acquire a totally different visual content.
Whether the story would follow an action approach would depend on how we
felt about the characters, the emotional slant, the intended audience of the
work, and what we found to be inspiring about the notion.

Grand Images

Grand images are moments when the film shows a glory of nature, a cityscape,
a beautiful home, or vistas and panoramas that are visually stunning. *Legends
of the Fall* contains many such images. The opening scene of *Witness* presents
grand images of Amish farmland. The images can be gruesomely grand, as in
Gone with the Wind when Atlanta burns and when the streets are littered with
hundreds of dead and wounded soldiers. *The Light Horsemen* contains one of
the grandest cavalry charges ever filmed. Such moments, which often grow
out of research, are briefly mentioned in the script: "They step out onto the
balcony and are dazzled by Paris, spread out like a tray of diamonds sparkling
in the night."

Visual Metaphors

Visual metaphors represent a story value or a visual moment that demonstrates character. Without getting into semiotics or ascribing meanings to incidental shadows and shapes, it should be noted that most films contain visual metaphors. There is an example of this in the scene from *Witness* (Shot 124), mentioned previously in the chapter, when Rachel removes her Amish cap, places it on the kitchen table, and steps outside to be with Book. Rachel's business with her cap is a visual metaphor that signals she is putting aside her Amish traditions. The hot-dog lunch in Shot 52B is a visual metaphor that suggests Book's junk-food life-style. When one of the corrupt cops "drowns" in the Amish corn silo (not scripted), the incident is a visual metaphor for traditional goodness triumphing over big-city corruption.

Fatal Attraction contains a number of visual metaphors that suggest Glenn Close's steamy character (Alex). She exudes cigarette smoke; she dances to wild music; her loft apartment is in an industrial zone where workers tote sides of raw beef past barrels of trash that burn hellishly in the night. Alex is so hot that she must drench herself with tap water to cool down while making love to Michael Douglas.

Creating metaphorical images begins when writers learn to recognize these conventions in movies and then create them to illustrate points of character or plot. The writer must also imagine the scene in sufficient detail and intensity to invent a prop, a situation, or a moment that can be used as a visual metaphor.

Symbols

Symbols are used to represent a need, a loss, an emotion, or a value that reflects on the story and its characters. The puppy in *Apocalypse Now*, the hero's pigeons in *On the Waterfront*, and the super-posse in *Butch Cassidy and the Sundance Kid* represent, respectively, innocence, gentleness, and danger (in those films).

Most symbols present themselves quickly and do not require the extended treatment of a visual metaphor. *The Piano* works this way because the title instrument symbolizes the tortured psychology of the heroine (Holly Hunter's Ada). In the end, after abandoning her spouse, Ada orders the boatmen who are rowing her to a ship anchored offshore to jettison her piano. For years the instrument was the beloved companion and the voice of this obsessive woman, and it reacts like a rejected lover by ensnaring her foot in a coil of rope and jerking her into the ocean. At the last moment, Ada breaks free and returns to life.

The dowry money of Mary Kate (Maureen O'Hara) in *The Quiet Man* is a symbol because her brother (Victor McLaglen's Red Will) refuses to give it to her, claiming he was tricked into granting his sister permission to marry the quiet American (John Wayne). Without her dowry money, which represents her independence, Mary Kate feels incomplete. In the end, her brother gives her the dowry, whereupon Mary Kate and her spouse fling it into a furnace—showing that it was only a symbol for something more important than money.

Symbols can reveal character. Wedding rings represent fidelity, so when someone removes or displays a wedding ring, the gesture assumes symbolic meaning. As a symbol, the wedding ring can be a source of conflict or anguish that affects the scene, as in *Sleepless in Seattle* (Shot 165) when Walter gives Annie his mother's wedding ring, which symbolizes her reluctant acceptance of this man. Later (Shot 200) Annie returns it to him, which symbolizes her determination to pursue her dream. Other symbols: Galvin's class ring in *The Verdict* symbolizes the young idealistic lawyer he once was; the pinball machine symbolizes Galvin's empty life; the bell in *Witness* symbolizes the communal nature of the Amish. (The logic of the bell relates to the fact that the Amish do not have telephones to call neighbors for help.)

Continuity Visuals

Continuity visuals are images created when characters travel from one setting to another. These visual interludes reveal scenery that orients the audience to terrain, architecture, or whatever has interest. The opening of *Witness* uses continuity visuals to pull the audience into the antique world of the Amish. Good writing uses visual continuity to make elegant story points, as in this transition from *Witness* (Shot 12A), which uses fifty seconds of continuity visuals to move the story from one century to another:

```
A few brief shots of a lone buggy containing the Lapp
family take us from the 18th century into the 20th from
the reassuring RATTLE OF THE CARRIAGE WHEELS on a quiet
backroad, to the ROAR OF TRAFFIC as the buggy waits
patiently for a chance to cross a busy interstate highway.
```

Witness, written by William Kelley and
Pamela and Earl W. Wallace, 1984

Continuity visuals can create the emotional setting for a scene or story. Even though a continuity moment may only play for a minute or so, it can add considerable visual content. The visuals that open *Jurassic Park* show the scientific team on a dig in the American West. Next the group flies to the dinosaur island and drives into the compound, where we see huge gates, waterfalls, electric fences, and other amazing sights. The purpose of these continuity visuals is to create a sense of the scientists' leaving the known world and being closed into a huge chicken coop that contains ravenous dinosaurs.

Continuity visuals can be as simple as having characters walk to a car and drive to the next scene. Scenes can be played in a moving car that reveals passing scenery. (Note that a convertible with the top down provides more visual content than does a hardtop.) During the drive, the audience registers on whatever visuals appear on-screen—kids playing stickball, a train loaded with huge logs passing nearby, neighbors chatting as they rake leaves. Upon arriving at the new location, the character might be seen passing through the lobby of a building, walking through a wheat field, passing a landmark sports stadium, or whatever. The screenwriter creates the visual opportunities that help tell the story. This visualization strategy, one of the simplest to use, is illustrated throughout the four main study films.

Mood and Setup Visuals

Dramatic scenes are usually prefaced with danger, suspense, sensuality, horror, or whatever mood or emotion seems justified. Movies set the stage and ease into the moment, rather than shoving a character into, say, a haunted house where he or she is immediately attacked by the monster. To pursue this example, the setup visuals exploit a scene's dramatic potential by making the audience feel apprehensive long before the character enters the haunted house. Thus, a character might be sent on a journey, despite friends who plead with the person not to go. But it is to no avail, and before long, the traveler passes into a sinister, foreboding landscape. After a bit, the character (and the audience) sees the destination looking malevolent, even from afar. Fear increases as the character draws closer. There might be a fright moment when a character or animal bursts forth and startles the audience. After entering the grounds (often after darkness has descended), the traveler nervously approaches and enters the dreaded castle or building. It is usually a spooky place that is explored room by room, always (as indicated by the music) moving closer to the menace. The setup visuals continue until the character steps into the wrong room (often the attic or the cellar), where the ghastly confrontation occurs. This worn example of how mood and setup visuals operate is cut from the same cloth as the following excerpt from *Jurassic Park:* Two touring vehicles are disabled because of computer failure, and the passengers are unaware that the dinosaurs are free. The adults are preoccupied, so the kids are the first to notice danger:

```
TIMMY PULLS GUM out of his pocket.  Feels a tiny shake,
looks around.  He puts it in his mouth, chewing quietly.
SUDDENLY, the whole car VIBRATES.  Regis' sunglasses jump
off the dashboard and fall to the floor.  The kids look at
him.


                    REGIS
          Must be turning on the
          electricity.

EXT.  T-REX PADDOCK - NIGHT

The T-Rex's huge hind feet crash down, one large foot
following after another in long, powerful strides.

BACK ON CRUISERS, REST AREA - FIRST CRUISER
```

```
There is a thud, and then a THUD, and then a THUD.   Tim
and Lex share a worried look.   Now the thud grows LOUDER.
There is a CRASHING SOUND, the whole cruiser SHAKES.   Then
silence.   Then another SHAKE.
```

Jurassic Park, written by Michael Crichton and
Marla S. Marmo, 1992

The scene intercuts between the two vehicles to register reactions to the approach of the T-Rex in ways that place the audience in the stranded vehicles as the beast approaches. Thus mood and setup visuals act like a drumroll that draws the audience into the mood and situation of the story.

Wallpapering

This television news term refers to the background settings used to enhance an interview. Politicians, for example, might stage a speech in front of a national monument or some such inspirational "wallpaper." Movies use sporting events, fashion shows, saloon activity, gambling, and the like as wallpaper against which scenes are played. The "wallpaper" of a scene presents visual details so the audience does not notice that the beat is mainly exposition. In *Witness* (Shot 52B), Book, Rachel, and her son eat a fast-food lunch at a small table next to a busy window. As noted in earlier chapters, the script had the lunch break occur in a park, but the filmmakers decided to use a location that displayed Book's life so it could be contrasted with Rachel's. Such changes occur when the scripted location seems dull, is unavailable, or is off-limits because of bad weather, logistics, or traffic—or when a more dramatic location is found. (Filmmakers have an advantage over writers because they can actually see, touch, and smell the locations, characters, and props. That physical presence inspires creativity; writers must imagine such details.)

Wallpapering is most effective when it is *interactive*, i.e., when it influences the characters and the story. Example: The final scene in *An Officer and a Gentleman* could have taken place in the heroine's kitchen, in a motel room, or on a street corner. Instead, it was staged in the factory where the heroine (Debra Winger) works, which is also where she will probably spend the rest of her life—unless her white knight rescues her. This is what happens, and as the other factory workers cheer, the hero (Richard Gere) arrives in Navy dress whites and carries Winger off to a Cinderella–Prince Charming ending. Thus the factory setting provides interactive wallpaper that adds visual content and drama to the story.

Walk-and-Talk Scenes

Walk-and-talk scenes provide another handy way to enhance visual interest. The strategy describes itself: the characters converse as they walk, which allows them to pass through backgrounds that show whatever the writer imagines—storefront displays, children ice-skating, shoppers in an open-air market, or whatever. The strategy is similar to wallpapering and continuity visuals. With a bit of thought, you should be able to create walk-and-talk backgrounds that visually add more to the story than static interior talking-heads scenes.

The Verdict, which mainly takes place in interior rooms, acquires visual content through numerous walk-and-talk moments, as in Shot 15, in which Bishop Brophy and Joseph Alito (the insurance agent) discuss legal strategy while walking through the cleric's impressive headquarters. There is another walk-and-talk incident in Shot 19, when Galvin talks with Dr. Gruber as they walk through a hospital. Throughout these walk-and-talk scenes, the audience is receiving visual information while also absorbing plot exposition. If these scenes had been played in a drab office, in the front seat of a car, or as telephone conversations, the movie might have appeared stagy and visually starved.

Some walk-and-talk scenes allow characters to interact with the background settings and to influence the content of the scene. Example: Early in *Rocky,* as the hero walks home after a boxing match, he meets friends from the neighborhood. They socialize around a fire and Rocky shares a swig of wine. Then, as he walks home, he chats up a tough teenager about her foul language. The exchange allows Rocky to interact with the wallpaper of his neighborhood and to reveal that he has earned the respect of the locals.

Business

"Business" in filmmaking means physical activities that the characters perform as they converse. Business is why characters are often shown grooming animals, painting fences, arranging flowers, tuning auto engines, and the like. Almost any physical activity can supply visual information and create a sense of verisimilitude that works for the story. A character may tie fishing flies *(A River Runs Through It),* assemble and test a rifle *(Day of the Jackal),* adjust a hearing aid *(Rambling Rose),* or manipulate sound equipment *(The Conversation).* Well-written scripts relate the visual business to what is happening in the scene. This is done in *Unforgiven,* when the hero is unable to shoot accurately or mount a horse; the business tells us that Munny is old and unprepared to take on a dangerous bounty hunt.

There is business in Shot 92 of *Witness* when Rachel comes upon Book as he is showing Samuel how to handle a pistol. The business causes a confrontation that touches on the movie's theme. Later in the film (Shot 99), Rachel brings Book a glass of lemonade as he planes a board in the barn. Book's carpentry is business, an activity that the audience can look at while the characters converse. In this case, director Peter Weir realized that barns in the summer can be hot, so he used this as motivation for Rachel to bring Book a glass of lemonade, which he chugs. His hearty thirst impresses Rachel and indicates her attraction to Book. In this way, a minor piece of business reveals subtle character feelings as it supplies visual content. The carpentry business has additional payoff when Book is enlisted to help the Amish build a barn, when he makes Samuel a wooden toy, and when he repairs the birdhouse that he knocked over when he first arrived at the Lapp farm. Such moments are possible when one looks closely at what the characters are doing and feeling. Ask questions; be aware of the setting, the weather, what your characters are wearing, and what they are thinking.

Additionally, there is a *how-to* quality to business that displays an interesting process or a skill. The barn raising in *Witness* (Shot 106) presents a how-to example as it shows how the Amish raise the massive timbered frame of a barn without machines. *The Terminator* has a gripping how-to incident that occurs (Shot 152) when the cyborg repairs damage to its arm and eyeball.

If you take this route, tie the business to what is happening in the scene, as in *The Terminator* (Shot 208) when Reese shows Sarah a skill from his childhood: making pipe bombs from household products; later these weapons will be used against the cyborg. Unless the activity connects to the drama, it may come off as empty business that has little value.

Settings

Do your best to avoid settings that lack interesting visuals. Scenes that take place in modern low-rent apartment buildings tend to be bland unless the rooms are dressed with bookcases, furniture, art objects, and hangings. However, when such fixtures are skillfully selected, positioned, and lighted, they can offer interesting visual content. If your setting seems dreary, think about restaging the beat at a location with more visual potential. For example, a scene set in a drab room might play better if staged in a chemistry lab, next to a swimming pool, in a gym, in a workshop of some kind, or in a location that contains interesting things to look at. Also, consider whether the beat can be wallpapered or done as a walk-and-talk scene.

You should also appreciate that filmmakers create interest by methods as simple as distressing the walls with splotchy paint and finger stains, especially around a light switch (as in Shot 34 of *The Verdict*). Settings can be visually textured with lighting effects such as reflections from a swimming pool, neon light flashing in through windows, or shadows cast by curtains, venetian blinds, trees, and the like. Visual information can result from steam rising from a kettle or the glint of ice in a glass. It is not necessary to mention these small visual sources in the script; what is important is imagining scenes that contain such visual potential and suggesting it in the script: *Jack's room reflects his fascination with sports/black magic/science* or *Jane's home is a Rorschach of her disturbed/organized/passionate personality.*

Exterior settings, which are usually more visual and more adaptable to visualization than interiors, can be salted with flowers, machines, or games that allow physical activity. Even a lawn sprinkler or greenery that sways in a breeze is a source of visual content and sound. Exterior settings allow characters to work in a garden, play badminton, putt a golf ball, build a fence, and perform all manner of outdoor activities that have visual content.

Image Systems

An image system is a recurring visual motif that can be found in certain films. The image system may make a thematic point or generate a metaphoric comment. For example, the various water images that occur in *The Graduate* symbolize the hero's sense that he is drowning in middle-class values. The watery image system begins during the opening party scene when Ben (Dustin Hoffman) looks out at the swimming pool. Throughout this sequence, the house is infused with reflections from the pool. Ben has an aquarium that appears in several scenes. Mrs. Robinson (Anne Bancroft) tosses her car keys into this fish tank. Water imagery occurs when Ben shows off his scuba equipment before sinking to the bottom of the pool. After his first tryst with Mrs. Robinson, Ben is seen floating on a rubber raft in the same pool. He looks sated, no longer the innocent young graduate of earlier scenes.

There is an eye image system in *Witness,* where various shots suggest the watchfulness of a witness. This shows in Shot 19, where Samuel, a goggle-eyed youngster, notices an eyeball-shaped hot-air balloon through the window of the train. In Shot 23A, Samuel notices a statue of an angel that gazes down at him in the train station. Then the shot reverses so it looks down on the boy. Shot 25 presents a close-up of the boy's eye as he witnesses the murder in the men's room. Shot 57 presents another close-up of the boy's eyes as he points to the news photo of the killer cop.

In *Angel Heart,* recurring images of revolving fans and descending elevators are an image system that hints at the debt that the hero owes to the Devil. The revolving fan images suggest that the debt is coming due; the descending elevator suggests that the debtor is heading down to hell.

The audience may scarcely be aware of the image system that has been worked into the script, and most films do not use this device. Nevertheless, this sly and elegant strategy can add visual interest to a story. The strategy should be briefly mentioned in the stage directions: *As Jim ENTERS his car, he again notices the odd glint of sunlight, this time off the windshield.*

Visual Triggers

As a film is researched, the production team combs the script in search of moments with visual promise. Cinematographers sometimes refer to such opportunities as **visual triggers**—moments that suggest interesting images. Such an opening occurs in Shot 57 of *Witness,* when Samuel identifies the killer. This visual trigger orchestrates the confusion of the squad room by focusing attention on Samuel as he points to McFee in a news photo.

Blown Away contains a scary scene with many visual triggers, as when the hero's wife returns home, unaware that the diabolical bomber has prowled her house. Armed with superior position, the audience catches its breath every time she turns on a gas jet, opens the refrigerator door, or picks up the telephone, fearing that she will trigger an explosion. This action is shot in extreme close-up, which heightens the expectation of disaster. These homely but potentially deadly moments are intercut with shots of the hero motorcycling home at breakneck speed to prevent an explosion. The combination of these elements creates a suspenseful sequence in which visual triggers become possible bomb triggers that keep viewers on the edge of their seats.

This final remark on visual storytelling: Although these strategies can enhance visual content, do not rely on them to save an undramatic story. Good stories are constructed around interesting characters who conflict over an interesting problem. Today's filmmakers are skillful at dressing bland locations with light, smoke, and other effects that add visual content. Modern film stocks allow shooting in extremely low levels of lighting, which adds another interesting dimension to visualization. But to get your scripts past readers who care about strong, entertaining stories more than modern production methods, make sure that your work indicates its visual potential through drama. Analyzing scripts and their films is a useful way to develop this ability.

SUMMARY

Filmmakers create movies that flood the mind with visual details and information. If the flow of images slackens, the audience may become restless or bored because the work lacks visual interest. *A key to writing visually rich stories is appreciating how quickly audiences absorb and process visual information.* Some writers acknowledge this statement, then ignore it by writing scene after scene of characters talking, often in a plain room. Such locations are often visually boring. Movies are about images; they are not illustrated radio. This is especially true regarding characters, who should be revealed by action, i.e., by what they *do* rather than what they *say*. Stories conceptualized in terms of action are more likely to acquire visual content, although the decision to go for action must be appropriate to the story concept and the writer's interest.

This advice on writing visually interesting scenes is not meant to encourage you to abandon intimate scenes in which characters express their deepest feelings, for strong dramatic moments can play well in any setting. But because our job is to write motion pictures that have visual content, screenwriters should understand visual storytelling. Accordingly, this chapter discussed the four elements of visual design: lighting, movement, color, and space. These values form the basis of the work of cinematography and how filmmakers turn script pages into movies that have visual content and drama.

The chapter also examined how cinematographers, production designers, and other filmmakers seek scripts that tell their stories with the visual content. In this regard, the interplay of sound and images should be understood as well. Finally, the chapter presented a dozen strategies for enhancing visual content. They are visuals from action, grand images, visual metaphors, symbols, continuity visuals, mood and setup visuals, wallpapering, walk-and-talk moments, business, settings, image systems, and visual triggers. If you familiarize yourself with these strategies, which show up in most films, you can use them to dramatize your story and add visual interest to your script.

Exercises

1. Mute the sound on a study film of your choice for a half hour or so and jot down how it uses visuals to make its various points. Follow along with the script as the silent version plays. Note where you lose the thread of the story, and why.
2. Study an action scene and a dialogue scene from the same film regarding their use of color, space, light, and movement.
3. As you study the two scenes, jot down how they employ wallpapering, walk-and-talk moments, business, setting, image systems, and other visualization conventions noted in this chapter. Keep an account of how, when, where, and for how long each strategy is used.
4. If you have a camcorder, tape someone (an actor or friend) getting ready for a date. Tape the person leaving home, entering a car, and driving off. Then tape the person coming back home. Do several versions: one in which the person is looking forward to the engagement, another in which the person dreads it; one in which the person had a good time, another in which the person did not enjoy the date. Use the pause button of the camcorder to do in-camera editing of the footage. (With practice, fairly tight edits can be accomplished this way.) Use this exercise to practice the visualization strategies noted in this chapter.
5. Tape an actor or friend delivering Concannon's speech from *The Verdict* (Shot 172), when we learn Laura is a spy. Or use any one of the following: Walter's aria from *Sleepless in Seattle* (Shot 200), after Annie returns his ring; Annie's aria to her brother (Shot 70); Schaeffer's speech to Carter in *Witness* (Shot 105); Sarah's voice-over aria at the end of *The Terminator* (Shot 259). The purpose of this exercise is to observe how the close-up of the character reveals inner content. Compare your version of the aria with how it was done in the film.

(For media that illustrate the points made in this chapter, see Appendix A.)

CHAPTER 9

Writing Stage Directions

Screenplays are written in a cramped format that must convey the sweep of the story and the inner feelings of the characters. This chapter discusses how screenwriters deal with these tasks.

During a 1990 CBS television interview, producer Richard Zanuck stated that it would cost about $25 million to remake *The Sting,* a film he made in 1973 for $5 million; this amount would not pay for one star actor in 1995. The point here is that movies have become a very expensive roll of the dice that is largely based on the production company's ability to judge a script. Because much of the script is taken up with stage directions, their presentation—the topic of this chapter—is important.

Stage directions are everything in the script except the dialogue. Stage directions convey what is happening in the story and sketch the settings and the characters; they set up scenes and dramatic situations and describe the physical and emotional actions that the actors must perform. Stage directions indicate the pace and energy of the movie, as well as the continuity that connects the scenes into a story. Stage directions use marks of punctuation and line-reading instructions (often in parentheses), which actors often resent but which help buyers[1] to understand the story and the intent of a line. In sum, stage directions present the writer's research, vision, and passion in a manner that allows the buyer to imagine what is happening in the story and between the characters.

Because the story imagined by the buyer should be the same as the one envisioned by the screenwriter, the surest way for this to happen is to write stage directions in the accepted industry style and format. Movie stage directions touch upon most of what we have discussed so far, that is, story, character, conflict, scene construction, dramatization, and telling the story visually. Most important, stage directions accomplish this task in as few words as pos-

---

[1]For convenience, we shall refer to anyone who reviews, critiques, recommends, or purchases a script as a *buyer*. This person can be an agent, story editor, actor, reader for a production company, teacher, or development executive for a studio or production company. Most of these people can only recommend or reject scripts; they cannot approve them for production. Green-lighting scripts for production is done by people who are higher up on the production ladder—heads of production at a studio, network, or production company.

sible. Such a style will realize advice mentioned throughout this volume: *The script should flow through the mind of the reader like film flowing through a movie projector.* This means that the stage directions should be devoid of snags, glitches, or anything that disturbs the flow of the story.

Turbulence in the stage directions is caused by obscure language, skips in the narrative, and sloppiness that cause buyers to lose the thread of the story. Avoidance of these pitfalls will allow a swift, easy read of the script. The spare style of a movie script also allows potential buyers to quickly determine if they are interested in the property. That judgment is based on the appeal of the story and its characters.

Stage directions came to the movies from the theater and from silent films, where playwrights and scenarists used stage directions to set the scene, to introduce the characters, and to dictate their actions, exits, and entrances. Because stage plays rely mainly on dialogue, their stage directions are less prominent than those used in movies. Silent films, for example, were told mainly with stage directions that described what happened in the story. If the actors required more direction about what to convey, the explanation came from the director during production. Occasionally, when something could not be conveyed through the silent images, it was printed on title cards and edited into the movie. During a Writers Guild of America interview in June 1994, Billy Wilder told me that when he began writing movies in the 1920s, a silent film could be contained on twenty or so pages. In the 1930s, after the industry had sorted itself out after the rush to talkies, scripts standardized regarding length, style, and format; little has changed since then. As noted in earlier chapters, one page of script (typed in the industry format) usually plays for about one minute on-screen, which allows buyers to use the page count to time the script.

In addition to indicating length, script format allows the buyer to judge the plucked bird, stripped of literary feathers and ornamentation. Although the cramped style of script format inhibits the screenwriter's ability to elaborately express the story being imagined, writers learn to work within its confines. The process has been compared to playing a violin with a string missing: it can be done, but it takes fancy fiddling and considerable fretting. The resulting script allows a faster review, which is important to companies that must read a yearly tonnage of scripts. To compensate for the stylistic limitations of script format, screenwriters create stage directions that use strong, simple language to draw buyers into their stories.

The shorthand style of movie scripts enables buyers to envision the story and its characters and to complete a fast read in an hour or so. Canny writers therefore present their work in the style and format that buyers are accustomed to reading. If our style or vision is fuzzy, weak, or vague, such flaws will show in the script. If our vision is clear and heartfelt, that too will register. A script is like a fingerprint or a personal signature that reveals how strongly the writer feels about what he or she has written, as well as how much the writer knows about his or her craft. William Goldman, who always has interesting things to say about screenwriting, noted one of the approaches that he applies to his work:

> I try to make my screenplays as readable an experience as I can, for a good and greedy reason—I want the executives who read them and who have the power to green-light a flick to say, "Hey, this wasn't such a bad read, *I can make money out of it.*"[2]

In the end, what matters is how well the story tracks, how well it has been dramatized, and how well the script reveals interesting characters—and much of this content is revealed in stage directions.

Well-written stage directions do not ensure a sale, but readers appreciate scripts that display reasonable facility with grammar, spelling, and word selection. Carelessly written scripts make buyers wonder if the writer is committed to (or understands) the craft. Having made countless numbers of them, I appreciate that typos and grammar mistakes are difficult to avoid. Even so, they should be hunted down and fixed. Ask a friend or pay a reader to proof your script. Some computer programs have spell-check and grammar-check features that point out and correct mistakes. The script should reflect the work of a person who takes writing seriously.

Script format tells the buyer how well the writer knows screenwriting, for it often happens that small but telltale aberrations creep into a beginner's script and are noticed by the reader. Although they are not a death sentence, format mistakes tend to lower a script's appeal. Buyers are not out to nail new writers; they understand that new writers should be judged on the quality of their stories, not on niggling errors of format. Even so, care with stage directions is important because most screenwriters are anonymous within the motion picture industry. In many cases, a writer drops out of sight for a year or so, then steps out of the wilderness of work with a wonderful script slung over his or her shoulder. As a result, the buyer may know nothing about the screenwriter except that this person has written a script of a certain quality. This cloak of anonymity means that scripts are judged on their merits, rather than solely on the writer's reputation. The lesson here is that the slight advantage of anonymity should not be tossed away because the beginning writer has ignored traditions and standards of format and stage directions. You can avoid this pitfall by studying scripts that you admire until you acquire a solid standard of good screenwriting style. Do your best to create work that blends in with that of professionals in terms of format and style. Writing professional stage direction is not a mighty task, and working within the format involves simple mechanics that can be learned.

Finally, you should know that most of the scripts in the production pipeline are far below the quality of the four main study scripts; in other words, the competition is not nearly as ferocious as you might think. Indeed, one of the most difficult lessons for new writers to grasp is how few good scripts are submitted for production—and here I am speaking of professionally written scripts submitted by reputable literary agents. There is always a

[2]*Esquire,* November 1994, p. 128.

shortage of good scripts, so if you have an idea for a story, write it in a way that appeals to buyers—they are willing to pay dearly for good work.

WRITING STAGE DIRECTIONS

Because stage directions should be brief, avoid exotic words that might slow the read. Keep your writing lean and trust the readers to understand what you have written. For example, if the stage directions indicate a scene that takes place in a greasy-spoon diner in the desert or a posh tennis club, you should assume that the buyer will visualize these generic locations without elaboration. If you write a description that says "EXT.   THE DESERT - NIGHT Windy, cold, and lonesome," you can trust the buyer to catch your drift without describing the obvious. Skimpiness encourages the buyer to participate in the read. The opposite is a script that overexplains everything in a way that diminishes the read. As mentioned earlier, many buyers skim over stage directions and follow the story by reading the dialogue.

Stage Directions That Indicate Time and Continuity

Screenwriters use various strategies to keep the buyer abreast of time passing and to bolster story continuity. The main convention is the slugline stage direction that contains the DAY or NIGHT designation: INT.   EMMA'S KITCHEN - DAY. Because some stories range freely over time, screenwriters help readers to track the story by writing stage directions that state how much time has passed between scenes: *The partygoers are gone and the house is quiet.* Or: *Later that evening.* Or: *A short time later.* Or: *Several months/weeks/years have passed.*

As discussed on page 214, time passing can be noted through graphics that are superimposed on the film. Visuals such as newspaper headlines, plants blooming, seasonal changes, and the like can indicate time passing. Or it can be done with dialogue: *Jack, it's been a year since she left!* Passing time can be noted in voice-over, or by a combination of these strategies, as in this example:

```
INT - PRISON LIBRARY/ANDY'S OFFICE - DAY (1950)

Andy is doing taxes.  Mert Entwhistle is seated across
from him.  Other off-duty guards are waiting their turn.

                        RED V/O
              The following April, Andy did
              tax returns for half the
              guards at Shawshank.

INT - PRISON LIBRARY - ONE YEAR LATER (1951)

Tax time again.  Even more guards are waiting.
```

                    RED V/O
          Year after that, he did them
          all . . . including the
          warden's.

EXT - BASEBALL DIAMOND - DAY (1952)

A BATTER in a "Moresby Marauders" baseball uniform WHACKS
the ball high into left field and races for first.

                    RED V/O
          Year after <u>that</u>, they
          rescheduled the start of the
          intramural season to coincide
          with tax season.

The Shawshank Redemption, written by
Frank Darabont, 1993

Stage Directions That Describe Locations

Screenwriters overexplain settings when they fail to appreciate the minimal amount of camera instruction that readers require to imagine a scene. When your script suggests an interesting location, trust the filmmakers to imagine it and to film it properly. This was done in the following example from *Green Card*, which describes a roof garden that Andie MacDowell's Bronte hopes will be donated to her environmental group:

EXT. ADLERS' ROOF-GARDEN - NIGHT

ALFRED ushers BRONTE out onto the roof-garden. It is even
more magnificent than she remembered. Several mature
trees stand in fascinating contrast to the towering city
buildings. Other plants and flowering shrubs surround the
walls.

Green Card, written by Peter Weir, 1990

A novelist might spend a page or so describing such a location; writer-director Peter Weir did it in a few sentences. If you are moved to flap your prose wings, pinch yourself and remember that buyers are interested in how the characters are revealed and stressed, how the story is dramatized, and how the plot unfolds. Overblown stage directions work against the read if they are seen as an attempt to compensate for failings in these three areas. Your script style can be cool, humorous, unadorned, racy, or whatever—as long as it is consistent and not oppressively overwritten. Note how the following examples sketch locations:

```
INT.   RICK'S - NIGHT
```

An expensive and chic night club which definitely
possesses an air of sophistication and intrigue. A woman
just past the first blush of youth is singing to the
accompaniment of a four-piece orchestra. The piano is a
small, salmon-colored instrument on wheels. There is a
Negro on the stool, playing. He is dressed in bright blue
slacks and sport shirt.

Casablanca, written by Julius Epstein, Philip G. Epstein,
and Howard Koch, 1942

*   *   *

```
EXT.   THAYER HOUSE - DAY
```

A wonderful rustic place, two stories high, rambling
porch, a widow's watch. On the bank are piled sections of
a dock, and a float with a diving board. The yard is
covered with pine needles. The board storm doors have
been taken off the front of the house and now lean on the
porch. There's an old washtub in the back, full of dirt,
where later flowers will grow.

On Golden Pond, by Ernest Thompson, 1979

*   *   *

```
INT.   TRASK'S OFFICES - RECEPTION AREA
```

Sweeping across a room just smaller than a football field,
all onyx and rosewood and vast Oriental carpets with a
conference table about the size of a tennis court. Suits
all over the place, huddled over papers, talking in
corners. All look up, at Tess. PICK OUT Jack, spotting
Tess, starting towards her.

Working Girl, written by Kevin Wade, 1986

Stage Directions That Suggest Visual Content and Style

Despite restrictions imposed by writing in script format, screenwriters are able
to communicate the energy, the style, the mood, and even the look of the
movie imagined, as in the following examples:

```
INT.   82ND PRECINCT WAITING ROOM - DAY
```

Patrolmen drift into the room -- pour coffee, gather round
the radio, polish shoes on the automatic shoeshiner, check
themselves in the full-length mirror. Serpico, in
uniform, examines the circulars for wanted criminals, the
precinct <u>TARGET OF THE MONTH</u>, bulletins describing lost
property and missing persons. He straightens one of the
notices which hangs at an askew angle, one of the thumb
tacks having fallen out. He sees the teletype, looks at
the list of stolen cars on it, copies it down. Hansen
enters, clapping his hands, snaps off the radio. . . . The
cops start to fall into line-up formation. Serpico finds
himself standing next to PELUCE, an older cop -- solid,
friendly -- with a chestful of citations. Serpico's eyes
rivet on the citations in admiration and awe.

Serpico, written by Norman Wexler, 1973

* * *

A BOLT OF LIGHTNING! A CRACK OF THUNDER!

On a distant, rainy hill, the old Frankenstein castle, as
we knew and loved it, is illuminated by ANOTHER BOLT OF
LIGHTNING.
MUSIC; AN EERIE TRANSYLVANIAN LULLABY begins to PLAY in
the b.g. [background]

We MOVE SLOWLY CLOSER to the castle. It is completely
dark, except for one room -- a study in the corner of the
castle -- which is lit by candles. Now we are just
outside a rain-splattered window of the study. We LOOK IN
and SEE:

INT. STUDY - NIGHT

An open coffin rests on a table. We cannot see its
contents.

Young Frankenstein, written by Gene Wilder and
Mel Brooks, 1973

Stage Directions For Action

The script should briefly describe the action so it is understood. Although
writers occasionally choreograph an action scene in detail—the final donnybrook at the end of *The Quiet Man* requires sixteen pages—in most cases the
stage directions are brief.

Stage directions for action should define anything unusual in the scene. The car chase in *Bullitt,* the final battle with the creature in *Predator,* and the oil truck sequence in *The Terminator* present action scenes that are not generic car chases or run-of-the-mill fights. The action showdown between Ripley and the creature in *Alien* is a fight to the death that takes up four pages of stage directions; *The Terminator*'s final battle spans twenty pages. Like all good stage directions, these examples suggest the visual excitement of the action and the emotion felt by the characters. They also indicate the progression of the visuals. To get an idea of how action visuals are written, note these outstanding examples:

```
Tim looks up through the sun roof.  The massive head of
the Tyrannosaurus Rex appears.  Tim watches, transfixed.
Lex looks up.  Irrational with terror, she aims her
flashlight like a gun.  Blasts him.  Her flashlight beam
cuts through the dark and rain -- she sees the beast
plainly for the first time and SCREAMS!

The POOL OF LIGHT bathes the Rex's face.  He smashes his
head down onto the Plexiglass bubble.  It crunches, and
falls into the car, crushing the children.  Tim uses his
feet to push it to the side.

Above, the Rex displays its gaping maw, drooling toward
the opening.

GRANT -
watches the Rex raise his mighty head again, above the
kids' cruiser.

TIM AND LEX
have a half-instant of relief.  Then SLAM.  The Rex butts
his head against the cruiser.  The Rex comes back down,
tries to discover his prey inside the cruiser.  Pushes his
head close to the glass, looking.
```

Jurassic Park, written by Michael Crichton and
Marla S. Marmo, 1992

The *Witness* filmmakers imagined the subtle action of the 150-second police station scene that was contained in the following stage directions:

```
INT.  DETECTIVES ROOM, NARCOTICS DIVISION - DAY

Through glass partitions we can see Book on the telephone
in a cubicle of an office.
```

Samuel has drifted out of the office and is idling amid
the bustle of the squad room. He crosses to a glass case
which holds a collection of plaques and framed newspaper
accounts which denote instances of outstanding duty and
achievement.

ANGLE THROUGH GLASS CASE

as Samuel moves along, only half interested in what his
eyes are taking in, not really old enough to comprehend
anyway. Until suddenly he freezes.

SAMUEL'S POV - NEWSPAPER ACCOUNT

Enlarged, prominently displayed. The headline reads:
Division Chief McFee Honored For Youth Project.
Accompanying the item is a mug-shot of McFee, clearly the
black man who murdered the young cop in the train station
men's room.

BACK TO SAMUEL

He stares transfixed.
A long beat, then Book, lowering himself to one knee next
to Samuel, ENTERS THE FRAME.

He's watching Samuel, knowing from the boy's expression
that they've found their man. Samuel slowly raises his
hand to point at the photograph. Book gently takes the
boy's small hand in his, concealing the accusation from
watchful eyes. He smiles gently at the boy.

> *Witness*, written by William Kelley and
> Pamela and Earl W. Wallace, 1984

    These stage directions are the beginning of a turning point in which Book
uncovers a police conspiracy. Notice how they set up the revelation that McFee
is the killer: "Samuel has drifted out of the office and is idling amid the bustle
of the squad room." The sentence (and particularly the word "bustle") suggests a large room crowded with cops and robbers. This instructs the filmmakers to create the squad room and police activities that eventually make up
the scene—the woman who offers Samuel a cookie, the felon who rattles his
handcuffs at the boy, and similar atmospherics. None of this was spelled out
in the stage directions, since the location and the activities are routine police
business that filmmakers understand.

Samuel wanders about the squad room for almost two minutes before he notices McFee's picture. Having Samuel spot the killer in a newspaper clipping was not the only way to make this point. The boy could have seen McFee in the lineup of suspects that occurs in Shot 51A, or noticed him as he walked through the squad room. The news clipping disclosure was effective because the location surrounded Book with possible conspirators. This is why Book conceals Samuel's pointing finger—the killers may be watching the boy as he points at McFee's picture.

Although the camera instructions are minimal, the script presents the movie that the Wallaces and Kelley imagined: "Through glass partitions we can see Book on the telephone in a cubicle of an office" suggests a long shot that places the hero in a large, busy room. When the stage directions read "Until suddenly he [Samuel] freezes [when he sees the mug-shot of McFee]," they are suggesting a close-up that communicates Samuel's reaction when he sees McFee's picture. The stage directions also suggest a close-up of the photo; otherwise the audience might not understand Samuel's reaction.

The stage directions then indicate Samuel's expression ("He stares transfixed"), which tells Book that the boy has seen something important. These stage directions nudge the buyer to imagine a close-up of Book: "He's watching Samuel, knowing from the boy's expression that they've found their man." As discussed on page 233, when a character experiences strong emotion, the moment is usually recorded with a close-up of the actor's face that conveys what he or she is feeling. The stage directions should indicate when the story should be imagined in wide-angle and when it might require a closer shot. When reference is made to how a character reacts, it signals that the angle is tight. When the stage directions state that *John grabs the bomb, runs to the window, and hurls it away,* the viewer is being encouraged to see wide-angle images, because a wide-angle shot is most effective for showing movement and physical action. As noted, it is not necessary to list specific angles in the script; master shots are usually sufficient.

Finally, the *Witness* scene makes its point entirely with images, for except for a few throwaway lines, the beat does not use dialogue. I recommend studying this scene as an example of tight, effective stage directions.

WRITING CHARACTER DESCRIPTIONS

Characters should be introduced in a sentence or two, in a way that does not narrow the casting choices. It is of little importance that the writer worked hard to create the roles and would gladly churn out pages of backstory, family history, and psychology on them. Script format advises that characters should be introduced quickly, as in these examples:

```
Munny [Clint Eastwood] is thirty-five or forty years old,
his hair is thinning and his mustache droops glumly over
```

his stubbled jaw. If it were not for his eyes he would
look like any pig farmer with his canvas overalls tucked
in his boots pushing on a hog.

Unforgiven, written by David Webb Peoples, 1984

* * *

DR. HANNIBAL LECTOR [Anthony Hopkins] is lounging on his
bunk, in white pajamas, reading an Italian *Vogue*. He
turns, considers her. . . . A face so long out of the sun,
it seems almost leached -- except for the glittering eyes,
and the wet red mouth. He rises smoothly, crossing to
stand before her: the gracious host. His voice is
cultured, soft.

The Silence of the Lambs, written by Ted Tally, 1990

* * *

DR. ELLIE SATTLER [Laura Dern], late 20's, sharp-eyed,
tough if she wants to be, runs like a gazelle across the
arid land. Exuberant, she leaves a trail of dust behind
her.

Jurassic Park, written by Michael Crichton and
Marla S. Marmo, 1992

* * *

NOW WE SEE LORETTA FOR THE FIRST TIME

She's entering a few final figures in the ledger. LORETTA
[Cher] is Italian, 37. Her black hair, done in a dated
style, is flecked with gray. She's dressed in sensible
but unfashionable clothes of a dark color.

Moonstruck, written by John Patrick Shanley, 1986

* * *

LOUISE is a waitress in a coffee shop. She is in her
early-thirties, but too old to be doing this. She is very
pretty and meticulously groomed, even at the end of her
shift.

Thelma and Louise, written by Callie Khouri, 1990

* * *

SAM BALDWIN [Tom Hanks] is in his thirties. His neck is
pinched into a crisp dress shirt and tie. His expression

```
is vacant, faraway.  A breeze blows but he doesn't react
to it.
```

Sleepless in Seattle, written by Nora Ephron, David Ward,
and Jeff Arch, 1993

These examples identify the main characters as to age, style, and general appearance. Unless a trait is essential to the character and story, do not ascribe precise physical characteristics or anything that might require specific casting decisions. Write generalized characters according to their physical type and age: *Jack is a large man in his fifties. Diane is a no-nonsense banker in her forties.* It is sufficient to describe secondary characters as *attractive, 30ish* or *overweight and loving every ounce* or *scrawny with wild eyes.* Unless it is essential for a character to be tall, blond, blue-eyed, athletic, or the like, do not use specific descriptions. Do not slow the read by overwriting character descriptions. Instead, reveal your characters through dialogue and action.

Stage Directions That Deal with Character Interaction

Dialogue is the main vehicle for showing character interaction, but stage directions also serve this function, as in the examples given below. Stage directions describe what the characters are doing in the scene—dancing, playing chess, cooking, or whatever. The first example, from *Dave,* finds the presidential double (Kevin Kline's Dave) and the First Lady (Sigourney Weaver's Ellen) in a limousine that is taking them to visit a homeless shelter. The stage directions describe the moment when Ellen realizes that the man sitting next to her is not her husband. It occurs when Dave ogles her exposed thigh, which is something that her despised husband would not do:

```
She turns suddenly away from him, twisting in the seat.
The bottom of Ellen's skirt hikes up her thigh, exposing
the top part of her leg.  Dave looks down at it suddenly,
drawn to the sight of naked flesh.  After a second or two,
she senses something and glances back to her right. . . .
Their eyes lock for a moment.  Dave smiles quickly and
glances out the window.  Ellen looks down at her own leg a
little puzzled.
```

Dave, written by Gary Ross, 1992

This excerpt from *Fatal Attraction* describes what happens when Dan (Michael Douglas) tries to end his affair with Eve (Glenn Close). Note that the description is direct and unflinching as it conveys the horror of the moment:

```
She kisses him again, more fiercely this time, holding his
face in both hands.  She releases him and takes a step
back.  She has a triumphant gleam in her eyes.  He raises
a hand to his cheek.
```

```
                         DAN
              Your hands are wet.

He looks at his own hand, which is smeared with red.   Then
back at her.   She brandishes her wrists, giggling crazily.
Blood oozes from two ugly gashes.
```
Fatal Attraction, written by James Dearden, 1985

After you have studied a few dozen scripts and their films, you should acquire a feel for how stage directions convey character interaction. Screenwriters invest their writing energy in the story, in dramatizing the scenes, and in writing emotionally dimensional characters, as in this example:

```
They sit opposite each other luxuriating in the occupation
of a snug table for two.   The atmosphere is comfortable
and relaxed.   They're getting on well.   Eve [Glenn Close]
laughs at something Dan [Michael Douglas] has just said.
```
Fatal Attraction, written by James Dearden, 1985

Buyers respond favorably to moments when characters interact dramatically, without dialogue, as in this example from *Unforgiven*, when the foppish killer called English Bob (Richard Harris) ignores a deputy's notice that guns are not allowed in the town of Big Whiskey:

```
And English Bob gives a smart bow, turns with a swirl of
coat-tails that allows a brief glimpse of not one, but two
holstered pistols, and marches off.   As WW [Saul Rubinek]
follows English Bob, he glances nervously back to see what
young Andy will do but Andy just stares nonplused.   In
that quick glimpse, Andy saw how the weapons were tied
down with thongs, meaning the owner wanted a quick pull
. . . and this shit is out of his league.
```
Unforgiven, written by David Webb Peoples, 1984

Stage Directions That Connect to the Dialogue

Subtextual content is often indicated by stage directions. *Thelma and Louise*, for example, has a scene in which Harlan (the man murdered by Louise) tries to pick up Thelma. The subtext of this moment is underscored by stage directions that suggest the attitudes of the three characters. Callie Khouri writes that "Harlan laughs. Thelma laughs, too, but doesn't really get the joke. Louise does not laugh." These stage directions are actable because they indicate what the characters are thinking. This is not always the case, and occasionally writers reveal sloppiness with stage directions that ask the actors to do the impossible:

```
Tom is attracted by Tina's beauty, yet she reminds him of
someone he knew when his life was not good.  So he resists
her flirtations by pretending to be disinterested.  At the
same time, part of him is excited, and Tom anticipates
Tina's next move -- sexual or otherwise.
```

When the foregoing stage directions are rephrased, the moment becomes more actable:

```
Although Tom finds Tina attractive, her intensity makes
him uneasy.
```

The simplification asks the actor to express two specific things—uneasiness and interest—simultaneously. Although it requires a slight stretch, most actors could communicate these two feelings. The advice here is to simplify the stage directions so the actors can respond emotionally.

Because buyers know when a scene is "actable," they become nervous when the stage directions repeatedly describe internal thought processes of the characters and backstory considerations that are not being expressed through dialogue and action. To avoid this, remember that even though movie audiences can usually "read" the faces of the characters and intuit what they are feeling, viewers are not mind readers. They must hear the dialogue and see the action to understand what is happening in the story. The following example, from *Five Easy Pieces*, concludes a spat between Bobby (Jack Nicholson) and Rayette (Karen Steele) over where he spent the night. The couple have been exchanging hurtful looks at opposite ends of a diner; then Bobby exits to the car and waits until Rayette joins him outside, where she continues to display a look of "suffered injustice." Notice how the stage directions indicate the inner turmoil of the characters and set up dialogue that is thick with bruised feelings:

```
                    BOBBY
          I was with Elton last night
          . . .
```

```
Rayette says nothing.  A PAUSE. Then Bobby raises his
right hand:
```

```
               BOBBY (continued)
          I swear.
```

```
She reaches past him to the car door.  He puts his hand
atop hers on the door handle: She tries to open the door.
He reaches up and runs his hand down the back of her hair
to her neck, soothing her:
```

                          BOBBY
              Rayette . . .

She gives up, drops her hand from the car door and looks
down to the ground:

                         RAYETTE
                        (softly)
              You son of a bitch . . .
                    Five Easy Pieces, written by Carol Eastman, 1970

The line-reading instruction "(softly)" indicates how the writer envisioned
Rayette's surrender to Bobby.

BREAKING THE RULES

Although you have been advised to stay in the mainstream of script format, there are interesting variations on the norm. One example, from the
work of David Giler and Walter Hill in their script for *Alien*, presents the
story as a series of shots, each with its own line of stage direction. This style
isolates important moments of the story and signals the vision of
the writers:

INTERIOR. PASSAGEWAYS

Ripley, Parker and Brett walk along.

INTERIOR. HATCHWAY
Outside an airlock.
The trio moves past.
Crouching, staring at the deck.
Nets poised.
Brett trailing Ripley and Parker.
None of them notice something in the airlock above.

THE ALIEN
Now seven feet tall.
It leaps down and grabs Brett.
He shrieks as it presses him close.
Snaps his spine.
Killing him as he screams.
Ripley and Parker turn.
Stand horrified as the Alien bounds down a companionway.
Moves out of sight carrying Brett's still writhing body.
                    Alien, written by Walter Hill and David Giler, 1979

DESCRIBING SECONDARY CHARACTERS

Minor characters can often be identified en masse: *three local yokels; four PTA mothers in their best outfits; five beery ballplayers celebrating*. It is usually not necessary to assign names to characters who have no lines or who say a line or so and then disappear from the movie. Such characters can be identified by their appearance or function: *First Thug, Tall Waitress, Silent Cop, Skinny Teacher, Old Cowboy*, and so on. Use the label to indicate the character's appearance or function. When a number of minor characters must be sketched, do it briefly. As the examples below suggest, the description should hint at the character's personality and appearance. The first excerpt (from *Single White Female*) occurs early in the film, when Allie (Bridget Fonda) interviews prospective roommates. The beat is a montage of bits, each of which plays for ten seconds or so:

```
INT.  ALLIE'S APARTMENT - LIVING ROOM - DAY  (MOS)³
```

```
The applicants: A FAT ONE, who chats continually as she
fills out an application.  Inside her purse Allie can see
a pack of cigarettes.  A THIN ONE, who walks around the
apartment, touching everything, while Allie tries to
interview her.  A DYKEY ONE, older, with sensible shoes,
discusses renovations, gestures to a wall she is
suggesting be taken out.  A FINICKY ONE who has a
measuring tape with her on a tour of the apartment.  AN
INSISTENT ONE, who, despite Allie's protests, shows her
pictures of her pet cats.  A PERKY ONE, friendly and
enthusiastic.  A SCARY ONE, very Tony Perkins-ish, with a
direct, unsettling gaze.
```

Single White Female, written by Don Roos, 1990

The actors performing these roles were allowed to create dialogue for their bits, but only the dialogue of the Scary One, who rambled on about undiscovered incest, is heard on screen. As these examples illustrate, a minor character type can be suggested in a sentence or so.

When the secondary characters have more to do in the story, they can be introduced briefly, often by age, physique, clothing, and/or attitude. The first example, from *Basic Instinct*, introduces police officers who arrive on a murder scene:

---

[3]The stage direction (MOS) derives from the early days of sound when German technicians were hired from Europe to operate recording equipment. MOS means (in mock German) "Mit out sound" (without sound). This stage direction expresses the writer's instruction that the action be filmed as a montage that does not require the voices of the actors.

```
NICK CURRAN is 42.  Trim, good-looking, a nice suit; a
face urban, edged, shadowed.  GUS MORAN is 64.  Crewcut
silver beard, a suit rumpled and shiny, a hat out of the
50's: a face worn and ruined: the face of a backwoods
philosopher.
. . . . . . . . . . . . . . .
It's like a convention in here.  LT. PHIL WALKER, in his
50's, silver-haired, the Homicide Chief.  CAPTAIN MARK
TALCOTT, 50's, well-kept, an expensive suit: an Assistant
Chief of Police.  Two homicide guys: JIM HARRIGAN, late
40's, puffy, affable; SAM ANDREWS, 30's, black.  A
CORONER'S MAN is working the bed.
```

Basic Instinct, written by Joe Eszterhas, 1991

These introductions and stage directions are sprinkled through the first three pages of the script, which illustrate a strategy for introducing multiple characters: Avoid long, confusing lists of introductions and exposition; introduce the characters gradually. Note how the technique was used to introduce a group of Secret Service agents in *In the Line of Fire*:

```
SAM, jovial, solid, mid-fifties, is standing behind his
desk going over presidential schedules and routes with
BILL WATTS, MATT WILDER, and LILLY RAINES.

WILDER is forty and easy-going; LILLY is thirty-five and
looks like she could be a network anchorwoman; WATTS is
thirty-five with a three-piece suit and an attitude.
```

In the Line of Fire, written by Jeff Maguire, 1992

Although the characters are described briefly, the reader is given a sense of each one, whether through appearance, personality, style, or profession. Buyers become confused when they must quickly plug five or ten characters into a story and imagine what they look like and how they relate to what is happening. This problem can be minimized by assigning sex-distinctive names to the minor characters. For example, avoid names such as Pat, Bobby, Dee, Fran, Lee, Jerry, etc., which could be male or female. Also, it helps to avoid names that sound similar—Bob/Rob, Sally/Sissy, Helen/Ellen, Mary/Marie, Tom/Tim, and the like. Distinctive names work better: Benny the soda jerk, blonde in the Ford, the chubby cop, the gargoyle librarian.

USING CAPITALIZATION AND PUNCTUATION IN STAGE DIRECTIONS

There is easy, general advice on when names, words, or stage directions are capitalized. Most scripts CAPITALIZE the character's name the first time he or she appears in the script. The capital letters flag the name, indicate a first appearance, and introduce the character. Thereafter, when the character is mentioned in the stage directions, the name is usually typed in caps and lowercase letters.

Many writers use capitals to emphasize when a character ENTERS or EXITS the scene. Or when someone OPENS the door or CROSSES to the window. Capitals are used to punch up a sound effect, as when characters respond to the loud THUD of an approaching dinosaur. Capitals can indicate proximity, as when a character stands CLOSE to someone. Capitals can indicate a PAUSE in the dialogue (also indicated by BEAT). Capital letters call attention to whatever the writer wants the buyer to notice. Of course, when this handy convention is overdone, the capitalization strategy loses its effectiveness.

Punctuation marks are another way to signal the writer's intent. It is a modest device—like trying to direct a cavalry charge with hand signals—but it is better than nothing. Some writers use an exclamation point to emphasize a line or moment; some use two or three of these marks to indicate intensity: *Karen gasps! John is ALIVE!!!* Other writers become virtuosos with question marks and ellipsis dots: *Are you . . . talking to me?* Attention to page spacing can make a story more enticing, as noted by Stephen de Souza *(Die Hard):*

> I realize that the first audience I have to win over are the people who are going to read the script. So I really try to make it a good read. In fact, I get so compulsive I'll even manipulate my prose to have a tense moment happen right at the page break: "He opens the closet and out falls . . ." turn the page. I actually contrive to have page turners.[4]

SUMMARY

Next to writing them, the best way to learn how to handle stage directions is through script and film study. Stage directions should be lean, strong, and readable. Locations, characters, and actions should be suggested quickly so the script reads easily. Smooth, flowing stage directions are appreciated, but do not attempt to dazzle the reader with glittery prose. Avoid heavy blocks of exposition. When lengthy (eight lines or more) description is necessary, space out the text by breaking it into four- or five-line slugs.

The stage directions should not divert attention away from the story or the characters. Do not tell the actors, the director, the cinematographer, the production designer, or the other experts how to do their jobs. Use the stage directions and dialogue to simply describe the movie you imagined. Your script will indicate how well you understand your characters and their story universe, so research what you write and trust that the reader will appreciate your work.

---

[4]"Interview with Stephen E. de Souza: *Die Hard*," in Jurgen Wolff and Kerry Cox (eds.), *Top Secrets: Screenwriting*, Lone Eagle Publishing, Los Angeles, 1993, p. 74.

Check the script for spelling and grammar. Occasional typos may occur, but too many send out negative signals. If you are unsure of the usage or spelling of a word, look it up in the dictionary before allowing it in your script. If you are unsure about a point of grammar, check it in a grammar book. Writing good stage directions can help to sell your script.

Exercises

Complete one or more of the following:

1. As you look at the videotape of a study film of your choice, select three moments and write scene headings and stage directions that describe what is happening on-screen. If possible, compare what you have written with how these moments were written in the script of the film.
2. Hand-copy one or more of the above moments from the script to acquire a better feel for how the screenwriter wrote them.
3. Imagine a location for a scene. Then imagine a character who must enter the location three times. Write stage directions that describe the character and setting. Then write the entrance three times: as if in a horror film; as if in a comedy; and as if in a drama, thriller, or romance.

(For media that illustrate the points made in this chapter, see Appendix A.)

CHAPTER 10

Script Format for Feature Films and Television

This chapter presents the traditional format for writing and typing a movie script and describes how to use format to hook the buyer into the writer's work.

THE FIRST PAGES OF YOUR SCRIPT

Spacing and layout errors indicate that the author knows so little about the craft of screenwriting that he or she has yet to learn standard script format. Barbara Alexander, a Los Angeles literary agent, has useful information on this point:

> A writer should do his or her homework before he comes to town with a script. Learn the industry format for scripts. Go to the library. Get samples. Font, length of script, even covers are important. Don't try to make the script look different. Don't try to reinvent the wheel because it only makes you look like a novice. The most experienced and professional writers work within a certain accepted format.[1]

As noted earlier, sloppy writing demeans the script and prejudices the buyer against the material. Sloppiness can involve not only the content of a script but also the movie industry's formatting traditions. Therefore, you should appreciate that use of correct format tells buyers that the writer has studied scripts sufficiently to understand why submissions should be written in the style that buyers are accustomed to reading. Although mastery of script format will not guarantee a script's commercial appeal, it is equally certain that formatting errors will not encourage buyers to look favorably on the submission.

Writing in format means working within a few standard margins and space requirements. This task can be performed by one of the computer formatting programs (Scriptor, Movie Master), it can be done manually, or it can be done by a typing service. (*The Journal of the WGA* publishes ads by various

---

[1] K Callan, *The Script Is Finished, Now What Do I Do?*, Sweden Press, 1993 (Box 1612, Studio City, California), p. 36.

typing services, which charge $1 to $2 per script page typed, depending on how difficult it is for the typist to decipher the original text.)

There is plenty of room within format to create a script that moves buyers emotionally—that makes them laugh, that sets their hearts to pounding with worry, or that makes them sad. When a submission expresses the passion of the writer, all sorts of bells and whistles go off. Passion, interesting characters, and a dramatic story arc are what buyers hope to discover, because they know that scripts that stir emotions during a read are a sign of a good story and the possibility of an entertaining movie. This reaction counts highly among people who are concerned with script evaluation.

Part of format involves a few simple measurements. One is the aforementioned rule of thumb that states that one page of script, written in the format, plays for about one minute on-screen. If your script is more than 125 or 130 pages in length, do your best to reduce the page count: long scripts turn into long movies that reduce the number of shows that theaters can run in a single day. Fewer showings reduce the turnover at concession stands, where theater owners make much of their profit. I realize the absurdity of tailoring the most influential art form in history so that merchants can sell popcorn, but that's why movies are called *show business:* we write the *show,* and the popcorn and ticket sellers take care of *business.*

Television scripts should also be "netted out," i.e., written to meet the time requirements of the show, minus the commercials. A typical sitcom nets out to about twenty-two minutes; an hour show nets out to about forty-eight minutes; and a two-hour movie-of-the-week plays for about ninety-eight minutes.

SAMPLE SCRIPT: "TRY AGAIN TOMORROW"

The basics of script format are illustrated in the sample script presented here as Figure 10-1, which exhibits all of the formatting conventions needed to write a script for features or for episodic television. The demonstration script contains notes that are explained at the end of the chapter. Situation comedies (sitcoms) employ a somewhat different formatting style, which is also explained at the end of this chapter. (An example of sitcom format is given as Figure 10-2.)

The title page shown is for a feature film. If this had been a television script, the name of the series would have been underlined, capitalized, and centered six spaces above the title of the script.

"Try Again Tomorrow"

written by

Harold MacIntyre

244 Golf Street
Los Angeles, CA 90444
213/383-4310

March 17, 1995

FIGURE 10-1. Sample script to illustrate format for feature films and television.

1" (approximately)   1

FADE IN[1]

◄—1.25–1.5"—► EXT. HIGHWAY - ARIZONA DESERT - ESTABLISHING - DAY[2]

An 18-wheeler roars through   ◄— Minimum of 1" —►
the silent landscape, past a forlorn roadside DINER,
fronted by a "FOR SALE" sign.

CLOSER ON THE DINER[3]

A dream-killing aluminum box on the wrong side of
the wrong road. Off to one side of the diner we
notice a WOMAN sitting on a box, smoking a
cigarette.

THE WOMAN[4]

Her name is BETTY, a 40-ish sensual woman in a
waitress uniform. She feels trapped and unhappy.

◄——— approx. 4"————————► MAN'S VOICE/OFF[5]
                     Sweetie-pie!

The woman stands, flicks away her cigarette and
ENTERS the diner.

                                      DISSOLVE TO[6]

INT. THE DINER - NIGHT[7]

A short time later. The bleak mood continues inside
the shabby little cafe. FRAME ON the pass-through
window that connects the kitchen: we see COOKY, the
50-ish man who called to Betty. He senses her mood.

                         COOKY
◄——— approx. 3" —►How do things look? ◄—Minimum of 2" —►

                            ↕
                         1–1.5"

2

Betty shrugs as Cooky ENTERS the counter area: he's
a defeated little man in a T-shirt and soiled apron.

                    COOKY (continued)
            He loves the place, right?

                    BETTY
                 (cynically) [8]
           It's the song of my heart.

FAVORING BETTY [9]

She crosses to the jukebox, flips a switch in the back
that gives her a free play. Something bluesy SOUNDS
OVER Cooky's AD-LIB droning about selling the diner
. . . and we segue into a MONTAGE of how Betty ended
up with Cooky.

MONTAGE - HOW BETTY AND COOKY GOT TOGETHER [10]

1. Angry trucker ejects Betty from his big-rig.
2. Betty walks along highway with her suitcase.
3. Betty checks out the cafe, and ENTERS. [11]
4. Cooky is attracted to Betty's sexy desperation.
5. Cooky looks at Betty, gives her a piece of pie.
6. Betty in uniform, joshing with Cooky: she's his waitress.

COOKY AND BETTY BESIDE JUKEBOX - PRESENT [12]

Montage ends when Cooky UNPLUGS the jukebox. He
doesn't like Betty dreaming herself away from him.
Off Cooky's look, Betty shrugs. PAUSE. Cooky crosses
to the telephone, dials.

INT. THE BUYER'S OFFICE - NIGHT

A sleazy hotel room that perfectly reflects the BUYER,
an unpleasant man with gold chains and a toupee. He
flirts with the aging SHOWGIRL who lounges on the sofa
as she does her nails.

3

                         BUYER
             Love that color -- blood red.

                        SHOWGIRL
             Blood! This is Tahitian Dawn,
             dummy!

Before the Buyer can grab her, the TELEPHONE RINGS.[13]

                         BUYER
             Cooky!

INTERCUT DINER/OFFICE PHONE CONVERSATION[14]

                         COOKY
             Are you coming tonight?

                         BUYER
             I thought it was tomorrow!

                         COOKY
             Hey! Be serious!

                         BUYER
             (privately to showgirl:)[15]
             Do we hafta go to that thing?
                 (Showgirl nods YES)
             I need to think about this.

                         COOKY
             You said you'd make an offer!

The phone goes dead. Cooky is shattered.

INT. ANTIQUE AUTOMOBILE AUCTION - NIGHT

Buyer and Showgirl push through crowd at an all-night
auto auction. Frantic bidding booms over the PA
system.

4

                    SHOWGIRL
          What about that guy with the
          diner?

                     BUYER
          I'm negotiating, doll -- like
          you do with me!

Showgirl laughs and slips away through the crowd.
The Buyer follows her.

EXT.   GARAGE NEXT TO HOUSE - NIGHT

Cooky tosses a rope over a rafter.

INT.   BEDROOM OF HOUSE

                     BETTY
                 (calling him)
          You coming to bed or what?

                   COOKY/V.O.
          I'm gonna hang around for a
          while.

INT.   THE GARAGE

Cooky removes his apron and folds it neatly over a
chair, moves a small step ladder under the rope,
stands on it, slips noose around his neck.

BETTY IN BED

She snubs out cigarette when she hears an odd <u>THUD</u>
<u>SOUND</u>. Betty pauses, shrugs, and turns out the light.

FADE TO BLACK. [16]

EXPLANATION OF NOTES IN SAMPLE SCRIPT

The discussion that follows relates to the sample script in Figure 10-1, which presents standard script format for both features and television (sitcoms excepted). Although the main formatting conventions are discussed in this chapter, you will encounter variations as you read scripts, since screenwriters are as inventive on this point as they are with their stories. Even so, this chapter presents the formatting instruction needed to write scripts for features and television. The notation numbers (in parentheses) attached to various items in the sample script (Figure 10-1) refer to the explanations given below.

(1) FADE IN   First image fades in.

(2) EXT.   HIGHWAY - ARIZONA DESERT - ESTABLISHING - DAY

This stage direction, called a *slugline,* establishes the location and time of the story; in this case it tells us that this is an EXTerior scene that plays during the DAY. (An INT. designation is used when the action plays in an INTerior location.) Interior/exterior designations are always part of the slugline, along with a brief statement of where the scene plays, as in *JIM'S MANSION, BACK SEAT OF ANDY'S BUICK, LOBBY OF THE CASINO, MAIN DINING ROOM, FRANK'S LABORATORY*, and so on.

In addition to the interior/exterior and location designations, sluglines include a DAY/NIGHT time designation that indicates whether the action plays in daytime or nighttime. (DAWN, DUSK, or EVENING may also be used.) Once oriented by the first slugline, readers use subsequent sluglines to locate themselves in time and place as they track the story. For this reason, careful attention should be paid to the *INTerior/EXTerior* and time designations, for *they indicate that a new scene has begun and the action is not continuous or simultaneous.*

When two incidents occur at the same time in two different locations, the slugline should indicate the simultaneous nature of the action, as in *EXT. JANE'S HOUSE - SAME TIME - DAY*, or *INT.   THE WAR ROOM - SIMULTANEOUS ACTION/CONTINUOUS ACTION - NIGHT*. There is no iron rule or exact style that dictates how to manage these shifts in locations; just be clear and consistent so the buyer can easily follow what is happening in the story.

Similar to a slugline is a stage direction called a *shot designation*, which presents specific angles or shots that occur within the scene. An example of this can be found in the second stage direction of the sample script, which reads *CLOSER ON THE DINER*. This is not, however, a slugline; it is a *shot designation* that has been included to help buyers visualize the story. Although shot designations are capitalized and spaced away from the body of the stage directions, they are not assigned shot numbers[2] and they do not include the

---

[2]Shot numbers are not included in the script until after it has been sold and is being prepped for production. The shot numbers help the filmmakers to quickly locate incidents in the script. Shot numbers are assigned to each INT/EXT/DAY/NIGHT slugline. Numbering begins at 1 and extends for as many shots as the writer feels are necessary. (*The Verdict* uses 97 shot numbers; *Witness* uses 164; *Sleepless in Seattle* uses 210; *The Terminator* uses 259.)

INT/EXT and DAY/NIGHT designations used in sluglines. For example, the slugline of *The Verdict* scene analyzed in Chapter 4 (in which Concannon, Sweeney, and Galvin meet) reads "38   INT.   JUDGE SWEENEY'S CHAMBERS - DAY." This slugline tells us that the beat designated as Shot 38 plays in an interior location, in Judge Sweeney's chambers, during daytime. Later, as the scene progresses, Mamet adds several shot designations to help the reader imagine the drama of this scene.

Shot designations are usually written as *angles* or *shots,* as in *ANGLE - THE JUDGE, CONCANNON, GALVIN,* or *CLOSE SHOT OF THE CYBORG'S EYEBALL.* Because the matter is important, let me say again that the INT/EXT/DAY/NIGHT designations are *not* included with the shots that are subordinate to the master-shot sluglines. If the INT/EXT/DAY/NIGHT designations were to be included with the subordinate shots, they would indicate that a new scene, playing at a different time (and possibly a different location), had begun.

Script study will reveal that there is no end to how shot designations are written, but usually they are included to help the reader imagine the script by spotlighting a dramatic moment, as in *WIDER, TIGHTER, NARROWER, FULL SHOT, CLOSE-UP/MEDIUM SHOT/TELEPHOTO OF BOOK AND RACHEL LOOKING FOR THE RING/OF THE CREATURE WATCHING FROM THE SHADOWS/OF MARY MAKING THE INCISION/OF THE BABY ASLEEP IN THE CRIB.* Do not overuse shot designations, which are yet another way that writers try to direct with the script. Let the other filmmakers make the movie; the writer's job is to create an entertaining story.

(3) CLOSER ON THE DINER   This shot designation draws the reader into the story by moving from a wide-angle shot of the desert to a closer shot of the diner, which focuses the action. Note that there is no time designation in the shot heading, indicating that the action is continuous. "Off to one side of the diner we notice a WOMAN" further focuses attention on the character that the reader should be noticing.

Note the progression of shots here, which begins with a wide-angle view of the desert and narrows to a closer shot of the diner; the next shot calls for a close-up of the woman. This narrowing of the setting orients viewers to the bleak desert location and then draws them into the story. Wide-angle establishing shots such as this are one way that movies enable audiences to tune in on the story. Although the progression of shots may seem like a simple and perhaps unnecessary convention, if this story were to open with an interior shot of the diner, viewers would be disoriented until they figured out where the diner is located. Similarly, if a scene opens in the interior of an apartment or office building, the audience has no way of knowing what the exterior location looks like, whether the location is up scale or down scale, or in the city or the country. Although stories occasionally begin this way, usually to disorient or confuse the audience, it is advisable to show the exterior of a setting before going inside to where the scene is playing.

The establishing shot need only play for a few seconds, perhaps showing a wide-angle shot of the exterior of a building. The shot might also show the character entering the building, or only the character's car parked on the street fronting the building. After a few seconds of this, the action cuts or dissolves to the interior location.

(4) THE WOMAN   This instruction indicates a closer shot of Betty, whose looks and mood are suggested: "She feels trapped and unhappy." The stage direction encourages a close-up (CU) because "trapped and unhappy" will not show in Betty's eyes unless the camera is close on her face. As noted earlier (page 233), the tighter the shot, the more intimately the audience connects to the interior state of the character. The reader is also encouraged to notice Betty through details—her uniform, her business with the cigarette, and her plaintive manner. These stage directions suggest Betty's character and offer clues about her inner state.

If the script wished to show what Betty sees as she stares into the desert, the stage directions would call for a point-of-view (P.O.V.) shot, which would be sluglined as BETTY'S P.O.V. -- THE DESERT.

A P.O.V. shot presents what the character sees, that is, a subjective point of view. P.O.V. shots might be used to show what a driver sees through the windshield of a racing car, what a batter sees when the pitcher throws the baseball, and the like. The end of the P.O.V. shot is indicated by a new shot designation that reads SCENE, RESUME SCENE, or BACK TO SCENE.

Another useful stage direction is the term INSERT, which indicates a close-up of an object or something other than a character. For example, if a man checks his watch and it is important that we note the time, the shot designation might read *INSERT WRISTWATCH: THE TIME IS 10:25.*

Inserts are isolated shots, usually of inanimate objects, that can be inserted into the film or tape during editing. Examples: *INSERT: BOMB IN CABINET; INSERT: PIPE LEAKING OIL.* In both this and the point-of-view shot, it is preferable to return to the scene by writing a new designation that states SCENE, RESUME SCENE, or BACK TO SCENE. Insert shots are often "cutaways" that can be useful during editing.

A close-up (CU) of a character generally shows a person from the chest to the top of his or her head. An extreme close-up (ECU) fills the frame with the head or object filmed. A medium shot (MS) would show several people from the waist up. A long shot/wide-angle shot (LS) shows a panorama or many characters or objects. (Writer-director Garry Marshall offered a simple summary of the three prime camera angles during a Writers Guild of America seminar in June 1994: long shots show characters from the feet up; medium shots show them from the waist up; close-ups show them from the chest up. TV close-ups are tighter, showing characters from the neck up.)

(5) MAN'S VOICE/OFF   OFF indicates that we hear the man's voice but do not see him because he is off camera. OFF can also mean VOICE-OVER (also written as V.O., VOICE/OFF, O/S, VOICE ONLY, and OFF STAGE). If a narrator is used, write NARRATOR/V.O. If the voice we hear comes over a telephone, an intercom, or a radio, this is indicated by NARRATOR/V.O./FILTERED.

(6) DISSOLVE TO   This continuity direction usually indicates that time has passed. In this case the story has shifted from day to night. As noted on page 215, a dissolve overlaps the images from Take A with images from Take B

for a few seconds, whereupon Take A fades out. Because the use of a dissolve is determined by the director and the film editor, writers often ignore whether scenes are connected with a dissolve or a cut. Accordingly, neither designation needs to be included.

(7) *INT.   THE DINER - NIGHT*   This slugline indicates that the action takes place inside the diner. Because of the time designation NIGHT, the reader will assume that time has passed. If this stage direction were written without the designation NIGHT, the script would be telling the reader that no time had elapsed since the previous shot. If you suspect the reader might be confused as to time, location, or incident, write on-the-nose stage directions that clarify: *A short time later. Same time. The next day. Three days later. The other side of the room. In the basement below the kitchen. Another view of the action. The action as seen from the roof of the stadium.*

INT.   THE DINER - NIGHT is another master shot. Within this slugline, the director and cinematographer will commit to specific shots that accomplish the goals of the scene. Except for an occasional shot that directs attention to a character or view, do not muck up the master shot with camera directions or technical mumbo jumbo regarding angles, tilts, lenses, trucks, dollies, or other continuity conventions. It is enough to imagine these things, as long as they help you write the script.

On rare occasions, writers suggest an antiquated visual effect for a spoof or period piece, such as a keyhole or shimmer dissolve or similar optical effect. Such a suggestion could be written as follows: *It might be fun to use an old-fashioned flip for the transition here.* In most cases, however, the director, cinematographer, and film editor decide such matters.

The stage directions that follow the slugline referenced by Note 7 use the term FRAME, which suggests a wide-angle orientation shot of the interior of the diner that tightens and centers on Cooky.

(8) *(cynically)*   This parenthetical stage direction indicates the subtext of Betty's inner anger. Be sparing with such instructions to the actors; reserve line-reading advice for dialogue that has an oblique meaning that might otherwise be misinterpreted. Scripts that are being offered for sale sometimes are written with a bit more stage direction, description, and line-reading instructions than would be found in a production version. They are written "fat" to ensure that readers understand what is happening in the story.

(9) *FAVORING BETTY*   This instruction suggests that Betty is positioned in the shot so that the audience is drawn to her. This designation is often used with a tracking shot or a two-shot; it tells the reader which character or object is most important at the moment. Writers use stage directions such as this to help readers visualize the story. In this case, the directions indicate that the writer imagined that the focus would be on Betty as she crosses to the jukebox.

Note the generalized music cue, "something bluesy." Although the musical director chooses or composes the music, many writers work better while imagining (or listening to) an underscore that dramatizes important moments in the film. As noted on pages 174 and 241, musical cues are not generally included, except for moments such as this, when a character is involved with recorded music or performance.

Also note that the music plays "OVER Cooky's AD-LIB droning about selling the diner." Ad-libbed lines are improvised by the actors. Because the lines are "throwaways" (i.e., they are not essential to the story), they do not need to be written out. If throwaway lines are scripted, they will be read and given importance they may not deserve. If a line of dialogue is meant to be heard over noisy background sounds, it can be designated by a parenthetical:

```
                     JIM
           (over the hubbub)  [or]
     (yelling over the noise/confusion/din)
```

(10) MONTAGE refers to an overlapping series of incidents and shots that fill in backstory or compress a longer sequence into a minute or so of screen time. Montages are usually done over music and/or off-screen narrative, without dialogue. (Discussed on page 133.)

(11) Indicate when characters ENTER or EXIT by using capital letters. Capitalizing this way helps readers to track the story.

(12) COOKY AND BETTY BESIDE JUKE BOX - PRESENT This shot indicates that the montage is over and that we are back in the scene.

(13) TELEPHONE RINGS Sound cues are usually capitalized. If you have a unique sound effect in mind, mention it, but do not write excessive instructions or descriptions. Capitalization of the word SOUND helps readers to spot where audio effects are needed. Sound designers create audio effects and present them to the director for his or her approval.

Capital letters are also used to punch up the names of characters when they make their first appearance in the script. Occasionally there may be an important moment or story point that the reader should notice. If so, it can be punched up with underscored boldface type, spacing, and/or capitalization, as in:

NOTE: BEFORE SHE CAN CLOSE HER PURSE, JIM NOTICES MARY'S PISTOL.

(14) INTERCUT DINER/OFFICE PHONE CONVERSATION means cutting from one person to another during the phone conversation. This convention avoids ping-ponging the stage directions between the people who are talking to each other on the phone.

(15) (privately to showgirl) This stage direction indicates an aside to the showgirl; the direction *(showgirl nods YES)* allows her to register her response quickly. Shorthand such as this can speed the read.

(16) FADE TO BLACK A traditional ending of a scene or the story. FADE OUT and FADE TO WHITE are also used.

SITCOM FORMAT

There are specialized texts that present sitcom (situation comedy) formats, which vary between production companies and whether the script is shot on

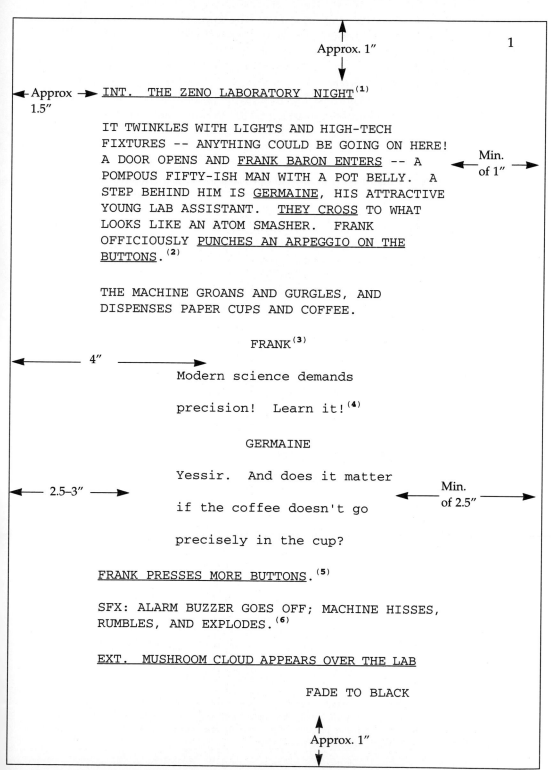

Approx. 1"

1

Approx → INT. THE ZENO LABORATORY NIGHT[1]
1.5"

IT TWINKLES WITH LIGHTS AND HIGH-TECH
FIXTURES -- ANYTHING COULD BE GOING ON HERE!
A DOOR OPENS AND FRANK BARON ENTERS -- A
POMPOUS FIFTY-ISH MAN WITH A POT BELLY. A
STEP BEHIND HIM IS GERMAINE, HIS ATTRACTIVE
YOUNG LAB ASSISTANT. THEY CROSS TO WHAT
LOOKS LIKE AN ATOM SMASHER. FRANK
OFFICIOUSLY PUNCHES AN ARPEGGIO ON THE
BUTTONS.[2]

Min.
of 1"

THE MACHINE GROANS AND GURGLES, AND
DISPENSES PAPER CUPS AND COFFEE.

FRANK[3]

4"

Modern science demands

precision! Learn it![4]

GERMAINE

Yessir. And does it matter

2.5–3"

if the coffee doesn't go

Min.
of 2.5"

precisely in the cup?

FRANK PRESSES MORE BUTTONS.[5]

SFX: ALARM BUZZER GOES OFF; MACHINE HISSES,
RUMBLES, AND EXPLODES.[6]

EXT. MUSHROOM CLOUD APPEARS OVER THE LAB

FADE TO BLACK

Approx. 1"

FIGURE 10-2. Sample script illustrating format for situation comedies.

tape or on film. Even so, the sample format, presented herein applies to most sitcoms. (For more on the various script formats, see Judith H. Haag and Hillis R. Cole, Jr., *The Complete Guide to Standard Script Formats*, CMC Publishing, Los Angeles, California, 1985.)

There are differences between the sitcom format and the format used for features and episodic television. Figure 10-2 presents a sample of a script for a sitcom. The notes (in parentheses) attached to various items in the sample script refer to the explanations given below.

(1) Sitcom sluglines and stage directions are capitalized and <u>underlined</u>.

(2) Sitcom stage directions are capitalized and typed in 12-point capital letters, single-spaced. Stage directions begin approximately 2 inches from the left edge of the page and extend to within 1 inch of the right edge of the page.

(3) Character names are typed in capital letters and underlined when first introduced. Names of characters are typed about 4 inches from the left edge of the page. There is a double space between the character names and their dialogue.

(4) Sitcom dialogue is double-spaced and typed in upper- and lowercase, beginning 2.5 to 3 inches from the left edge of the page and extending to within approximately 2.5 inches of the right edge of the page. Avoid extending a speech onto the following page, especially when a joke is involved. It is preferable to end the page before the long speech. Keep the names of the characters and their speeches together on the same page; do not leave an orphan name at the bottom of the page while typing the associated speech at the top of the following page. Long speeches can be continued onto the next page by writing [MORE] at the bottom of the page. In such cases you should repeat the name of the character who is continuing the speech at the top of the next page with (CONT'D) or (CONTINUED) appended. This convention also applies to non-sitcom scripts for features and TV episodic shows.

(5) Sitcom action, movement, and business are capitalized. Key business and entrances and exits are usually underlined in sitcom format.

(6) Sound, lighting, and other effects[3] are placed on a separate line.

SUMMARY

The measurements that follow are approximate because there are variations in script format. Without becoming slaves to a ruler, new writers should stay close to the margins and spacing measurements outlined in this chapter. Additionally, the following advice applies:

Paper: Use standard white photocopy paper or bond. Do not use colored, rough-textured, slick, erasable, or onion-skin paper or any type of paper that might smudge. Bind the script in a simple spread-pin folder.

---

[3]SFX (or FX) refers to either sound effects or special effects (also designated by FX). A sound effect can be as common as a canary chirping, or it can consist of an extraordinary sound montage that dramatizes or punches up a dramatic moment. A special effect refers to an extraordinary visual moment that requires the work of special-effects experts.

Typeface: Use a standard typewriter font (10 pitch/12 point Pica, Elite, Prestige, Courier, etc.). Do not use book type or decorative typefaces. Scripts are more readable when typed with a fresh black ribbon. Retain your original manuscript and submit a sharp photocopy that is easy on the eyes. *Avoid dot-matrix printing or anything else that might make reading your script more difficult.*

Page numbers: Type page numbers in the upper right-hand corner of each page. Since spec scripts do not contain shot numbers, page numbers are important to the editorial process and they should *always* be included.

Margins for stage directions: As marked on the feature and sitcom scripts above, stage directions should begin 1.25 to 2 inches from the left edge of the page. There should be at least a 1-inch right margin for features and sitcoms.

Dialogue: Dialogue begins approximately 2.5 to 3 inches from the left edge of the 8 1/2- by 11-inch page. The dialogue should not extend beyond 7 inches from the left edge of the page. The dialogue should run down the center of the page in a column that is approximately 4 inches wide. Do not hyphenate words; rather, type the entire word on the next line. Sitcom dialogue is double-spaced; dialogue for features and episodic television is single-spaced.

Character names: Capitalize character names, which begin 4 inches from the left edge of the page.

Spacing: As shown in the sample feature script, single-space the stage directions. Space approximately 1 inch at the top and 1 to 1.5 inches at the bottom of each page. Do not crowd the page. Make it "airy" by leaving white space around the text. To give readers a breather from masses of stage directions, break them up by inserting an extra space every six or lines so. Do not compensate for a long or short script by taking liberties with spacing.

For both features and sitcoms, place a double space between the slugline that introduces the scene location and the stage directions. Place a double space between the stage directions and the character name that precedes the dialogue. Double-space between the speeches of different characters. Single-space stage directions for features and sitcoms. Sitcom stage directions are typed in capital letters only; television and feature scripts are typed in caps and lowercase. Unlike scripts for features and episodic television, sitcom sluglines are underlined.

Do not justify the right-hand margin of the script. The left margin should be flush left; the right margin should be ragged. Scripts are typed on only one side of a sheet of paper.

Exercise

Select a scene from one of the four main study films and view it three or four times. Make whatever notes you feel are necessary to remind you of what happens, then write the scene in script format. When you have typed up the scene, compare your version with how the scene was written in the actual script. Repeat as necessary.

(For media that illustrate the points made in this chapter, see Appendix A.)

CHAPTER 11

Rewriting

*Movie scripts are not written—they are rewritten.
A writer may complete five or ten drafts before the
"first" draft is submitted, at which point more rewrites
may be required. This chapter deals
with how this process works.*

Once upon a time, someone told me that a writer must learn to wear four hats, being, at different times, an explorer, an artist, a warrior, and a critic. The explorer investigates the world and the self for the raw materials of writing. What has been discovered is interpreted and organized into story and script by the artist. The warrior defends the work as well as the artist who wrote it. The critic is the hawkeye who reviews and rewrites as necessary.

The "four hats" theory reflects the organization of this book: the preceding chapters deal with developing yourself as an explorer and as an artist who discovers, organizes, and dramatizes plot, story, scene, and character. The final chapter deals with becoming a warrior who protects and nurtures the script, as well as the author who wrote it. This chapter asks you to put on your critical hat during rewriting.

Rewriting is the next-to-last layer of story sense that we began piecing together when we discussed locating and developing an idea and expanding it into a plot and story. Additional layers dealt with scene construction, characterization, dialogue, dramatization, writing for the camera, stage directions, and script format. Now the topic is rewriting, which can be tedious, for after working for weeks or months, it is easy to become convinced that one has created an Oscar-winning script. Reality intrudes when the material is sent out to a reviewer who lacks the writer's blood bond with the script and looks at it with a cool, distant eye that may see areas that are less than perfect. These readers—agents, teachers, producers, story editors, and studio executives that we shall again call buyers—invariably locate weaknesses that they feel diminish the commercial appeal of the script. So varied are these rewriting problems that they span most of the topics covered in this book. That's the bad news; the good news is that the range of rewriting problems allows this chapter to be used as a review of everything presented thus far in *Story Sense*.

Problems arise because scripts are poorly written or because readers fail to imagine the same movie as the screenwriters. Whatever the cause, most scripts have problems; most scripts are also rejected—some of them many times. Most of these works are lost, but some are rediscovered and shot as originally written. *The Verdict* is such a script; it was initially passed over, then was rediscovered by the director and the production company after various writers submitted their rewrites of Mamet's original work.

Experiences such as these occur when movie executives respond negatively to a script and decide that it "needs work." Sometimes this is true, but when it is not, insisting on a rewrite can be like painting a mustache on the *Mona Lisa*. Desecrations happen. *The Wizard of Oz* presents a ghastly example of studio tampering, in which one executive argued for dropping one of the scenes because "nobody wanted to see a fat little girl sing next to a pigpen." Righteous in his conviction of what needed to be done to save the movie, he proposed that the studio cut Judy Garland singing "Somewhere over the Rainbow." Fortunately, other views prevailed.[1]

Although script wreckers make inviting targets, there are also many creative story executives who work with writers to help improve material. So, if only for peace of mind, let us assume that creative, enlightened souls will be involved with the rewriting process being discussed. This is not fantasy, for there are many hardworking, intelligent story executives who are committed to developing good scripts, and the compass that guides these buyers is their instinct for what will entertain an audience. Although this spin places a commercial focus on their judgements, it also places a reality perspective on rewriting: the process must accommodate the wishes of those who operate from the business side of show business.

Business concerns are at work as movie executives read, read, read, read, and read some more in search of good scripts. They confer with colleagues about scripts; they study what their analysts say about the scripts they have reviewed; and then they go home for weekends and holidays and read more scripts. It is through such labors that studio executives try to locate what they hope will be golden needles found in the haystacks of scripts that they read. The prize they seek is a good story with interesting characters that will attract an audience. Although this is an obtainable goal, it is not as easy as it might seem, which is why, despite hard work and legions of readers, the batting average for a successful movie executive is similar to that of a successful ballplayer—one hit in every three times at bat. However, although a hitter with a .300 average has a good chance of being inducted into baseball's Hall of Fame, for movie executives the number means that two-thirds of their movies will fail at the box office—hardly enough to keep them in business. Small wonder, then, that movie executives are picky about the scripts they approve for production and that they call screenwriters into their offices to discuss a script's commercial appeal. These story conferences are the true beginning of rewriting; everything that went before is part of writing the first draft. Story conferences, however, are where writers must address whatever problems fretful studio executives feel might jeopardize the millions required to turn a script into a movie. The uneasi-

[1]See Aljean Harmetz, *The Making of the Wizard of Oz* (Proscenium Publishers, New York, 1984), for more on this classic movie.

ness of buyers is based on their sense of story and an ancient bit of movie wisdom: *Movie scripts are not written—they are rewritten.*

Writers should also remember that story conferencing is merely another
phase of screenwriting. Many writers prepare for this showdown by asking
friends to evaluate their scripts, but be aware that these advisers tend to dance
lightly on the negative and stomp hard on the positive. The writer's goal at
this stage is to get suggestions that are worth considering before wading back
into the work for a final rewrite before sending the script out for sale. Most
scripts would benefit from Paddy Chayefsky's approach to rewriting:

> My own rules are very simple rules. First cut out all the wisdom; then cut out
> all the adjectives. I've cut some of my favorite stuff. I have no compassion
> when it comes to cutting. No pity, no sympathy. Some of my dearest and most
> beloved bits of writing have gone with a very quick slash, slash, slash . . .
> these four pages out. Because something was heavy there. Cutting leads to
> economy, precision, and to a vastly improved script.[2]

All of this—the writer's drafts, critiques by friends, and notes from buyers—is part of the first postpartum rewrite. The second postpartum rewrite
occurs during production, when the script is given to actors and filmmakers,
who may shorten or change speeches, or drop them entirely, along with characters, staging, and action. These changes and fixes, made during production,
are part of the creative ferment of moviemaking.[3]

The third postpartum rewrite happens in postproduction when cans of
film are edited; selected story moments and characters are highlighted or
downplayed, and music, sound, and special effects are added. During the
weeks (or months in the case of most features) of postproduction, filmmakers
and studio executives study the film during its metamorphosis from raw
footage to finished film. If they do not like what they see, they may create new
scenes, reshoot existing scenes, or decide that the movie is so bad that it cannot be salvaged. In such cases, the film will not be given theatrical release;
instead, it will be sent directly to video or else shelved (not released to any
venue). Although very few treasures are lost as a result of such decisions,
movie judgments are imperfect, even when evaluating a finished film—which
is a much easier task than evaluating an unproduced script. For example,
despite starring two Academy Award winners (Jessica Lange and Tommy Lee
Jones), *Blue Sky* was shelved by the studio that made it. After languishing in a
storage vault for nearly three years, it was released to generally glowing
reviews by critics. The movie eventually earned Jessica Lange an Oscar nom-
ination. Despite being a succès d'estime, *Blue Sky* did not turn out to be
another *Bonnie and Clyde,* an earlier film that was yanked from distribution
when nervous executives decided that it would not entertain mainstream
America. The examples are cited to indicate the highly subjective nature of the

---

[2]John Brady, *The Craft of the Screenwriter,* Simon & Schuster, New York, 1981, p. 55.
[3]This is an interesting process that has generated literature that writers should know about. For
example, see Sidney Lumet, *Making Movies,* Alfred A. Knopf, New York, 1995, and Rudy Behlmer,
Behind the Scenes, Ungar, New York, 1982.

evaluation of movie material and to acknowledge that the judging of movies and scripts is an imperfect system. It is also the only system, and despite its lowly batting average, Hollywood's literary machinery works well enough.

Perhaps unfairly, I have tied the discussion of how scripts inch their way through the movie pipeline to a statement made earlier in this book: *80 percent of what shows up on the screen is in the script.* Some writers, upon first hearing this remark, are inclined to puff up with pride, especially when it is applied to good films. However, the 80 percent figure has two edges, so scripts should also be held responsible for 80 percent of what shows up in a bomb, a turkey, a stinker, a dud, a loser, and on and on through the negative characterizations of movies that are rejected by audiences. Even longer is the list of reasons that cause rejection, and these are what executives try to anticipate and correct during rewriting.

The first things that a buyer's notes address are problem areas that are easy to fix or explain away—excessive dialogue, scenes that do not work, characters who do help the story. Other problems run deeper and are less accessible. We feel defensive when these larger problems show up, especially in view of the keen critical abilities that most writers display when reviewing someone else's work. Unfortunately, our piercing critical gaze often becomes feeble when applied to our own work, especially the story. This happens because of the curious nature of screenwriting: As we create the images of a scene, the bright light of imagination reveals what happens in vivid detail; at the same time, however, we are blinded by that light and are unable to see flaws in the overall pattern of our work—the story. Sometimes we seem to pass through the mirror of imagination and become so accustomed to the story universe we have created that its flaws become invisible. At other times, we have merely convinced ourselves that the drivel we have written is great stuff! Whatever the reason, the initial work of rewriting usually concerns problems with the story, which are quickly spotted by buyers and their advisers. Pointing out story weaknesses is the easy part; fixing them, which is often left to the writer, can be much more difficult.

The buyer's concerns are not unreasonable; they usually echo the questions the writer asked during the initial writing: Is the story original, different, exciting, entertaining? Is the script a page-turner, one that demands to be read nonstop from beginning to end? Will audiences pay to see this story? The buyer thinks about the writer's intentions and whether they have been realized. Buyers ask whether the script has thoughtful content, that is, is it *about* something, or is it merely feel-good entertainment? Buyers think about the characters and whether they display willfulness, conflict, felt emotion, and thoughtfulness. The buyers also study the dialogue—is it sharp, clever, lean, insightful, laden with subtext and acting opportunities that will attract top actors and entice audiences to buy tickets? They ask whether the story presents powerful conflicts that cause secrets to be pried from characters. Buyers seek scripts that answer all these questions in the best possible way, which is why so few scripts survive the rewriting process and why fewer still become movies.

You will now be given advice on the main areas where story and script problems abound. You can use this discussion to troubleshoot your script before sending it out. Although it is the nature of books to sequence topics so they line up into what seems to be an order, there is no tidiness or order when writers zigzag through the writing process. Keep this in mind and feel free to hop back and forth between areas and topics in whatever order suits your needs.

REWRITING PROBLEMS WITH THE STORY

Is the Story Concept Flawed?

If the story concept is weak or uninteresting, the script may lack audience appeal regardless of how well it is written. However, think carefully before discarding the story notion in which you have invested energy, as many writers are inclined to do when negative feedback arrives; when an idea inspires a writer to devote weeks or months to develop it, there is often more value and substance to the notion than the author may realize. This caution is based on hundreds of story conferences with writers who have presented me with stories that they feel are broken birds that cannot fly. In some of these cases, the problem is not whether the idea can fly; it is whether the writer can stop flying, that is, stop flitting from idea to idea. Such a writer is never satisfied with the story concept at hand because he or she is unable to solve story problems that arise—and there may be a passel of them.

Flitting is an unproductive pattern that can indicate insecurity, weak thinking, and lack of craft, which is why moving from idea to idea and abandoning unfinished stories and scripts should be avoided like a disease! The cure is to appreciate that story concepts do not automatically write themselves into plots. Writers should also appreciate that the story phase of the work is difficult and that an idea cannot be blamed for failings that occur because the writer has not used craft and imagination to exploit the dramatic potential of the original story concept.

Unimagined stories are also the fault of weakly imagined characters who are so dimly seen that they have limp, undeveloped backstories. Such characters lack distinctive personalities and are often dull and predictable. Feeble characters like this cannot create conflict or drive the story or realize the potential of the story concept because the writer has not given them enough energy. Weak characters must be pumped up during rewriting. This does not mean merely slapping on new names or memories, for zombie characters cannot come to life until they have been charged with the writer's life force. This is what is involved with imagining so intensely that we bring our characters to life in our mind. Seen from this view, the second main screenwriting ability—imagining and writing characters—involves giving characters enough life energy for them to emerge from the limbo of the unconscious and have life on the pages of a script. If your characters seem weak and dull, invest them with abilities, problems, dreams, and hang-ups that energize them and bounce them off other active, energetic, willful characters.

It is, of course, easier to believe in the founding idea of a story when you believe in your ability to do this work—and you must believe you can do it or the harpies who haunt writers will sense your weakness and undermine your will to write. We fight this by hard work, by husbanding our investment of time and energy, and by appreciating the work we are doing and the profession of screenwriting. In the course of this reality check, we also should entertain the thought, nasty as it is, that a story concept and its characters are not developing because we are not imagining the story in a crafty, thoughtful, and creative manner.

This pep talk does not mean that all story concepts are worth rewriting, for an idea can lose its appeal or a flaw may emerge that sours an idea. Occasionally, films containing conceptual flaws make it through the pipeline, but their faulty genes show up on-screen and defeat them (as in *Mr. Jones, The Savage Is Loose, Last Exit to Brooklyn*). If your story does not come together or if you end up disliking it, the best move may be to put the idea aside. At some future time, you may find a way to revive the notion. At the least, the experience can be used as a lesson: *Because the story concept organizes both the plot and the script, do not proceed until the idea feels totally right.* (See Chapters 1 through 3 for more on plotting, story concepts, and blocking the story.)

Are There Problems with the Structure of the Story?

Even if the story concept is solid, the structure and organization may require rewriting. The considerations described below may help identify and correct weaknesses in this area.

First, be certain of your intentions and be clear about what you are trying to say in the story. Know what the story is *really* about, on a thematic level. It can be helpful to reduce the story to a brief statement. For example, *Jurassic Park* is about the dangers of playing games with nature; *The Terminator* is about destroying an indestructible agent of technology. Sometimes it helps to compare your story with another that follows the same developmental pattern. For example, *Braveheart* has been called *Spartacus* in kilts, which is a fairly accurate assessment because of the similar way in which the two stories develop: warrior leads revolt against tyrants, is defeated in final battle, and is crucified. *Under Siege* has been described as *Die Hard* on a battleship, or a horizontal version of a vertical story (warship instead of skyscraper).

Writers try all manner of strategies to acquire this overview of what happens in their stories, for once a story concept is firmly in mind, it is easier to work out the incidents of plot supporting it. Put simply, *you must know what you wish to say before you can say it.* There should be no compromise or fuzziness on this point. Knowing the *event* in the story—what happens after everything happens—is an essential perspective here. The event is usually synonymous with the solution of the problem that occurs in the climactic scene.

To sustain audience interest in how the problem resolves, be sure that the first-act setup contains enough dramatic potential to sling the story through the long span of the second act. A strong dramatic setup often presents a likable but flawed hero who takes on a difficult problem that puts this person in conflict with a more powerful and dangerous antagonist. *A strong first-act setup will make it more likely that the drama will arrive at the climactic moment with a story that is intensely dramatic.*

The second act, which may take up half the movie, sees the trouble promised in the first act engulf the hero. The hero's condition goes from bad to worse until it appears that he or she is heading for defeat. As the hero slips deeper into trouble, subplots appear that deal with backstory, inner struggles, relationships, and the theme. Most films have three or four subplots, which are introduced in the first act or early in the second act.

The third act of most stories is taken up with the climactic scene that solves the problem. As noted, the solution to the problem is usually synonymous with the event of the story, as in *The Terminator,* a story that organizes around solving how to destroy the creature. In this example, the story problem seemed beyond solution, but in the end, the heroes found a way to emerge with at least a degree of victory or vindication. Additionally, the third act ties up loose ends of the plot and the subplots.

To solve the problem and to save the hero, writers often invent a lifeline—a device, an ability, or an ally that enables the hero to tip the balance. (Lifelines are discussed on pages 87 and 208.)

Act III should be the easiest to write because it is mainly about how the hero solves the problem. The details of the solution require ingenuity, but screenwriters excel in solving such problems. (See Chapter 3.)

Is the Story Boring?

Stories that lack drama and interesting characters are boring. Stories are boring when they lack conflict and a rising arc of tension that causes the audience to worry whether the hero will solve the problem. Some stories need rewriting because nothing is at stake and there is no hero to root for; hence, there is no drama. Stories are boring when they overexplain, which tends to eliminate mystery and surprise. Stories are boring because the characters talk too much and because the plot stands still. Stories are boring because the locations and action are not interesting.

Although story-related problems such as these often arrive in a swarm, they can be picked off one by one. For example, ask if the script has a sense of story takeoff; if not, create one. Does the story seem to be heading toward a goal, or is it wandering? Does it track the problem, or is it confused and vague? Do the stakes escalate until they are life-shaping or life-threatening? Does the story address the dramatic problem that organizes the plot: will the hero kill the monster, win the case, win the love interest, or the like? Does the problem force protagonist and antagonist to make difficult choices that escalate the drama? Is there a showdown at the end in which the dramatic question is resolved? Ask yourself such questions as you write, as you review your script, and as you rewrite.

Many stories can be energized when an engine is invented to drive the action.

The engine can be a villain who is made more menacing and active. Stories can also be brought to life with a new dramatic situation that organizes the material. Many science fiction stories work this way: a monster from hell escapes and the hero(es) is(are) the only one(s) who can eliminate it *(The Andromeda Strain)*. More modestly, a character may be confronted by a need or a goal that organizes the story. *Sleepless in Seattle* and its clone, *Only You,* work this way. *Unforgiven* is organized around the hero's need to win the bounty that will save his farm. *Immortal Beloved* was tied together by a mystery that needed to be resolved.

A boring script can be energized by characters who are so full of life that they almost write the story. The characters in *Bullets over Broadway, My Favorite Year, Moonstruck,* and the top television sitcoms illustrate the point. This strategy requires distinctive characters who are emotionally charged and bursting with attitudes and hang-ups.

Some scripts are larded with so much exposition that they lack forward momentum. You can spot this weakness when characters spend too much time examining their past, their present, their motives, and other soporific topics. Too much exposition can dilute the emotional focus on the dramatic problem. *The story should focus on the problem being tracked in the A-storyline or the work may lack drama.* This point does not conflict with earlier advice on the importance of writing characters enriched with backstory and internal conflict. A balance must be struck here, so that the backstory and the exposition do not interfere with the momentum and focus of the drama. On each of these points, a sense of story should guide the writer to a proper balance between the A- and B-storylines. This story sense should indicate where the script is dragging, when characters are over- or underrevealed, and when the pace and tension require adjustment. (See Chapter 7, pages 211–217.)

Does the Plot "Work"?

Most plots are based on how the problem is presented, tracked, and resolved. Think of the dramatic problem as the arch of the spanning bridge; the incidents of the plot are like the blocks that are shaped and arranged so they form the supporting arch of the plot that spans from beginning to end. Most plots follow a three-part pattern: the problem asserts, it aggravates, and it is resolved.[4] This evolution allows the writer to exercise the characters as they struggle with the problem. Three-act structure offers a reliable progression for organizing an idea into a concept and then into story. The progression from idea to concept to plot to story is easily summarized:

$$\text{Idea + Problem = Concept}$$
$$\text{Concept + Sequence of Incidents = Plot}$$
$$\text{Plot + Characters = Story}$$

---

[4]Exceptions to three-act structure are uncommon, but *Full Metal Jacket* and *Guarding Tess* seem to contain two acts; *Thelma and Louise* and *Apollo 13* seem to have four acts.

Without a viable plot, scripts bog down. Soft spots in the plot include situations, characters, and dialogue that are predictable. These problems can be fixed by adding a twist, inserting a surprise, and/or making the problem more intractable. *Pulp Fiction* demonstrates unpredictability and loopy menace. When writer-director Quentin Tarantino added interesting characters, pounding dialogue, and a bizarre story universe, the result was a special film.

A good plot avoids gaps in story logic, pacing, and intensity; if you find them in your script, they should be tightened and dramatized. Examine your plot for what is real. What might happen to surprise the audience? If the plot seems contrived, manipulative, and fake, rewrite until it feels honest and true. Avoid "plotty" stories populated with dull characters who try to entertain with empty spectacle, violence, and cheap thrills.

Fixing the plot sometimes requires disassembling the incidents, sorting them out, discarding what feels false and contrived, saving what is worthwhile, adding new actions, and then bolting the entire contraption together again. If this requires rethinking everything—the theme, the backstory, the problem, the conflict, the characters, the frame, and the emotional slant—do it. These are major tasks, but if the story concept seems worth saving, go for it. Until the story is right, it is unlikely that the script will work. *The main cause of script failure is story weaknesses.*

After the story is reworked, the scenes and sequences are woven together so there is logic and motivation for what happens. The scenes should make their points clearly as they build in intensity. When you are sure that the story concept and the event of the story work, redo the beat sheet, rewrite the scenes, and correct the story problems. A friend or collaborator may be helpful as you carry out this difficult work. (See Chapters 2 and 3.)

Is the Story Logical?

Audiences will accept a giant leap in logic for stories that are fanciful *(Babe, Peggy Sue Got Married, Back to the Future)*, but they are less tolerant toward realistic stories that abuse common sense. This problem, quite fixable, occurs because the writer is so close to the material that illogic and sappiness are not noticed. Example: In *Impulse*, the heroine (Theresa Russell, portraying a detective) is driving when her car breaks down. Russell manages to make it into a service station, but she must wait for her car to be repaired. Glancing about, she notices a nearby saloon, which she enters. Sitting at the bar, Russell orders a drink and discovers that the man sitting next to her is the criminal who is being sought by every cop in the city! This extremely coincidental meeting does not seem to bother her, and the pair leave and spend the night together. The illogic of this chance meeting and their affair broke the back of the story for me. *Die Hard with a Vengeance* also suffered this way.

Logic problems can be corrected by rewriting the plot on one or two pages; the brief length should make it easier to ask, *How likely is it that such-and-such could happen, given the circumstances of the story?* If the answer is not very, adjust the circumstances, justify the incident, and eliminate whatever is causing the logic problem. Even though such fixes can be difficult, your invest-ment in the story's credibility should make the added effort worthwhile. Logic problems often arise when a script's characters are so undeveloped that the writer must turn to incidents of plot to make the story entertaining. (See Chap-ter 3).

Is the Script Too Angry or Too Grim?

Some new writers are drawn to stories that are relentlessly unhappy, grim, depressing, and angry. Such stories may negatively assault the audience, despite the writer's passion. Writers lighten heavy stories by "fizzing" the work with humor, irony, metaphor, or adventure that mask angry passion. *Pulp Fiction, My Favorite Year,* and *Postcards from the Edge* use humor to defuse their underlying seriousness. (See Chapter 1.)

Does the Script Target One of the Primary Audience Groups?

The script should target at least one of the three audience groups—youth, young adult, adult—and should not drift away from this focus. (See Chapter 1.)

Does the Script Address One of the Basic Emotional Slants?

The script may need to be rewritten so it makes the audience laugh, feel sad-ness, experience fear, or have some combination of these emotions. A clear fix on the story's emotional slant will make dramatizing more likely. Do not slight this topic, for it is the key to dramatizing the story and the characters. (See Chapter 1.)

Does the Story Play a Single Emotional Note?

When the main character is written on a single emotional note throughout, the script may be diminished. I felt this happened with Kathy Bates's character in *A Home of Their Own.* As does a symphony, a movie story should swing through a range of emotional "colors." The audience should laugh, cry, gasp with fear, worry, tense up, and experience dramatic ups and downs. Even the most intense thrillers often include moments of comic relief so the audience can relax and brace for the next terror.

Does the Story Begin Early Enough?

Many stories take too long to begin. They dawdle along while introducing characters, establishing the story universe, and setting up the story. A large part of the first act of *Only You* is spent setting up a story that does not begin until the heroine arrives in Venice and meets the man of her dreams—twenty minutes or so into the story. Most stories benefit when they are started on the first page, as in *The Terminator*; at the least, do your best to get the story under way within the first five pages or so. If ten or fifteen minutes of preliminaries precede the "button" that starts the story, the script may need to begin sooner. Exceptions? Absolutely. If the setting of the story is complex and exotic, its revelations may sustain interest, as in *Jurassic Park, Alien,* and *Cool Hand Luke*.

Starting the story in the first few pages of the script can be done subtly, as in *The Verdict* and *Sleepless in Seattle*. These films introduce the main characters in ways that connect directly to the problem of the story. This point is another that is difficult to define because the question of how much warm-up should front-end the story depends on so many variables. However, the beginning of wisdom on this point is appreciating that stories can seldom start too early, but they often start too late.

Stories can be jump-started through voice-over from a narrator or a character *(Shirley Valentine)*, or a graphic can fill in backstory *(Star Wars)*. Another fast-start strategy is to interrupt the status quo by having a stranger enter the story *(High Plains Drifter)*; or the problem can immediately present itself as a character *(The Terminator)* or as a dramatic incident *(All the President's Men)*. *The Fugitive* combines several of these ploys to launch its story.

It is not necessary to explain everything in the opening minutes of the story. Audiences will usually put up with intriguing confusion for five or ten minutes as the setup gradually reveals itself, as in *In the Heat of the Night* and *Three Days of the Condor*. Scripts generally benefit from strong openings that let the audience know that the story is under way. (See Chapters 1 through 3.)

Is the Plot Too Complicated?

Audiences can lose the thread of a story when the plot contains too many characters, subplots, and twists. This is doubly damaging when playing time is squandered on setting up the plot instead of developing the characters. The fix here hinges on the advice that *audiences care about what happens in the story when they care about what happens to the characters*. Also, audiences have seen most movie plots in one way or another, so that despite disguises and new settings, they are at least vaguely familiar with most story situations. As a result, viewers, like the sultan in *Arabian Nights*, are not easily impressed with plot machinations. Characters, by comparison, have infinite variability. For this reason I recommend using quirky, complex characters to energize simple plots. If this proposition is reversed, the story may be in trouble. (See Chapters 1, 2, 3, and 5.)

Does the Story Have Something to Say?

Does the story connect with a major life concern—family, success, identity, inner peace, love, belonging, or the like? Part of the success of films such as *Forrest Gump, Pulp Fiction,* and *Sleepless in Seattle* is their connection to popular values and opinions. When a film touches on such a value, audiences are more likely to turn out to see it. *The Terminator* had this effect because it touched upon the public's mistrust of technology and "star wars" weaponry. However, because there is usually a one- to three-year lead time on most movies, it is difficult to anticipate what the public will be thinking when the movie is released. Even so, writers tend to go with the message in their hearts.

Writers dig into thematic values by thinking about what they wish to say in their story and how it seems to relate to what is happening in the world. If the script lacks a theme or deeper meaning, the writer rewrites until the material contains this content. Often it takes but a line or two of dialogue and/or an incident to make a social, philosophical, or ethical comment. The goal is to give the script a thoughtful observation or a life lesson that is based on the subtextual meaning of the story. Once the notion has been grasped, it can be kneaded into the script. (See Chapter 2.)

REWRITING PROBLEMS WITH THE CHARACTERS

Are the Characters Motivated?

Characters are energized by conflict, by their responses to one another, by their psychology and backstory, and by the incidents of plot. Interesting characters have identity. They have professions, lives, needs, and dreams. Motivated characters make dramatic choices that lead to conflict and apparent defeat for the hero during the Act II confrontation. In the climactic scene, the hero's victory is all the more sweet because it has been earned through struggle. This development shows when Galvin turns down Bishop Brophy's settlement offer in *The Verdict* (Shot 26) and hence must confront Ed Concannon. Their legal battle leads to Galvin's apparent defeat in the courtroom and then to final victory when he locates his surprise witness. (See Chapters 4 and 5.)

Characters, Plot, and Story

Plot is what the author wants to happen; story is what the characters want to happen. This is not a slogan; it is a plan for writing, because when the author becomes the vessel that allows characters to speak, they can help to write their stories. This approach is the opposite of one that arbitrarily defines who the characters are and what they should say and do. Learning to mind-surf with the characters so they are given enough freedom to live their stories and express their hearts takes time, but it is a collaboration that I recommend highly. More than any single strategy, creating fresh, unpredictable characters will help you to write original stories. Without this approach, the characters may end up delivering empty plot contrivances that fail to work because the characters are not "alive." Avoid writing scripts like this by searching out the characters' beliefs and values. Do they have interior lives—problems, backstories, and passions? Are the characters opinionated and distinctive? Do they have conflicting traits that drive the story? Have they distinguished between what they *want* and what they *need* to be complete? If these values are lacking, write them in. When you give life to your characters, they should give life to your story. (See Chapter 5.)

Does the Story Contain a Powerful Conflict Between Hero and Villain?

Most stories take off when a problem connects the hero to a powerful villain. The hero should be someone for whom the audience can root. Usually, the villain is more powerful than the hero. Is the villain complex and motivated? Does the villain have a counter-theme that suggests his or her motivation? Are there moments when external forces create eruptions of conflict and emotion in your characters? When they are stoked emotionally, characters behave dramatically, even when the provocation seems slight (as when the heroine's friend in *Sleepless in Seattle* [Shot 151] becomes tearful while summarizing the plot of *An Affair to Remember*). The emotional explosion can be based on a major incident, as when the hero's warning of the cyborg's impending attack on the police station is ignored in *The Terminator* (Shot 159).

Most scripts benefit when there is an unequal conflict between hero and villain—the poor kid against the snob from the ritzy school, the old-timer against the neighborhood bully, sodbuster against gunfighter, and so forth. If your story lacks drama, crank up the hero-villain conflict. This can be done by investing your scenes with injustice, unfairness, and outrage that connects to the hero's suffering.

Be clear on the nature of the conflict. For example, *The Verdict* focuses on how a wrecked lawyer is redeemed when he manages to pull his life together. It is this conflict, not whether Galvin will defeat Concannon, that is tracked throughout the script and that informs every scene in the movie. *Strong stories have strong internal and external conflicts.* (See Chapter 2.)

Are the Characters Interesting?

Do the characters have distinctive personalities? Do we care what happens to them? Characters should contain imperfections and vulnerabilities that are part of what motivates them. Characters who lack faults and weaknesses may be too perfect for audiences to care about. These questions relate to the nature-nurture influences that drive the characters.

Your sense of story must be used here, for if the characters are too needful, the material can become sentimental. The reverse is a story so stuffed with selfish, nasty characters that there is no one for whom the audience can root. *Good Fellas, Basic Instinct,* and *House of Games* have so many scuzzy characters that I didn't much care what happened to any of them. When there is no one to root for, it is easy to lose interest in the movie. *This simple point is ignored with surprising frequency, and many stories are diminished because of it.*

Most films contain characters who are admirable, although they may appear to be otherwise. Humphrey Bogart, Tommy Lee Jones, Harvey Keitel,

Jennifer Jason Leigh, Linda Fiorentino, and Whoopi Goldberg excel in playing characters who occupy a shady corner of the moral high ground. Despite imperfections, their characters are appreciated by audiences.

It is human nature to want heroes and antiheroes to triumph over villains. If the underdog hero seems about to be defeated by the villain, the audience worries. Worry leads to suspense and tension that increases as the climactic scene approaches. Whether the hero wins or loses with grace, the audience should leave the theater feeling satisfied. As noted elsewhere in this text, the plan for making this happen is simple but demanding: *Make audiences want something, make it seem unobtainable, then find an unexpected way to give it to them.* This advice asks you to figure out what you are promising the audience, especially regarding the main character and his or her struggle over the problem of the story. Are you promising them the right thing? Is the promise of the story delivered? In most cases, what is being promised is the event of the story, which occurs in the climactic scene. What happens in this beat should be what the audience has been encouraged to expect—and what it wants to see occur— victory for the hero and his or her allies. (See Chapters 3 and 5.)

Is There Positive Change in the Hero?

To test for positive change in your story, ask whether the challenge of the dramatic ordeal has made the hero stronger or more insightful in some way. Positive change in the main character usually occurs when he or she resolves a problem connected to the B-storyline, such as the quest for love, trust, confidence, respect, or the like. Unlike the villain, the hero must struggle to victory while maintaining the moral high ground. At times, the hero's moral posture may seem like a disadvantage, but in the end (as in *The Verdict*) it is often the source of courage and endurance that provides the ultimate margin of victory.

In some cases, the inner problem may not be entirely cured, but it improves sufficiently for the story to end on an optimistic note. All of this is referred to as a "positive arc of character," i.e., the hero changes for the better. *The Verdict* makes us believe that Galvin changes for the better because he wins the case and (apparently) stops drinking. These events connect to Galvin's inner problem because they signal that he is finally free of the humiliation of the Lillibridge case. Unless there is positive change in the hero, the audience may feel that there was no point to the movie. (See Chapter 5.)

Other Character Problems

Does the story have a hero? Does the story focus on the right character? The main character is usually the person who experiences the most emotion, solves the problem, undergoes the most change, and is the one the audience wants to see win. Shortcomings on this point occur when the focus of the story keeps shifting from one person to another or when the story is populated with dull characters who lack interior life and motivation. Emotionally enriched characters have strong feelings that cause them to react, often unpredictably, to the incidents of the plot. When characters are alive in the writer's imagination, there is a chance that they will be alive on the page and on the screen. Examples abound: Harvey Keitel in *The Piano*, Glenn Close in *Fatal Attraction*, Marlon Brando in *On the Waterfront*, Geraldine Page in *The Trip to Bountiful*, or the cast of *Bullets over Broadway*. (See Chapter 5.)

REWRITING PROBLEMS WITH THE SCENES

Do the Scenes Lack Focus?

First, ask whether each scene makes its point. Many new writers are unsure about what they wish to say in the beat, and this vagueness shows in the script. To correct the problem, examine whether the scene makes its point clearly and dramatically. *Weakness on this point is one of the main causes of script failure.*

Is the outcome of the scene in doubt until the last possible moment? Locate the moment when the scene climaxes and makes its point. If that moment is vague or does not exist, sharpen the focus.

Sometimes a weak scene can be cut or combined with another. Test each scene to determine whether it is fuzzy or weak, or whether it is even necessary. Do the conflict and the drama of the scene reveal the characters, or does revelation occur without a struggle? Review the Galvin-Sweeney-Concannon scene from *The Verdict* (Shot 38) that was analyzed in Chapter 4; note how dramatically and clearly this scene makes its point.

Has the Emotional Juice Been Wrung Out of the Scenes?

Professional scripts set up and exploit moments when characters experience powerful emotions. Does your script contain such "hits"? Do they reveal the inner fears, needs, dreams, and goals of the characters? Some writers set up emotional incidents, but instead of exploiting them, they leapfrog over them because they are unable to handle the feelings stirred up. If you feel discomfort at such times, change your attitude, for emotional moments are what you should be exploiting. Intense emotions are what characters should be feeling, so wring this juice from every opportunity. If there is no juice, rewrite the scene until it contains emotion. This is done by investing conflict, emotion, and passion in the characters, making them lonely, angry, fearful, mistrustful, horny, or whatever makes them vulnerable and edgy. The scene should find a way to tap into that emotion, as when Reese tells Sarah that he has traveled across time to be with her (*The Terminator*, Shot 211), or when Brad Pitt's character goes berserk when his wife is killed in *Legends of the Fall*. Screenwriters whip up emotion in characters and capture it on paper. If the action becomes excessive, it can be tidied up during rewriting. *Scenes are more likely to suffer from too little emotion than from too much emotion.*

Are the Scenes Emotionally Flat Because They Deal with Exposition?

When characters spend too much time discussing the plot, they have little time for emotional interaction. As a result, the audience is subjected to the movie equivalent of a party where everyone chitchats politely about trivial matters, sips mineral water, and goes home. Boorrrinng! Even when the story is reserved and formal (*Remains of the Day*), emotional undercurrents can rustle like snakes, quietly energizing the characters and the story. Sex, disputation, and/or violence—subdued or blatant—can energize dull scenes.

Scenes play as long as they do because they need time to unleash the characters emotionally. Flat scenes often use their time to explain the plot rather than to heat characters emotionally. Scenes with too much exposition often lack conflict and drama, so avoid this by focusing the confrontation on characters who are emotionally charged. Work your exposition into the dialogue in a way that reveals the characters. For an example of this approach, see *Witness* (Shot 77), when Rachel pleads with the Amish Elders until they agree to hide Book in their community until he recovers. Her speech is loaded with plot exposition and emotional content as she pleads for protection of her son. (See Chapters 4, 5, 6, and 7.)

Do the Scenes Lack Energy?

Energy is the emotional intensity that the writer has invested in the plot incidents and the characters. Writing at this level requires intense focus and concentration so that plot incidents will seize attention so tightly that the audience can scarcely breathe. Examples: *Pulp Fiction,* when Samuel L. Jackson outmaneuvers a pair of trigger-happy robbers; *The Verdict* (Shot 40), when Galvin is confronted by Dick Doneghy—the latter is so angry over the hero's refusal of the bishop's settlement offer that for a moment it seems that the two men will come to blows. Moments such as these grow out of backstory, how the characters are imagined, the dramatic situation, and the location. For an example of how these values combine, note Shot 122C of *Witness,* when Book phones police headquarters and learns that his partner (Carter) has been murdered. The news of Carter's death puts Book in a dangerous mood, so when three toughs hassle him, Book reacts violently. The energy of this scene comes from the backstory, the situation, the location, and the nature of the characters.

To energize a weak scene, make the characters edgy, grumpy, annoyed, needful, or whatever winds them with emotion. That energy can be latent or snoozing, as in *Unforgiven,* which presents William Munny as an aging man in homely overalls and a cheap haircut who is reputedly a legendary killer. The story almost convinces us that Munny has lost whatever killer instinct he might have had, but in the climactic scene his terrible nature roars forth.

Scenes can be energized by restaging them in another location. A love scene or a fight would play one way if staged in an apartment or a campsite but would play differently if staged at a church picnic or beneath crowded stands during a football game. A scene can be energized by a change in the weather, as in *Fatal Attraction,* when a sudden rain forces Glenn Close and Michael Douglas to seek shelter in a restaurant.

An effective energizer is the "dog heavy," a character who appears in a scene so the hero can demonstrate how she or he responds to trouble. The haughty salespeople who embarrassed the heroine of *Pretty Woman* illustrate.

Desperate circumstances can energize a scene, as when Sarah discovers that Reese has been wounded after the attack on the police station in *The Terminator* (Shot 182). (See Chapters 2 and 4.)

Are the Scenes Too Long?

Double-check scenes that extend beyond three or four pages; the characters may be talking too much. Also be sure that your scenes are not expanded bits that deal with plot. Although every bit and scene should reveal the characters while advancing the plot (however slightly), movie scenes are mainly used to reveal what the characters are feeling. To see this advice in action, reread the Galvin-Sweeney-Concannon scene analyzed in Chapter 4 or read any of the scenes cited in the media notes for Chapter 4 in Appendix A.

A long, talky scene can sometimes be replaced with visuals that play more quickly and more dramatically. Some scenes are too long because they begin too early. A scene need not start when the parties initially arrive and meet. Instead, cut into the scene after it has been under way and disagreements are flaring. This strategy eliminates warm-up discussion, as shown in Shot 15 of *The Verdict,* when insurance agent Alito informs Bishop Brophy of Galvin's shoddy record. The preliminary chitchat is out of the way when this expositional beat begins, which allows it to focus directly and immediately on Galvin's record.

It is impractical to generalize about when a scene is too long or when it should begin or end, but we can note that dialogue should address the point of the scene and not wander. Dialogue in most scenes can be cut when the writer is alert to dramatic silences that indicate that something important has occurred. Silences are treasured by actors, because such moments allow them to express emotions nonverbally, through close-ups.

Although you should be sparing with instructions about where the actors should pause in your dialogue (this is an example of directing with the script), there are times when judicious use of such instructions can help readers appreciate key plot and character moments that might otherwise be missed. Examples of how writers use the "pause" convention can be found throughout the four main study films: Mamet uses "(BEAT)" to signal a pause for a dramatic moment; other writers use "(PAUSE)" or a series of three or four dots (ellipses) to indicate hesitation and silent moments that enhance the drama. Stage directions can signal a pause or a silence: *Suddenly everyone looks at John.* Or the person speaking might perform a piece of business. In *The Verdict* (Shot 30), as Concannon preps his legal staff, he writes the trial date on a blackboard. This action encourages a pause that punches up the moment. Whether the actors and director utilize such guidance by the screenwriter depends on whether it suggests a pace and energy that they feel is appropriate. Such concerns arise during production when certain lines refuse to play as written and thus require on-the-spot rewriting by the filmmakers. This happens frequently.

If you bog down on scenes that are too long, study the scene examples in the list of media for Chapter 4 in Appendix A for a sense of how long scenes play. If this does not work, hand-copy a scene from a script, then read what you have written while the movie version plays on video. Review the scene three or four times. It takes an hour or so to study a scene this way, but it can enable you to figure out how the beat organizes, how it is driven, and how long it plays. This exercise should help you write your own scenes. Also look at the breakdown of *The Verdict* in Appendix C, which times each scene and sequence. Many writers time scripts to overcome the movie's emotional rush (which can confuse how long the beats play). Timing scenes and sequences can help you sense when to start and end scenes, and how long they should play. (See Chapter 4.)

Are the Scenes Too Short?

Scenes that are too short may not be necessary. Or they may be making the wrong point. Or the point may need to be reworked. Or perhaps the beat can be combined with another scene or restaged. Or another character can be added. When characters get together for a scene, it should be for a reason: something must be decided, an issue or question raised, old business settled. Movies are too intense to support a weak scene that does not work for the story. (See Chapter 4.)

Do the Scenes Lack Structure, Tension, and Conflict?

When a scene does not feel right, check its structure. Most scenes have a beginning-middle-end shape that mirrors the three-act structure of the overall story. Does the scene build to a climax? Does the scene contain twists or surprises that increase the drama? Does the scene change polarity? Does the scene involve a chase-and-capture or a chase-and-escape dynamic? Does the scene contain conflict? Most important, does the scene make its point clearly? The writer should be totally certain about the point to be made in the scene.

Most scenes should contain conflict. Scenes that lack conflict usually lack the purposefulness expected of drama. You can create conflict by introducing dispute—someone lied, failed to appear, behaves strangely, broke a promise, or whatever. The goal is dramatic conflict that physically or mentally threatens the characters and causes tension. *Lack of motivated conflict is another cause of script failure.*

Although we have discussed how scenes operate, this advice must be kept general, because screenwriters are a contentious lot who delight in creating scenes with wonderful originality. Do your best to strike a balance here. On the one hand, do not become ensnared with the fetish of scene structure or anything that cramps your creativity; on the other hand, acknowledge that screenplays contain structures that have become traditional because they work. Here again I am splitting the middle: yes, standards exist, *but* . . . do not become a slave to them. Freedom, spirit, creativity, the high-wire-trapeze without a net is where the good stuff is. If the result is a broken story, fix it. Try for scenes that are so far out that they seem unusable, then save the wackiness and rewrite it into a scene that works. (See Chapter 4.)

Would Scenes Benefit from Torquing?

Torquing creates a diversionary context that allows scenes to entertain as they reveal exposition. As noted in Chapter 6, torquing occurs in *The Terminator*, when the spectacular visuals of a car chase hold the audience's attention while Reese tells Sarah about his mission.

Scenes can be torqued by subtext, as in Shot 53 of *The Verdict* when Concannon simultaneously baits and preps Dr. Towler. Torquing can relate to the backstory, as in *In the Line of Fire* when the villain blames the hero for failing to prevent the assassination of President Kennedy. Scenes can be torqued by the chemistry that flashes between two characters, as in *Body Heat, Miami Blues,* and *Fatal Attraction.* (See pages 172 and 199.)

REWRITING THE DIALOGUE

Tape recorders and camcorders are tools for checking the rhythm and quality of your dialogue. Tape your work and listen to the playback. Taping can help you spot what is strong and what is weak in your dialogue. Rewrite as needed. Dialogue can also be sharpened by having friends act out your material. Tape them, take notes, and ask questions about what the dialogue reveals about the characters being portrayed and what it reveals regarding subtext. Such exercises may expose one or more of the dialogue problems discussed below.

Dialogue from Weak Characters

Effective dialogue springs from characters who are imagined so vividly that they seem to acquire life and independence from the writer. If characters are boring in imagination, their dialogue will probably be boring as well. Dialogue that does not reveal the characters requires digging deeper so that your characters speak their hearts to you. Although becoming one with the characters requires work, this ability is essential to quality dialogue. Count on spending at least a year learning how to imagine at this level. Until then, connecting with the characters and writing their dialogue may be difficult. (See Chapter 6.)

Dialogue That Lacks Subtext

If the dialogue lacks subtextual meaning, the story may seem superficial. To fix this, explore what your characters think and feel, then work that content into the dialogue—but make the character interesting. If Aunt Mary lacks interest, energize her with a rich inner life and passionate nature. Pump things up, dramatize! The police psychologist in *The Terminator* (Shot 153) could have questioned Reese in a straightforward manner. Instead, his dialogue had a sneering subtext that enriched the scene because the audience realized the truth of Reese's warning about the cyborg.

Repetitive Dialogue

Repetitive dialogue repeats what the audience already knows. When rewriting, examine each speech for what it reveals about the character, the plot, the theme, and the relationships. If a word or a line is unnecessary, cut it.

Dialogue that overexplains excludes audiences from the movie and makes them spectators rather than participants. When the dialogue is too on-the-nose—when it sounds as though Morris the Explainer has slipped into the show—review a favorite script while the movie plays on video. Absorb its rhythms and use that insight to pace the dialogue in your script.

Repetitive dialogue shows up in small ways, as when character names are repeated to the point of distraction. Usually a script needs only one or two mentions to let the audience identify a character. Name only those characters who require names, for audiences have a limited capacity for connecting movie names with movie faces, so when a character says, "John's sick," the audience must know who John is. One way around this is for the dialogue to refer to characters by their appearance—the blond with the tattoos, what's-her-name with the hair.

Preachy Dialogue

Do not tout your favorite cause in the dialogue, because it may intrude on the story and take the audience out of the movie. Scripts that deal with abortion, welfare, drugs, ecology, ethnicity, religion, and other hot-potato issues must be handled delicately, because movies aim to entertain, not to create controversy that jeopardizes the commercial prospects of the movie. When writers step onto a soapbox, the audience must not become defensive; rather, it should be swept along by the drama. Proselytizing in a movie is sure to be spotted and just as surely to be resented by one group or another.

This does not mean stripping your story of content, whatever it might be. Movies can deal with any topic imaginable, but they are dramatic entertainment, not propaganda. *Scripts that address serious issues should do so entertainingly.*

Dialogue touting a cause is usually more effective when it reflects a character's attitude than when it states the issue outright. This is done by insinuating the issue so the audience is encouraged to support or to reject the position. For example, *The Verdict* does not rail against corruption within the Boston legal system, yet that value shows through indirectly and as subtext. Similarly, *Under Fire*, a drama about journalism and the Nicaraguan revolution of the late 1970s, chides the role of the press in such historical events. Less successfully, *Medicine Man* deals with saving the rain forests, but the dialogue is so preachy and shrill that the film was not successful. In most cases social content can be marbled into the story subtextually, as in Galvin's summation speech in *The Verdict* (Shot 94). (See Chapter 6.)

Dialogue That Lacks Emotion

Lack of emotion in dialogue can be due to the writer's spending too much time on plot and backstory, or it can result when the characters are dead inside. Flat dialogue can also be the result of tweedy, platonic speeches that fail to get into what the characters are feeling emotionally. When a beat extends for more than a page, it is probably a scene that should be dealing with the inner feelings of the characters, not working out travel plans or philosophizing. This, too, is a judgment call, and though movies should have intellectual content, they are mainly about what characters feel and do, not what they think. The thoughtfulness of a film often arrives via the thematic observation that is implied by the story. (See Chapters 5 and 6.)

Dialogue Rhythms and Patterns

When the dialogue clumps along with metronomic regularity, give it a hot foot or slow it down. *Pulp Fiction* does this when Samuel L. Jackson's character shifts gears by quoting from Ezekiel; the measured cadence of the biblical citation creates an effective break from discussions of hamburgers and other banal concerns of the assassins.

Dialogue can be rewritten so it is salty, humorous, embittered, colorful, intense, or in some other way interesting. Inventory some of the people you know and select those who have distinctive speech patterns; or recast a character with a person or an actor who has a distinctive way of speaking. Rewrite the dialogue to suit the temperaments, ethnicity, education, and life styles of the characters. Indicate your intention in the stage directions: *Vince speaks with a hissy, poisonous lisp; Betty's chirpiness cannot hide her melancholia.*

Most important, listen to how your characters speak in imagination. If they all speak with the same rhythms and energy, change their dialogue pattern to something fresh and distinctive. If Beth the schoolteacher is flat, change her into a Valley girl, a drill instructor, a worrier, or whatever makes her character work for the story. If a character speaks without energy, imagine someone like Martin Scorcese in the role and use his warp-speed speaking style to help you to rewrite the dialogue.

As noted earlier, conflict energizes dialogue because angry characters often become contemptuous, cynical, nasty, annoyed, and emotionally hot. Use that heat to pop kernels of dialogue. If you follow this advice, make sure that there is a reason for the fight you concoct; otherwise, the exchange may sound like nagging or bickering, which is seldom entertaining. (See Chapter 6.)

Writing in Dialect

Often, a note in the stage directions is enough to cue readers that characters in the story speak in dialect. Using stage directions to set up dialogue spoken in an accent or dialect allows writers to avoid typing tricks, elisions, and other contortions aimed at communicating the flavor of the dialogue. Indicate a foreign accent by stating that the character speaks in a thick, moderate, or slight Irish, Italian, or whatever accent.

When characters speak in a foreign language, use stage directions that inform the reader that the dialogue will be spoken in Greek, Chinese, or whatever. The speech itself is then written in English, not the foreign language.

Dialogue for period stories should avoid words that are inappropriate to the period; an anachronistic word or phrase can jolt an audience out of a film. *The Oxford English Dictionary* presents the origins and first usage of many words. Specialized volumes on slang may be useful as well.[5]

Researching antique dialogue often requires researching newspapers and plays from the period, as well as films set in the era, since many movies have been enriched by advice from historians and other specialists. Period stories may also require writers to research costumes, architecture, life-styles, and other antique elements that connect to the dialogue. (See page 167.)

Marks of Punctuation and Dialogue

Exclamation marks can be used to indicate excitement! Several such marks indicate considerable excitement!! Dialogue typed in capital letters often means the words are SHOUTED!!!

A speech that is broken with three dots indicates hesitation . . . or a pause. Four dots at the end of a speech indicates that the line . . . trails off. . . .

Dialogue that is bracketed by single or double quotation marks indicates that the words have a context and/or a special meaning. In *The Verdict* (Shot 65), Concannon accepts Dr. Thompson as an "expert witness." The quotation marks (implying *so-called*) indicate the subtext of Concannon's contempt for Thompson—and for Galvin's sorry case. As scripts are read and written, screenwriters accumulate punctuation tricks, so I will not extend the list. Although these marks also aim to direct the movie, occasional judicious use of them can give the dialogue a bit of shape and flavor. (See pages 166, 270.)

REWRITING TO IMPROVE DRAMATIZATION

One of the keys to dramatizing is appreciating the basic emotional slant of the story—will it make the audience feel sad, amused, or fearful? Such thinking

---

[5]Among the interesting titles on this topic are Esther Lewin and Albert E. Lewin, *Thesaurus of Slang,* Facts On File, New York, 1988, and Robert L. Chapman, *New Dictionary of American Slang,* Harper & Row, New York, 1986.

connects to whether the story will appeal to children, young adults, or adults. Dramatizing also means deciding whether the story will favor physical action or the emotional life of the characters and whether the story will be done in a real, unreal, or surreal manner. Once you decide these points (they can be thought through gradually, as the material develops), the story has a better chance of being dramatized effectively. These are simple, important values that should not be slighted.

Many new writers do not appreciate how intensely movies are dramatized, because filmmakers make the screen action appear to be normal when it is not. Movie characters are eased into extraordinary situations so gradually that the audience is persuaded to believe they are watching a realistic tale. Much of the work of screenwriting involves making the plot incidents and the character motivations believable to the audience. Movies are persuasive on this point, as can be seen even in *The Verdict*, which is tightly written in terms of credibility. Yet it might be asked whether a lawyer as powerful as Concannon would risk hiring Laura as a spy to beat a lowlife such as Galvin, when such an action would place the Catholic Church in the position of paying a woman to prostitute herself. This decision raises another improbability, which is to convince a woman such as Laura to debase herself as she did. Still another unlikelihood is the hero's decision to turn down Bishop Brophy's settlement offer without consulting with his client. The persuasive rush of the story, however, easily plasters over these flights of fancy, which show up in many scripts when they are examined closely. In most cases, such flaws can be justified, eliminated, or made invisible with additional work.

Dramatization stresses the characters and forces them into life-shaping or life-threatening crises. This ties into another of our primary mantras: *Drama is the reaction of character to crisis.* The crisis in *The Verdict* is caused by the hero's decision to fight the case against the most powerful lawyer in Boston. Despite Galvin's foolhardy action, we are persuaded (because of the Lillibridge incident) that he might do such a thing. With Galvin battling impossible odds, a crisis ensues that almost destroys him before he wins the case. Thus, dramatization adds to the tension, conflict, and problem in ways that hold the attention of the audience. (See Chapter 7.)

Dramatizing the Story through the Locations

There is drama to be had when the writer appreciates and exploits the settings used in the story. *The Verdict*, for example, plays mainly in interior settings, yet the locations used were able to add drama as well as visual content. *Nobody's Fool* uses a small town in upstate New York during winter in ways that make everything that happens seem personal and believable. One of the keys to making the location work was the cold weather. Unlike most movies, this story makes it obvious that it is about people in a *cold*, wintry town, because we see the breath of the actors as they speak. The snow looks real because it is real, and when Jessica Tandy asks Paul Newman to fix her railing, or when he steals off with his boss's snowblower, the cold weather supplies credibility to their actions. The story's believability also extends to its colorfully quirky characters—a flawed mix of people that seem so real that we forget that we are watching Paul Newman in a star turn. Instead, we are caught up in a yarn about a sixty-year-old guy named Sully who is boarding with his former elementary school teacher. We believe that everybody in Sully's clique knows everybody's business—and nobody cares because they have grown up with each other in the town and they accept each other, warts and all.

The advice from this example is to examine your story for how it uses its locations. Are they interesting? Have they been carefully selected and researched? Are the characters motivated or influenced by the settings, or are the backgrounds unimportant wallpapering that has not been thought through? Most important, ask if the settings are working for the story and helping you to write the script. (See Chapters 2 and 8.)

REWRITING FOR THE CAMERA

The strategies listed in Chapter 8 ("Writing for the Camera") suggest dozens of ways to add visual content. Some of these may require restaging beats so they play in exterior locations rather than in interior settings. Talky scripts can be improved with scenes that can be told with images, rather than with dialogue. A certain amount of editorial distance may be needed for this work, so do not be shy about asking for help. For an example of how imaging works, note how *Sleepless in Seattle* (Shot 137) visualizes the love between father and son by showing Sam and Jonah on a boating trip. Also, examine your story for a value or a custom that can be exploited visually. The barn raising in *Witness* demonstrates the Amish tradition of neighborly cooperation. *Little Women* makes skillful use of antique settings, weather, and a sense of time to enhance its story. If a lake, mountain, cave, swamp, or other natural occurrence is part of the story's frame, why not use it? If the frame has no such locations, think about adding something along these lines.

Stories can be made more visual when characters reveal themselves by what they do, rather than by what they say. Clint Eastwood and other action stars have built careers on scripts that allow them to display character through action. Action does not always mean violence; *My Favorite Year, City Slickers, Bite the Bullet,* and many other films employ visual sequences (one in each act is usually enough) that allow characters to demonstrate who they are through physical action.

When the story is top-heavy with indoor scenes in which characters sit around and talk, rewrite to add visual content. *Movies are motion pictures; they are not illustrated radio.* When a story plays mainly indoors and is talky, invent ways to feed the eye of the audience. *The Verdict* is a useful study in this regard because it mainly uses six interior locations: Galvin's apartment, Concannon's headquarters, O'Rourke's Saloon, Bishop Brophy's headquarters, the hospital, and the courthouse. The interior focus of the story is logical because it deals with mature people and a malpractice suit. The assorted doctors, lawyers, and priests in their respective costumes come together during a cold Boston winter, so naturally they stay inside where it is warm. Even so, the only low-visual interior setting is Galvin's apartment, and its bleakness deliberately reflects the drab life of the character. The other scenes play in spacious interior locations that present considerable visual information. (See Chapter 8.)

REWRITING EXPOSITION AND FIXING FORMAT PROBLEMS

During a television interview, Victor Borge remarked that he gave up the concert hall when he realized that he would never be able to make the piano "talk." This ability—to coax emotion, color, and nuance from a piano—is essential to greatness as a keyboard artist and Borge felt he lacked it. Screenwriters have an easier time when writing stage directions that convey emotion, style, and energy in scripts, but we too must make our work "talk." This task is not made easier by the demands of a script format that insists on a writing style that must be brief, yet colorful and easy to read as it describes the interior and exterior lives of the on-screen characters. The four study films and examples cited in earlier chapters illustrate how this is done.

Writers develop personal styles of writing stage directions and descriptions. Some prefer a lean approach (*The Verdict*), while others like to charm the reader (*The Quiet Man*). *Alien* uses a stark format, while *Ruthless People* is raucous and *The Shawshank Redemption* is straightforward. Script styles can also be novelistic (*How Green Was My Valley*) or whatever catches the writer's fancy. Whatever the style, stage directions should be spare. Readers should be able to zip down pages without being confronted with clunky blocks of exposition. This is mentioned because some buyers skim the script by reading the dialogue and the scene-heading sluglines; these readers give only glancing attention to the stage directions.[6] So, already hobbled by format, we must also avoid lengthy stage directions, camera advice, and secretive instructions to the actors. In spite of these limitations, screenwriters are able to shoehorn their stories into script pages that describe the drama. Doing this means avoiding language that slows or defocuses the read. As discussed in Chapters 9 and 10, the script should read swiftly, without glitches, snags, or confusion.

---

[6]Perhaps you will be less discouraged by this news if you can appreciate how many scripts must be read before a good one turns up. Like any other intelligent person who reads a story, the script reader wants to be hooked into it and to enjoy the read. When this fails to happen after twenty pages or so, the reader shifts into overdrive and begins to speed-read. Readers slow down when a scene or a moment catches their attention. When a reader is pulled deeply into the story, the read slows down; in some cases the reader will reread the entire script if it comes to life and begins to hold interest. Note that readers will not always persevere if the beginning is uninteresting. This seems to have been the case with *Rambling Rose*: Calder Willingham's excellent script was passed over for twenty years, apparently because of a dozen or so pages of prologue. When these were torn off and discarded, the script could be shot almost exactly as written.

Making the Script Fun to Read

Unlike a book or magazine article, screenplays tend to be a special reading experience, because even though millions may see the film version, only a handful of people ever read the script version, and there is something privileged about that. Good scripts are fun to read when the writer conveys the basic energy of the story, whether suspense, humor, drama, or whatever. I know of no better way of learning this skill than by reading scripts carefully and studying the films made from them. (See Chapters 9 and 10.)

Parenthetical Instructions

There are two types of parentheticals: one relates to the dialogue and the other indicates action and business. Dialogue parentheticals are usually centered and placed under the name of the character and above the dialogue. Parenthetical instructions are used when the meaning of a line is not what it seems, i.e., it may have a subtext that involves irony, sarcasm, humor, or whatever. In such cases, use a line-reading parenthetical. For example, in *Witness* (Shot 118) Book tells a tourist that he will rip off her brassiere and strangle her with it if she takes his picture. The dialogue is preceded by the parenthetical note "(smiling)," which indicates that Book is joking. In *Sleepless in Seattle* (Shot 21), Annie is with her mother in the attic trying on an antique wedding gown when their discussion turns to "adjustment" to married life. When the tone shifts from small talk to sexual matters, the parenthetical "(lowering her voice)" indicates the mother's modesty regarding intimate topics. This small but telling moment of family values helps define Annie, her mother, and their social class.

Dialogue parentheticals also are used to indicate which character in a crowd is being addressed: *JOHN (to Mary)*. They also can indicate a pause— (SILENCE); (NO REACTION); (BEAT); (PAUSE)—or a hesitation in a speech. Although parentheticals sometimes annoy actors, writers use them to ensure that their scripts are understood by buyers and other readers. As noted previously, when spec scripts are first offered for sale, they may be a bit heavy on parentheticals. Fat "selling scripts" are often trimmed after sale, when they are rewritten.

Parentheticals connected to action and business can be placed under the character's name, or the parentheticals may break the speech with a brief action description. Thus the dialogue might read: *JOHN (tearing open the letter); MARY (crossing to the window); BILLY (loading the pistol).* Small assists such as these can be found throughout the four main study films; they make scripts easier to visualize, while speeding the read.

Do not use parentheticals to tell the actors when their veins should bulge, when tears should flow, or when their voices should quaver or rage. Actors do not need to be coached on how to perform, so trust them to do their job. The writer's task is to create dramatic scenes that allow actors to do what they do best, to *express emotion* and the inner being of the characters they are portraying. Proper use of parentheticals can be learned by studying scripts while you watch the movies made from them.

WHAT ABOUT THE TITLE?

Although everyone seems to have an opinion on how to title a story, finding one that feels right is a problem. This is especially true because studio marketing and publicity people often argue for titles that will convince the public to buy tickets to the movie. Many scripts are retitled before being released: *The William Munny Killings* was retitled *Unforgiven, Diversion* was retitled *Fatal Attraction,* and the list goes on and on. Thus, titling a movie is not as easy as one might think. As with everything else in a screenplay, the title should work for the material, i.e., it should suggest something about the story that attracts public attention. Sometimes it is enough for a title to describe the task of the story, as in *Breaking the Sound Barrier, Sink the Bismarck, Educating Rita,* and *Quest for Fire.*

Serviceable titles can be tied to the name of one or more of the characters, as in *Sid and Nancy, The Wild Bunch, Young Frankenstein, The Thing, The Outlaw Josey Wales, Norma Rae, The Terminator,* and *Patton.* A location can be used, as in *Paris, Texas; Nashville; Outland; Planet of the Apes;* and *Casablanca.* Titles can be based on a real or fanciful time period, as in *Year of the Gypsies, Groundhog Day, My Favorite Year, Day of the Jackal,* and *Once upon a Time in the West.*

Titles can be graphic—*The Texas Chain Saw Massacre, Kiss the Blood off My Hands, Dying Young*—or they can be more poetic, as in *Of Mice and Men, In the Name of the Father, Inherit the Wind,* and *The Grapes of Wrath.* Some titles are based on a line of dialogue from the movie: . . . *And Justice for All, I Never Sang for My Father, The Gods Must Be Crazy.* Titles can hint at or suggest the story, as in *A Bridge Too Far, The Best Years of Our Lives, Gone with the Wind, When Harry Met Sally,* and *For Whom the Bell Tolls.*

Rather than continuing to scratch my itch for compiling lists and categories, let me conclude this topic by cautioning against titles that do not seem to connect with anything *(The Shawshank Redemption, Legends of the Fall, Choose Me)* or titles that are so long that they cannot fit on a theater marquee. Naturally, even this routine advice does not always apply, since some titles are noteworthy simply because they are so long—e.g., *The Englishman Who Went up a Hill and Came down a Mountain* and *The Positively True Adventures of the Alleged Texas Cheerleader-Murdering Mom).* Another strategy for learning about titles is to browse through a video store and observe which titles are most noticeable. Examine how movies are advertised on the cassette box and which titles are most outstanding or easily remembered.

SUMMARY

Scripts organize around the story concept. This statement of the story idea, plus the problem, usually determines whether the notion is worth writing and rewriting. If the story concept is weak, then chances are the script will be weak as well. If the story concept is interesting, then the story may work. Rewriting the story concept asks writers to think about why they were drawn to the idea and what they wish to say in the story. Rewriting the story concept is a major task that can involve rethinking the inner struggle of the main character, the thematic statement, and how the material is interpreted by the writer. It can also mean enhancing the characters emotionally, thinning the dialogue, sharpening the conflict, creating more interesting settings, and finding ways to visualize and dramatize the story. The root question for doing this work is quite simple, but the writer must not shirk on the answer. It asks the writer one question: *What is the story really about?* This question is central to the entire writing process because it tells authors of their intentions and what they should be saying in the work.

Rewriting involves more than changing lines of dialogue or thinning stage directions. It often means reworking the story, energizing the characters, and creating visually interesting scenes. Rewriting means being sensitive to the dramatic opportunities of your story and its characters so the work's dramatic potential can be realized.

Scripts suffer when they are populated with empty characters who lack inner life because they have been relegated to driving the plot. Such characters serve as human furniture—the bimbo, the bad guy, the bully, and the like. Moments after appearing on-screen, such stereotypical characters define themselves by how they look, dress, and behave. They lack mystery, quirkiness, and humanity. They are the opposite of characters who have complex emotions, who grapple with inner problems, and who are driven to discover who they are. This advice touches on what is arguably the primary lesson in this volume: *Write simple stories with complex characters.*

Rewriting is not penance or a sign of failure; it is a normal part of screenwriting. A positive attitude is important for this phase of the work. Writers endure review and rewriting by accepting that it is better for friends to point out errors than to have buyers discover weaknesses that lead to rejection of the script. Be alert for advice that might improve the material, but be certain that it serves the needs of the story that you wish to write. Be cautious about taking on ideas and "suggestions" that you cannot write or that you do not like.

Exercises

Rewrite the scene that follows on p. 316. As you do, consider the dramatic point to be made in the beat. Ask what is happening with the characters and what images are on the screen. Rewrite the scene as you wish.

The scene is the opening beat of a feature film about immigrants who have left city tenements to find better lives on the Great Plains in the 1880s. The scene, which plays out in a boxcar that is transporting the newcomers to the frontier, immediately introduces the characters and tells what happens to the main characters (Mary and her family).

As written, the scene makes its story point—that the old West presented a hard face to immigrants. Some of the characters are foreign-born, and the scene as written indicates that many of them are afraid of the surrounding wilderness. Although their fear is suggested by the sound of the wind, imagine what else might happen with these people. How can the images be enhanced? The rewrite asks you to reveal more about the settlers, to exploit the dramatic opportunity, and to make the scene more dramatic.

When you finish your rewrite, you might wish to look at Appendix E to see how the scene was professionally rewritten.

```
INT.  RAILWAY BOXCAR - DAY

MARY, a two-year-old, lies awake and watchful in her
sleeping mother's arms.

EXT.  RR TRACK

Wheels whirl over the tracks and smoke pours out of the
chimney.

INT.  BOXCAR

The dark and rattling car is full of immigrants; most of
them are asleep.  In the corner a woman breast-feeds an
infant.  A man with rotting teeth snores.  A young boy
sings to himself, the tune almost inaudible over the noise
of the train.

CAMERA FRAMES on a twenty-ish Irishman named ROMAN, who
peers through a crack in the boxcar.  Light streams
through the opening and flickers across his face.

Mary whimpers.  Her mother, CLEONA, wakes to discover the
baby has wet her diapers.  Roman holds the crying child as
Cleona searches through her bundles for a fresh diaper.

The train slows down.  Cleona and Roman look at one
another for a moment before Cleona hurriedly fishes out a
rag from her bag.  The immigrants begin to chatter in
German, Swedish, and other languages.

A few of the men stand in the rocking car and try to see
through the cracks in the wooden siding.  Their legs are
unsteady.  One almost falls.  Excitement mounts as the
train slows further.  Roman presses his face close to his
peephole.  The families draw their possessions close
around them.

Cleona restrains a fussy Mary in her lap.  The train comes
to a halt.  The immigrants fall silent.  All are alert and
still.  Slowly a low and deep moaning rises from the
silence.  The wind.
```

(*For media that illustrate the points made in this chapter, see Appendix A.*)

CHAPTER 12

Career Counseling for New Screenwriters

After the script is written, what happens next? How does the unattached writer get an agent and "pitch" the script to a potential buyer in a story conference? This chapter discusses how screenwriters manage such tasks.

The fourth and final hat that a screenwriter wears is that of a warrior. This mode is important, because screenwriters must endure a grueling apprenticeship to learn their craft. This is an accomplishment that deserves protection, especially when dealing with those who make script decisions. We become warriors to stay active in an industry that is overrun with meddling executives who have wildly varying degrees of script expertise and story inclinations. We become warriors to protect our work when it is criticized, trashed, or ignored. We become warriors to combat bouts of fear and insecurity that would cripple our ability to write.

New (and not-so-new) writers create scripts every day. Some of these are sparkling and fresh; others are rewrites of previous works. Old and new, these projects crowd around Hollywood's production pipeline, jostling for movie success. To outsiders and newcomers, the business of motion pictures may seem like disorganized tumult, but it is part of the selling ritual that writers endure and that this chapter will examine. To begin with, the chapter offers general advice on how screenwriters relate to the Hollywood system. Next, we examine where writers do their work—in Los Angeles, at home, or elsewhere in the country. This discussion is followed with advice about securing an agent. Finally, the chapter discusses how to pitch your story in story conferences. Although there are specialized books that deal fully with these topics, they are presented here as advice for those who might be contemplating a career in screenwriting.

ADVICE FOR NEW WRITERS

In many ways the movies are similar to businesses that feed capital, energy, and raw materials into one end of the production pipeline so that vacuum cleaners, ball bearings, or whatever roll out of the other end. Movies differ only because the raw materials fed into the Hollywood pipeline are the ideas and the energy of those involved with film production. At its heart, there is not much physical machinery involved in making movies—a camera, a few lights, and sound equipment make up the hardware essentials. What Hollywood feeds on are meetings and conferences where movie people discuss casting, financing, scripts, budgets, distribution, and the like. A key element in all this is the selection and review process that deals with film scripts. Decisions are made about which of the hundreds of scripts—all claiming to be sure box-office winners—should be developed. It is in this stage of trying to select scripts that bear the promise of successful movies that the industry suffers most cruelly from Goldman's Law[1]: *In Hollywood, nobody knows anything.*

Script selection is a source of anxiety and contention, and if the studios could invent a computer program or a machine that would reveal which scripts would pay off at the box office, their business would be much, much easier. As it is, turning script pages into cans of film is somewhat of a guessing game in which studios and production companies bet millions on their script choices. Although their decisions are made carefully, the selection process is inexact and exasperating, as illustrated by *Howard the Duck, Last Action Hero,* and *Radioland Murders,* to single out a few of the titles that did not sell a lot of tickets. Such disappointments are part of the movies, which is why a major studio usually reviews thousands of movie ideas in a year.[2] Twenty or so of these will be made into films. Another fifty or so stories and scripts are funded for possible production in the future.

Screenwriters should have a sense of how much money the script selection process involves and the economic dimension of the movie industry. For a time it was difficult to acquire such information because the founding moguls did not wish competitors and employees to know how well or how poorly their studios were doing. In recent years, however, weekly box-office grosses and star salaries have been published in newspapers as if they were sports scores. In a way they are scores, because the numbers establish box-office winners and losers among the studio players.

The industry's belated candor is connected to the exponential growth of ancillary markets (overseas feature box office, video rentals, and video sales in the United States and overseas). The increased income from these sources means that U.S. filmmakers can spend more on their films, which now employ international stars, lavish productions, and astounding technical expertise that foreign filmmakers are unable to match. As a result, U.S. movies and TV

---

[1]From screenwriter William Goldman, who coined this advice in *Adventures in the Screen Trade* (Warner Books, New York, 1983). The remark asserts that it is all but impossible for anyone to predict which scripts or movies will be successful.
[2]The major studies include Disney, Universal, Warner Brothers, Columbia, TriStar, Paramount, MGM, United Artists, and 20th Century Fox. In addition, movies are produced by fifty or so smaller production companies such as Morgan Creek, Castle Rock, Miramax, New Line, and Imagine. These firms affiliate with studios, which advertise and distribute the production company's films for a share of the profits.

shows have become the preferred motion picture entertainment of audiences nearly everywhere.

The price of our success is being paid by overseas filmmakers, who have suffered precipitous box-office and production declines. *The Los Angeles Times* (July 1, 1994) reported that the European Union lost half of its theater movie audience to American films in the decade between 1984 and 1993. The same decade saw yearly revenues of U.S. films shown in Europe increase from $330 million to $3.6 billion, while those European Union producers who managed to find distributors and theaters that would show their films lost money in most cases. As shown in Table 12-1, the total income of U.S. film and television from all markets amounted to $16 billion in 1993, giving the U.S. movie industry a balance-of-payment surplus that is second only to our aircraft industry. Projections indicate that the movie business will continue to grow for years to come.

TABLE 12-1. Global U.S. Film and Television Sales
(In millions of dollars)

				Average Growth per Year	
Exhibition Window	1988	1993	1998*	1988–1993	1993–1998*
Domestic home video	$2,245	$4,053	$6,027	16.1%	9.7%
Foreign home video	1,531	3,166	4,276	21.4	7.0
Domestic theater rentals	1,875	2,597	3,315	7.7	5.5
Foreign theater rentals	1,463	2,501	3,848	14.2	10.8
Domestic pay television	692	961	1,383	7.8	8.8
Foreign television sales	752	961	1,424	5.6	9.7
Foreign pay television sales	167	604	1,113	52.3	16.8
Domestic TV syndication	306	368	387	4.1	1.0
Domestic basic cable	133	316	460	27.5	9.1
Domestic broadcast networks	111	186	232	13.7	4.9
Cable/CBS/PPV	18	62	282	48.9	70.8
Hotel, motel, other PPV	23	39	57	13.3	9.4
Total Revenue	$9,316	$15,814	$22,804		
Percentage Growth				14.0%	8.8%

*1998 figures are an estimate.
Source: Hollywood Reporter. Data published by *Motion Picture Investor Newsletter,* Paul Kagan Associates.

As noted in earlier chapters, it is difficult for screenwriters to escape the gravitational pull of these figures. They bend the commercial mainstream and the work of screenwriters. The numbers flex their muscles as the gorilla of cost that sits in on every meeting and story conference. The same numbers look over our shoulders as we write, nudging us to create dreamy stories that will attract the international mass audience. If this sounds stressful, it's because it *is* stressful.

Some writers manage to lessen this pressure by living away from the two main production centers, New York and Los Angeles. Regardless of where they reside, screenwriters invent various schemes for living and working. Some teach, or write novels, or run businesses. Some work with partners; others work alone. Some subsist on menial jobs. Matters such as these are discussed in our next topic, where to live.

TO BE OR NOT TO BE IN L.A.?

Because most American prime-time television drama originates in Los Angeles, those wishing to break into TV writing will find it advantageous to live in L.A.[3] For those interested in writing features, living in L.A. is less important. In her book on the business side of screenwriting, K Callan reports that most agents and production companies are indifferent about where writers live.[4] Their interest is in the script, not where it was written.

Even so, many writers respond well to the creative rush of Los Angeles and New York. They are drawn by movie traditions and the charm of living a bohemian, surfer, or whatever life-style they fancy. Some writers wish to escape their hometowns, while others prefer to remain close to home and the familiar well from which they draw their stories. A few writers live elsewhere but work with a partner who lives in Los Angeles or New York (Jack Epps and Jim Cash wrote *Top Gun* and other films this way; one partner works in Los Angeles, and the other teaches and lives in Michigan).

A number of actors, directors, and screenwriters visit L.A. from outlying cities, as needed. Commuters who lack money may ask pals to put them up on a couch for a week or so because these visits are costly, and it can take five years or so to become established and to build a record of work. During this time, money to live on can be a problem.

If it is any consolation, the financial pinch during (and after) break-in is also felt by actors, dancers, and other performers. However, artists have always found ways to endure this period, regardless of what it takes—and it

---

[3]Each month *The Journal of the WGA* publishes a TV marketing list of the shows on the air, reporting those shows that are open to free-lancers and the name of each show's contact person, as shown in Appendix F. The names and phone numbers cited do not guarantee access, however.

[4]K Callan, *The Script Is Finished, Now What Do I Do?*, Sweden Press, Studio City, California, 1993. p. 34. This book presents extensive listings and descriptions of agents in Los Angeles and New York, as well as information on how to approach agents. Also see Carl Sautter, *How to Sell Your Screenplay: The Real Rules of Film and Television*, New Chapter Press, New York, 1992.

can take everything! Michael Blake knows, for while he was writing the novel that became *Dances with Wolves,* he lived out of his car and washed dishes in a Chinese restaurant in Arizona. Blake was forty-two at the time and felt that his life was a failure. Bruce Joel Rubin wrote for twenty-five years before *Ghost* launched his career. The point is that anyone who is contemplating a career in screenwriting should be braced for the lean times that go with the apprenticeship. Most of us see our work rejected at a time when it seems that everyone on earth is writing a screenplay. Our mightiest efforts may be ignored while newcomers score with their first attempts. All this may be happening at the same time we find that the day job we use to pay the rent is so draining that we have no energy to write. To make the torment complete, we often must submit to people whose only qualification as reviewers seems to be their ability to savage our work.

Bitter jokes and painful struggle are the downside of screenwriting, but we stay with it because it is part of the dues we pay for writing movies and because this work is not something that we choose; rather, it chooses us. Like martyrs, we learn how to transform frustration into self-righteousness and to turn privation into a spiritual state. Even so, like all artists, we hear the wolf scratching at the door in the night. At such times we must be a warrior and remember that we chose the writing life; we must not yield to fear.

Regarding living arrangements, the most practical situation is to connect with an agent in New York or Los Angeles. This allows telephone conferencing and mail and fax exchanges. When a script is offered for sale, production company executives can read it and decide if they wish to speak with the writer. If they do, conferencing by telephone can be arranged. When a sale is imminent, the writer can travel to L.A. or New York for a face-to-face meeting. Thus, modern communication gives screenwriters a much longer leash than when Jack Warner insisted that his screenwriters sign in a 9:00 A.M. and sign out at 5:00 P.M. when they left the studio for home. (Warner reasoned that because he paid his writers a banker's salary, they should keep a banker's hours.)

Of the many good things that Los Angeles offers, one of the best is UCLA Extension (UCLAX), the largest continuing-education program in the world. UCLAX is especially strong in screenwriting and motion picture production. In screenwriting alone, UCLAX offers forty low-cost ($300 or so) courses each quarter throughout the year. They are taught mainly at night on the UCLA campus by excellent screenwriting teachers, some who moonlight from local film schools. UCLAX is open to anyone, and there are no requirements for admission. Although UCLAX courses cannot be transferred or applied to university degree programs, they are an excellent educational investment.[5]

Low-cost courses in screenwriting and filmmaking are also offered by Los Angeles community colleges. Additionally, the Writers Guild of America, the Director's Guild, and the Academy of Motion Picture Arts and Sciences, as

[5]For a copy of the UCLAX catalogue, write to UCLA Extension, P.O. Box 24901, Los Angeles, CA 90024, or call (310) 825-9971.

well as museums and other area colleges, offer free or low-cost lectures throughout the year. By sifting through these opportunities, newcomers can piece together a practical, low-cost program in screenwriting without the expense of traditional film school.

It should also be noted that many of the people that one meets in the UCLAX writing courses work in the motion picture industry, which means that consorting with classmates presents opportunities to share information on how the business works.

I also recommend that new writers think about teaming up with a partner who can share writing and living expenses. As these arrangements are sorted through, the new writer should be thinking about seeking representation with a literary agent.

THE LITERARY AGENT

Los Angeles and New York support most of the nation's literary agencies. Some are firms that employ dozens of agents; others are one- and two-person operations. A typical agent usually works with fifteen or twenty writers, whom they read, counsel, and manage. Since all of this takes time, agents seek clients who can write professionally and who seem capable of dealing with buyers. This is as it must be, for if the ABC Agency continually sends out unprofessional scripts or troublesome writers, the firm's reputation will suffer. Thus, literary agents protect their good names by sending out scripts and writers that they feel are worth reading. The work goes out to production companies under the agency's imprimatur, which tells potential buyers that the agency has read the script and believes it has commercial potential. Additionally, the agency's cover and logo on the script reassures the production company that it will not be entangled with lawsuits claiming plagiarism.

There is nothing magical about agents; they are intermediaries between writers and the production companies. When an agent comes upon a script that has commercial appeal, he or she contacts buyers and uses his or her selling skills to induce the contactee to read the script and, if all goes well, to buy it. Agents may offer clients occasional suggestions for improving the salability of their scripts, and they also pass along their sense of what the market is buying. Agents comfort their writers when disappointment occurs, but mainly they are the writer's negotiating partner. The one irreducible fact of the writer-agent relationship is the quality of scripts: *The writer must submit professional work that the agent can sell.*

For their part, agents develop personal contacts with story editors, producers, and story executives in TV and in features. These relationships, carefully nurtured over time, are one of the agent's most valued assets. Another asset is reputation, for even though Hollywood has a global reach, the scripting side of the movies is not large, and those involved with it—producers, writers, agents—often know each other personally or by reputation. Because many script deals are based on trust and a handshake, agents value their reputations, which they have earned. This trust and the social skills of many movie higher-ups help moderate a business that is highly stressful.

Agents do most of their work by telephone, using fast, efficient calls to busy executives who often handle a hundred calls and callbacks every day, many about scripts that claim to be brilliant. Agents also understand movie contracts and how to negotiate, and they usually initiate the selling process by calling production companies to introduce their writers, to set up meetings, and to announce scripts for sale. By schmoozing over the telephone and in personal meetings, agents keep abreast of what the trends are, who is buying, and what buyers are looking for. Keeping abreast also means that agents read the trade press (*Daily Variety, Weekly Variety, The Hollywood Reporter, The Los Angeles Times, The Journal of the WGA,* and similar publications).

Agents realize that the production companies are in a bind when it comes to reading material, for within the mass of submissions there are only occasional scripts that are worth every effort to find. However, to stay in the script game, studios and independent production companies have to stretch out a net of readers in order to snag the best writers and scripts that are circulating. It is a wasteful system, but it does ensure that most of the scripts submitted by agents will be read at least once. The best way for a screenwriter to become part of this game is to team up with a literary agent.

Securing a Literary Agent

There is no official way to sign with an agent, except through good writing, which rises as cream and is certain to be recognized. The first step toward finding representation is to determine which agents are taking on new clients. Such a list of agents is published by the Writers Guild of America, West.[6] A new writer peruses this list, selects an agency (or two), and sends a brief (one-paragraph) query letter that introduces the writer and makes a request for representation. If you do this, also send along a page of story ideas that indicate how your mind works. If you have news clippings or performance awards that bolster your appeal, send that material, too. Include your phone number and a SASE for the reply. Your goal at this stage is a personal meeting or at least a phone conference in which you can try to finesse the agent into reading your material. Agents are more likely to respond favorably when these preliminaries are done politely and professionally. (Note that typos and sloppy writing on a query letter are not professional.) Avoid agents who charge a fee for reading your scripts. But be aware that literary agents are not writing teachers. Therefore, newcomers should improve their work until it seems salable. Until this level of writing is achieved, there is not much point in launching a campaign to find an agent, who must have professional work in order to do business.

---

[6]Contact the WGA, West for a copy of its current list of agents. (Include a $2 check or money order and a SASE.) The WGA, West is located at 8955 Beverly Boulevard, Los Angeles, CA 90048, telephone number (310) 550-1000. There are two branches of the Writers Guild of America. The WGA, East is located at 555 West 57th Street, New York, NY 10019, (212) 767-7800.

When an agent agrees to meet with you, a conference is arranged; you meet with the agent, and you submit writing samples. If this process must be done from out of town, mail the samples and conduct the meeting by telephone—the writing samples are what matter most at this stage. Send the agent what he or she requests, which is usually two or three television scripts (for different shows) or a feature script or two, to demonstrate your capability. The agent will evaluate the storylines, energy, characters, dialogue, format, and overall writing style. A personal meeting will indicate to the agent whether the writer can handle a story conference, i.e., is the writer reasonable and intelligent, or is he or she too excitable, nervous, or aggressive?

Most agents are experienced script readers who recognize professional work. Agents also appreciate writers who tell their stories with passion, who can spin a yarn that holds together, who create interesting characters, and who write with thoughtfulness and humor. If the agent turns you down, ask for feedback so you can evaluate your work. You need to know what is wrong with it and how your writing can be improved. Not all agents will give such a critique, but some will, especially since a cursory evaluation of a script can be done in ten minutes or so, enough time to indicate the writer's level of skill. Most scripts are rejected because of weak stories—not much happens, what does happen happens too slowly and is not dramatic, and/or the characters are drab. A weak story (and/or a sloppy writing style) usually shows in the first twenty pages or so. If nothing is happening by then, the read usually ends.

Rejection means moving on to the next agent on your list. This continues until someone approves of your work and you are offered a contract whereby the agency agrees to represent you as a client. If none of the agents signs you (or agrees to look at your work, without a contract), continue to write and to study until your work comes up to the mark. You must believe in your ability to write screenplays. This willpower is what enables "wanna-be" screenwriters to persevere.

Writers who sign with an agency contract to pay the agency 10 percent of the gross sale price of each script sold. The contract also stipulates that the writer will deal exclusively with the agency. After the writer is taken on by an agency, an agent is assigned to offer guidance, encouragement, and business savvy concerning which production companies to approach with which scripts and how the approaches will be made. Once the writer-agent relationship is established, the next step is to send the writer's work to a potential buyer for evaluation and possible sale.

HOW SCRIPTS ARE EVALUATED

Scripts that are submitted by a reputable literary agent go to one or more movie studios and production companies. In some cases, the script (when submitted by a well-known writer or a prestigious agent) bypasses the first step of the review process and goes directly to a development executive or a producer, who judges the commercial potential of the work.

For most scripts, the evaluation begins when the script is sent to the production company's story department, where professional readers evaluate one or two scripts per day. In a week, the dozen or so readers on the studio's staff might approve six to ten scripts—one in every twenty or thirty scripts that are reviewed.[7] This identifies those scripts that have commercial possibilities so they can be sent on to the next rung on the ladder. This rung is occupied by a dozen or so development executives and producers who read their share of the recommended scripts and discuss their choices at weekly story meetings. Most of what they read will be rejected for one reason or another, but a few scripts will be sent into development for rewriting, and every month or so a script will be approved and green-lighted by the studio for production. This same process goes on, although with fewer scripts and reviewers, at smaller production entities throughout the nation. Although it is difficult to determine the attrition rate between submitted scripts and those that are produced, my calls to readers, agents, and development executives suggest that one in every hundred or so submissions sells, and about one in five of these is made into a movie. The odds are not as dire as they might seem, because most scripts are submitted to a number of production companies. These numbers are not cited to discourage you; they are to remind you that rejection is the norm, and though it can be heartbreaking, being turned down is almost unavoidable, given the odds cited above.

During review, readers and development executives ask the same questions you probably would, if you were in their shoes: Does the script present interesting characters who are caught up in a good story? Would the public pay to see this story? Does the story say anything philosophically? Was the script a page-turner? Did it stir the reader's emotions? Through basic questions such as these (and those in the evaluation forms in Appendix G), reviewers hope to locate a good script that validates their work.

In sum, script selection is not a vast, bureaucratic process; it is a personal operation in which a few people screen out weak material so that attention can focus on those properties that have commercial promise. In the end, the head of production and two or three of his or her closest advisers decide which scripts to fund and turn into movies. Green-lighting a script for production is based on a highly intuitive sense of what the diverse global movie market is interested in seeing. Admittedly, it is a less-than-perfect process that funds turkeys such as *Exit to Eden* and *The Road to Wellville* while gems such as *Platoon* and *Terms of Endearment* are passed over for years. Even so, fallible human beings do their best to pick winners.

One final point before leaving this topic: Good scripts are rare, despite thousands of submissions and the best work of everyone. As a result, when a good script comes along, even when written by an unknown writer, it attracts attention. That so few good scripts show up every year should be taken as a measure of how difficult they are to write, rather than as the result of an unfair or arbitrary review process. It is important for new writers to appreciate that *good scripts sell.*

---

[7]Appendix F presents examples of the reviewing forms used by movie studios and production companies.

THE PITCH MEETING

During my years of taping at the WGA, no topic has drawn more attention than pitching. This happens because pitching is a performance skill that defeats many writers. Pitching is the writer's opportunity to present a prospective buyer with the story that he or she has written. The pitch is done as a verbal presentation that is like a sales ritual that has been compared to the rendezvous of trappers who once emerged from the woods, opened their packs, and spread out their prize pelts for inspection and sale. In the writer's rendezvous, we open our briefcases and unpack a prize story or two that have been fluffed for sale. We palaver, feint, and bluster, but if we do not truly believe in the script for sale, the buyer usually will sense our lack of commitment and will react negatively. This is the first lesson of pitching: *Believe in the wonderfulness of your work.*

A pitch meeting is an opportunity that should not be wasted, so prepare for it by timing and practicing the pitch. Some writers audiotape or videotape their pitches beforehand, for practice; many other writers practice their pitch on friends. Another approach is to have a friend pitch your story to you, so you can evaluate it from this perspective. Should you feel that such preparation is excessive, note what *Witness*'s William Kelley said on the subject:

> There's no way to stress too much the preparation for a pitch. . . . Plan what you're going to say, go in and say it, be polite; and then get the hell out. They'll appreciate the saving of time and they'll appreciate your directness and positive approach and your positive departure.[8]

Kelley's remarks offer the second lesson of pitching: *Prepare the pitch carefully.* Such preparation acknowledges that a pitch meeting is a business meeting. Be sure to arrive on time, dressed in a way that shows respect for the other person while expressing who you are. Pitch meetings are brief, usually taking twenty minutes or so. Do not waste the buyer's time or act green, artsy, or geeky. Sit up as straight and tall as you can manage; act alert, polite, and interested. Do not slouch. Do not smoke. Do not accept coffee if it is offered. Do not tense up if the buyer is interrupted by phone calls or if other people wander about the room. Be tolerant: the buyer may be on edge after a day of hassling with job problems, worrying about his or her child's tonsillitis, or dealing with any number of other stresses.

After the writer and the buyer exchange preliminary pleasantries, the meeting will get around to the verbal presentation of the story. When new writers pitch a feature, their goal is to persuade the buyer to read the finished script. It is therefore advisable to pitch just one feature story, since these are complicated and require careful explanation. When pitching for TV, some writers are prepared to pitch six or ten story concepts that can be recited in ten or twenty seconds each. Others arrive with a single idea plotted in detail.

---

[8] "Interview with William Kelley: *Witness*," in *Top Secrets: Screenwriting*, p. 172.

Whatever is being pitched, the buyer should appreciate the wonderful yarn being spieled. As you pitch, do not sound apologetic, self-deprecating, craven, or desperate. Do not mumble or rush your presentation. Speak clearly and forcefully. Maintain eye contact. If you babble or stumble during the pitch, if your knees shake and your tongue sticks to the roof of your mouth, buyers will discount your afflictions as a normal case of the jitters. Buyers know that many writers would as soon eat a bug as pitch a story. What matters is the story, not how it is spieled. Do your best to tell the story dramatically. Listen to a few of Garrison Keillor's monologues on public radio for how he tells a story; such a style is ideal for pitching. Do not read the pitch from notes or recite it in a singsong, memorized manner. Instead, be a storyteller.

A good pitch has shape and rhythm. It is of a piece. It holds attention. It is inventive. The pitch should indicate if the story favors plot or character (or both). The pitch should suggest the story's three-act structure and where the act breaks occur. It should describe how the problem is set up and tracked, and how the audience is hooked into the yarn. The pitch should mention a few key character motivations. It should suggest the visual content of the story. A good pitch is like a joke; the punch line is the payoff, when the problem that has organized the story is resolved. The story should end cleanly, conclude the subplots, and answer lingering questions.

Commercial "heat" should shine through the pitch, i.e., the story should have interest because the idea is inventive and different. No one knows for sure what creates heat, but it seems to touch on dramatic contrast, as in *Forrest Gump*. Magical originality (*Like Water for Chocolate*) can generate heat. In some stories, remarkable characters leap out (*The Last Seduction*). Or the story situation may be unique (*Speed*) or inventive (*Babe*). In other instances, a special location (*The Shawshank Redemption*) draws interest. Some movies contain a number of these ingredients, as in *Amadeus, Bullets over Broadway, Apocalypse Now, Dr. Strangelove, The Grapes of Wrath,* and other outstanding films.

All of the foregoing elements should be packed into *a two-minute oral pitch.* The pitch is kept brief because most writers cannot sustain listener interest for much longer than this. For such reasons, the pitch should encapsulate the story and trigger questions from the buyer that can be answered. Details of the story can be filled in as the questions are answered.

The pitch presents a polished and extended version of the concept statement, that is, the basic idea plus the problem that organizes the story (see examples in Chapter 2). Most buyers are skillful at plucking out the core idea of the story, but the pitch should clearly present the concept statement. *The story concept is usually what hooks or turns off the buyer.* Producer Lauren Shuler-Donner (*Dave, Free Willy*) has been pitched hundreds of yarns; her comments on the topic, given at a WGA seminar in November 1993, are instructive:

> Tell the person you're pitching to—in two or three sentences—what the movie is about. It's the *TV Guide* version, which I know sounds frivolous, but what happens when you're being pitched to is that your mind is jumping ahead, trying to see the movie—you're trying to figure out what it is. The summary spares you from that. If somebody says this is about a shark that terrorizes a

small town, then okay, I know what you're going to say and now you can start to tell me the story. I listen for a story that is generally worked out in three acts; what the conflict is; good, original, fleshed-out characters; and an unexpected resolution at the end. An original story, and something that I like.

Experienced buyers have heard five or ten variations on every plot imaginable, so they are seldom knocked out by a story idea. As indicated by Shuler-Donner's remarks, buyers often tune in on the plot by associating it with a familiar genre. They also listen for how the writer has freshened the notion in ways that swing it in an unexpected direction, making it different from other variations that the buyer might have heard. The idea's specialness need not be profound, but it should make the buyer perk up and take notice. An idea about a big-city cop who takes refuge with a beautiful widow in Amish country is interesting. A story about a young woman who wants to escape the mean hills of Tennessee and make a life for herself by working in a store is so unadorned that it too is interesting. The idea of a hoodlum rewriting a play for a gaggle of theatrical twits is interesting. An adaptation of *Heart of Darkness* that is set in Vietnam is interesting. (These concepts all became popular movies, respectively, *Witness, Ruby in Paradise, Bullets over Broadway,* and *Apocalypse Now.*)

During the pitch session, jot down the buyer's comments and suggestions. Writers freely exchange ideas, and we are honored when one of our suggestions is used to improve a script. Often, pitching turns out to be a creative and a critical process that can nurture a script. Bruce Joel Rubin told a 1991 WGA seminar that he pitched *Ghost* for months before he sold it. Along the way, Rubin was given suggestions by various potential buyers, who liked the idea but felt it needed work. Rubin listened, took notes, remembered ideas from the pitching sessions, and used a few of them to rewrite his script. Eventually it sold and became the hit movie that launched Rubin's career.

Being open-minded about the buyer's ideas does not mean accepting everything that this person suggests. Writers spend weeks or months writing a script, while the buyer spends only a few minutes listening to a pitch, so do not roll over for anyone's quick judgment of your work. Also, do not be charmed into accepting a buyer's vision of your story; otherwise, you may discover that your lovely creation has been switched with an ugly changeling that you cannot write. If you dislike the buyer's ideas, be deferential. In 1992, Susan Jansen, a former student who became the story editor for the TV series "Home Improvement," spoke to my class and offered her favorite editorial noncommittals: "That's interesting." "Let me think about that." "Interesting idea!" Nodding wisely also works, as does a well-timed "hmmm"!

If the buyer is not interested in your idea, say good-bye and leave in a pleasant and upbeat manner, as though you have a dozen deals lined up. Also remember that only the story idea was rejected, not the writer. Rejection is part of working in the movies, as one might expect in a business that buys fewer than 1 percent of the ideas pitched. The remaining scripts are rejected for reasons that may have nothing to do with the writer or the story idea. Screenwriters work from their creative energy and self-confidence. When that fire is dampened by rejection, it must be rekindled before it creates a writer's block.

On the positive side, view the pitch session as a learning experience that demystifies the selling process. Prepping for the pitch session should sharpen your sense of what the story is about, what buyers find appealing about it, and which areas need additional work. Finally, you should experience professional growth because you have written a story, taken it into the marketplace, and had the gumption to show up for the meeting and to take criticism; you have been in combat and survived. That experience will make the next pitch meeting easier. Another plus is realizing that feature ideas can be polished up and pitched to another studio or production company. There are hundreds of potential buyers out there, all looking for good scripts.

Much of the foregoing feature film advice was echoed by Stanley M. Brooks in a speech given to the Academy of Television Arts and Sciences. His 1990 lecture "Pitching Your Project to the Networks" included ten commandments of pitching, reproduced below:

1. Know the product that the network buyer is producing (watch TV).
2. Rehearse your pitch. Don't ever try to wing it.
3. Be prompt and look presentable. Think of the pitch session as a job interview.
4. When getting criticism, be strong, yet flexible. If the buyers pass on the project, be understanding. You'll have to pitch them again.
5. Have ideas for casting (the names of actors you feel can play key roles).
6. Never lie about your project, especially about "attached" stars or "owning the rights."
7. Keep your pitch short and concise. Tell the concept, sketch the characters, and then summarize the story.
8. Never stay too long. Don't oversell.
9. Do not pitch outside the meeting, as in a restaurant.
10. Enjoy yourself! They are buying more than the idea. They are buying your passion and enthusiasm.

If the buyer is drawn to your story idea, he or she may jot down notes or an outline. While this may not mean that you've made a sale, it does indicate that the person is interested and may use the outline to pitch the idea to associates. If the firm decides to buy your idea, your agent will negotiate a deal. Although the press occasionally reports huge payments for scripts, first-timers are more likely to be paid close to WGA minimums (listed in Appendix H). The sale will lead to a deal memo, which is a standard agreement between the production company and the writer's agent that lists the conditions of the sale. (A sample deal memorandum is presented in Appendix I.) The Writers Guild of America has procedures and advice for how this is handled, but new writers should be on guard for clever promoters who entice them into doing free rewrites of scripts and stories. If they want you to write, you should ask them to pay. The deal memo sets this up.

The deal memo usually signs the writer to a payment schedule that allows the production company to terminate the project should the writer fail to deliver an acceptable treatment, or script, or polished script. Periodically, the writer will be called in for story conferences as the script is being written, which brings us to the next stop along the production pipeline—the story conference, in which the story or the first draft of the script is discussed.

THE STORY CONFERENCE

How Scripts Are Developed

Let us assume that you have pitched your story and have signed a deal memo. Now the production company (usually in the person of the producer that you have been working with) calls you in to discuss what you wrote in exchange for your writing fee. These meetings are where writers slip into heavy armor to defend and explain their work. Initial meetings deal with the story, which is often the most vexing phase of the work. After the beats of the script have been hammered out—which can take weeks or even months—there will be more conferences, in which individual scenes and speeches will be discussed. During these sessions, the production company usually flags points in the story or script with notes that indicate areas of confusion. The writer is expected to fix or explain away what the buyer did not like or did not understand.

Writers stay with their work to protect it; for financial reasons; and so they will not be labeled as *uncooperative, difficult,* or *unable to deliver a viable script.* Despite the best of intentions, the original writer may be unable to deliver a script that pleases the studio. When this happens, or when the original writer runs out of energy, a new writer may be hired. Rewriting can continue for several years, with the script floating from one office to another, until someone decides that the story problems cannot be solved. In these cases, the script will be abandoned and filed away. No literary morgue contains more lost treasure than the thousands of rejected scripts shelved in Hollywood's dead files. Recently, studios have dusted off some of these rejects, hoping to come up with a good script that was passed over. Some of the works being considered were written before World War II! It remains to be seen if anything will come of these attempts at resurrection.[9]

However it is done, developing scripts is expensive. The major studios, for example, typically invest several hundred thousand dollars in each script being developed. Because a major studio usually has 50 to 100 projects in development during a given year, it spends upward of one-quarter of its yearly overhead expense developing scripts. Tom Pollack, who heads Universal Studios, told a WGA meeting in December 1993 that his company's overhead figure came to about $100 million per year. Universal releases about twenty films a year, which means that each movie bears a $5 million charge to compensate for overhead costs. About $1 million of that overhead charge is

---

[9]Studios are also becoming more interested in remaking old movies; to date, however, nothing very special has resulted. Comic books, TV shows, and prequels and sequels are also being recycled into movies. Despite this grave robbing, the need for new stories remains unabated.

spent on developing scripts for the studio. Industrywide, hundreds of writers are paid for scripts and rewriting assignments each year. Even though most of these properties are never made into movies, they provide writers with considerable income.[10]

Responding to Notes and Editorial Suggestions

The annotated script or story is returned to the writer before or at the time of the story conference so the comments of the buyer can be studied. Many of the items tagged will be minor—clarifying or trimming dialogue, beefing up a character, restaging a scene, and the like. Such matters are not difficult to rewrite. Some of the notes, however, may cut into the spine of the script, and these require careful review. The buyer may be unhappy with the story conflict, the logic of the story, or how the scenes and characters are dramatized and motivated. The editorial notes may point to real or merely perceived dead spots, drift, and meanderings in the storyline, or to scenes that do not work. Be prepared to defend your work and to explain away such criticism. At the same time, deal forthrightly with the buyer's criticism because it may be accurate or partly accurate.

This phase of story conferencing usually goes easier when writer and buyer are imagining the same movie. Getting all parties tuned to the same wavelength is more likely to happen when the writer follows the format advice given in earlier chapters. A lucid writing style and mastery of format permit all parties to be in agreement on story, style, theme, conflict, problem, what motivates the characters, and how they interact. Also, be prepared to state your casting choices; some buyers like to put faces on characters to make it easier for them to imagine the movie. The concerns of the buyers are often tied to what they feel will please moviegoers, so do your best to explain away their objections and reservations. Jot down their comments and suggestions. You will need time to evaluate your notes and perhaps to phone-confernece with the buyer before coming back in a week or so with new ideas. In some cases, script repairs are worked out on the spot and polished when the writer goes home and has time to rewrite what was worked out during the story conference. During this crucial final phase of the work, even though you know the material better than anyone, you may be oblivious to weaknesses or opportunities that are obvious to the buyer.

In a classroom, multiple critiques give student writers many opportunities to rework their material. The teacher's insistence on an improved story or script may seem demanding, but it is a trifle compared to how the movie industry works. U.S. studios and production companies run a world-class business and they insist on world-class work. For such reasons, writers in a story conference must keep in mind that the buyer's suggestions may actually be commandments implying *make it better or we'll hire another writer!*

---

[10]Unlike scripts for features, television scripts are more likely to be produced, because staff writers are available to rework the material until it meets the show's standards.

Screenwriters are paid professional fees to deliver professional material. The production company, not the writer, determines when that quality has been delivered. However, the ice wears thin when the writer contests every suggestion. Conversely, some writers cave in and attempt to write whatever the buyer suggests. A balance must be struck between independence and hackdom. Writers who are unable to do this either drop out of the pipeline or become so accommodating that they lose their personal vision and scramble to deliver flavor-of-the-month work. Joe Eszterhas *(Basic Instinct)* has commented on this trap:

> A lot of young writers get caught in this process and change everything just to get the movie made. In the course of it they completely dilute the strength of what it is they wrote, but on a much deeper level they hurt themselves by compromising something inside them. They stop being a writer and start taking dictation, and that's going to catch up to them the next time they sit down at the typewriter.[11]

Eszterhas is advising the warrior ethic here, telling us to defend our material and our vision as artists. That vision is our talent; it is why we were hired in the first place, so that ability should not be ignored or slighted. When pushed into a corner and ordered to change the material, we usually do our best to accommodate the buyer. However, if changes are demanded that seem unacceptable, three options are available: return the money and try to sell the script elsewhere; keep the money and tell the buyer to find another writer; or make the changes suggested and change your definition of "unacceptable"!

I recommend working with the buyer and making the suggested changes, if only to preserve your reputation as a cooperative writer. In some cases, writers complete the requested script changes, but after the new ideas have been grafted onto the script, they do not work. Often, buyers realize this and return to the original version.

Writers build their careers one script at a time. We are professionals, and like all professionals we are expected to perform on demand, in this case, to write a commercial script that can be made into a movie. Often before a producer hires a new writer, calls are made to someone who has worked with the writer and an evaluation is requested. When the word is good, it leads to assignments; when it is not, the writer may need to rebuild his or her reputation.

There may be ups and downs in your career as a writer, but whatever happens, believe in your talent. Without being fanatical, remember that there will be other scripts and other opportunities, but there is only one unique and special *you.* Your mind, heart, and soul are the source of your stories and characters, so do not allow yourself to be diminished. Be a tough, intelligent writer who can wear four hats at once and create scripts that come out *sssssssssmoking!*

---

[11]*Journal of the Writers Guild of America,* May 1994, p. 17.

CASE STUDY: THE SANTA CLAUSE

To give you a sense of how pitching, agents, and the market for good scripts operate, note how the hit movie *The Santa Clause* came into being. In 1992, two first-time screenwriters (Steve Rudnick and Leo Benvenuti) submitted a script to their agent. He liked it and pitched it by phone to various production companies, including Outlaw Productions. Outlaw, a three-person shop, began operations with *sex, lies and videotape*, which cost $1.2 million to make and grossed $25 million. Along with a tidy profit, this film gave Outlaw enough clout to talk with major studios about scripts that might make successful films. Unfortunately, their best efforts led to a string of duds (*The Opposite Sex, Crossing the Bridge, Don't Tell Mom the Babysitter's Dead, Indian Summer, Mr. Baseball, Wagons East*).

Eager to secure another hit, Outlaw responded to the agent's pitch and asked for *The Santa Clause* script to be delivered to its office. Several days later, after Outlaw read the material, the two screenwriters were called in for a story conference. The meeting ended with a deal memo that paid the writers $10,000 in option money in exchange for giving Outlaw the right to develop the script. Thus began a series of story conferences in which Outlaw gave its suggestions for improving the script to the writers. Several drafts later, Outlaw felt that the script was good enough to pitch to a studio, which would then put up the money needed to turn the script into a movie.

As is often the case with a script with "heat," *The Santa Clause* found an audience; in this case it involved the managers of *Home Improvement* star Tim Allen. Although they felt the property was an ideal launch vehicle for the TV star, Allen was tied up with commitments and unavailable for a year. While negotiations continued, Allen contacted Disney chairman Jeffrey Katzenberg, who knew the comedian from his top-rated TV show (which is a Disney production). Disney had been searching for a script that would showcase the star and launch his career in theatrical films. Katzenberg reportedly read *The Santa Clause* script on Thanksgiving Day, 1992, five months after the initial pitch call to Outlaw, and his reaction was so positive that Robert Newmyer, one of the Outlaw partners, said that "Katzenberg fell in love with the script for Tim." Such language is movie code for "let's make a deal—fast!" Pressure was applied over the holiday weekend. Disney phone calls piled up, and after an intense round of negotiations between Disney and Outlaw's three partners, Katzenberg insisted that Outlaw take the script off the market and sign a deal by midnight of that night. Outlaw agreed, which led to Disney's paying the screenwriters $500,000 for *The Santa Clause* script.

When Allen became available the following year, production began in April 1994. Budgeted at $17 million, the movie was given a major advertising campaign that cost Disney an additional $20 million. *The Santa Clause* earned close to $150 million in North America alone. Forty to fifty percent of this goes to Disney, which will pay Outlaw a share. The theater owners keep the rest. For its involvement with *The Santa Clause*, Outlaw Productions will not only earn many millions but will also have in place a bridge to one of the major movie studios, which could lead to future coventures.

The Santa Clause experience is fairly typical of how movies happen: someone writes a good script, it is recognized for its commercial and/or artistic potential, and the wheels begin to turn—fast! In similar situations, hot scripts have set off bidding wars. Often arranged by agents, these can be frenzied affairs in which copies of the prize script are hand-delivered by motorcycle messengers. The recipients are top studio executives who can say yes to projects that they feel have merit. Such an executive is given a day or so to read the script, and then the bidding begins. The negotiations are done by telephone and are often concluded in a day.

The Santa Clause is cited to add a ray of hope to the sobering reality that has been scattered in this chapter. Although screenwriting is challenging, it is exciting. Like *Thelma and Louise* and many other scripts, *The Santa Clause* was written by new writers who had never sold a movie, yet they were paid handsomely.

This example illustrates a big-budget studio production that was lavishly advertised. However, some films are made much more modestly, so let us close our discussion by examining the low end of moviemaking, where newcomers—with luck, brains, and work—might be able to gain experience and financial reward. At the least, what you read in the following section may set you to dreaming.

MAKING MOVIES OUT OF THE MAINSTREAM

This final broadside concerns advice on developing a low, low, low budget version of Outlaw Productions. The plan also touts the benefits of working with a writing partner or with people who can serve as an expert sounding board. Whether the team writes scripts together or meets once a week to share ideas and complaints, such an association can be productive.

You can extend the writing collaboration by adding people who are interested in production and in the movie business. Three to five such people are enough to form a production team that is committed to writing, directing, producing, and editing a low-budget feature film. The starting point for this is the same one used by a studio: a script that everyone believes in. With the script in hand, the next task is getting it financed and made into a movie.

The team should agree on how to divide up future income (if any). This should be drawn up as a legal contract that spells out the nature of the partnership. The team should learn the movie business so that the members can work out production costs and sources of actors, equipment, locations, unions, legal matters, distribution, and tracking the profits (if any). A practical first step on this point is to read *The Hollywood Reporter*, the daily and weekly editions of *Variety*, and other industry sources. Some of the basics of how movies are made can be culled from books on production, advertising, and distribution. Understanding motion pictures, which are a huge, complicated business, takes several years of intense study, so do not take this proposal as a lark or a casual thing to be done on weekends. Independent production requires knowledge, determination, courage, and hard work, which are the essentials for doing good work in any career that is fulfilling.

A sweat-equity group of movie fanatics could be set up anywhere in the country, because the new information technologies have both scattered production centers and connected them through computers and telephones. Hook into the network by giving your production team a production goal and going after it by establishing an office, printing stationery, getting a telephone and registering in the yellow pages—and making a commitment to the team. Begin by setting aside a month to write and shoot a short (fifteen-minute or so) movie. Shoot the script on 16mm film or use the best video format available. If nothing better is available, shoot the show on VHS or Hi8 equipment. If you crave better equipment, rent it (do not buy it). Beware of tech-heads whose true love is hardware; go instead with those who are interested in software (writing scripts, working with actors, and making movies).

Edit the short film at a commercial studio or tape house in the nearest metropolitan center. In some cases, the production team may be able to beg/trade/barter assistance from a school, a local cable company, or an industrial firm that uses professional video for training. Repeat the short-film exercise once every month for three or four months while the team works on a feature script. As the team accumulates experience, connect with local theater groups. Research the local acting talent and tap into it; some of these actors may have professional ability. Public access channels on cable TV can be combined into a makeshift regional network that showcases the team's work and touts what the production team plans to do. Use the exposure to draw in additional writers, actors, and other production types who are willing to invest their energy in the venture.

Cultivate the local press for publicity. If initial short productions turn out well, the team should submit its work to festivals, solicit grant money, and offer a forum to writers who can create character-oriented stories that are honest and real because they are about people, not special effects, stunts, and empty spectacle. Once good scripts accumulate, good productions can follow. How do you know when the script is good? You'll recognize it when you see it!

Interestingly, the main production centers are no longer the only places where good work and the writers who create it can be found. To take a few cases that I know personally: Not long ago I served as a judge for the state of Louisiana when it initiated a search program to find new screenwriters who could help develop the state's motion picture industry. I read several dozen scripts and found six of them to be of professional quality; many others were almost as good. I have seen similar work from new writers who submitted scripts to a summer workshop conducted by the North Carolina School of the Arts School of Filmmaking. The point here is that good writers can be found everywhere. Although their work is far from being perfect, these writers can do the work if they are encouraged and counseled until their scripts are good enough to be made into movies. Small, local production teams who know what they are doing could be the inspiration that makes this happen.

Although all this may sound optimistic, it is a plan for organizing a production company—and, as Outlaw Productions demonstrates, such small, "let's put on a show" groups have proven successful in the past. Creative opportunities for new writers and filmmakers exist, and a small, hungry production team that can produce entertaining dramatic programs for less than $1 million per hour can make those breaks happen. Such a price tag would undercut the $2 million per hour that cable companies and independents were paying in 1995 for their low-budget features. Additionally, there are satellite, cable, fiber-optic, and other distribution schemes taking shape, all of them geared to sending movies into our homes and theaters. Whether Off-Off-Broadway, in a small repertory theater, or in a regional motion picture production company that does local stories, good writing attracts artists. This is not a radical idea, for independent filmmakers have been eking out a living this way for many years.

Perhaps these are pipe dreams, or it could be that entertainment history is repeating itself. During the era of silent pictures, for example, gutsy filmmakers took to city streets with hand-cranked cameras and little or no experience—and they made movies. In the 1950s, the golden age of television created another art form—live television drama. Paul Newman, Sidney Lumet, Horton Foote, Paddy Chayefsky, Robert Redford, and hundreds of other artists began their careers creating large characters who operated in small stories that were performed and broadcast live from tiny studios. The shows that were aired to an appreciative national audience (*Philco Playhouse, Studio One, Playhouse 90*) are still remembered fondly, decades after the fact. Independent regional video could reopen this window of opportunity. It would not be easy. Five or ten years of hard work might be needed before the team could create programming that rivaled low-budget Hollywood shows. Even so, the need for inexpensive programming could inspire regional production companies. The programming hunger is already evident, as can be seen by the way cable TV has roped in exercise shows, talk shows, government hearings, court trials, comedy clubs, home shopping, wrestling, infomercials, and other oddments that attract viewers. As the number of channels extends, the demand for dramatic programming should increase as well.[12]

The trend toward regionalism is already under way, as shown by mainstream production companies that have set up shop in Canada, Florida, Texas, North Carolina, Europe, and wherever movies and TV can be produced economically.

Here again we return to the starting point for all this—a script that allows actors, directors, cinematographers, editors, and other artists to do their work. These people will read scripts and decide which ones seem worth their time and energy. The models for such shows have already appeared in the form of

---

[12]In 1995, a new pay-TV channel dealing exclusively with independent films was launched. In the same year, the Sundance Institute announced plans to release independent works on cable TV. Such developments indicate new opportunities for those bold enough to seize the chance.

The Brothers McMullen, Smoke, Nobody's Fool, Food Gas Lodging, El Mariachi, Passion Fish, Boyz N the Hood, and *sex, lies, and videotape,* to name but a few.

The likelihood of a production team succeeding in any of this is, of course, slim to none. However, these are the same odds that apply to most artistic enterprises, which does not deter those seeking careers in the arts. A regional independent production company could be another route for new talent to showcase new work. There is a double appeal to this plan: it challenges writers to put up or shut up, i.e., to stop complaining about commercial restrictions and write what they feel in their hearts. Additionally, the plan allows members of the production team to take charge of their careers instead of waiting for the happenstance of Hollywood to discover their talent. The plan being proposed short-circuits the Hollywood system by allowing direct creation of movies. The product would be distributed through alternative film and video outlets such as public access channels, local television stations, foreign distribution, direct-to-video cassettes, cable television, Public Broadcasting Service, and, when the work is good enough, in standard theatrical release. Such exposure would allow filmmakers to gain experience, to tell stories with motion pictures, to showcase their work, to have fun, and to move on to bigger things.

The plan being proposed was put into effect by two young producers of low-budget direct-to-video movies, Aron Schifman and Richard Munchkin. Schifman and Munchkin operate Century Film Partners, which *The Los Angeles Times* (February 22, 1995) describes as one of the "new actioneers" that export American-made action movies to the global market, that is, the cable/TV/satellite/home-video markets in Europe, Latin America, and Asia. There are already several hundred of these lowest-budget independent companies in operation. Century Film Partners is part of this activity, turning out feature films for $1 million to $3 million. The process of how the company does this is described by Munchkin and Schifman in a no-nonsense style that reflects their company's practical, in-the-trenches business style:

MUNCHKIN: Say a writer we know comes in and says here's an idea. OK, we say, great. Then we say, give us three pages, just outline the beats.

SCHIFMAN: His idea might be one paragraph, say a chicken crossing the road has only one leg and talks Spanish.

MUNCHKIN: And it's being chased by a motorcycle. So the writer works on those three pages, doing a scene-to-scene breakdown. We say change this scene to this and change this scene to that.

SCHIFMAN: Take that chicken and make it a beautiful blonde.

MUNCHKIN: Yeah, and add some humor. The writer makes those changes and then we say go for the script.

SCHIFMAN: He asks for some money, we give him some money. Then what happens next is we call up a number of our people, investors, and we say there's this project called "The Chicken Crossing the Road" that looks like the best chicken script I ever read.

MUNCHKIN: The reality is that I have yet to have one of our investors ask me what the story is about.

SCHIFMAN: Right. We say we want to shoot "Chicken" in January. They say OK. Now we know that the "Chicken" project will be acceptable to the foreign buyers because we've been in touch with them about it. We go forward shooting the film, notifying the buyers who is in it, what's happening, giving them one potato chip at a time. We just do as we did a year ago, when we got together in October, shot our first film in January, found another in April, shot another in June, got another script in August. The process is a relatively quick, uncomplicated one with everything paid cash on the barrel.

Although these two entrepreneurs are bottom-feeders in terms of Hollywood production companies, they are making movies. With titles like *Texas Payback, Fists of Iron,* and *Breakaway* (Tonya Harding's debut film), their work has managed to entertain audiences so that buyers keep coming back for more. As a result, Schifman and Munchkin are making movies instead of dreaming about them. Their go-out-and-do-it attitude made this possible. They didn't wait for their big break; they went into the marketplace and made it happen. You can do the same. I advise you, kind reader, as I advise my students: *Nothing ventured; nothing gained.*

SUMMARY

Movies are big business that pressures screenwriters to create scripts that will attract large international audiences. Scripts for these projects can be written in Los Angeles or New York, or arrangements can permit the writer to work in a distant city. However the writer works, he or she should sign with a literary agent. The key to securing such representation is to write scripts that have commercial appeal.

Agents arrange meetings that introduce writers and their work to buyers. The selling process often begins with the pitch meeting, where writers orally present their ideas to story editors and development executives. A movie pitch is carefully prepared as a concise, clear summary of the story. The pitch should give the buyer a sense of the three-act structure and the characters; the story should come across as being fresh, inventive, and told with passion. The buyer uses such values to judge the script's commercial appeal: is the story good enough to attract an audience?

Story conferences take place after the buyer has read the completed story or script. In these meetings, writer and buyer discuss the intentions of the material and how to improve it. The buyer works with the writer to improve the story's dramatic potential and to correct flaws, whether real or imagined.

Editors base their work on two questions: What is the writer trying to say in this? Is it being said in the best way? The writer must answer these questions, explain the material, work with the editor, and consider suggestions. Be cooperative, but do not give up your integrity.

Independent regional production is another route for those who wish to control their work, from writing to distribution. It is not an easy path, but it is a path that leads to experience and creative opportunity.

Exercises

Complete one or more of the exercises below.

1. Prepare a one-minute pitch of your favorite film. Without mentioning the title, pitch the movie to a colleague, who should be able to identify the film. Repeat as needed.
2. Prepare a two-minute pitch of the same film and carry out the previous exercise. Repeat as needed, then videotape the pitch and review it for effectiveness.
3. Videotape a story conference in which one colleague pitches your story to a second colleague, who acts as editor and critic. The writer of the script observes but does not take part in the review. The story conference should last for ten minutes or so. Then the writer reviews the tape with the colleagues. Discuss all story and character problems, confusions, and thematic weaknesses, as well as how to improve the material. Review the tape as needed.

(For media that illustrate the points made in this chapter, see Appendix A.)

Media That Illustrate Points Made in the Chapters

CHAPTER 1

1. Screen three or four video trailers that preview upcoming movies. Consider which segment of the audience the movie seems to be targeting. (The video trailers can be taped off the air or found at the beginning of many rental videos.)
2. From the same trailers, determine if the films being advertised have been done in a real, an unreal, or a surreal style.
3. From the same trailers, determine if the films being advertised intend to frighten audiences, to make them sad, or to make them laugh.
4. *The New York Times Magazine,* January 9, 1994, contains an essay by Mary McHugh entitled "Telling Jack." The article contains at least five possible ideas for stories. Write a one- or two-page story based on this article.
5. Examine art slides or a book of narrative paintings and identify the dramatic idea that organizes each work.

CHAPTER 2

1. Screen short films that demonstrate three-act structure. Any of the following can be used: *The Unicorn in the Garden,* a five-minute animated film based on a James Thurber short story (James Thurber, *Fables for Our Time,* Harper & Row, New York, 1940); *Lunch Date,* an Oscar-winning ten-minute student film; and such twenty-minute films as *Molly's Pilgrim, I Know a Secret, Crac, An Occurrence at Owl Creek Bridge, The Red Balloon, Paddle to the Sea, Sergeant Swell, The Man Who Planted Trees,* and *A Time Out of War.* Episodes of *Cheers, Barney Miller, Frasier, M.A.S.H., Taxi,* and *The Wonder Years* are also recommended.

*This appendix is referenced at the end of each chapter.

CHAPTER 3

1. Screen excerpts from one or more of the four main study films (*The Verdict, Witness, The Terminator,* and *Sleepless in Seattle*) that illustrate the ending of the first and second acts. Because blocking the story is so important, media clips that illustrate story structure are useful tools for learning to plot a yarn.
2. To study effective dramatic setups, see the first act of *Molly's Pilgrim, Rocky,* or *Paths of Glory.* To study story logic, see *I Know a Secret, Of Mice and Men* (1939), or *The Andromeda Strain.* To study continuity, see *Cool Hand Luke, Ruby in Paradise,* or *Tiger Bay.*

CHAPTER 4

1. Almost a month of my U.S.C. graduate screenwriting course is spent on writing and analyzing scenes, during which the class studies the scripts and tapes of twelve scenes that illustrate various aspects of this topic. The scenes used are: when Gerard Depardieu plays the piano in *Green Card;* when Julie Walters chews out Michael Caine near the end of *Educating Rita;* the opening scenes of *Body Heat* and *Roxanne;* when Mrs. Robinson seduces Ben early in *The Graduate;* when the heroine of *American Gigolo* learns that the hero is a hustler; when Gene Hackman visits the social club of the Klan in *Mississippi Burning* and disables their toughest man with one hand; when Jack Nicholson seduces Susan Sarandon in *Witches of Eastwick;* when Sally meets Harry in the bookstore in *When Harry Met Sally;* when father and son visit the university in *Breaking Away* and talk about the boy going to college; when the lovers in *Moonstruck* first consummate their affair; when father and daughter meet in a restaurant after many years in *Running on Empty.* There are hundreds of additional scenes to choose from, but those noted above are quite dramatic. The twelve scenes can be analyzed using the questions listed in the exercises section at the end of Chapter 4.
2. To illustrate action scenes, screen the police station attack from *The Terminator* (Shot 60). Or screen the car chase sequences from *Bullitt* or *The French Connection.*
3. To illustrate character scenes, screen the sequence from *The Verdict* (Shot 24) when Galvin turns down Bishop Brophy's settlement offer. Also screen the character scene from *Sleepless in Seattle* (Shot 89) when Sam goes on his first date with Victoria.
4. To illustrate the montage, screen the beat in which the heroine biplanes over the veldt in *Out of Africa.* Also screen the rise of the hero's team in *The Natural* and the end montage from *Our Daily Bread.*

CHAPTER 5

1. Collect and screen a half hour or so of television news clips that illustrate people who have been shaped by short-term trauma and long-term conditioning.
2. Collect and screen excerpts from feature films or television shows that present character types who display the effects of short-term trauma.
3. Screen the flashbacks in *Breaker Morant, The Terminator* (Shots 46, 183FX), and *Sleepless in Seattle* (Shots 7, 53D). Note the visual conventions that allow these films to transition to a different time.

CHAPTER 6

Screen the video excerpts from *The Verdict* listed below, which illustrate the dialogue points made in this chapter.

1. Dialogue freighted with exposition: Shot 21 of *The Verdict* (Dr. Gruber's long speech).
2. On-the-nose dialogue: Shot 31 of *The Verdict* (when Mickey and Galvin begin to research their case in the library).
3. Dialogue with subtext: Shot 72 of *The Verdict* (in Concannon's office: his aria to Laura, when we learn that she is his spy).
4. Dialogue that advances the plot: Shot 86 of *The Verdict* (when Galvin first meets the admitting nurse [Kaitlin Costello] at her school in New York and talks her into testifying).
5. Dialogue that reveals character: Shot 61 of *The Verdict* (when Laura chews Galvin out for wanting to quit the case, telling him that she can't invest in failure again).
6. Dialogue that affects relationships: Shot 58 of *The Verdict* (when Galvin first meets Nurse Rooney in the doorway of her apartment).
7. Dialogue that addresses the theme: Shot 33 of *The Verdict* (when Galvin has dinner with Laura for the first time in O'Rourke's Saloon and tells her of his belief in the law).
8. Dialogue that reveals backstory: Shot 47 of *The Verdict* (when Mickey and Laura have supper in O'Rourke's and he tells her what really happened to Galvin during the Lillibridge scandal).

CHAPTER 7

1. Prepare a reel of film clips that illustrate each of the dramatizing strategies mentioned in this chapter. To excerpt scenes, you must borrow or buy a second VCR. The two machines can be linked together with video dubbing cables. Usually the salesperson in the video store that sells the cables can explain how to connect the VCRs and how to cue them and copy the video excerpts. Record at SP speed using 30-minute cassettes (the shorter length makes it easier to index and locate what has been recorded).
2. Review the tape of excerpts that you made to illustrate various dramatization strategies and identify and explain how each excerpt functions and how each adds drama to the film.

CHAPTER 8

Create a cassette of video excerpts that illustrate dramatizing by visual storytelling.

CHAPTER 9

Assemble video clips of the script excerpts cited in this chapter. Compare each excerpt with how the writer presented his or her vision in the script.

CHAPTER 10

Note how the four main study films deal with script format in the following areas: spacing, parentheticals, stage directions, character descriptions, action descriptions, and camera instructions.

CHAPTER 11

Compare the scripted version of Shots 87–88 and Shots 93–97 of *Sleepless in Seattle* (when Annie meets with Detective Wheedle) with the film version. (Detective Wheedle was all but eliminated from the movie.) Similarly, check Shot 17 of *The Verdict*, which deals with Galvin's secretary (Claire Pavone). Compare this with the film version. Also see Shot 49 of *Witness*, when Book's sister (Elaine) conflicts with Rachel; Shot 124, when Rachel spats with Book about staying among the Amish; Shot 129A–132 as Schaeffer and the local sheriff ready plans to deal with Book. Note how the scripted versions of these scenes vary from the way the film versions handled these moments. Note how the continuity of the story was sustained during these cuts.

CHAPTER 12

Excerpt scenes from films containing story pitches. See *Nothing in Common*, midway through, when the hero and his team pitch an airline commercial. Also see the opening of *The Player*, which shows various characters pitching their story ideas; Zero Mostel pitching "Springtime for Hitler" in *The Producers*; and the scene from *I'll Do Anything* in which Nick Nolte (portraying an actor) auditions for a role (his performance shows how actors pitch for roles, revealing the needfulness and intensity that go into these key selling moments).

The Screenwriter's Reference Shelf

Script readers expect factual accuracy and respect for the craft of writing, which includes spelling and grammar. Some writers employ editors or ask a housemate to proof pages and circle what seems questionable. If you request such help, don't become testy when mistakes are pointed out. Although I have studied the English language for most of my life, grammar and spelling mistakes continue to slip past me, regardless of how carefully the pages are proofed. They will probably slip by you, too, so don't be shy about asking someone sharp-eyed to edit your material.

One way to minimize factual and grammatical error is to use reference books. They are also handy for answering many of the questions that arise as we write, which can save treks to the library. You might wish to gather a yard or two of reference books onto a nearby shelf for such situations. If you've been wondering what might belong on such a reference shelf, here are a few titles and categories you might wish to check out. (Some of these titles are also listed in the Bibliography at the end of this book.)

Encyclopaedia Britannica (a used set is often sufficient)

The New Columbia Encyclopedia

The American Heritage Dictionary of the English Language (third edition)

What's What (R. Bragonier and D. Fisher)

Webster's New Collegiate Dictionary

The American Heritage Dictionary

The People's Almanac

The Bible

A few books on English grammar

The Oxford American Dictionary

*This appendix is referenced in Chapter 2, p. 58.

Will Durant's *History of Civilization*

A large unabridged dictionary

Introductory college textbooks in physics, biology, geology, botany, oceanography, astronomy, and chemistry

A technical dictionary

A collection of maps and atlases and a globe

Two or three world almanacs and books of facts

A physician's general reference and *Gray's Anatomy*

Standard references in medicine, pharmacology, physiology, and psychology

Four or five books of quotations, great thoughts, and aphorisms

A few references in philosophy

Anthologies of poetry and your favorite works of fiction (for when you need to be inspired by good writing)

Bulfinch's *Mythology*

Picture histories of the United States

Pauline Kael's movie reviews

A Biographical Dictionary of Film (David Thomson)

Filmgoer's and Video Viewer's Companion (Leslie Halliwell)

The Film Encyclopedia (Ephraim Katz)

Picture histories of the movies (*The Parade's Gone By, The Movies,* etc.)

A dozen or so books on playwriting and screenwriting

A dozen or so books about film actors, cinematographers, editors, directors, and screenwriters and their views on the profession

Two or three up-to-date video movie guides (Scheuer, Maltin, Martin, etc.)

Best American Screenplays I, II (Sam Thomas)

Thesaurus of Slang (Esther Lewin and Albert E. Lewin, Facts On File, New York, 1988)

New Dictionary of American Slang (Robert L. Chapman, Harper & Row, New York, 1986)

The Family of Man (timeless photographs about the human condition, created by Edward Steichen for the New York Museum of Modern Art, Simon & Schuster, New York, 1983)

Cast List, Sequence Breakdown, and Shot Numbers of The Verdict

CAST OF *THE VERDICT*

Paul Newman as *Frank Galvin*
Charlotte Rampling as *Laura*
James Mason as *Ed Concannon*
Milo O'Shea as *Judge Sweeney*
Jack Warden as *Mickey Morrissey*
Edward Binns as *Bishop Brophy*
Julie Bovasso as *Nurse Rooney*
Lindsay Crouse as *Kaitlin Costello Price*
Joe Seneca as *Dr. Thompson*
Wesley Addy as *Dr. Towler*
Roxanne Hart as *Sally Doneghy*
James Handy as *Kevin Doneghy*
Kent Broadhurst as *Joseph Alito*
Lewis Stadlen as *Dr. Gruber*

FEATURE FILM ANALYSIS: THE VERDICT

The Verdict is the primary film analyzed in *Story Sense,* and I recommend that you secure a copy of the script and a VHS or laser disk copy of the film. Watch the film scene by scene, sequence by sequence. Stop the playback when a scene concludes and read the commentary on the next scene. You may need to review a particular scene more than once to understand how it was written and filmed.

View the film from varying perspectives—visual design and style, sound and music, dialogue and subtext, scene construction, dramatization, and characterization. Movies are dense with the contributions of many artisans; if you study films as outlined in this lesson on *The Verdict,* you should become more aware of the contribution of each craft and what it takes to turn a script into a movie. Let a month go by and then study *The Terminator* as you studied *The Verdict.* In the same way study the tapes and

---

*This appendix is referenced in Chapter 3, p. 70, and elsewhere in this book.

scripts of *Witness* and *Sleepless in Seattle*, if possible. After the four study films have been reviewed analyze a new script and its tape each month for a year. Spend about ten hours studying each film and script. Read *American Cinematographer, Film Comment,* and other magazines and press reports about how various films are made. By studying films in the manner described, you will gain an understanding of how movies are written, and how the acting, blocking, dialogue, music, and other components contribute to the film.

STRUCTURE OF THE VERDICT

David Mamet's script for *The Verdict* is based on Barry Reed's novel of the same title (Simon & Schuster, New York, 1980). Mamet added the personal redemption theme that supplies the B-storyline of the movie. The story's structure is based on Galvin's struggle to win a malpractice suit (A-storyline) and to regain his self-respect and belief in the law (B-storyline). Years of alcohol and disreputable lawyering have reduced Galvin to the wrecked person we meet in the first scenes. Gradually, he struggles out of his hopelessness, wins the case, and at the end seems headed for a brighter future. This is the *event* in the story: what happens after everything happens. The story shows positive change in the main character. It also presents an ending that is both "up-tick" (he wins the case) and bittersweet (his relationship with Laura ends badly). This movie contains sixty scenes and bits that combine into ten sequences, which is typical for a feature film.

SUBPLOTS IN THE VERDICT

The Laura Subplot

This subplot tracks Laura's struggle to resume her legal career after a failed marriage. To do this she is reduced to spying for Concannon. Laura is more than a traditional love interest because of her needfulness. This was barely suggested in the script, yet it worked. Charlotte Rampling's portrayal of Laura gives depth and complication to *The Verdict* by making us empathize with this desperate woman.

Laura also illustrates the importance of the love interest which provides private moments when characters can express interior thoughts and feelings that might not be spoken otherwise. Such revelation can enrich a story and dimensionalize the characters.

The Laura subplot complicates when she agrees to go home with Galvin. It twists again when the audience discovers she is a spy for the opposition law firm. The climax of this subplot occurs when Galvin strikes Laura in the bar. Note the way the complications in the subplots cluster around the twists and the climax in the A-storyline. Clustering the action this way adds to the drama. To detect clustering and appreciate its importance requires close study of films and scripts.

The Mickey Morrissey Subplot

Jack Warden's Mickey Morrissey helps to complicate the story when he joins Galvin to fight the case. The second twist in this subplot occurs when Mickey wants to quit because he feels that Galvin has lost the case. The climax of this subplot happens when

Mickey hears the jury foreman ask if the jury can increase the amount awarded to the claimant.

Other Subplots *in* **The Verdict**

In addition to the Mickey and Laura subplots, this story has subplots that deal with (1) Doctor Towler, who is being sued for negligence; (2) the admitting nurse and the operating room nurse; (3) Dr. Thompson; and (4) the Doneghys. Although these four subplots are in the story, they are not developed as strongly as the Mickey subplot and the Laura subplot. Even so, these secondary characters become active around the first- and second-act twists. The first twist in the Doneghy subplot is when the husband shoves Galvin in the courthouse for refusing the settlement (Shot 40). The second twist (albeit a minor one) is when Sally Doneghy communicates despair over the direction of the case (Shot 67).

Nurse Kaitlin Costello doesn't appear until the final act (Shot 86), but her seven minutes of testimony (Shot 91) provide the hero with the lifeline he needs to win the case.

This final word on subplots: Since there are usually four to eight key players in a feature, that many subplots are possible. But rather than just letting subplots happen to characters, you may wish to assign characters specific "voices" that create variation and texture in the script. Thus, one subplot character might be the voice of the author, while another might be that of the trickster or the alter ego. A character may play the voice of reason, or fear and doubt or temptation. (See page 29 for more on this topic.)

ADDITIONAL STORY ELEMENTS

Much of the backstory in *The Verdict* is passed on by the hero's former law partner, Mickey Morrissey. We also pick up backstory from the insurance man, Joseph Alito, who lets us know that Galvin did well in law school but became involved in a jury-tampering scandal, turned to drink, and has almost no law practice remaining. The jury tampering occurred when Galvin reported his father-in-law's illegal action during the Lillibridge case. The revelation backfired when Galvin was blamed for the shenanigan and was almost disbarred. As it was, the incident led to the breakup of Galvin's marriage and began his slide into the pit where we meet him. The scandal is known throughout Boston's legal community, as are the reputations of the lawyers in this case.

The case being tried asks if two doctors lied when they swore that their patient ate *nine* hours prior to entering the delivery room. Gradually, through repeated references, the facts of the case accumulate around this question. When Galvin finally locates the nurse who convinces the jury that the doctors lied, the audience shares the hero's victory.

Charlotte Rampling creates her character's history out of a few lines of dialogue, such as "I can't afford to invest in failure again," implying that her husband's failure wrecked her marriage and her life. This one line is enough to suggest Laura's motivation: she is willing to do anything that will get her law career and her life started again—even if it means prostituting herself.

The frame, or setting, of the story is Boston and the legal world that surrounds an old courthouse. Director Sidney Lumet uses the cold winter light of the city to create shivery but effective settings. In this regard, the film makes excellent use of New England weather, the area's traditions, and Boston's faded Victorian elegance as it tracks the problem of saving Galvin's soul. The music (by Johnny Mandel) that colors this frame is somber, heavy, and sparing. It is used mainly to indicate the hero's inner conflict.

Thematically, the movie implies that the decency in humanity and its laws are worth preserving. In the course of the story, Galvin wins the case in a way that restores his spirit and his belief in the law. Those twin solutions (to the outer and inner conflict) are the event in *The Verdict*, what happens after everything happens. Note that a number of different events could have been wrung from the situation of the story. For example, the event could have been how Galvin saves himself by falling in love with Laura. Or it could have focused more on Judge Sweeney and how he deals with two greedy lawyers. Or it could examine how the jury decides which side is telling the truth (as in *Twelve Angry Men*).

SCENE-BY-SCENE BREAKDOWN OF THE VERDICT

Each shot number is listed below, along with the playing time of each bit and scene. Elapsed playing times are given to indicate how long the movie has been playing and how long each beat plays.

ACT I: THE SETUP
(THE HERO TAKES ON THE PROBLEM.)

SEQUENCE 1
STORY POINT MADE IN THIS SEQUENCE:
Introduce the hero. (Seven minutes)

(Shot not scripted) (1:22): Opening credits: slow dolly in on Galvin (Paul Newman) playing pinball, drinking beer. *Story point (SP) made:* Orientation scene to introduce Galvin and the wintry frame of story.

Shots 1–5 (3:26): Three bits show how Galvin operates: he follows obituaries and pays off two funeral directors so he can hustle business with the bereaved. The three bits end when he is given the bum's rush out of the second funeral home. "Soul" theme cues us to Galvin's inner pain. *SP:* Show how Galvin operates. Elapsed time: 4:48

Shot 6 (:37): Galvin jokes with the guys at his bar. *SP:* Shows Galvin's loneliness. Elapsed time: 5:25

Shot 7 (:46): Galvin drunkenly tears up his shabby law office. Music suggests his misery. *SP:* Indicate Galvin's inner pain. Elapsed time: 6:11

Shot 8 (1:17): Mickey (Jack Warden) arrives at Galvin's office and finds him passed out on the floor, the office a mess. The end of the soul theme signals the end of the first sequence and the beginning of the second sequence. *SP:* Introduce Mickey. Elapsed time: 7:28

SEQUENCE 2
STORY POINT MADE IN THIS SEQUENCE:
Introduce the problem. (Thirteen minutes)

Shot 8 (1:46): This beat is a continuation of the preceding action in Galvin's office, after the hero awakens. We are seven minutes into the movie when the "button" occurs that initiates the plot. It occurs when Mickey asks Galvin what he has done about the Doneghy case, soon to come to trial. Mickey announces that this is Galvin's last chance to do something right. *SP:* State dramatic problem and start the story. Elapsed time: 9:14

Shot 9 (:28): A bit indicating Galvin's shabbiness as he types a fake note that belies that he has no secretary. *SP:* Show Galvin's craftiness. Elapsed time: 9:42

Shot 10 (:40): Galvin stops off at a bar for a beer-and-egg eye-opener before visiting his client. *SP:* Show Galvin's unhealthy life-style.

Shots 11–12 (1:02): Galvin visits his brain-dead client in the back ward of an old hospital. *SP:* Begin to build Galvin's motivation for refusing the easy settlement.

(Shot not scripted) (:22): A bit in the lobby of Galvin's building, where the elevator fails and he must walk up the stairs. At this stage, nothing works right for him. *SP:* Reveal Galvin's character and advance the plot. Elapsed time: 11:24

Shots 13–14 (3:10): Sally Doneghy (sister of Galvin's client) enters Galvin's office, where he lays out their case. Sally's husband arrives and he too is a decent sort. They want the case settled so they can begin a new life in Arizona. *SP:* The Doneghys will be pleased with settlement and Galvin can make a lot of money for doing almost nothing—if he chooses the easy way out. Elapsed time: 14:34

Shot 15 (1:30): A bit between Bishop Brophy and insurance man Alito. A talky exchange that is broken up by a walk-and-talk through the prelate's palatial residence, to his waiting limo. *SP:* Church doesn't want the publicity of a trial, so it will offer to settle the case out of court. Scene also introduces the powerful forces opposing the hero. Elapsed time: 16:04

Shots 16–17: A bit between Galvin and his secretary, Claire Pavone, was cut from the production and her role was eliminated because it was not needed to tell the story.

Shots 18–22 (2:20): Galvin visits Dr. Gruber, his expert witness. A walk-and-talk scene where Gruber offers to nail the doctors who turned Galvin's client into a vegetable. *SP:* Galvin secures a key witness who is willing to testify because "it's the right thing. Isn't that why you're doing it?" This exchange stirs Galvin's unconscious and awakens his conscience. Elapsed time: 18:24

Shot 23 (1:30): Galvin, pleased with the Gruber meeting, drops into his bar and spots Laura (Charlotte Rampling). He puts a move on her but she slips away. *SP:* Galvin meets the love interest. Elapsed time: 19:54

SEQUENCE 3
STORY POINT MADE IN THIS SEQUENCE: Hero's conscience
causes him to take on the problem: he intends to fight the case.
(Eight minutes)

Shot 24 (1:55): Galvin in his shabby apartment talks to Sally Doneghy about the case. Again, something stirs within Galvin as he sips his Bushmills. *SP:* Galvin's conscience is awakening. Elapsed time: 21:59

Shot 25 (2:08): Galvin returns to the hospital, where he takes Polaroids of his client. As they develop, so does his conscience, causing him to announce to the nurse that it's okay for him to be in the ward because he is the patient's attorney. *SP:* Galvin's conscience is alive again. Elapsed time: 24:07

Shot 26 (4:08): Galvin takes his swollen conscience to the settlement meeting with Bishop Brophy. This is an "or else" scene in which the hero must choose the difficult path that will spin the story into a new and dangerous direction. The first twist in the scene is when Galvin comments on the easy arithmetic of the bishop's figure; the scene hinges again when Galvin flashes Polaroids of his brain-dead client. The climax of the scene occurs when Galvin refuses the bishop's offer for the sake of conscience. *SP:* Galvin refuses the offer, which sets up a confrontation with superior opponents, i.e., *the hero takes on the problem.* This reversal (twist) ends Act I. Elapsed time: 28:15

Act I playing time: twenty-eight minutes

ACT II: THE CONFRONTATION
(THE HERO SEEMS DEFEATED BY THE PROBLEM.)

SEQUENCE 4
STORY POINT MADE IN THIS SEQUENCE: *The two sides
prepare for battle. (Seventeen minutes)*

Shots 27–28 (2:18): Galvin meets Mickey at the courthouse and tells him about refusing the settlement. *SP:* Despite warnings from Mickey, the hero decides to take on Ed Concannon (James Mason). Elapsed time: 30:33

Shots 29–30 (2:54): Introduction to Concannon as he preps his team of lawyers for the upcoming battle with Galvin. *SP:* We meet the antagonist. Elapsed time: 33:27

Shot 31 (1:19): We cut from Concannon's grand offices to Galvin and Mickey working out of what appears to be a musty law school library that contrasts dramatically with Concannon's posh offices. Throughout the film Lumet packs his frame with visually dense settings to cover for a talky script that lacks visual action. Mention is made of the OB nurse who will connect Galvin to the admitting nurse—the one who turns out to be the lifeline that Galvin uses to win the case. *SP:* To inform the audience about the details of the case. Elapsed time: 34:46

Shot 32 (2:28): Galvin drops into his bar again where he meets Laura. Galvin asks her to have dinner with him. *SP:* Their relationship takes hold. Elapsed time: 37:14

Shot 33 (1:43): Galvin and Laura are chatting about the law as they finish up dinner. Galvin's speech grazes the theme as he muses about there being "no justice . . . but in their heart the jury's saying 'maybe.'" *SP:* Galvin reveals that he plans to fight the case, but he seems unsure. Elapsed time: 34:57

Shot 34 (1:57): A shabby little scene between Laura and Galvin in his apartment. He fixes drinks, kisses her, but she is uncomfortable until he puts the photo of his ex-wife away. There is a curious "commercial" quality to Laura's easy acquiescence, as though entertaining older men in bed was something that she did regularly. *SP:* Their affair is launched. Elapsed time: 40:54

Shots 35–37 (:30): Another barroom bit. This time Galvin beats the pinball game, but his involvement with the machine makes him late for his meeting. *SP:* As we saw earlier, Galvin is not taking care of business.

Shot 38 (4:16): A tense scene (analyzed in Chapter 4) that takes place in the chambers of the judge. The beat's three-part structure segments initially when Galvin remarks that his client can't walk; the second segment ends when Galvin announces that he will try the case and not take Concannon's final settlement offer; the third segment, which climaxes the scene, ends when Galvin tells Sweeney that he is sure that the judge would "take the money and run like a thief." *SP:* Galvin refuses the final settlement offer and antagonizes the judge who will try the case. Elapsed time: 45:40

SEQUENCE 5
STORY POINT MADE IN THIS SEQUENCE: Hero is stripped
of his star witness and must face his opponent without a defense.
(Sixteen minutes)

Shot 39 (:35): Brief stage directions tell us that Galvin is rusty as he tries to select a jury ("Galvin has flop sweat."). *SP:* Galvin appears to be a weak lawyer who is totally overmatched by Concannon. Elapsed time: 46:15

Shot 40 (3:35): A dense little scene sets up the trial. It begins outside the jury room when Mickey tells Galvin that Concannon is planting stories in the press. At the tobacco stand Galvin remembers his date with Laura and asks Mickey to fill in while he meets with Dr. Gruber. On the way out, Galvin is accosted by Dick Doneghy (Sally's husband), who is angry over Galvin's refusal of the settlement offer. Strong scene where the human dimensions of the case are evidenced. *SP:* If Galvin loses, the Doneghys will pay for his arrogance and Galvin will be disbarred. Elapsed time: 49:50

(Shot 41 cut)

Shots 42–43 (:25): The first bit in a three-bit scene begins in a doctor's lounge, where Galvin waits for Gruber. *SP:* Gruber does not show up.

Shot 44 (1:05): The second bit in the scene shows Galvin leaving the waiting room and moving through the hospital to the nurse's station, where he is told that Gruber is off-duty. Galvin gets Gruber's address from a phone book. *SP:* Still no Gruber and Galvin is worried.

Shots 45–46 (1:55): The third bit takes place a short time later as Galvin rings the front doorbell of Gruber's house: no answer. It starts to snow. The gloomy soul theme sounds as Galvin goes to the rear door where the housekeeper informs him that Gruber has gone to an island in the Caribbean where there is no phone. The three bits play for 3:25, during which Galvin realizes he has no case. *SP:* Galvin has lost his star witness and is in deep trouble. Elapsed time: 53:25

Shot 47 (1:37): Mickey and Laura eating in O'Rourke's Saloon; Mickey tells what really happened in the Lillibridge scandal. *SP:* Galvin was framed by the establishment, which makes the audience feel guilty for having suspected him of improprieties. An example of "undeserved suffering." Elapsed time: 55:02

Shots 48–49 (1:04): Galvin calls on the judge, who refuses to delay the trial. *SP:* Galvin gets no help from a hostile judge. Elapsed time: 56:06

Shot 50 (:27): A bit with Galvin in phone booth calling the insurance company. *SP:* Galvin is desperate and afraid.

(Shot not scripted) (:53): Laura and Mickey are still in O'Rourke's discussing Galvin's history. *SP:* Mickey explains how Galvin lost control of his life. Laura seems touched. Elapsed time: 57:26

Shot 51 (3:38): Galvin in his office trying (unsuccessfully) to cut a deal with the insurance company. Mickey arrives and witnesses his friend's desperation. Galvin calls a new expert witness. *SP:* Galvin is falling apart but he hires a new expert witness. Elapsed time: 61:02

Shot 52 (:50): A sympathy bit between Galvin and Laura as she tucks him into bed. *SP:* Laura senses that Galvin is falling apart.

The "clock" used in *The Verdict* started to tick 10 days before the start of the trial. The filmmakers use this time frame to create suspense and urgency. Note how visual content is supplied by exteriors of the neighborhoods, visits to the train station, and shots of large, ornate public buildings. Also note how these scenes begin to show Galvin acting with more courage as his lawyering skills begin to return. Elapsed time: 61:52

SEQUENCE 6
STORY POINT MADE IN THIS SEQUENCE: *Further collapse of the hero, who seems to be without a case and without hope.*
(Fourteen minutes)

Shot 53 (2:27): Concannon and company groom Dr. Towler to be part of the steam-roller that will crush Galvin. *SP:* Despite Galvin's sorry reputation, Concannon is taking no chances with this case. This dramatizing strategy makes the villain appear more formidable and places the hero in greater jeopardy. Elapsed time: 64:19

Shots 54–56 (1:59): Galvin picks up his expert witness, an aged black doctor. *SP:* Galvin's witness is not as impressive as Concannon's elegant Dr. Towler. Elapsed time: 66:18

Shots 57–58 (2:20): Galvin arrives at Nurse Rooney's tenement. Rooney gives Galvin the solution to his problem, but he's focused on what went on in the operating room, instead of what Rooney meant by "You guys are all the same! You've got no loyalty! You're a bunch of whores." Although Rooney seems to present a dead-end obstacle, later Galvin will figure out that she was referring to what happened to her friend Kaitlin Costello, the admitting nurse. *SP:* Galvin gets a clue, but it barely registers. Elapsed time: 68:38

Shot 59 (1:04): This bit plays in Concannon's office, where he learns about Dr. Thompson and his record of malpractice testimony. How did Concannon's people acquire this information? This exchange is a clue that Concannon has a spy. *SP:* Concannon is tracking Dr. Thompson and everything else that Galvin does.

Shot 60 (1:26): Galvin and Mickey figure out that Dr. Thompson doesn't even know what "Code Blue" means. However, a key question arises: when did Galvin's brain-dead client eat her last meal? Was it one hour or nine hours before admission? *SP:* Dr. Thompson is a weak witness. Elapsed time: 71:08.

Shot 61 (3:28): Laura's hotel room, where Galvin whimpers that he's going to lose the case. She berates him for quitting: "You said the trial wasn't over until the jury came in!" The scene ends when an anxiety attack sends Galvin retreating into the bathroom. *SP:* Laura's refusal to comfort Galvin is upsetting, and he stays awake all night, sipping whiskey, which is hardly the way to ready himself for trial. Elapsed time: 74:36

SEQUENCE 7
STORY POINT MADE IN THIS SEQUENCE: *Hero's blunders make it seem that he has been defeated. (Eleven minutes)*

Shots 62–63 (4:39): Galvin's opening remarks summarize the legal and medical issues and make us aware of his dubious legal talents. This story is unusual for the number of times it explains the details of the case, which the audience must understand in order to follow the plot. *SP:* Galvin is rusty and in over his head in a difficult case. Elapsed time: 79:15

Shot 64 (:27): A bit where one of Concannon's aides tells Alito of Galvin's visit to see Nurse Rooney. *SP:* Offers another clue that someone is spying on the hero. Elapsed time: 79:42

Shots 65–66 (4:39): A three-part scene that loads a monstrous trap for Galvin. First Concannon undermines the authority of Dr. Thompson, whom he condescendingly accepts as an "expert witness." In the second part of the scene the judge maneuvers Thompson into admitting the defendant doctors were not negligent—based on the narrow but confusing nature of the judge's questioning.

The trial recesses and the lawyers retire to the judge's chambers, where the argumentative third segment of the scene plays out. Galvin goes toe-to-toe with the judge, and for the first time we see real fire in our hero, as if the unfairness of the trial has connected him with what is right and good. *SP:* Galvin is losing badly but he continues to fight back. Elapsed time: 84:21

Shot 67 (:22): Galvin storms away from the meeting with the judge and sees Sally Doneghy. *SP:* The hero's case is sinking badly and he is unable to offer hope that things will improve. Elapsed time: 84:43

Shot 68 (1:44): The complication scene that ends Act II. In an example of on-the-nose writing that again explains what the case is about, Galvin tries to break Dr. Towler, but a reversal occurs when the doctor tells him that Deborah's brain damage could have occurred because she was anemic to begin with: "It's right there on her chart." Camera close-ups on various characters' reactions indicate that everyone feels that Galvin has lost his case. *SP:* This is the story's darkest moment. Elapsed time: 86:27

Act II playing time: fifty-seven minutes

ACT III: THE RESOLUTION
(THE HERO SOLVES THE PROBLEM.)

SEQUENCE 8
STORY POINT MADE IN THIS SEQUENCE:
Hero fights on, even though his case seems
hopeless. (Nine minutes)

Shot 69 (1:04): A bit outside the courtroom when Dr. Thompson offers a glimmer of hope by telling Galvin that people have a great capacity to hear the truth. *SP:* To hammer home Galvin's disaster while keeping hope alive. Elapsed time: 87:31

Shot 70 (:23): Galvin and Laura in snow outside courthouse discussing the case. *SP:* Galvin is unsure of what to do next. Elapsed time: 87:54

Shot 71 (:48): Galvin in his office getting a back rub from Mickey. *SP:* Mickey wants to quit, feeling that the case is over. Galvin refuses to quit. Elapsed time: 88.19

Shot 72 (1:49): In Concannon's office, where we learn that Laura is Concannon's spy. This is a major plot twist. *SP:* Laura is a spy. Elapsed time: 90:08

(Shots 73 and 74 cut)

Shot 75 (1:35): Galvin and Mickey search for a way to connect Nurse Rooney to the admitting nurse. Galvin exits to deal with Rooney personally. *SP:* They may have found a lead. Elapsed time: 91:43

Shot 76 (1:25): Galvin visits the hospital chapel, where he tricks Rooney into revealing that the admitting nurse lives somewhere in New York City. *SP:* Galvin learns that the admitting nurse lives in New York City. Elapsed time: 93:08

Shot 77 (1:26): Momentum accelerates as Galvin and Mickey attempt to locate the admitting nurse in New York. *SP:* They are unable to locate this witness. Elapsed time: 94:25

Shot 78 (:22): Laura thinks about phoning Concannon regarding the lead that Mickey and Galvin are pursuing. *SP:* For reasons of the heart, Laura does not call Concannon. Elapsed time: 94:47

SEQUENCE 9
STORY POINT MADE IN THIS SEQUENCE: *Hero locates his missing witness, who will become his lifeline. (Eleven minutes)*

Shots 79–80 (1:40): Galvin's chances improve when his telephone bill arrives in the morning mail and suggests an idea. *SP:* Though desperate, Galvin has landed another clue in his search for the admitting nurse. Elapsed time: 96:27

Shots 81–82 (1:25): Galvin pries open Nurse Rooney's mail box, where he finds her phone bill containing three calls to New York. *SP:* Once Galvin has the phone number (Kaitlin's), he has the lifeline needed to win the case. Elapsed time: 97:52

Shot 83 (:55): Galvin calls the number from Rooney's phone bill and locates Kaitlin Costello. A weight lifts from his shoulders when, finally, he speaks to her. *SP:* Galvin locates his witness. Elapsed time: 98:47

Shots 84–85 (1:25): Galvin calls Laura at his office and she senses that he is onto something. She agrees to meet him in New York City; meanwhile, Mickey is rummaging through her purse for a cigarette when he discovers the check from Concannon's firm. *SP:* Mickey discovers that Laura is a spy. Elapsed time: 100:12

Shot 86 (1:42): In New York City, Galvin meets the admitting nurse, played by Lindsay Crouse. *SP:* Galvin asks for Kaitlin's help. Elapsed time: 101:54

Shots 87–88 (:49): Mickey meets Galvin in New York City. *SP:* Galvin learns that Laura is a spy. Elapsed time: 102:53

Shot 89 (1:12): Galvin slaps Laura in a New York City lounge. *SP:* To express Galvin's contempt for Laura's betrayal. Elapsed time: 104:15

Shot 90 (:47): Galvin and Mickey are on a shuttle plane returning to Boston. *SP:* Though he has grounds for a mistrial, Galvin chooses to fight. Elapsed time: 105:02

Shot 91 (:47): A bit in Mickey's office, where Galvin refuses a phone call from Laura. *SP:* Galvin is turning his anger toward Concannon. Elapsed time: 105:49

SEQUENCE 10
STORY POINT MADE IN THIS SEQUENCE:
Hero wins case. (Sixteen minutes)

Shot 92 (11:49): This long beat is a scene-sequence, so-called because it is a single scene that plays like a sequence and makes a major story point. Scene-sequences, which are distinguished by their length and their importance to the story, are like short one-act plays in that they often segment into three parts; a few, like this one, may contain an epilogue-like ending. The barn raising in *Witness* and the three action scenes in *The Terminator* are also scene-sequences. *The Verdict*'s scene-sequence presents the climax of the story, when the hero solves the problem and wins the case. It begins when Galvin gets Dr. Towler to testify that the claimant ate *nine* hours earlier. The point of this first segment of the beat deals with how Galvin baits a trap for Concannon that sets up the climax.

The confrontation segment of the climactic scene begins when Galvin calls in his lifeline (Kaitlin Costello). She testifies that the claimant had a meal only one hour before anesthesia, not the nine hours claimed by Dr. Towler.

In this third segment of the scene-sequence, Concannon cross-examines Kaitlin. He gets careless and bullies her into saying that the doctors forced her to change the admitting form so it read that Deborah ate nine hours before anesthesia rather than one hour before anesthesia. With this, Concannon's case falls apart. This key moment uses a triple reversal to prove that the doctors lied. The story climaxes with Kaitlin's impassioned speech about wanting to be a nurse. *SP:* Concannon falls into Galvin's trap. Mamet sustains the climax, delaying the moment until the jury comes in with its verdict.

In this fourth segment of the scene-sequence, which is like an epilogue, Concannon tries to salvage his case. The judge agrees with him, but the jury has heard the truth and will decide. *SP:* Issue in doubt. Elapsed time: 117:38

Shot 93 (:27): Bishop Brophy frets over the morality of the case. *SP:* Sustains the climax and ends this storyline.

Shot 94 (3:49): Galvin's summation speech. *SP:* Galvin posits the moral basis of his case: Act as if you have faith (in the law) and you will be given faith—and justice. Elapsed time: 122:04

Shots 95–96 (1:15): The moment of climax. *SP:* The jury finds for Galvin's case. Elapsed time: 123:19

Shot 97 (:10): A bit where Galvin glimpses Laura as he leaves the courthouse. After a moment she disappears.

The film ends with two unscripted bits that play for two minutes. One shows Laura drunk as she phones Galvin; the other shows Galvin as he sips coffee in his office, refusing to answer Laura's call. *SP:* Their relationship is over.

Act III playing time: thirty-eight minutes
Total playing time: approximately 125 minutes

SUMMARY

The Verdict employs a three-act structure that is based on the tracking of a problem. As in most feature films, it employs an A-storyline and a B-storyline. As is usually the case, the A-storyline deals with plot (winning the case); the B-storyline deals with the internal struggle of the main character (believing in the law, the self). Features can also have as many as a half-dozen subplots that develop secondary characters who comment on the theme and the conflict of the story.

Most motion picture stories work from a situation that is suggested in the story concept. In *The Verdict*, the situation/concept involves a boozy lawyer who blunders into a battle against a powerful lawyer. Whether attached to a sitcom, an hour episodic, a movie-of-the-week, or a feature, the story concept is the starting point for developing a story with a three-act structure that is organized around the tracking of a dramatic problem.

Many writers begin their stories by writing a backstory that provides a history for the location and for the main characters. (As noted in Chapter 5, backstory concerns what happens before the story began.) In *The Verdict*, the key backstory incidents involve the hero's disgrace over a jury-tampering charge, the brain death of a young mother, and Laura's need to reestablish her legal career. Backstory influences such as these are used to create the interior lives of the main characters.

The Verdict illustrates how a plot summary, written like a simple short story, can help organize a story idea into three acts. The first act of most features sets up the story by introducing the hero, the villain, and the problem. The second act gets the hero in deep trouble as he or she conflicts with the villain over the problem. The third act sees the hero solve the problem in a surprising yet logical manner. This three-act pattern is used by most stories, regardless of length or outlet (TV or features).

Although traditional three-act structure may strike some as being a formulaic approach (especially anyone wishing to invent a new storytelling approach), this organizing strategy has provided writers with ample room to experiment during the past several thousand years of western drama. I suggest that those who feel constricted by the three-act structure begin by mastering the "formula." When this task has been accomplished, invent or adapt your own scheme. The movie industry is forever trying to invent something new, and it seems to have an unlimited ability to absorb innovation. What remains constant is the need for a good story that is told with imagination, passion, and flair.

Professional Version of the "Marry Me—or Else" Scene

The Situation: A woman (Leslie) is weary of waiting for her lover (Frank Serpico) to marry her, so she delivers an ultimatum: Marry me or I'll marry my friend in Texas. Below you will find the scene from the film (Serpico), written by Waldo Salt and Norman Wexler. Compare your scene with theirs and then view the scene to see how much can be said with minimal dialogue.

INT. SERPICO'S BATHROOM - NIGHT

Leslie [Cornelia Sharpe] and Serpico [Al Pacino] in a bubble bath. The room is lit by candles. There is incense burning. Music can be heard from the other room. Leslie scrubs Serpico's back.

> LESLIE
> This is a good place to tell you, Paco. That guy in Texas I was telling you about -- I'm going to marry him in two months.

Leslie climbs around him in the tub, faces him, smiles.

> LESLIE (continuing)
> Unless . . . you marry me.

> SERPICO
> What about the theater, your dancing?

---

*This appendix is referenced in Chapter 6, p. 188.

                    LESLIE
          A girl has to get married
          sometime.

                    SERPICO
          You're a long time from
          sometime, Leslie.

He gets out of the tub, starts to dry himself.

                    SERPICO
          I thought you were committed.

                    LESLIE
          I am but . . .

                    SERPICO
               (cutting her off)
          You are . . . but . . .

                    LESLIE
          I can keep working, studying
          there.

                    SERPICO
          In Fort Worth?

                    LESLIE
          Amarillo.

                    SERPICO
          Am I invited to the
          wedding . . .

                    LESLIE
          I'll ask Roy.

                    END OF SCENE

Rewrite of Immigrant Scene Exercise in Chapter 11

REWRITE OF SCENE

The only "right" way to improve a line of dialogue, a scene, or a story is to rewrite the material so it is more dramatic and more entertaining. A hundred writers would find at least that many ways to rewrite the scene in this exercise. Some work fast, and some work slowly: rewriting takes as long as it takes. The rewrite below required two days. It is longer than the original, but it retains focus on Mary and her family, since they are at the center of the original scene.

```
EXT.  THE GREAT PLAINS OF THE DAKOTA TERRITORY -
ESTABLISHING - DAY
```

```
An empty land.  Without trees or mercy.  A silvery glint
becomes the tracks of the transcontinental railroad and a
steam engine (1870s) pulling railroad cars.
```

```
INT.  BOXCAR OF TRAIN - DAY
```

```
Two dozen families crowd into a stifling boxcar.  At first
they look like bundles of rags, but as the angle tightens
we pick out a teenager fanning his mother, a man holding
up a ragged cloth to screen his wife as she bathes from a
bowl of water, a boy playing chess with an old man.
```

```
Fresh air and light are so precious that the immigrants
take turns being pressed up to cracks and vents.  A man
peers outside, then says something in Swedish to his
family.
```

*This appendix is referenced in Chapter 11, p. 316.

The Swede's wife pushes past him for a look, bumping into one of her children, who begins to cry. The wife shakes the kid . . . causing a German family to converge on the viewing crack. In seconds, FEAR grips the immigrants; everyone is talking excitedly, trying to see what's outside.

ANGLE OF THE MORRIS FAMILY

MARY, a six-year-old, joins her father (ROMAN) as he looks outside. Roman's wife (CLEONA) and their two smaller children join her husband and Mary.

                    MARY
          He says there's no trees.

                    ROMAN
          There'll be trees. There's
          nothing bad out there. . . .
          it's -- just . . . !

The kids sense their father's fear. Someone sees something through the cracks in the siding, and Mary and her four-year-old brother TIMMY rush to their crack for a look-see.

MARY'S P.O.V. - THROUGH CRACK - THE DAKOTAS - DAY

The empty land intimidates everyone.

BACK TO SCENE

Mary turns from the crack and looks sadly at her father and mother. Children are weeping now.

ANGLE SHIFTS as a thin Welsh woman begins singing a hymn. She is joined by other women, and then the children and the men until they are all singing to God to drive away their fear. Mary watches in silence.

EXT. THE HIGH PLAINS

                    SUPER: DAKOTA TERRITORY 1871

SOUND of the locomotive fades in.
As the train ENTERS the
FRAME, we hear the SOUND of the immigrants singing.

The camera soars down the track. The singing fades out so
there is only the HISSSSS of the wind. Then another SOUND
fades in: a strange metallic HAMMERING.

Camera swoops toward something bright in the distance. As
the helicopter shot moves down the track, the hammering
grows LOUDER . . . until we see a Sioux warrior in war
regalia . . . hacking mindlessly on the railroad track
with a steel ax. He does no harm, but it doesn't matter.
He is preparing to die.

ANOTHER ANGLE OF SIOUX WARRIOR

In the distance, the locomotive shimmers into view.

INT. CAB OF THE LOCOMOTIVE

Fireman stokes boiler while Engineer looks down the track.

ENGINEER'S P.O.V. - SIOUX WARRIOR STRIKING THE TRACK

BACK TO SCENE

The Engineer reaches for the whistle cord.

INT. THE BOXCAR

Immigrants are singing when the SOUND of the train whistle
renders them silent and FEAR reasserts.

INTERCUT TRAIN, BOXCAR, SIOUX WARRIOR

The trainmen realize the warrior is ignoring their
warning whistle. The two men exchange looks, then the
Fireman returns to stoking; the Engineer SOUNDS the
whistle.

INTERCUT SIOUX WARRIOR, ENGINEER, AND FIREMAN AS THE TRAIN
APPROACHES.

SIOUX WARRIOR IS GROUND UNDER THE LOCOMOTIVE

REACTION OF ENGINEER AND FIREMAN TO KILLING THE WARRIOR

INT. BOXCAR - MARY AND HER FATHER

Mary's face is pressed to a crack in the floor when she suddenly jerks upright, shocked by something she'll remember for the rest of her life: the dismembered warrior flashing beneath her, his scream mixed with that of the train whistle. BLOOD splatters her face. Mary gasps for breath. Then others react to the horror of the blood that has splattered through the boxcar. Mary's mother grabs her.

                    MARY
          A man! I saw a man!

Cleona sees the blood and quickly wipes it off Mary's face, tossing Roman a ferocious look.

                    CLEONA
          You had a dream.

                    MARY
          A man was all --

                    CLEONA
          You had a dream!

Cleona restrains Mary, looking at her warningly. The train shudders to a halt. The immigrants fall silent.

Mary understands her mother's admonition and controls her terror. Slowly a mournful moaning rises from the silence. The wind.

ANALYSIS OF SCENE

The rewritten scene adds a few incidents and details to the original. To beef up the scene's visual content and to explain what is worrying the immigrants, additional exterior shots were included. To punch up the clash of the old and new, the incident with the Sioux warrior was added. He prays to his God for strength and courage to defeat the machines invading his lands. The fear of the settlers is represented by the hymn that asks the Christian God for strength. Mary and her family are used to organize the scene and to help define the settlers.

The warrior's death is a strategy for settling the audience into a mood that is consistent with the story unfolding; it is a serious drama, like *The New Land*. The blood that splatters up through the cracks in the floor of the boxcar makes the point of the scene: Although the settlers try to turn a brave face to the new land, it holds them in a fearful grip.

The scene divides into three parts: the first segment ends when the immigrants sing for courage; the second segment ends when Mary screams in horror; the final segment deals with the aftermath of the warrior's death. The "red dot" (point of the scene) occurs when Mary obeys her mother's warning look and behaves courageously, even after the warrior's blood splatters people in the boxcar. The polarity of the scene shifts from positive to negative. Subtext is supplied by the fear and uncertainty of the immigrants.

The Engineer and the Fireman were added to dramatize the death of the Sioux warrior. The scene is basically a chase-and-capture scene, because the immigrants are "captured" by their fear. The rewrite would add about two minutes to the original two-minute playing time of the scene. Unless told specifically that the rewritten material is to be of a specific length, we write to the length that seems to make the material work best. If a scene proves to be too long or too expensive, then the rewrite would be rewritten until it felt acceptable.

Writers Guild of America
TV Market List

*Source: *Journal of the WGA,* June 1995. This appendix is referenced in Chapter 12, p. 320.

Please note that this is the most current information we have available.

SHOW	TYPE/LENGTH	SCRIPT STATUS	COMPANY	CONTACT	NETWORK
Almost Perfect	EC/30 min.	▲	Paramount		CBS
Babylon 5	ED/60 min.	▲	Babylonian Prods.		SYN
Baywatch	ED/60 min.	★	Baywatch Prod. Co.	Michael Berk or David Braff (310) 302-9135	SYN
Beverly Hills, 90210	ED/60 min.	▲	Spelling TV Inc.		FBC
Bless This House	EC/30 min.	▲	Warner Bros.		CBS
Boy Meets World	EC/30 min.	▲	Walt Disney Pics.		ABC
Brotherly Love	EC/30 min.	▲	Witt-Thomas/Disney		NBC
Burke's Law	ED/60 min.	▲	Spelling TV		CBS
California Dreams	EC/30 min.	★	NBC Prods.	Diane Farrell (818) 840-7780	NBC
Caroline In The City	EC/30 min.	▲	CBS Entertainment Prod.		NBC
Central Park West	ED/60 min.	▲	CBS Prods.		CBS
Charlie Grace	ED/60 min.	▲	Warner Bros.		ABC
Chicago Hope	ED/60 min.	▲	20th Cent.		CBS
Coach	EC/30 min.	▲	Universal TV		ABC
Courthouse	ED/60 min.	▲	Columbia		CBS
Cybill	EC/30 min.	▲	Carsey-Werner		CBS
Dave's World	EC/30 min.	▲	CBS Ent.		CBS
Diagnosis Murder	ED/60 min.	▲	Viacom		CBS
Double Rush	EC/30 min.	▲	Shukovsky/English Ent.		CBS
Dr. Quinn: Medicine Woman	ED/60 min.	▲	CBS Ent.		CBS
Dream On	EC/30 min.	★	Melkis Prods.	Bill Sanders (818) 777-5013	HBO
The Drew Carey Show	EC/30 min.	▲	Warner Bros.		ABC
Due South	ED/60 min.	▲	Alliance Comm.		CBS
Ellen	EC/30 min.	▲	Walt Disney TV		ABC
ER	ED/60 min.	★	Warner Bros.	Lydia Woodward (818) 954-3826	NBC
Family Matters	EC/30 min.	★	Warner Bros. TV	Fred Fox, Jr. (818) 954-7435	ABC
The 5 Mrs. Buchanans	EC/30 min.	▲	20th Cent.		CBS
Frasier	EC/30 min.	▲	Paramount		NBC
The Fresh Prince of Bel-Air	EC/30 min.	▲	NBC Productions		NBC
Friends	EC/30 min.	▲	Warner Bros. TV		NBC
Grace Under Fire	EC/30 min.	▲	Carsey-Werner		ABC
Hangin' with Mr. Cooper	EC/30 min.	▲	Warner Bros.		ABC
Hearts Afire	EC/30 min.	▲	Mozark Productions		CBS
The Home Court	EC/30 min.	▲	Witt-Thomas		NBC
Home Improvement	EC/30 min.	▲	Wind Dancer Prods.		ABC
Homicide: Life on the Street	ED/60 min.	▲	Baltimore Pics.		NBC
Hope and Gloria	EC/30 min.	▲	Warner Bros. TV		NBC
Hudson Street	EC/30 min.	▲	TriStar TV		ABC
In The House	EC/30 min.	▲	NBC Prod.		NBC
Jag	ED/60 min.	▲	Paramount/NBC Prod.		NBC
Kung Fu: The Legend Cont.	ED/60 min.	★	Warner Bros.	Michael Sloan (818) 972-0052	SYN
Larroquette Show	EC/30 min.	▲	Witt Thomas		NBC
The Larry Sanders Show	EC/30 min.	▲	Brillstein-Grey Ent.		HBO
Law & Order	ED/60 min.	▲	Universal TV		NBC
Legend	ED/60 min.	▲	T.L. Productions		UPN
Living Single	EC/30 min.	▲	Warner Bros. TV		FBC
Lois and Clark: The New Adventures of Superman	ED/60 min.	▲	Warner Bros. TV		ABC
Lonesome Dove	ED/60 min.	★	Canadian Dove Prods.	David Wilks/Allison Hock (403) 252-8115	SYN
Love & War	EC/30 min.	★	Love & War Prods., Inc.	Ian Praiser (818) 760-6100	CBS
Mad About You	EC/30 min.	▲	TriStar TV		NBC
Marker	ED/60 min.	▲	Cannell Studios		UPN
Married...with Children	EC/30 min.	▲	Columbia Pics. TV		FBC

TV Market List Legend: **L**=Anthology **AA**=Action-Adventure **AD** = Action-Drama **DC**=Dramatic Comedy **V**=Variety **MD** = Musical Drama **EC**=Episodic Comedy **ED**=Episodic Drama **RC**=Romantic Comedy **SF**=Science Fiction **S**=Serial **CV**=Comedy-Variety **MC** = Musical Comedy

The person named as contact for each TV series is not necessarily the one empowered to make commitments to writers. For information as to authorized representatives, please call or write the Equal Employment Access Dept. at the Guild, (310) 205-2548. For the most up to date information, call the TV Market List Hotline: (310) 205-8600.

SHOW	TYPE/LENGTH	SCRIPT STATUS	COMPANY	CONTACT	NETWORK
The Marshal	ED/60 min.	▲	Paramount		ABC
Martin	EC/30 min.	▲	HBO Indep. Prods.		FBC
Maybe This Time	EC/30 min.	▲	Disney		ABC
Melrose Place	ED/60 min.	▲	Spelling TV Inc.		FBC
Minor Adjustments	EC/30 min.	▲	Witt-Thomas		NBC
The Monroes	ED/60 min.	▲	Warner Bros.		ABC
Murder One	ED/60 min.	▲	Steven Bochco		ABC
Murder, She Wrote	ED/60 min.	▲	Universal TV		CBS
Murphy Brown	EC/30 min.	★	Warner Bros. TV	Jana Barto (818) 954-3700	CBS
The Nanny	EC/30 min.	▲	TriStar		CBS
Newsradio	EC/30 min.	▲	Brillstein-Grey		NBC
Northern Exposure	ED/60 min.	▲	Finnegan-Pinchuk		CBS
NYPD Blue	ED/60 min.	▲	Steve Bochco Prods.		ABC
Off Duty	ED/60 min.	▲	Rysher		CBS
Paradise Beach	ED/60 min.	▲	New World Int'l.		SYN
People V	ED/60 min.	▲	NBC Prods./Universal		CBS
Picket Fences	ED/60 min.	★	20th Century Fox TV	Ann Donahue (310) 203-2692	CBS
Pig Sty	EC/30 min.	▲	Paramount Network TV		UPN
Platypus Man	EC/30 min.	▲	Kevin Bright Prods.		UPN
Pointman	ED/60 min.	▲	Warner Bros. Dom. TV Dist.		SYN
Pursuit of Happiness	EC/30 min.	▲	Grub St. Prod./Paramount TV		NBC
Renegade	ED/60 min.	▲	Stu Segall Prods.		SYN
Robin's Hoods	ED/60 min.	▲	Spelling TV		SYN
Roseanne	EC/30 min.	▲	Carsey-Werner Co.		ABC
Saved by the Bell: The New Class	EC/30 min.	▲	NBC Prods.		NBC
seaQuest DSV	ED/60 min.	▲	Universal/Amblin		NBC
Seinfeld	EC/30 min.	▲	Castle Rock Entertainment		NBC
Silk Stalkings	ED/60 min.	▲	Stephen J. Cannell		CBS/USA
The Single Guy	EC/30 min.	▲	Castle Rock/NBC Prods.		NBC
Sisters	ED/60 min.	★	Warner Bros. TV	Ron Cowen or Daniel Lipman (818) 954-3403	NBC
Sliders	ED/60 min.	▲	Universal TV		Fox
Somewhere in America	EC/30 min.	▲	ABC Prods.		ABC
Star Trek: Voyager	ED/60 min.	▲	Paramount TV		SYN/UPN
Star Trek: Deep Space 9	ED/60 min.	●	Paramount TV	Michael Piller (213) 956-5910 (Non-Agent Sub. (213) 956-8301)	SYN
Step by Step	EC/30 min.	▲	Lorimar Productions		ABC
Tales from the Crypt	ED/30 min.	▲	Tales from the Crypt Prods.		HBO
Touched by an Angel	ED/60 min.	▲	CBS Ent.		CBS
Thunder in Paradise	ED/60 min.	★	J.G. Business Mgmt.	Michael Berk or Tom Greene (310) 301-7655	SYN
Under One Roof	ED/60 min.	▲	Katy Films		CBS
Under Suspicion	ED/60 min.	▲	Warner Bros.		CBS
Unhappily Ever After	EC/30 min.	★	Disney	Sandy Sprung/Marcy Vosburgh (818) 560-7865	WBC
University Hospital	ED/60 min.	▲	Spelling TV		UPN
Uptown Undercover	EC/30 min.	▲	Universal		FBC
VR.5	ED/60 min.	▲	Rysher Ent.		Fox
Walker: Texas Ranger	ED/60 min.	▲	CBS Ent.		CBS
The Watcher	ED/60 min.	▲	Paramount Network TV		UPN
Weird Science	EC/30 min.	▲	Universal		SYN
Wilde Again (Tea Leoni Show)	EC/30 min.		Brillstein-Grey		ABC
Wings	EC/30 min.	▲	Paramount TV		NBC
Women of the House	EC/30 min.	▲	Mozark Prods.		CBS
Wright Verdicts	ED/60 min.	▲	Wolf Film Prod.		CBS
The X-Files	ED/60 min.	★	20th TV	Chris Carter (310) 369-1130	FBC

★ *Submissions through agents only*   ▲ *All scripts committed for the current season*   ● *Open for submissions*
■ *For terms and conditions regarding this series, please call the Contracts Department*   ? *Information unavailable*

APPENDIX G*

Script Evaluation Forms

The reader evaluation forms that follow have been gathered from different movie studios and production companies. Called "coverage," the evaluations are performed by professional readers, who review one or two scripts per day. These summaries are then read by executives, who use them to select the scripts that have been given favorable ratings. Scripts that pass this second read are reviewed by the development staff, usually consisting of a half dozen or so executives. Some scripts will be rejected, some will be put into "development" (to be discussed and rewritten by the original writer or a new writer), and a select few will be approved for production.

---

*This appendix is referenced in Chapter 12, p. 325.

STUDIO READER EVALUATION FORM

1: SUPERIOR: 2: OUTSTANDING 3: SATISFACTORY
4: ACCEPTABLE 5: UNSATISFACTORY

QUALITIES	DESCRIPTION	COMMENTS
Sense of character 1 2 3 4 5	Story shows a clear sense of leads, heroes, supporting characters in their involvement with the story.	
Sense of concept 1 2 3 4 5	Concept used is an interesting springboard that audiences can relate to.	
Movement 1 2 3 4 5	Quality of emotion or physical energy.	
Warmth 1 2 3 4 5	Quality of rooting interest—what is the reader's reaction to the story's emotional content?	
Jeopardy 1 2 3 4 5	Presentation of what is at stake, danger faced by hero or heroine, life or death stakes.	
Conflict 1 2 3 4 5	Presentation of the depth of the conflict.	
Humor 1 2 3 4 5	Quality of humor presented. Is it forced? Is there a natural flow?	
Plot/Subplot 1 2 3 4 5	The extent of the linear progression. Are story and substory delineated and followed through? Resolved?	
Hardware 1 2 3 4 5	Utilization of equipment in the story.	
Resolution 1 2 3 4 5	Story concludes fully resolved, with no loose ends.	
Presentation 1 2 3 4 5	Professional appearance.	
Format 1 2 3 4 5	Length is appropriate for the form of the film.	

READER'S COVERAGE OF A FEATURE SCRIPT (SAMPLE)

Here is an example of a reader's coverage of a feature script that was submitted to one of the major motion picture studios. Names have been altered for confidentiality.

Type of Material: Screenplay, 122 pp.

Title: The Winged One

Submitted by: BCC Agency

Author: Vic Taylor

Analyst: C. J. Carter—

Circa: Future

Location: Alien earth-like planet

Date: June 12, 1994

Drama Category: Fantasy Adventure

THEME: On the distant planet of Vignolo, a renegade Prince and rightful heir to the throne tries to wrest rule of the planet from an evil High Priestess who usurped her station from the Prince's father.

Sometime in the future, on the distant planet of Vignolo. AVISTA, High Priestess of Vignolo, holds supreme and evil reign over the seven tribes, or races, of the planet. She has held such a position for over 3000 "cycles" when she took power from the "Winged One" and sent him into banishment. It is now time for Avista to initiate new leaders of the seven tribes—leaders specifically chosen by her to follow her orders. One of those new leaders happens to be DOLGER, of the Talish tribe, who— unbeknownst to both himself and Avista—is the son of the "Winged One" and thus the rightful heir to the throne which Avista occupies.

It is during Dolger's initiation that he has a strange vision that tells him of his heritage. Dolger is confused, but he knows he can no longer be a part of Avista's tyrannical rule. Dolger flees into the desert and the other six tribe leaders pursue him with strict orders from Avista to bring him back or kill him as she now realizes who he truly is. It is not easy for the other leaders to find and stop Dolger.

Meanwhile, Dolger is taken in by a tribe of Nomads where he meets the beautiful SALONNA, with whom he falls in love. It is also with the Nomads that Dolger encounters LORD SEENO, whom he finds out is his true father. Lord

Seeno and VRANN, a Nomad leader, take Dolger across the
desert to the City of Krimm, where Dolger will gain
strength from the Spirit of Knowledge.

    The leaders of the other tribes track Dolger to the
City of Krimm. A mighty battle ensues and Dolger is able
to wrest his rightful power from Avista. Back in the
throne room of the Temple of the King, Dolger is joined
by Salonna and justice is restored to the planet.

COMMENT:

Regrettably, "The Winged One" is a tediously overwritten
screenplay which ultimately fails to reveal any sort of
storyline that is easily decipherable. The material is a
fantasy adventure which attempts to paint an almost fairy-
tale-like saga about a renegade prince who is attempting
to regain his rightful throne. The piece is full of
magical incantations, hallucinatory visions, thunderbolts
that dance off fingertips, etc., and a final battle
between the forces of good and evil in which good, of
course, triumphs. There is nothing new, fresh, or original here in either the basic storyline or the accompanying
story elements. Characters are thinly developed, dialogue
is archaic and sometimes baffling in meaning, settings
aren't clearly specified or described, and the general
structure of the piece is much too confusing. Unfortunately, this is a screenplay which meanders haphazardly
and offers nothing exciting or imaginative in the fairy-
tale/fantasy-adventure genre.

NOT RECOMMENDED   December 12, 1994

STUDIO EXAM GIVEN TO PROSPECTIVE READERS

This studio exam is given to prospective readers. Applicants have six hours to read a test script and to write a review of it. The questions cited are representative of those that readers are expected to apply to scripts evaluated.

    Write a complete synopsis of the script, not more than two pages in length. In doing your analysis please use the following questions as a guideline in assessing the strengths and weaknesses of the script. It is not necessary to answer all of the questions as they may not always apply to the script you have been asked to read.

1. Short outline (3 lines).
2. What is the genre of the film?
3. Describe the content of the film.
   (a) What is the main conflict of the story? Is it clear? Is it satisfactorily resolved?
   (b) Is the story best suited as a feature film?

   (c) Is there enough material for a feature film?

   (d) Does the writer make good use of the cinematic medium?

4. Comment on the characters.

   (a) Are they believable and fully developed within the context of the story?

   (b) Does the lead character have a clear intention or goal? Is it properly motivated?

   (c) Do the characters change as a result of the story? Are these changes properly motivated?

   (d) Is the opposing character (or characters) interesting?

   (e) Has the writer made good use of bit parts?

5. Comment on the plot structure.

   (a) Does every scene reveal new information about the characters or the main action of the story?

   (b) Does the writer have a sense of introducing new elements of the story at appropriate times?

   (c) Does the tension build?

   (d) Does the writer make good use of suspense, or is the action of the story predictable?

   (e) Are there enough subplots to make the story interesting and do they tie into the main action?

6. Comment on the dialogue.

   (a) Is it well-written?

   (b) Has the writer used dialogue where visuals would better convey the meaning, and vice versa?

   (c) Do all the characters have their own distinctive dialogue or do they all tend to sound the same?

7. What type of audience do you think would be interested in seeing this film in the United States and outside of the United States?

Writers Guild of America Minimum Basic Agreement 1991–1995

*This appendix is referenced in Chapter 12, p. 329

WGA 1992 THEATRICAL AND TELEVISION BASIC AGREEMENT*
[Partial listing only. Actual payments may be negotiated higher.]

THEATRICAL COMPENSATION—EMPLOYMENT, FLAT DEALS

	To 5/1/93		To 5/1/95	
	(low)	(high)	(low)	(high)
Original Screenplay, Including Treatment	$35,076	$65,793	$37,938	$71,847

Installments:

Delivery of Treatment	15,894	26,319	17,356	28,741
Delivery of First Draft Screenplay	13,813	26,319	14,366	28,741
Delivery of Final Draft Screenplay	5,369	13,155	5,583	14,365
Original Treatment	15,894	26,316	11,970	28,741
Rewrite of Screenplay	11,510	17,546	11,970	18,248
Polish of Screenplay	5,757	8,772	5,987	9,180

WEEK-TO-WEEK EMPLOYMENT

14 out of 14 weeks	2,855 per week	3,117 per week
20 out of 26 weeks	2,449 per week	2,895 per week
40 out of 52 weeks	2,250 per week	2,457 per week

LOW BUDGET: Motion picture costing less than $2,500,000.
HIGH BUDGET: Motion picture costing $2,500,000 or more.

TELEVISION COMPENSATION
NETWORK PRIME TIME

(Note: Latest WGA contract agreements will increase these payments by approximately 10 percent between 1995 and 1997.)

Effective	**May '92–May '93**	**May '93–May '94**	**May '94–May '95**
Length of Program:	120 minutes or less (but more than 90 minutes)		
STORY	$14,546	$15,128	$15,733
TELEPLAY	24,842	25,846	26,880
STORY AND TELEPLAY	37,826	39,339	40,913
Length of Program:	90 minutes or less (but more than 60 minutes)		
STORY	10,891	11,327	11,780
TELEPLAY	19,367	20,142	20,948
STORY AND TELEPLAY	28,750	29,900	31,096
Length of Program:	60 minutes or less (but more than 45 minutes)		
STORY	8,152	8,478	8,860
TELEPLAY	13,443	13,981	14,540
STORY AND TELEPLAY	20,434	21,251	22,208
Length of Program:	30 minutes or less (but more than 15 minutes)		
STORY	4,631	4,816	5,009
TELEPLAY	9,966	10,365	10,831
STORY AND TELEPLAY	13,894	14,450	15,028

Writer's Deal Memorandum

The deal memo shown on the following pages is typical of the contracts struck between writers and production companies. Deal memos are signed after the buyer expresses interest in a pitch and story concept. In this example, note the various cutoff options available to the producer should the writer fail to deliver the story or script expected.

1. NAME: John Smith

2. ATTORNEY OR AGENT: XYZ Associates, 4214 Wilshire Blvd., Beverly Hills, CA 90201

3. CAPACITY: Screenwriter

4. PROPERTY: "Zebra Man," a novel by Phillip Jones

5. START DATE: Upon signing of this deal memo.

6. TERMS:

a. $60,000 for a first draft screenplay payable $30,000 upon signing of this Deal Memo, and three additional payments of $10,000 each upon delivery of each of three approximately equal installments of the screenplay, the last installment of which shall be delivered no later than December 10, 1995. It is understood that the Producers may require Smith to restructure the first of such installments without additional compensation therefore.

b. $30,000 for a rewrite and/or polish payable $10,000 upon commencement of such rewrite and/or polish and $20,000 upon delivery thereof. Such delivery shall be made within four weeks after Producer's notification to Smith to commence said rewrite and/or polish. This notification must be given Smith, by not less than 14 days' written notice, within 120 days after delivery of the first draft screenplay. During this 120 days, Smith may accept other assignments, provided, however, that upon receipt of appropriate notice, as aforesaid, Smith shall render to Producer four consecutive weeks of nonexclusive services in connection with such rewrite and/or polish.

c. In addition to the above payments, if Smith receives sole screenplay credit, Producer will pay Smith an additional $100,000 on commencement of principal photography, if no other writer has been assigned to the project by Producer. If another writer has been assigned to the project but Smith still receives sole screenplay credit, Producer will pay Smith such additional $100,000 within ten days after final determination of such sole screenplay credit. In the event another writer has been assigned to the project and such writer receives joint screenplay credit with Smith, Smith's payment of $100,000 shall be reduced by the compensation to the writer who receives joint screenplay credit, to a maximum of $50,000. Screenplay credits will be determined by the Arbitration Committee of the Writers Guild of America, West, Inc.

Reference to "other writer being assigned to the project" shall refer to another writer engaged after Smith delivers his first draft screenplay and not any writer previously assigned to the project. Additionally, if another writer has been assigned to the project by Producer but it is reasonably clear in the sole judgment of Producer at the time of commencement of principal photography that Smith shall receive at least shared screenplay credit, then Smith shall be paid $50,000 upon commencement of principal photography, which $50,000 shall be a credit toward the additional payments due to Smith, if any.

d.   In addition to the cash compensation as above, Producer will pay Smith 2 percent of 100 percent of the net profits of the film, if Smith receives sole or split screenplay credit.   The definition of net profits shall be the same as the most favored definition given any other participant in this production.

7. <u>BILLING:</u>	Single card credit worded approximately: "Screenplay by John Smith." In the event of any other writing claims, the final credit will be determined by the Arbitration Committee of the Writers Guild of America, West, Inc.
8. <u>RIGHTS:</u>	All motion picture, television, and allied rights.
9. <u>MISCELLANEOUS:</u>	If Producer shall require Smith's services more than 50 miles from Los Angeles, Producer shall provide first-class transportation, if available, and $300 per day for expenses during the period that Smith shall be required to remain out of town.

<u>ACKNOWLEDGMENTS:</u>
Until a more formal contract, mutually satisfactory to our respective attorneys, is executed, the foregoing represents the full and binding agreement.

_____	_____
JOHN SMITH	PRODUCER
Date: _____	Date: _____

Glossary

act   The traditional dramatic segment in stage plays and motion pictures. Most films follow a three-act structure. Most acts are made up of two to five sequences. Discussed in Chapter 3.

angle   A camera shot. The three prime shots (angles) that writers should understand are the *long shot,* the *medium shot,* and the *close-up.* The latter shot shows the eyes of the actors, which reveals their emotional state. Long shots are useful for orienting the audience to the location, for showing who is in it, and for revealing physical action. Medium shots allow audiences to see characters confronting each other face-to-face; they are also used for showing action. You can quickly learn how these three angles or shots work by studying the scenes noted in Appendix A, Chapter 4. Knowing how the three basic angles or shots work will make it easier for you to visualize the movie that you are imagining. Discussed in Chapters 4 and 8.

antagonist   Usually the villain of the story; the person or force opposing the protagonist, who is usually the hero. James Mason's Ed Concannon is the antagonist in *The Verdict.* In most cases the antagonist creates conflict and dramatic tension. In a few films *(Lost Weekend, Thirty Two Short Films about Glenn Gould)* the antagonist is an aspect of the main character, and the conflict is internalized within the character. Discussed in Chapter 2.

arc   Refers to the overall span and progression of the story as well as to what happens to a character during the drama. For example, the arc of the story in *The Verdict* traces the hero's rise out of the ashes of his wasted life. Concannon's arc moves him from the top of the legal profession to a position where he is not only defeated but also may face disciplinary charges for hiring Laura as a spy. Discussed in Chapters 1 through 3.

archetype   A story model or character type that occurs frequently in art and literature. To help new writers organize an idea or notion, six basic story archetypes are presented in Chapter 1. They organize around Heroes, Buddies, Breaking Away, Impossible Dream, Faust, and Medea archetypes. The archetypes are especially useful during the early stages of plotting, when the writer is figuring out which way to develop the story.

aria   A longish, impassioned speech that often reveals a character's innermost values and thinking. Example: *The Verdict* (Shot 26), when Galvin's aria turns down Bishop Brophy's settlement offer. Discussed in Chapter 6.

A-storyline The external action line of a story. The trial forms the A-storyline in *The Verdict*. Discussed in Chapter 2.

backstory What happened to the characters before the story began. Eastwood's character in *Unforgiven* had been a renegade and killer, and this backstory was touched upon throughout the movie. In the climactic scene, the old murderous instincts prove to be intact, and Munny punishes his adversaries. Backstory also can involve the history of a situation. For example, the Native Americans in *Dances with Wolves* had difficulties with the Army before the story began; these backstory experiences make them hostile to the hero when he first enters their territory. Backstory is often the source of character motivation. Discussed in Chapter 5.

basic dramatic units Refers to acts, bits, scenes, and sequences, discussed in Chapter 4.

beat This term has several meanings. It can refer to a story point that is made by a bit, a scene, or a sequence. An outline of such points is called a beat sheet. The term *beat* also refers to a pause that occurs in a scene or speech, as when something registers on the characters. The term, used interchangeably with *pause,* is often capitalized and placed in parentheses in a speech to indicate that someone is thinking or reacting to something. Do not overuse this convention; actors and directors know when to pause. The writer's task is to give them valid reasons for doing so. Discussed in Chapters 4 and 6.

bit The shortest of the three basic dramatic units. Usually a bit plays for a minute or so and tends to advance the plot. A number of bits can combine into a sequence, as in the opening of *The Verdict*, which presents a seven-minute sequence that is composed of seven bits. Each bit makes a dramatic point; together the seven bits combine into the sequence that begins to introduce the hero. Discussed in Chapter 4.

blocking This term has two meanings: the first refers to the process of deciding which beats best tell what happens in the script and then arranging the beats in the most dramatic order. For many writers, blocking the plot is the most difficult phase of screenwriting. If this task is not done correctly, the script based on the plot may fail. In most cases, blocking requires very careful thinking. Blocking—laying out the beats of the story—is one of two master skills that screenwriters must have. (The other is the ability to sustain scenes and characters in imagination until they do and say entertaining things.) The second meaning of *blocking* refers to the movement of the actors and the action within a scene. Discussed in Chapter 3 and 4.

B-storyline The internal (psychological) problem of the main character. Often this struggle connects to the character's backstory experiences or with inadequacies that must be corrected or set to rest. The ordeal of solving the problem connected to the A-storyline is what forces the protagonist to solve the personal problem that is connected to the B-storyline. In other words, *adversity introduces a man to himself.* Discussed in Chapter 2 and throughout the text.

business Physical action performed by one of the characters. Eastwood's marksmanship practice in *Unforgiven* is business—visual action that entertains the audience while advancing the story or revealing character. Discussed in Chapters 8 and 9.

button The moment when the story actually begins. In *The Verdict*, that moment occurs in Shot 8, when Mickey (Jack Warden) props the drunken hero up and lectures him about preparing his case. This dialogue, which clearly begins the narrative, occurs about seven minutes into the story. Discussed in Chapter 4.

character arc See arc, above.

climax   When the problem tracked in the story is resolved. This moment or incident is usually the event of the story—what happens after everything happens. Discussed in Chapter 3.

colors   Refers to the range of emotional states experienced by the characters. A term favored by actors, *colors* applies to the various emotional readings of a line or a scene. There is an example of actors demonstrating colors in *Passion Fish*, when the heroine is visited by actress friends. Usually a range of emotional colors makes a character and a script more entertaining than one that plays on a single emotional note. Discussed in Chapters 4 and 5.

continuity   This term has a number of meanings. The one used most frequently by writers concerns how the various scenes and sequences in a script flow from the opening shot to the final fade-out. A similar meaning refers to how on-screen incidents lead the audience through the story so they can understand what is happening in the plot and within the characters. Continuity can also refer to the stage directions that describe the motives of the characters and the action of the story. Additionally, filmmakers refer to the order of shooting and use of props (keeping track of which hand an actor uses to hold a teacup) as continuity. This is a major concern in the stop-and-start world of making movies because the filmmakers may forget whether the actor held the cigarette in the right hand or the left. Such details are easily missed when a scene requires hours to shoot. The person responsible for continuity (usually the script supervisor) must make sure that the various takes "match," so that they can be edited together. This means that items such as clothing or the food and drink not move about, change ingredients, or mysteriously reappear after being altered by the action. Discussed in Chapter 3.

craft   Like story sense, craft is the screenwriter's knowledge of story, human nature, dialogue, blocking, camera, dramatization, scene construction, and other dramatic skills. Craft is what writers use as they zigzag through the endless possibilities that attach to ideas, to characters, and to incidents of plot. The individual craft elements of screenwriting can be learned; what is done with these tools depends on how well they are learned and, of course, on the initiative and energy of the writer.

cut   Occurs when two "takes" are spliced together, without overlapped footage. Film editors cut and splice the various takes within a scene to present those images that best tell the story. When used within a scene, a cut indicates continuous action. When a cut connects two scenes that take place at different times and/or in different locations, it indicates either continuous action or action that occurs after hours or days have passed. The cut is the most widely used continuity device, especially in modern films, where it often replaces the dissolve and the fade-in/fade-out conventions. Discussed in Chapter 8 and elsewhere.

dimensional characters   Refers to characters that have backstories and emotional needs that give them an inner life. As with real people, emotionally dimensional characters have quirks, problems, humor, and flaws that make them seem real, imperfect, and interesting. Discussed in Chapter 5.

dissolve   Occurs when two or more images overlap for a few seconds on-screen. The dissolve is a transition device that often signals that time has elapsed between scenes. The dissolve is usually the work of the director or the editor, who tells the processing lab how long the overlap should last. The lab will then overlap images from the end of Scene A with the first images from Scene B.

When the dissolve dollies in to a close-up of a character, it may signal that the story is moving from an objective view of reality to a flashback or fantasy scene, as in *The Terminator* (Shot 183FX). Discussed in Chapter 8.

dog heavy   A stereotypical bad guy, frequently a huge man with a bald head and a nasty attitude. Dog heavies lack dimension as characters, but they can serve as convenient movie shorthand because they are quickly recognizable when they enter the scene. The three hoodlums who dab ice cream on the Amish in *Witness* (Shot 122A) are dog heavies. Discussed in Chapter 5.

dogleg   Occurs when a story spends time on a diversionary action or plot incident that does not relate to the main storyline. Doglegs diffuse the forward momentum of the story by presenting action that dead-ends without paying off, and for such reasons they should be avoided. Doglegs are rarely seen in mainstream movies because they are amputated during production or editing. Discussed in Chapter 3.

drama   The reaction of character to crisis. Drama often begins as a situation and progresses through incidents of plot that cause the audience to identify and empathize with the dramatic ordeal of the protagonist of the story. Discussed in Chapter 3.

dramatic conventions   Various strategies and craft skills used by writers to tell their stories. There are dozens of dramatizing strategies; these include engines, power tools, reversals, and surprises. Discussed in Chapter 7 and elsewhere in the text.

dramatic engine   A character, a force, a situation, or a task that organizes and drives the story. Lt. Gerard in *The Fugitive* is the engine that drives that film. The capsized ocean liner is the engine that drives *The Poseidon Adventure*. The cyborg drives *The Terminator*. The trial drives *The Verdict*. Discussed in Chapter 7.

entertain   As used in this text, the meaning of *entertain* is close to the root meaning of the word, which is "to hold between." Thus, an entertaining film causes individual viewers to combine into an audience that holds in common the thoughts and emotions stimulated by the movie. American films favor stories that create emotional reactions such as fear, love, anger, joy, sadness, humor, nostalgia, and the like. Such films therefore seek to have an emotional impact on the audience. In *The Verdict* and *Schindler's List*, the goals are more lofty than those of *Speed* or *Death Wish*, yet each film in its own way entertains its segment of the audience. Some films are "popcorn" or feel-good movies; others are more subtle and profound. All hope to entertain the largest audience possible. Noted in Chapter 1 and elsewhere in the text.

exposition   Refers to information that the audience must know to follow what is happening in the story. Exposition reveals plot, backstory, and who the characters are. This information is often marbled into the story through dialogue and visuals in ways that present information without slowing the forward momentum of the story. Discussed in Chapters 5, 6, and 7.

fade-in/fade-out   Occurs when the picture dims to black (or white) for a few seconds and then fades into the first image of the next scene. This strategy, the movie equivalent of a chapter break in a book, usually indicates that a major phase of the story or a character's development has concluded and a new phase is beginning. Fade-ins and fade-outs are used infrequently in American films, having been replaced by dissolves, cuts, and other continuity strategies.

filmmaker   Usually refers to the motion picture director, but this catchall term also includes writers, producers, editors, cinematographers, sound designers, production designers, musical directors, costumers, and dozens of other professionals who contribute to making motion pictures.

flashback   A presentation of a past experience of one of the characters or a previous incident that connects to the story. Flashbacks are used in *The Terminator* to show Reese's terrible world of the future. Discussed in Chapter 5.

focus   Cinematographers focus their lenses; screenwriters focus their scripts by pressing the characters with a dramatic problem that intensifies until it must be confronted and resolved in the climactic scene. Even though there may be occasional respites that slacken the emotional intensity, these breaks are only to give viewers a breather before they are hit again with an even stronger surge of drama. Focus and intensity are essential for successful scripts and motion pictures. Discussed in Chapter 5 and elsewhere.

frame   The physical scene as it is seen through the camera's viewfinder. It also refers to the story universe, and overall settings of a story. As an example and extension of the first definition given, characters are said to "enter the frame," which means they enter the scene and move to assigned floor marks so they can be filmed with preset camera and lighting positions.

Frame also has a movie-related meaning as a verb, as in "Frame on Jim," or "The shot/angle/camera frames on Jim," which means that Jim is the featured subject in the camera viewfinder and in the shot. Discussed in Chapters 2 and 8.

freighting   Refers to how writers slip backstory, exposition, and other story information into the script, usually by lacing dialogue with subtextual meaning or by use of images. Freighting is used interchangeably with marbling. Example: When he talks to the radio psychologist in *Sleepless in Seattle* (Shot 29), Sam's dialogue is freighted with melancholy because of the death of his wife. Discussed in Chapters 5, 6, and 7.

green-light   To agree to turn a script into a movie. This decision is made by a studio or a production company. For major studio productions green-lighted for 1995, this involves a commitment of about $40 million per film. Discussed in Chapters 11 and 12.

how-to factor   When a movie shows how something is made or how it is maneuvered or operated. The audience often has a curiosity about what is shown—how the Amish work together to build a timbered barn *(Witness),* how pilots land airplanes on an aircraft carrier *(Top Gun),* or how an assassin will slip his gun past the metal detectors guarding the president *(In the Line of Fire).* There is visual and entertainment value in certain actions and procedures. Discussed in Chapters 8 and 9.

intercut   To cut back and forth between characters or scenes. Intercutting is useful for showing simultaneous action, as when the camera ping-pongs (intercuts) between two people having a telephone conversation (in script shorthand this appears as INTERCUT FOR CONVERSATION). Discussed in Chapters 8 and 9.

love interest   Usually a man or woman who is romantically involved with the main character. The love interest allows the protagonist to express personal thoughts and feelings. Most films benefit by having some sort of love interest, even if the resulting relationship is platonic. Discussed in Chapter 2 and elsewhere.

mainstream   Any film that plays in a local movie theater. These films range from obscure *(Red Rock West)* to blockbusters *(Jurassic Park)* to art-house fare *(Red).* Because of cost factors, backers seek scripts that will appeal to the largest possible segment of the audience. Discussed in Chapters 1 and 12.

marbling How screenwriters slip backstory and exposition into a story via dialogue or images. Another word for freighting. Discussed in Chapters 4 through 7.

master shot The general stage direction heading (slugline) that indicates where and when the beat is staged, as in EXT. ZOOK'S BARN - DAY (a daytime exterior shot of Zook's barn). Although it may be the only shot described in the beat, the writer realizes that the director and cinematographer will probably break down the master shot into individual shots (also known as *angles* or *takes*). INT. ANNIE'S PARENTS' DINING ROOM - NIGHT (Shot 18 of *Sleepless in Seattle*) is the master shot of the scene in which Annie announces her engagement to Walter. Although there are no further camera instructions for three pages, the action was photographed using close-up, medium, and wide-angle shots. If permitted, most screenwriters could create a shot list for the entire movie as they imagined it. However, this would make the read more difficult, and the shots cited might not suit the location. Writers usually do include a few additional camera angles to help the reader to visualize the scenes. Discussed in Chapters 4, 8, 9, 10, and 11.

momentum A feeling that something is happening in the story, that dramatic forces are propelling the characters and the action toward a logical, inevitable, and unpredictable conclusion. Discussed in Chapter 7.

narrative The plot line of the story; the sequence of events that begins at the beginning and ends after the climactic scene or epilogue. The narrative of *The Terminator,* for example, tracks how the two heroes destroy the cyborg; in *Sleepless in Seattle,* the narrative deals with how Sam and Annie get together. Discussed in Chapters 2, 3, and 7.

panning When the camera follows the action by pivoting on its horizontal axis. Discussed in Chapter 8.

parentheticals Instructions to actors that indicate how an action or a line should be performed. These instructions are most useful when the moment in the script might be misunderstood. Thus someone might show that a line is to be read *(cynically)* by writing the word in parentheses under the speaker's name, indicating that there is a subtextual meaning to the dialogue. Use sparingly. Discussed in Chapters 5, 6, 9, 10, and 11.

plot A sequence of incidents in which characters contest over the resolution of a dramatic problem. Through this struggle, the characters discover their deeper nature and other truths. The incidents of plot intensify as the action rushes toward the climactic scene in which the problem will be resolved. Story is a more complete term that involves both plot and the emotional content supplied by characters who are stressed by the incidents of the plot. The story thus evolves out of the plot during the scriptwriting phase of the work. Discussed in Chapters 2 and 3 and throughout the text.

point of view (P.O.V.) A subjective shot in which the camera shows what one of the characters is seeing and experiencing. Discussed in Chapters 9 and 10.

prequel A story that has as its subject an established character portrayed at a younger age than in the original work in which the character first appeared. The "Young Indiana Jones" TV series depicts the legendary Harrison Ford character when he was a teenager. Discussed in Chapter 1.

producer There are various levels of producers in features and in television, so only a general definition will be given here. In television, the executive producer deals with the network and the talent and supervises the overall thrust of the show on a seasonal basis. In many cases the executive producer may be the creator and part-owner of the series. A television producer, by comparison, usually oversees the production of individual segments of a TV series. Associate producers on television are often staff writers and/or story editors.

In feature films, the producer is often the person who develops the script, deals with the studio, hires the talent, and is the contact between the filmmakers and the studio or production company. This person usually hires one or more line producers, who attend to the everyday operation and budget of the movie. Associate producers in features work for the producer. All of these are demanding jobs that are high in personal, political, and artistic stress. One of the key aspects of producing is being able to locate a good script—and then working with the writer to rewrite it (when necessary) and bringing together the right mix of talent and filmmaking skills needed to turn the script into a movie. If the principals do not get along, the production process can become an unhappy experience for everyone. Discussed in Chapter 12.

production team   The men and women who contribute to the movie. These filmmakers include the development executives and producers, directors, cinematographers, sound and picture editors, composers, special effects and stunt coordinators, sound effects experts, musical directors, set designers, production designers, painters, electricians, carpenters, people who handle lights, and so on. Other members of the production team include truck and stunt drivers, doubles, stand-ins, actors, extras, costumers, makeup artists, and, of course, writers.

protagonist   The main character in the movie. Usually this person is the hero, but sometimes the villain is the protagonist. This is the case in *Amadeus,* in which Salieri is the protagonist because he is used to tell Mozart's story. Jack Nicholson is the villainous protagonist in *The Witches of Eastwick.* Discussed in Chapters 2 and 3.

scene   A dramatic unit that usually plays for three to five minutes. Although scenes advance the plot, more often they are used to reveal character, establish relationships, and reveal the theme. Most scenes have a segmented structure that is similar to the three-part structure of the screenplay. A scene can also be made up of segments that take place in more than one location or time setting. Discussed in Chapter 4.

sequence   A dramatic unit that makes a major point of story. Ten or so sequences make up a typical movie. Sequences are composed of bits and/or scenes and usually play from five to fifteen minutes. Discussed in Chapter 4.

shot   A single "take" (photographic run) that is filmed from a particular angle. A shot becomes complicated when it is prolonged and/or involved with movement. *The Verdict* (Shot 51) presents a 220-second scene that is photographed with a single, unmoving, low-angle shot that shows Galvin in his office as he telephones a replacement expert witness. This is unusual, however, and most bits and scenes contain numerous shots that are edited together to make the dramatic point. Discussed in Chapters 8 through 11.

slugline   The line of stage directions that indicates the location and time of a new scene, as in EXT.   THE CASTLE - DAY. When a sold script is being readied for production, the slugline, which is usually the master shot of the beat, is given a shot number. Discussed in Chapters 9 and 10.

spectacle   The visual grandeur and look of the movie. This look depends on the quantity and quality of the cast, the elegance of the sets and costumes, the number of cavalry in the charge, and the production's overall scale and visual content. Epic films *(Braveheart, Lawrence of Arabia, Gone with the Wind)* and anticipated block-busters *(Batman, Waterworld)* usually present special effects, crowd scenes, and action that create visual spectacle. Such films tend to be expensive, costing $30 to $100 million. By contrast, intimate films *(The Brothers McMullen, Smoke, My Family)* have limited budgets ($2 to $15 million) and rely on the intensity of character inter-action to entertain the audience.

story   A dramatic summary of an event. Story is the sequence of incidents found in the plot, plus the emotion, motivation, reaction, and personal involvement of the char-acters. Plot is the springboard that allows the characters to interact with each other and to react to the incidents of plot. Discussed in Chapter 2 and throughout the text.

storyboards   Sketches that indicate specific moments in a scene. Storyboards range from highly detailed drawings by a storyboard artist to stick figures and layout drawings that writers and other filmmakers doodle so they can figure out move-ment, action, and camera angles within a scene. In most cases, storyboards and layout diagrams are not included in the script. Discussed in Chapter 8.

story point   A dramatic point that advances the plot and reveals character or relation-ships. This point, often made at the end of the scene, is sometimes referred to as the make-point moment or the "red dot" moment of the scene. Scenes that do not make their point clearly are a main cause of script failure. This is a difficult lesson to learn, so do not underestimate this writing task. Discussed in Chapter 4.

story template   A three-act summary of what is found in most screenplays: in the first act the hero takes on the problem; in the second act the hero seems defeated by the problem; in the third act the hero solves the problem. Discussed in Chapter 3.

story universe   The world of the story as suggested in the script. It includes the phys-ical location of the story, as well as the tone, style, and energy of the story. Thus, a film such as *Blue Velvet* presents a typical American town, yet it examines the malaise beneath the surface charm. In this way, the film presents an off beat, con-flicted story universe. Each of the four main study films presents a distinctive story universe: *The Verdict* deals with the faded elegance of the Boston legal scene; *Sleep-less in Seattle* is set in yuppie enclaves in Baltimore and Seattle; *Witness* shifts between the mean streets of Philadelphia and Amish farm country; *The Terminator* contrasts the dead world of the future with the troubled world of what seems to be Los Angeles (circa 1984). The story universe is an important value that should not be neglected. See also frame.

structure   The spine of a story, which is based upon the presentation and tracking of a problem through resolution. The structure of *The Verdict*, for example, is based on how the hero changes for the better as a result of solving the problem of the story (winning the lawsuit). Structure is shaped by the logic and values that connect to the problem being tracked. Structure also involves who the characters are, the nature of their internal and external struggle over the story problem, and what the story is saying thematically. These elements, which require considerable thought, combine into a spine upon which the incidents of story can be hung. If the basic story idea is entertaining and if the story has a solid structure, it is possible to rewrite and fix problems with dialogue, scene construction, continuity, and similar matters. Discussed in Chapters 2 and 3.

subplot   A secondary storyline that is subordinate to the A-storyline that organizes the plot. Subplots usually involve characters who have dealings with the protagonist and/or the antagonist during the struggle to solve the problem or to achieve the goal of the story. Thus in *Sleepless in Seattle,* the main storyline concerns how to get Annie and Sam together. Annie's friendship with Becky (Rosie O'Donnell) supplies a subplot that comments on and helps the heroine solve the problem that organizes the story. In *The Verdict*, the hero's affair with Laura creates a subplot that is secondary to the main storyline, which concerns how Galvin manages to win the lawsuit.

Most feature films have two to five different subplots, each one adding interest to the story. Subplots allow the drama to shift away from the A-storyline in order to examine the problem from thematic, romantic, and/or philosophical perspectives. Subplots also serve specific functions, such as allowing characters to discuss their inner thoughts and feelings. Laura in *The Verdict* does this for Galvin, and she also expresses her feelings. Another useful subplot is one that sets up a friendship between a protagonist and an alter-ego character. Their relationship allows the hero to verbalize what he or she is thinking. The character of Mickey in *The Verdict* is an alter-ego character who allows the hero to express his feelings and his motives. Discussed in Chapter 3.

subtext   What the character thinks and feels inside. This content is implied in the dialogue but not stated directly. Discussed in Chapter 6.

switchback   When a story goes over material that has already been covered in the story and that the audience already knows. Switchbacks should be avoided in most cases. Discussed in Chapter 3.

talking-heads scene   A scene that features two or three people talking in a visually starved location. Although such scenes can be memorable, screenwriters try to stage scenes in locations that present as much visual content as possible. For example, a talking-heads scene played in a library lined with shelves of books usually offers more to look at than does the same scene played in an ordinary motel room. Discussed in Chapters 7 and 8.

throughline   The dramatic question or goal upon which the audience focuses. In most cases that question concerns the dramatic problem that challenges the main characters through the A-storyline. The throughline is sometimes referred to as the plot, the spine, or the structure of the story. In *The Verdict*, the throughline of the story is the trial and how it affects the hero. In *The Terminator,* a story with a strong action throughline, the audience focuses on how Sarah and Reese battle the cyborg. Discussed in Chapter 3.

torquing   Refers to any situation, context, or "spin" that adds interest or diversion to a scene. Torquing a scene requires inventing a situation or visual, creating a moment of character, or juxtaposing elements that divert and entertain the audience. There is an example of torquing in *Sleepless in Seattle* (Shot 99), when Victoria has dinner with Sam and Jonah on their houseboat. During the meal, Jonah's dislike of Victoria creates such a negative context that it puts a humorous spin on the scene; thus, Jonah's attitude torques the scene. Discussed in Chapter 7.

treatment   A short-story version of the story. A treatment should be easy to read and should suggest the settings, what the characters want, and what happens to the characters in the story. A feature treatment is usually five to ten pages; a treatment for a television is usually two or three pages. Discussed in Chapter 3.

trucking   When the camera moves apace with the action, as when characters walk and talk. The camera can be mounted on rigid tracks for this, or it can be moved by a motorized vehicle that may employ gyro-stabilizers that ensure steady images. Also called a *moving shot, a tracking shot,* or a *dolly shot.* Discussed in Chapter 8.

twist   An unexpected happening, accident, discovery, revelation, coincidence, or occurrence that bounces the plot in a new and more dramatic direction. Creating twists, an important dramatic skill, usually requires very careful thinking. Discussed in Chapters 3 and 7.

voice-over   When a narrator or character in the story speaks off-screen and comments on the action. It is designated by V.O., OFF CAMERA, OFF, or VOICE ONLY. Discussed in Chapters 6 and 10.

wallpapering   Jargon for enhancing a scene by staging it against a visually interesting background. Exposition scenes played against visually interesting "wallpaper" often are more entertaining than those played in visually sparse settings. For example, the ornate headquarters of the bishop in *The Verdict* provides settings that are visually more interesting than the hero's dreary apartment. The characters walk through the bishop's headquarters as they talk, to further show off the location. Discussed in Chapter 8.

works   Is effective. Refers to a story, character, script, scene, action, or moment. Scripts are said to work because of character insight, story logic, and overall effectiveness, i.e., their ability to entertain. Often, however, what appears to work in the script may not work during production because of the location, budget, conditions on the set, or the attitudes or abilities of the actors and/or filmmakers. In such cases, on-site adjustments and last-minute fixes may be attempted to correct whatever is needed to make the story or the scene work.

Bibliography

SCREENWRITING

Armer, Alan A. *Writing the Screenplay: TV and Film,* 2d ed. Wadsworth Publishing. Belmont, California, 1993.

Brady, John. *The Craft of the Screenwriter: Interviews with Six Celebrated Screenwriters.* Simon & Schuster. New York, 1981.

Chayefsky, Paddy. *Television Plays.* Simon & Schuster. New York, 1955.

Corliss, Richard. *Talking Pictures: Screenwriters in the American Cinema.* The Overlook Press. Woodstock, New York, 1985.

Dancyger, Ken, and Jeff Rush. *Alternative Scriptwriting.* Focal Press. Boston, 1991.

Dmytryk, Edward. *On Screen Writing.* Focal Press. Boston, 1985.

Froug, William. *Screenwriting Tricks of the Trade.* Silman-James Press. Los Angeles, 1992.

Geller, Stephen. *Screenwriting.* Bantam Books. New York, 1985.

Goldman, William. *Adventures in the Screen Trade: A Personal View of Hollywood and Screenwriting.* Warner Books. New York, 1983.

Haag, Judith H., and Hillis R. Cole, Jr. *The Complete Guide to Standard Script Formats.* CMC Publishing. Los Angeles, 1985.

Horton, Andrew. *Writing the Character-Centered Screenplay.* University of California Press. Los Angeles, 1994.

Howard, David, and Edward Mabley. *The Tools of Screenwriting: A Writer's Guide to the Craft and the Elements of a Screenplay.* St. Martin's Press. New York, 1993.

Hunter, Lew. *Screenwriting 434.* Perigee Books. New York, 1993.

Karton, Joshua. *Film Scenes for Film Actors.* Bantam Books. New York, 1983.

McDougal, Stuart Y. *Made into Movies: From Literature to Film.* CBS College Publishing. New York, 1985.

McGilligan, Pat. *Backstory: Interviews with Screenwriters of Hollywood's Golden Age.* University of California Press. Los Angeles. 1986.

Root, Wells. *Writing the Script: A Practical Guide for Films and Television.* Holt, Rinehart and Winston. New York, 1979.

Saks, Sol. *The Craft of Comedy Writing.* Writer's Digest Books. Cincinnati, Ohio, 1985.

Sanders, Terry, and Freida Lee Mock, eds. *Word into Image: Writers on Screenwriting: Transcripts of the Award-Winning Film Series.* American Film Foundation. Santa Monica, 1981.

Schanzer, Karl, and Thomas Lee Wright. *American Screenwriters: The Insiders' Look at the Art, the Craft, and the Business of Writing Movies.* Avon Books. New York, 1993.

Seger, Linda. *Making a Good Script Great.* Samuel French. New York, 1987.

Server, Lee. *Screenwriter: Words Become Pictures: Interviews with Twelve Screenwriters from the Golden Age of American Movies.* The Main Street Press. Pittstown, New Jersey, 1987.

Swain, Dwight V. *Creating Characters: How to Build Story People.* Writer's Digest Books. Cincinnati, Ohio, 1990.

Thomas, Sam. *Best American Screenplays* (three volumes). Crown Publishers. New York, 1986–1995.

Vorhaus, John. *The Comic Toolbox.* Silman-James Press. Los Angeles, 1994.

Walter, Richard. *Screenwriting: The Art, Craft and Business of Film and Television Writing.* New American Library. New York, 1988.

Wolff, Jurgen, and Kerry Cox, eds. *Top Secrets: Screenwriting.* Lone Eagle Publishing. Los Angeles, 1993.

Yoakem, Lola, ed. *TV and Screenwriting.* University of California Press. Berkeley, 1958.

WRITING

Boyer, Robert H., and Kenneth J. Zahorski. *Fantasists on Fantasy: A Collection of Critical Reflections by Eighteen Masters of the Art.* Avon Books. New York, 1984.

Brande, Dorothea. *Becoming a Writer.* J. P. Tarcher. Los Angeles, 1934.

Bretnor, Reginald, ed. *The Craft of Science Fiction: A Symposium on Writing Science Fiction.* Barnes & Noble. New York, 1976.

Chapman, Robert L. *New Dictionary of American Slang.* Harper & Row. New York, 1986.

Egri, Lajos. *The Art of Dramatic Writing: Its Basis in the Creative Interpretation of Human Motives.* Simon & Schuster. New York, 1946.

Fergusson, Francis. *Aristotle's Poetics.* Hill and Wang. New York, 1961.

Gardner, John. *On Moral Fiction.* Basic Books. New York, 1977.

Gardner, John. *The Art of Fiction.* New York. Alfred A. Knopf, 1983.

Gessner, Robert. *The Moving Image: A Guide to Cinematic Literacy.* E. P. Dutton. New York, 1968.

Greenberg, Harvey R. *The Movies on Your Mind: Film Classics on the Couch, from Fellini to Frankenstein.* E. P. Dutton. New York, 1975.

Katz, Jack. *Seductions of Crime: Moral and Sensual Attractions in Doing Evil.* Basic Books. New York, 1988.

Lewin, Esther, and Albert E. Lewin. *Thesaurus of Slang.* Facts On File. New York, 1988.

Marcus, Fred H. *Short Story/Short Film.* Prentice-Hall. Englewood Cliffs, New Jersey, 1977.

Martin, Jay. *Who Am I This Time: Uncovering the Fictive Personality.* W. W. Norton. New York, 1988.

Poltarnees, Welleran. *All Mirrors Are Magic Mirrors: Reflections on Pictures Found in Children's Books.* The Green Tiger Press. La Jolla, California, 1972.

Polti, Georges. *The Thirty-Six Dramatic Situations.* The Writer. Boston, 1940.

Reed, Barry. *The Verdict.* Simon & Schuster. New York, 1980.

Strunk, William, Jr., and E. B. White. *The Elements of Style.* Macmillan. New York, 1972.

Surmelian, Leon. *Techniques of Fiction Writing: Measure and Madness.* Doubleday. New York, 1968.

Telford, Kenneth A. *Aristotle's* Poetics: *Translation and Analysis.* Gateway Editions. South Bend, Indiana, 1961.

Welty, Eudora. *One Writer's Beginnings.* Warner Books. New York, 1983.

MYTH

Bettelheim, Bruno. *The Uses of Enchantment: The Meaning and Importance of Fairy Tales.* Vintage Books. New York, 1977.

Bulfinch, Thomas. *Bulfinch's Mythology.* Avenel Books. New York, 1979.

Campbell, Joseph. *The Hero with a Thousand Faces,* 2d ed. Princeton University Press. Princeton, New Jersey, 1968.

Goodrich, Norma Lorre. *The Medieval Myths.* Mentor Books. New York, 1961.

McConnell, Frank. *Storytelling and Mythmaking.* Oxford University Press. New York, 1979.

FILMMAKING

Almendros, Nestor. *A Man with a Camera.* Farrar, Straus, Giroux. New York, 1984.

Behlmer, Rudy. *Behind the Scenes.* Ungar. New York, 1982.

Gallagher, John Andrew. *Film Directors on Directing.* Praeger. New York, 1989.

Givens, Bill. *Film Flubs.* Carol Publishing. Secaucus, New Jersey, 1990.

Harmetz, Aljean. *The Making of The Wizard of Oz.* Proscenium Publishers. New York, 1977.

Lumet, Sidney. *Making Movies.* Alfred A. Knopf. New York, 1995.

McBride, Joseph, ed. *Film Makers on Film Making: The American Film Institute Seminars on Motion Pictures and Television,* volumes I, II. J. P. Tarcher. Los Angeles, 1983.

Sayles, John. *Thinking in Pictures: The Making of the Movie* Matewan. Houghton Mifflin. Boston, 1987.

Schaefer, Dennis, and Larry Salvato. *Master of Light: Conversations with Contemporary Cinematographers.* University of California Press. Berkeley, 1984.

Seger, Linda, and Edward Jay Whetmore. *From Script to Screen: The Collaborative Art of Filmmaking.* Henry Holt. New York, 1994.

Walker, Joseph, and Juanita Walker. *The Light on Her Face.* The American Society of Cinematographers Press. Hollywood, California, 1984.

ACTING AND ACTORS

Caine, Michael. *Acting in Film: An Actor's Take on Moviemaking.* Applause Theater Books. New York, 1990.

Higham, Charles. *Brando: The Unauthorized Biography.* New American Library. New York, 1987.

Hunter, Allan. *Gene Hackman.* St. Martin's Press. New York, 1987.

THE FILM INDUSTRY

K Callan. *The Script Is Finished, Now What Do I Do?* Sweden Press. Studio City, California, 1993.

Kanin, Garson. *Hollywood.* Limelight Editions. New York, 1984.

Levinson, Richard, and William Link. *Stay Tuned: An Inside Look at Who and What Makes Prime-Time Television Prime.* Ace Books. New York, 1981.

Maltin, Leonard. *Movie and Video Guide.* Signet Books. New York, 1994.

Pinkerton, Linda. *The Writer's Law Primer.* Lyons and Burford Press. New York, 1990.

Sautter, Carl. *How to Sell Your Screenplay: The Real Rules of Film and Television.* New Chapter Press. New York, 1992.

Toohey, Daniel W., Richard D. Marks, and Arnold P. Lutzker. *Legal Problems in Broadcasting.* University of Nebraska Press. Lincoln, 1974.

FILM AND FILM HISTORY

Brownlow, Kevin. *The Parade's Gone By.* University of California Press. Los Angeles, 1968.

Griffith, Richard. *The Talkies: Articles and Illustrations from A Great Fan Magazine 1928–1940.* Dover Publications. New York, 1971.

Griffith, Richard, Arthur Mayer, and Eileen Bowser. *The Movies.* Simon & Schuster. New York, 1981.

Halliwell, Leslie. *Halliwell's Filmgoer's and Video Viewer's Companion,* 9th ed. Harper & Row. New York, 1990.

Huss, Roy, and Norman Silverstein. *The Film Experience: Elements of Motion Picture Art.* Dell Publishing. New York, 1968.

Kael, Pauline. *I Lost It at the Movies.* Bantam Books. New York, 1965.

Kael, Pauline. *Kiss Kiss Bang Bang.* Bantam Books. New York, 1968.

Kael, Pauline. *When the Lights Go Down.* Holt, Rinehart and Winston. New York, 1980.

Kael, Pauline. *Taking It All In.* Holt, Rinehart and Winston. New York, 1984.

Kael, Pauline. *State of the Art.* E. P. Dutton. New York, 1985.

Kael, Pauline. *Hooked.* E. P. Dutton. New York, 1989.

Katz, Ephraim. *The Film Encyclopedia.* Putnam. New York, 1979.

MacCann, Richard Dyer, ed. *Film: A Montage of Theories.* E. P. Dutton. New York, 1966.

Schatz, Thomas. *Hollywood Genres: Formulas, Filmmaking, and the Studio System.* Random House. New York, 1981.

Springer, John, and Jack Hamilton. *They Had Faces Then: Annabella to Zorina: The Superstars, Stars and Starlets of the 1930s.* Citadel Press. Secaucus, New Jersey, 1974.

Thomson, David. *A Biographical Dictionary of Film.* William Morrow. New York, 1981.

INDEX